Seeking the Common Ground

Seeking the Common Ground

*Protestant Christianity,
the Three-Self Movement,
and China's United Front*

Philip L. Wickeri

ORBIS BOOKS

Maryknoll, New York 10545

The Catholic Foreign Mission Society of America (Maryknoll) recruits and trains people for overseas missionary service. Through Orbis Books Maryknoll aims to foster the international dialogue that is essential to mission. The books published, however, reflect the opinions of their authors and are not meant to represent the official position of the society.

Copyright © 1988 by Philip L. Wickeri
Published by Orbis Books, Maryknoll, NY 10545
Manufactured in the United States of America

Manuscript editor: Joan Marie Laflamme

LIBRARY OF CONGRESS
Library of Congress Cataloging-in-Publication Data

Wickeri, Philip Lauri.
   Seeking the common ground : Protestant Christianity, the Three
-Self Movement, and China's united front / by Philip L. Wickeri.
      p. cm.
   Bibliography: p.
   Includes index.
   ISBN 0-88344-441-0
   1. Three-Self Movement (China)—History.   2. Protestant churches-
-China—History—20th century.   3. China—Church history—20th
century.   I. Title.
BR1288.W53   1988
280′.4′0951—dc19   88-17486
                                                           CIP

To the memory of
my mother,
Lydia M. Wickeri

Contents

Preface   xi

Acknowledgments   xv

Abbreviations   xvii

Introduction   xix
A Brief Note on Method   xxii
Sources   xxiv
Terminology   xxvi
Scope and Content   xxvii

Part One
The Church, Marxism, and Christianity in China

1. Perspectives on the Protestant Church in China   3
The Conservative Perspective   4
The Liberal Perspective   7
The Challenge of China: Emerging Perspectives, 1949–1979   11

2. Christianity, Marxism, and the Chinese Context   17
Christianity and Marxism   17
The European Experience of Christian-Marxist Dialogue   *17*
The Latin American Experience and Liberation Theology   *20*
Marxism in the Chinese Experience   *23*
Christianity and the Chinese Context   27
Religion in Traditional Chinese Society   *28*
The Missionary Movement and Imperialism   *32*
The Three-Self Idea   *36*

Part Two
The United Front

3. Ideology and Organization 45

Historical Background 46

Theory and Ideology 51

Dynamics of Unity 52

Working Style 60

Organizational Framework 65

The Chinese People's Political Consultative Conference 66

The United Front Work Department 68

The Religions Affairs Bureau 70

Mass Organizations 72

4. Religion and Religious Policy 75

The Chinese Communist View of Religion 76

Atheism, Religion and Superstition 78

The "Five Characteristics of Religion" 83

A New Departure in Chinese Religious Studies 89

The United Front and Religious Policy 92

Religion and Patriotism 94

The Policy of Religious Freedom 101

Conclusion 106

Part Three
Three-Self as a Chinese Movement

5. Seeking the Common Ground 113

Protestants and the Chinese Revolution 117

Christians within the United Front 122

The "Christian Manifesto" 127

Severing the Links with Imperialism: Denunciation and
Reeducation 133

The Denunciation Movement 134

Ideological Remolding 140

The Organization of Three-Self as a Patriotic Movement 146

6. Rejection and Renewal 154

Rejection from the Right 157

The Jesus Family 160

The "Little Flock" 162

Wang Mingdao 164

Rejection from the Left 170

The Cultural Revolution Era, 1966–1976 179

The Renewal of Three-Self 185

Conclusion 192

Part Four
Three-Self as a Christian Movement

7. Faith and Works 199
Christian Selfhood   203
Self-Support   205
Self-Propagation   210
Christian Unity   215
The Unification of Worship   219
Mutual Respect   222
Ecumenical Relations   227
Selfhood and Unity in the 1980s   233

8. Theological Reorientation 243
The Context and Orientation of Theological Reflection   250
Theological Fermentation at the Grass Roots   258
Christianity and the World   261
Christians and Non-Christians   266
Chinese Theology in the 1980s   273

Conclusion 281
The Particular in the Universal   281
The Universal in the Particular   286

Notes 293

Bibliography 331

Index 349

Preface

This book marks a turning point in Western understanding of Chinese Christianity and its development over the last four decades. A remarkable historical work, it tells the fascinating story of a church renewed and revitalized in the fires of revolution and lays the foundation for a new quality of dialogue and solidarity with Chinese Christians. If taken seriously, it will make an important contribution to a new era of ecumenical relations not only with China but with other Third World churches and peoples.

In a scholarly work that captures and holds the reader's attention from beginning to end, Philip Wickeri lays before us one of the most remarkable—and least known—stories of church renewal in our time. It is the story of a church that has not only survived forty years of Communism, including a decade of institutional suppression during the Cultural Revolution, but is now a vital and growing church, an authentically Chinese church, responding creatively to the challenges posed by revolutionary upheaval and the struggle for national reconstruction. As he does this, the author provides convincing evidence in support of his claim that "what is happening in China and in the Chinese church is important for the world" and that "all Christians need to gain a better understanding of what China has to say to the world."

This good news comes as quite a surprise to most of us. In 1949, the Communist victory in China sent shock waves throughout the Western Christian world. It brought with it the closing down of one of the largest—considered also to be one of the most promising—fields of missionary endeavor. It left many with a sense of loss as well as serious doubts about the possibilities for the future of Christianity not only in China but in other countries threatened by Marxist revolutions. It was a clear indication that an era in the world mission of the church was coming to an end.

For a few years, some missionaries felt the need to learn the "lessons of China" and called for a critical re-examination of the goals and patterns of the missionary enterprise. But this examination was carried on far from China and with little contact with the experience and thought of those caught in the midst of developments taking place there. The strong anti-imperialist and anti-missionary reaction on the part of some Chinese church leaders, together with the increasing difficulties of maintaining contact, especially during the Korean War, soon led to an almost complete breakdown in communications. Efforts to understand what was happening in the Chinese church were limited to a very small group of scholars and missionaries. Chinese Christians practically disappeared from the ecumenical screen.

In the last few years, that situation has begun to change as North Americans have an increasing number of contacts with the people of China, visit their country and begin to get some sense of what has been happening there. Some of us have met and talked with Chinese Christians, have read something about the Chinese church and realize that it is alive and well. The time is ripe for us to learn more about them, listen to their witness and explore new ways of relating to them.

Seeking the Common Ground will make an extraordinary contribution to that end. This book portrays, as no other I have seen, the life and experience of Chinese Protestant Christians over the last forty years. It brings this community of faith into our lives and churches and helps prepare us for a serious dialogue with them. And it lays before us the unique witness of the Chinese church on matters of importance to all of us.

Here is a church that dared to risk losing its life in order to find it. Guided by the Three-Self Movement, it sought to respond in faith to the challenge of the Chinese revolution. In doing so, it found a new Chinese identity, "made Christian faith more accessible to the average Chinese and the church more acceptable in Chinese society." As it gave up its patterns of dependency on foreign money and persons, its denominational structures, and much of its institutional existence, it found new ways of functioning and new forms of community life. Searching for its rightful place in the struggle for a new social order, it was able to face all the difficulties of relating to the Communist Party as well as to explore the openings offered by the United Front, and thus carve out a place for Christians to contribute to the future of their nation. Its witness, above all else, is to the power of the Holy Spirit to lead faithful Christians to recognize and respond to the working of God in revolutionary times, and to create new forms of church life on such frontiers.

Philip Wickeri, the author of this monumental work, belongs to a small company of a new generation of missionary scholars. Possessed of a deep love for the Chinese people and their culture, he has succeeded, to an amazing degree, in entering their world and living in dialogue with them. He has spent a decade studying the recent history of the Chinese church while working with the Chinese people. In this way, he has arrived at an unusual depth of understanding of the perspective of Chinese Christians, while at the same time recognizing that he is a Westerner. Struggling to free himself from Western biases which might block understanding, he realizes that he is an outsider and that this gives him an opportunity to look at what he is studying from a certain critical distance as well. And he is a missionary with a vital faith as well as a theological stance that enables him to understand the relationship of the Gospel to the struggles of Third World peoples.

It is this unique combination of personal qualities and academic expertise that led Philip Wickeri to immerse himself in the reality he was studying, and to allow the data he was gathering to suggest the best way to organize it as well as a way of knowing most appropriate to it. Along this path, he eventually concluded that the Three-Self Movement provided the clue to what had been happening in the Chinese church, and that the United Front strategy of the Communist Party of China was of central importance for understanding Chinese Communism as well as how it went about relating to the church. Working from this insight, he focuses his study on the Three-Self Movement and its efforts to renew and transform the church as it sought the common ground. The result is a study of the last four decades of Chinese Protestant Christianity that I believe goes far beyond anything produced by Western scholars until the present; a sensitive and in-depth portrayal of the struggle of Chinese Christians that allows us to follow their journey in a new situation for which they were not prepared, where they faced tremendous problems, and eventually discovered unexpected opportunities for witness.

As someone who has tried to follow these developments from afar but never succeeded in making sense out of them, I moved through the pages of *Seeking the Common Ground* with increasing fascination. For I found that it gave me answers to questions that had perplexed me; it opened new horizons of understanding of the faith journey of Chinese Christians and prepared me, as nothing else has done, for a new quality of relationship with them. This convinced me that Wickeri's decision to focus his study on the Three-Self Movement was a wise one, and that it enabled him to expand and deepen our understanding of developments taking place in China on a number of points:

1. In regard to Chinese Communism: the transformations that have taken place in Marxism as it has put down roots in Chinese soil, especially the strategy of the United Front as a "distinctively Chinese departure in communist thought" and the key to understanding the religious policy in contemporary China. By giving due importance to this, Wickeri has succeeded in correcting what he calls "the most egregious omissions in most of the standard works on Christianity in China which have been published in the West." And he helps us understand what the Three-Self Movement was trying to do in the fifties, what it accomplished by seeking the common ground, and the possibilities for new developments now in the interaction between the Communist Party of China and the Christian Churches.

2. On the Three-Self Movement: a new perspective within which we can better appreciate what it was and did as well as the contributions it continues to make. As I read this account, I got a new sense of the vision of this small group of Christians who were able to perceive the foreignness of their religion and its institutions and call for repentance—and also to claim that they could best serve their God and witness to their faith as they dared to respond positively to the revolution taking place in their country.

Wickeri tells their story as he lays before us what they did, their mistakes as well as their discoveries, and the results of their efforts. He makes no attempt to hide their mistakes, but he does help us to see what they did in historical context. And he enables us to see why, given the nature of Chinese Communism, the Three-Self Movement chose the path it did and was thus able to carve out a place for the Christian community in a revolutionary society; more than that, to develop "mutually supportive and interdependent relationships between Christians and Communists in the CPC, without seeking a Christian-Marxist synthesis or collapsing faith into ideology."

3. *Seeking the Common Ground* makes it possible for us to realize that the Three-Self Movement represents much more than an attempt to relate the Chinese church to a revolutionary situation; it contributed decisively to the spiritual renewal of the church as it helped it to find a new self-identity through a "self-conscious immersion into the historical development of the Chinese people." As a result, Christianity has become an authentic *Chinese* religion and developed new forms of church life, expressed in the churches-in-homes, a post-denominational Protestantism, an ecclesiastical structure less rigidly institutional, and a new quality of relationships between traditionally mainline and evangelical Protestants.

4. By focusing on the Three-Self Movement, the author of this volume makes it possible for us to understand and appreciate the extraordinary vitality and growth of the Chinese church in the eighties, after ten years of the Cultural Revolution. A church that was prepared to suffer through and survive that decade of upheaval, be enriched and renewed by suffering and thus view what had happened in the light of redemption. A church capable of responding to new opportunities as it was renewed by simultaneous movements from the top down and from the grass roots communities. A church experiencing the creation of new life spiritually, ecclesiastically and theologically. A church in which, unknown to the rest of the world, the work of theological re-creation was going forward, not unlike what has been happening in Latin America and elsewhere in the Third World, yet uniquely Chinese.

As I have read and pondered this book, I realize that the witness of Chinese Christians, mediated by Philip Wickeri, has brought me gifts of great value for which I'm grateful. It has given me an opportunity to know them, rejoice in their achievements and learn from them. It has encouraged me to look more hopefully toward a future which may well be increasingly revolutionary for many peoples. And their witness becomes a new call to repentance as I am compelled to look more critically at the continued dominance of the Western Christendom mentality in our church life as well as our patterns of relationship to our own society and the churches in other parts of the world.

Richard Shaull

Acknowledgments

My deepest debt of gratitude is to the Chinese Christians I have come to know over the last ten years. The names of the Protestant leaders whom I interviewed are listed in the bibliography. I would especially like to thank friends on the faculty and staff of Nanjing Union Theological Seminary who helped in so many ways, from the arrangement of interviews to the location of difficult to get resources. They patiently responded to my continuing questions and requests for information, and this book would hardly have been conceivable without their assistance. Although my perspective has been shaped through these encounters, responsibility for the interpretation presented here lies with the author alone.

I also wish to express my appreciation to the faculty and staff of Princeton Theological Seminary, where I did the writing and research that forms the basis of this book; and to the board and staff of the former Program Agency of the Presbyterian Church (U.S.A.) for granting the extended home assignment that enabled me to complete my doctoral research.

A number of people made valuable comments and suggestions as this book was being written. Richard Shaull, who contributed the preface, has continued to challenge my theological perspective, even as he helped to shape it. Charles West and Lynn T. White III made many helpful suggestions on the manuscript during the writing of my doctoral dissertation in Princeton. I also wish to thank Bud Carroll, Theresa Chu, Deng Zhaoming, Margaret Garvie, Winfried Gluer, Don MacInnis, Charles Martin, David Paton, Bob Whyte, Wang Xiuling, and Franklin Woo for their reflections on various chapters of this book.

Finally, I would like to thank my daughter Elisabeth and my wife Janice. It is our shared history of China and the church that has made the writing of this book possible. Janice, editor of the *Chinese Theological Review*, did many of the translations that appear in this volume, and she has also been a thoughtful editor and critic. Elisabeth has taught both of us something about seeking the common ground.

Philip L. Wickeri
Hong Kong
Easter 1988

Abbreviations

C & C	*Christianity and Crisis*
CB	*China Bulletin*
CC	*The Christian Century*
CCC	China Christian Council
CCA	Christian Conference of Asia
CF	*Ching Feng*
CN	*China Notes*
CNA	*China News Analysis*
CPC	Communist Party of China
CPPCC	Chinese People's Political Consultative Conference
CQ	*China Quarterly*
CTR	*Chinese Theological Review*
Documents	*Documents of the Three-Self Movement*
GMD	Guomingdang, Chinese Nationalist Party (also KMT)
HKCC	Hong Kong Christian Council
IRM	*International Review of Mission*
ISWR	Institute for the Study of World Religions
NEB	*The New English Bible*
NPC	National People's Congress
NSJ	*Nanjing Seminary Journal*
NSJ (NS)	*Nanjing Seminary Journal (New Series)*
PRC	People's Republic of China
RAB	Religious Affairs Bureau
RMB	One Chinese yuan
SAC	State Affairs Council
SCM	Student Christian Movement
SW	*Selected Works of Mao Zedong*
TF	*Tian Feng*
TF (NS)	*Tian Feng (New Series)*

TSM	The Chinese Christian Three-Self Patriotic Movement
UFWD	United Front Work Department
WCC	World Council of Churches
WSCF	World Student Christian Federation

Introduction

There has been a reawakening of interest in Christianity and the church in China over the past ten years. Stories from the home worship gatherings of Chinese Protestants at the grass roots tell of a people who have struggled, suffered and been sustained through their faith in Jesus Christ. Churches that have opened or reopened in towns and cities are attended by the young and the old, the progressive and the evangelical, men and women from Christian families as well as those who are newly baptized or are merely curious. Theological seminaries and training centers are educating a new generation of leaders in eleven major cities, and there are short-term leadership training programs for the laity in many other places. Chinese Christians have begun printing their own bibles and other religious publications, under the direction of recently reconstituted national and local Protestant organizations. In addition, there has been renewed contact and communication between Christians in China and overseas. Scores of official and unofficial visits to and from China have promoted mutual understanding and new ecumenical relationships.

What has emerged from all of this is a picture of a revitalized faith and fellowship, of a church that, despite all the problems and setbacks, has survived a period of great difficulty and is now flourishing. It is a situation about which people inside and outside China are raising many questions. What has accounted for the evident vitality of Protestant Christianity in China, especially since the restoration of institutional religious life after 1979? How are the more recent developments related to the experience of Chinese Protestants in the 1950s and 1960s? Given the fact that the church seems to be thriving in a socialist society, how are we to understand and interpret the relationship between Christianity and communism in the Chinese experience? The Protestant church in China is said to have entered a post-denominational era, and yet there is certainly a plurality of denominational backgrounds and a variety of forms of Christian life.[1] How then are we to interpret ecumenism and Christian unity in China, and what does this suggest about the nature of the church as it is found in the reemerging congregations? For more than thirty years Chinese Christians have been talking about their selfhood and their need to become identified with the Chinese people. What is the theological basis of such self-hood and unity, how is it related to a wider ecumenism, and to what extent has it been achieved?

These questions are by no means new. In the late 1940s and early 1950s, as Chinese Christians were facing a situation of great change and uncertainty, they were raising similar questions about their future in a new society. In the spring of 1950 a young Anglican priest wrote an essay entitled "Repent, for the Kingdom of God is at Hand," in which he put forward three questions, which were on everyone's lips. How can the church be unified? Should Christians study or discuss politics? How can the Chinese church develop its own theology? The author said that all three of these questions were very important, but they did not touch upon what was most basic. The most fundamental question, the question in light of which the other three should be seen, was that of repentance.

> If we do not approach these three questions with a deep sense of repentance, if we are only responding to the pressures of the times, seeking unity, study and service in a perfunctory way, then no matter how we try to transform ourselves, we will just be muddling through. If, on the other hand, we are earnest and sincere about repentance, then all Christians who love the Chinese church, whether Chinese or foreign, will be of one mind in making sincere efforts to seek reform in these three important areas, and the solution to all other problems will naturally proceed more smoothly.[2]

It is now more than thirty years since Zheng Jianye wrote those words, but his advice is still valid for those who are concerned about Christianity in the People's Republic of China (PRC). Since 1949, through the Chinese Christian Three-Self Patriotic Movement (hereafter the Three-Self Movement or TSM), Chinese Protestants have sought to establish themselves as an independent, self-governing, self-supporting and self-propagating church; to identify themselves with the Chinese people; and to seek a common ground with the Chinese Communist Party (CPC) in its efforts for modernization and socialist reconstruction. It has also been important that Chinese Christians have suffered *with* the Chinese people, during the various campaigns against rightists beginning in the late 1950s and especially throughout the ten-year-long Cultural Revolution era (1966–1976).

The restoration of religious life in China after the Third Plenum of the 11th CPC (December 1978) must therefore be seen in light of religious policy and practice in the 1950s. The political struggles and efforts for church construction in the 1950s must in turn be viewed against the background of the church in China before 1949, and particularly its relationship with foreign missionaries and mission boards. "A great new event is more than an additional paragraph to be inserted in the next edition of a book," wrote Eugen Rosenstock-Huessy. "It rewrites history, it simplifies history, it changes the past because it initiates a new future."[3] As far as the experience of the Protestant church in China is concerned, this is true for December 1978 almost, but not quite, as much as it was for October 1, 1949.[4]

This book seeks to interpret that experience in terms of the policy and practice of the Communist Party's united front and to understand the Chinese Christian response within that context. It is an approach based upon what Chinese Protestants have been saying about themselves over the years, one that can help to explain what the Three-Self Movement has been trying to do in China. In order to put this experience in historical and theological perspective, Christianity must be understood in the Chinese social context. This means that the Chinese Protestant experience has been part of a much broader revolutionary experience, sharing in its achievements and setbacks. Only after the attempt has been made to understand Chinese Protestants and the TSM on their own terms can we approach the questions now being raised about the Chinese church in a way that may also be significant for the faith of Christians in other situations.

This is not a history of the Three-Self Movement. Given the relative scarcity of documentary materials currently available, such a history could not now be written. Thus, no attempt will be made to cover all phases of its historical development, and the separate histories of particular churches and denominations will barely be touched upon. The emphasis throughout is on ideas and the interpretation of events around a particular dynamic; namely, how Chinese Protestants have sought to situate themselves in a socialist society within the unifying framework of the united front as advocated and practiced by the CPC. This dynamic will be discussed with reference to CPC religious policy, the patriotism and resistance of Chinese Protestants, and developments in church and theology.

The united front originated as a strategy of revolutionary involvement, not as a philosophical theory. In China it was practiced as early as the 1920s, although it did not reach its full development until the war against Japan and the subsequent struggle for liberation. Its purpose, both before and after 1949, has been to unite the Chinese people around a common goal or program under the leadership of the CPC. In this study our concern is with developments in the united front after 1949, during the periods of socialist reconstruction (1949–1956), the struggle between two lines and emerging ultra-leftism (1957–1966), the Cultural Revolution era (1966-1976) and the period of the Four Modernizations (1976-present). More particularly, the focus is on the united front and CPC religious policy, which means that the years between 1949 and 1958 and those after 1979 will receive special attention, as they relate to developments in Protestant Christianity.

The slogan that best summarizes the ideal of the united front as it has been understood since 1949 is *qiu tong cun yi*, meaning "seeking the common ground, while reserving differences."[5] With regard to religious policy, the common ground (*tong*) is that of patriotism, socialist reconstruction or modernization, while the differences (*yi*) are the differences in ideological or religious belief and in worldview. The idea of *qiu tong cun yi*, however, has much broader implications, both within the united front and outside of it. For example, it will become evident as we proceed that the idea has been important for the Protestants' principle of mutual respect as well as for the theological reorientation that began to take place in the 1950s. The title of this book is meant to suggest that *qiu tong cun yi* is the fundamental concept with which to interpret religious policy and the Protestant experience in contemporary China.

The first time I heard this phrase was in August 1979 in Princeton, New Jersey. I had been asked to serve as an interpreter for the first religious delegation from the People's Republic of China to visit the United States. They had come to attend the Third World Conference on Religion and Peace, which was meeting at Princeton Theological Seminary. Members of the delegation—Buddhists, Christians and Muslims—stressed again and again that they had come to seek the common ground with religious believers from other parts of the world, not to create controversies or debate differences. In China "seeking the common ground" provides the means whereby men and women holding different worldviews can cooperate in matters of common concern and at the same time retain their particular understandings of faith. While such a framework has definite limitations, it has also made possible a new understanding of religion and society in contemporary China.

A Brief Note on Method

In both theology and the social sciences there has been an increasing preoccupation in the last decade over the question of methodology. This is perhaps more a reflection of the state of the disciplines themselves than it is of the pursuit of a subject that can yield constructive results. The Lutheran theologian Joseph Sittler has suggested a more authentic approach for a book such as this one:

> My own disinclination to state a theological method is grounded in the strong conviction that one does not devise a method and then dig into the data; one lives with the data; lets their force and variety and authenticity generate a sense of what Jean Danielou calls "a way of knowing" appropriate to the nature of the data.[6]

Since 1979 I have literally lived with the data of this book, initially as a fraternal worker of the then United Presbyterian Church in the U.S.A. assigned to Hong Kong to be a liaison following developments in the People's Republic of China; from 1981 to 1983 as a teacher in the Foreign Languages and Literatures Department of Nanjing University; and since 1985 as the Overseas Coordinator for the Amity Foundation, based in Hong Kong, under secondment by the Presbyterian Church (U.S.A.). The doctoral dissertation I submitted to Princeton Theological Seminary represented a preliminary version of the book now before you.[7] My overall approach has been shaped by all of these experiences, and especially in the countless hours of conversations and informal visits with Christians and Chinese intellectuals during my visits to Nanjing. Combined with an abiding interest in understanding and interpreting the role of religious faith in movements of social change, life and work in China has afforded a deeper understanding of the problems and possibilities of Christian participation in a socialist society.

The purpose of this book is to describe, interpret and analyze the Christian experience in China in terms of the relationship between the Protestant Three-Self Movement and the Communist united front. There have been no book-length studies of the TSM in any language, and much of the material that appears here is being presented for the first time to non-Chinese readers. Therefore, a good part of this work will be devoted to the introduction of ideas and the narration of events that relate to our theme. It will be based upon the Chinese-language resources discussed below, supplemented by English-language materials of both a descriptive and interpretive nature. Because the purpose is to understand what Chinese Protestants in the TSM have been saying about themselves, my interpretation will draw primarily on the publications, statements and theological essays of the Protestant leadership in China. In turn, these will have to be analyzed and evaluated as we proceed. It must be acknowledged that any interpretation of contemporary China presents problems with the verification and corroboration of stories and events, and the present study is no exception. As a result, there are areas about which a certain amount of uncertainty remains. These will be noted in the text as they occur.

Parig Digan has called attention to five areas of interpretive disagreement among Christians who are concerned with China—the *theological*, the *missiological*, the *political*, the *ethnic* and the *sinological*, that is, the place of the contemporary church within the four-thousand-year pattern of Chinese history.[8] The task of interpretation has also been influenced by a sixth factor, the renewal of personal contacts with Chinese Christians and the desire for deeper *ecumenical* relationships. In each area there is a range of viewpoints that represents ideas and beliefs which have been formed by the interaction between Christian faith and the contemporary world. The question therefore arises as to how these may be brought together into an interpretive framework within which to view Protestant Christianity and China's united front.

A one-sided emphasis on any single area of interpretive disagreement misses the variety of ways in which Christianity has interacted with Chinese society and culture. In contrast, the relationship between Christianity and the united front suggests a framework of interpretation that focuses on the interaction between faith and society and can encompass all of the above-mentioned areas. Using such a framework, the primary *theological* concern is to understand how Chinese Christians interpret and give expression to their faith in God through Jesus Christ in a secular society. This is at the same time *missiological*, for it suggests the necessity of Christian witness and proclamation in China and is related to an understanding of the Chinese Three-Self Movement.

A consideration of the relationship between Christianity and society is necessarily *political*, because it revolves around the question of the church as a political institution, as well as the nature, extent and purpose of Christian involvement in political life. Moreover, the political dimension in China brings

Christians face to face with the challenge of Marxism. To the extent that our understanding and perspective on the church in China is shaped by our identities as overseas Chinese, white Europeans and North Americans, or as men and women of the Third World, our framework is also racial and *ethnic*. And lest we ignore the impact of Chinese tradition and thus misrepresent the place of religion in Chinese society, our concern must also be *sinological*. A perspective on the Protestant church in contemporary China derived from such a multidimensional understanding may, at the same time, provide a basis for more fruitful *ecumenical* relationships. It is therefore the relationship between faith and society that will guide our approach to understanding Protestant Christianity and China's united front.

Sources

Tian Feng (*TF*) is the official publication of the Three-Self Movement and thus represents the major documentary resource for the history of the Protestant movement in China after 1949. It began publication in February 1945 in Chongqing (Chungking) under the editorship of Y. T. Wu. Originally intended to provide a forum for the discussion of Christian opinion on social issues in China, *Tian Feng* was designated as the official organ of the TSM by the Three-Self Preparatory Committee on April 25, 1951, with editorial offices in Shanghai.[9]

There were also other Protestant journals available in the China of the 1950s. *Xie Jin*, the official publication of the National Christian Council (NCC), was reorganized in 1951 and continued to be issued until 1954. Nanjing Union Theological Seminary put out seven issues of *Jinling xiehe shenxue zhi* (*Nanjing Seminary Journal*, *NSJ*) between 1953 and 1957, each of which included important essays of an interpretive and theological nature. Specialized publications such as *Tian Jia* (*The Christian Farmer*) and *En yu*, a magazine for young people, had generally ceased publication by the mid-1950s. The same was true of most denominational publications. In addition to these magazines and journals, there were a small number of pamphlets, study manuals, devotional books and reference materials issued and distributed in connection with the TSM during the 1950s.[10]

Since 1979 Chinese Protestants have been publishing *Jiao cai*, a publication for lay theological training; *Tian Feng* in a new series (*TF* [*NS*]); the *Nanjing Seminary Journal*, also in a new series (*NSJ* [*NS*]); and *Jiangdao ji*, a quarterly collection of sermons.

There is also a great deal of material for internal circulation, including publications of local Three-Self Committees and Christians' contributions to *Wenshi shi ziliao* (*Resources on Literature and History*), which are unavailable to the researcher. Materials for internal circulation have been "classified" in China so as to restrict readership to certain sections of the population. The *Wenshi ziliao* are especially valuable collections by individuals who were involved in important events, movements and organizations before 1949. Solicited, organized and compiled by different levels of the Chinese People's Political Consultative

Conference (CPPCC), they include contributions by prominent Christians including Y. T. Wu, Liu Liangmo, Jiang Wenhan and T. C. Chao. In addition, local Three-Self organizations may preserve and collect their own *Wenshi ziliao*.

Innumerable books, articles and reports have appeared in Western languages about Christianity in China. After 1949 many first person accounts were written by former missionaries, most of whom tended to take an extremely critical view of both communism and the TSM.[11] Many of these same writers continued to reflect on China and the fate of the churches there throughout the 1950s. Perhaps the most influential publication on Chinese Christianity in that period was *The China Bulletin* (*CB*) issued by the Far Eastern Office of the NCCUSA between 1947 and 1962. Beginning in the mid-1960s, there was an attempt to rethink the China experience among Protestants and Catholics overseas. These studies attained wider recognition, and underwent significant reorientation, after the fall of the "Gang of Four" in 1976. Ecumenical publications such as *China Notes*, *China and Ourselves*, *China Message*, *Tripod*, *Ching Feng* and *Bridge* continue to play an important role in creating a dialogue on Christianity in China. The *Chinese Theological Review* (*CTR*) remains the major source of English-language translations from the contemporary Chinese church.

Both the perspective and the standard of reporting in Christian publications on China vary tremendously, and therefore they must be used with care. It has never been easy to know and understand China, and the problems of developing an accurate picture only increased after the founding of the PRC. For many years outside observers could only rely on their readings from the Chinese press and other reports filtered through Hong Kong, Taiwan and the occasional visitor or emigrant. With the increased opportunity to visit and experience China, some of the difficulties have been overcome, but there is still the danger of basing one's conclusions on a few experiences, "having seen the flowers on horseback" as the Chinese say. No account of the Protestant experience in contemporary China can ever claim to be perfectly objective, and this includes the perspective of Chinese Protestants themselves. It is therefore imperative to ground one's interpretation on the best resources that are available and, at the same time, to clearly indicate the perspective which shapes one's knowledge and understanding.

Chinese government, party and specialized academic publications are also essential for interpreting the Protestant experience in China. The analysis of the united front and religious policy presented here is based mainly on official statements; the writings of party and government leaders, particularly Mao Zedong and Zhou Enlai; and the writings of those entrusted with the implementation of united front policy such as Zhang Zhiyi and Li Weihan. Newspaper accounts, editorials and theoretical essays have also been consulted, primarily for an understanding of more recent trends including the critique of ultra-leftism. Specialized official publications on the academic study of religion have been useful for interpreting the Chinese Marxist view of religion.[12] Local newspapers have not been used extensively, although accounts from Shanghai's *Jie-*

fang ribao (Liberation Daily) did occasionally find their way into *TF* in the early 1950s. The difficulty of using Chinese newspapers and periodicals is well known, and the reader must continually bear in mind the political and educational functions of the media in a situation where the definition of "all the news that's fit to print" is quite restrictive by Western standards.[13]

A special feature of this study is the interviews, which have been conducted with Protestant leaders and several government officials concerned with religious policy. From 1980 to 1983 eighteen individual interviews were granted with Protestant representatives from Shanghai, Nanjing and Hangzhou. Among these were many of the leaders of the national TSM and the China Christian Council from those cities, as well as teaching faculty from Nanjing Union Seminary. In addition, separate interviews were conducted with the then deputy director of the Jiangsu Provincial United Front Work Department (UFWD); the director of research of the Central UFWD in Beijing; a deputy Secretary General of the CPPCC; and a representative of the Central Religious Affairs Bureau (RAB). These interviews were especially useful for interpreting the issues being raised by this study from different perspectives.

Terminology

Translation and terminology present a problem when dealing with a large variety of Chinese materials; for example, there are five different Chinese terms that are roughly equivalent to the English word *unity,* each having a different usage and connotation.[14] Even the word *Christianity* (*jidujiao*) presents difficulties, because it sometimes refers to all Christians and sometimes to Protestants alone.

For the purposes of this study we will generally follow the usage of Chinese Protestants for terminology and translations of a theological nature. Romanization will be according to the *pinyin* system, except in the case of personal names when another form has been widely used or is known to be personally preferred. It will therefore be K. H. Ting and Y. T. Wu rather than Ding Guangxun and Wu Yaozong. All translations, unless otherwise noted, are either my own or those of Janice Wickeri.

Political references and terminology will also be based upon current usage in the PRC. Thus, the designation of 1949 as "Liberation" will be used as an historical expression in common usage. Derogatory quotation marks, which are common in Chinese publications, will be avoided. What the Chinese now refer to as the ten-year-long "Cultural Revolution" (1966-1976) is technically a misnomer. In this study Cultural Revolution will refer specifically to the years between 1966 and 1969, while the longer period will be designated (with some misgivings) as the Cultural Revolution era. Other instances in which terminology is not in accordance with PRC usage will be noted or redefined contextually.

Terms and titles of publications will be translated into English for the convenience of non-Chinese-speaking readers. The *pinyin* titles of Chinese language works appear in the bibliography.

Scope and Content

This book grew out of an interest in theology and mission, of which the church of China is but one example. Based on the conviction that Christians involved in a particular context are the best interpreters of their own theology and experience, a major concern will be to introduce and describe the Chinese Protestant understanding of their own experience over the last forty years. This alone, however, would not be enough. To the extent that one has understood what Chinese Christians have been about, it also becomes necessary to offer a critical evaluation of their efforts. This helps to put the experience of one particular Christian community into a broader historical and theological perspective; at the same time it holds out the possibility of further dialogue.

The Chinese have a saying to the effect that a person observing a situation around the edges may see more clearly than one who is directly involved. This is one reason why the concerned and informed observer is compelled to reflect on the Chinese situation, but it is not the most important one. When all the talk of indigenization, contextualization and incarnation is said and done, this world still belongs to God alone. We participate equally in God's plan of creation, redemption and sanctification, and we have a stake in a common future. All persons, moreover, are subjects of God's judgment and grace. In this light Christians have a special obligation to share with one another what has been granted to each in his or her own portion, lest what was given as a gift be taken as a possession. However dimly and imperfectly we may see or hear, we have both the right and the duty to speak.

The Protestant experience in China is important on its own terms, but it is also significant for a better understanding of theology and the church in the world. An evaluation of that situation is in some ways no less critical for Christians in North America than it is for Christians in China. Today many Christians in different parts of the world are involved in a struggle for justice and are attempting to find a common ground with those alongside of them who do not confess Jesus Christ as Lord. At the same time there is a growing concern to reinterpret the meaning of Christian faith for contemporary society and to rediscover the sources of mission and ecumenism. In these areas in particular, the Chinese Christian experience will be of more general interest.

The point of departure for part 1 is the broader interpretive questions, which have shaped different understandings of the church, Marxism and Christianity in the Chinese context. Part 2 deals with the origin and development of the united front particularly as it relates to religious affairs and the life of the Protestant church in China. The two chapters in this section are concerned with religious policy and practice as they have been defined by the Chinese Communist Party. Part 3 treats the TSM as a *Chinese* movement, the Protestant response to the united front and the Chinese revolution. Beginning with the early involvement of Protestants in the united front, this section proceeds to a consideration of the organization of the TSM, the rejection of Three-Self from the right and the left, and the renewal of the TSM in the 1980s. In part 4 attention shifts to the TSM as a *Christian* movement, including a treatment of selfhood, unity and theological reorientation in Protestant Christianity since 1949. In each area the focus is on how developments in the TSM in the 1950s has helped to shape the restoration of Three-Self in the 1980s. Our conclusion explores the significance of universality and particularity in the Chinese Christian experience.

PART ONE

THE CHURCH, MARXISM, AND CHRISTIANITY IN CHINA

1

Perspectives on the Protestant Church in China

Protestants who are attempting to interpret the relationship between Christian faith and Chinese society would do well to bear in mind Dietrich Bonhoeffer's distinction between the ultimate (grace, justification, God in Christ) and the penultimate (the actual situation in which we are living). Justification in our understanding of Christian faith is the last word (ultimate), but we must go on living in this actual (penultimate) world. The penultimate must not be sacrificed for the ultimate—the radical extreme—nor can the ultimate be compromised by the penultimate. "The penultimate," Bonhoeffer writes in his *Ethics*, "remains even though the ultimate entirely annuls and invalidates it." Moreover, Bonhoeffer argues the case for Christian activity in the world: "Does one not in some cases, by remaining deliberately in the penultimate, perhaps point all the more genuinely to the ultimate, which God will speak in His own time (though even then through a human mouth)?"[1] As is true for any society, socialist China is the realm of the penultimate, and it must never be confused with the ultimate. But by the same token, Christians who have chosen to work deliberately within socialist China may point more directly to the ultimate than those who have not.

Bonhoeffer's Christocentric theology has never found many eager listeners in China, but it may help those of us outside to understand the different approaches conservatives and liberals have taken to church and society there. In the 1950s two perspectives dominated most writing and reporting about China and the TSM. The conservative approach tended toward the radical extreme, emphasizing absolute opposition between Christianity and Chinese society. This perspective, which is still with us, is characterized by bitterness and suspicion toward almost anything connected with the Three-Self Movement.

Although the liberal perspective also understands Christianity and Chinese society to be in opposition, it stresses the TSM's need to compromise in order for the church to maintain some sort of *modus vivendi* under communism. While the second approach was somewhat more sympathetic to the TSM, it tended to

3

be judgmental and thus misunderstand the type of relationship that Protestant leaders were trying to establish. Both conservative and liberal approaches tended to be static in their understanding of church and society, and they inhibited the development of any kind of relationship with Chinese Christians in the Three-Self Movement.

There were other voices in the 1950s pointing to a more dynamic understanding of the TSM and a more constructive approach to what our relationship with China should be, but these were largely neglected. It was only in the late 1960s and early 1970s that conservative and liberal perspectives were seriously challenged or, to be more precise, that the challenge of China was actually heard. Following the theological and social changes that were taking place all over the world, a new spectrum of interpretations began to open up Christian faith to the Chinese experience.

The terms conservative and liberal are vague and sometimes misleading. Nevertheless, they are useful in characterizing two spectrums of opinion about the Protestant church in contemporary China. The conservative approach is very definitely on the right politically, and theologically conservative-evangelical or fundamentalist. The liberal approach may either be conservative or liberal-democratic politically, and theologically has been associated with people from the mainline-ecumenical churches, which include a wide range of liberal, neo-orthodox, existentialist and other theological perspectives. The terms *conservative* and *liberal* as they are used here are only intended to facilitate discussion, not to draw hard and fast lines between opposing camps.

The Conservative Perspective

There is not one conservative perspective, but rather a range of conservative opinion, which has been evolving over the last three decades. It includes some former missionaries to China, often those who had been part of the China Inland Mission or smaller conservative churches. Also included would be many overseas Chinese, as well as a large number of the Christians who fled to Hong Kong and Taiwan around 1949. In the 1950s those associated with the China Lobby, such as Walter Judd, strongly supported the anti-communist stance of the churches and governments of Taiwan and the United States, and denounced anything connected with the TSM. There are still a large number of independent China-oriented mission groups and research centers that have generally been hostile to the CPC and suspicious of the TSM. The publications of these and similar groups and individuals have been voluminous.

Perhaps the most extreme position taken in the 1950s was that of Samuel Boyle, a former China missionary connected with the Independent Board for Presbyterian China Missions and a staunch fundamentalist. He saw the situation in China after 1949 as a special case of the more general fundamentalist-modernist controversy. Actively encouraging Christian disassociation from both the Chinese government and the NCC in the late 1940s, he extended his attack to include the Church of Christ in China, the National Council of Churches in the U.S.A. (NCCUSA) and the World Council of Churches (WCC). By 1960, drawing heavily on a fundamentalist interpretation of Luther and Calvin, he concluded that any Christian associated with the TSM was not of the "true" church. Churches that were members of the WCC, as well as the Roman Catholic Church, also lacked the marks of a true church, and so, "In today's crisis in Christendom our first task is to separate from all such organizations."[2]

Not all conservative interpretations of China have been as intemperate and overtly political, but the assumption that Christianity and communism should stand in fundamental opposition remains the same. For many, this position was strengthened or even vindicated by the experience of the Cultural Revolution. In 1969 Leslie Lyall proposed an apocalyptic understanding of China and of a world in turmoil based on Revelation 12:

> Throughout the world today—and nowhere more evident than China— the great red dragon confronts the church of Christ. The agelong war in the heavenly places is speeding to its climax (v.7). Satan, the deceiver, confusing men with his specious ideologies and attractive cults, has been cast out into the earth as a defeated foe (v.9, 10).[3]

As a result of the reforms and leadership changes in China since 1978, Leslie Lyall has developed a more sympathetic approach. But for many conservative Christian writers the problem remains the same. According to Carl Lawrence, "Any political changes we have seen over the past few years have been simply orchestrated undulations necessary to prepare China for the coming 'utopia.' "[4] His message is quite clear: there can only be confrontation between church and society in China no matter what kind of communist government is in power.

Jonathan Chao, director of the Chinese Church Research Center, has developed a conservative-evangelical perspective based on the need for an indigenous Chinese Christianity. His early advice that Western churches should discourage the return of their missionaries to China and not anticipate the conversion of Chinese Christians away from a socialist way of life is sound.[5] In Chao's view, there is a "house church movement" in China which is the only authentic voice of the Protestant community there. Its history since 1949 has been one of prolonged suffering, interpreted by Chao as a reflection of "the suffering, death, resurrection of Jesus and the Pentecostal gift of the Spirit." Christianity and the Chinese revolution are still in opposition, but Christians should see their suffering as "a gift of God's profound grace."[6]

Although he acknowledges the importance of Chinese Protestant efforts to eliminate denominationalism and free the Chinese church from foreign control, Chao persists in putting a question mark over the motives of the Three-Self leaders who organized the process. Instead, he imposes his own opposition to communism and theological liberalism onto the situation in China, abstracting his theological and missiological concerns from the socio-political realities of the Chinese situation. We shall see that the home worship gatherings are indeed a highly significant development in Chinese Protestantism. But they do not represent what Chao views as a popular tide rising across the Chinese nation.[7]

Moreover, by separating "Christian suffering" in China from the suffering of the Chinese people over the last 200 years, Chao perpetuates the idea that Christianity is alien to the revolutionary process. Franklin Woo has observed,

> Many Christians supported the Communist revolution out of religious conviction that life would be better for the majority of suffering Chinese people, just as many others did not. They did so by identifying themselves with the hopes and aspirations of their own people, and thus rediscovered their mission as God's witnessing people. Christians of the world who live with more material benefits need to see China, with its generations of deprivation and suffering, from a "God's-plan" for creation perspective, and ask themselves what God's love requires of them in doing justice today. (Mic. 6:8)[8]

By failing to understand Christianity in the context of the Chinese revolution, Jonathan Chao presents a one-sided approach to the Protestant situation in contemporary China. It is a perspective that, despite claims to the contrary, denies the creative possibility of Christian and Marxist cooperation in the Chinese situation.

Although there has been some evolution of the conservative perspective on China over the last three decades, the basic problem regarding church and society is the same. It is a problem common to all approaches in which Christians regard Communists as "the enemy."[9] In this view there is an inability to see any possibility of dialogue with Communists on a *human* level, and fellow Christians who have chosen to cooperate are either viewed with suspicion or dubbed as betrayers. Moreover, this approach is unrealistic for Christians who are living in a socialist society, because they are encouraged to take a stance that is at best passive and at worst apocalyptic. The conservative leaves no room for the individual to work deliberately in and *for* society, and thereby witness to Jesus Christ in a Marxist framework. Thus there is a failure either to take seriously the positive content of communism or to develop a creative theological response.

A second problem is ideological. Although most theological conservatives appear to be sincere in their evangelical motivations, their Christian understanding has been formed in social contexts vastly different from that of the People's Republic of China. As a result, their theological perspective is bound up with other presuppositions about the nature of society, politics and economics. To the extent that such assumptions remain unspoken and unchallenged, there is the problem that what on the surface seems to be "purely religious" in fact involves a great deal more. This is part of the argument that liberation theologians from Latin America have been making for the past twenty years against liberals and conservatives alike. So much of what is said about the political nature of the TSM leaders in conservative quarters is little different from the charges they have been making over and over against ecumenical churches and agencies since the 1920s. The ideological bias against socialism is evident in most of the writings cited in this section, and it remains a fundamental barrier to understanding the situation of Christianity in the PRC.

A final problem is that of ecclesiology. The Chinese church has only now begun the task of rebuilding and church construction. What will it look like in the next twenty or thirty years? No one has a ready answer. But it is clear that some more stable form of church structure will be needed, one that is truly Christian and truly Chinese. There are tens of thousands of churches and home worship gatherings scattered across China, but how will they grow and develop and be sustained? These are ecclesiological questions that Chinese Protestants must learn to deal with among themselves. Christians overseas should not attempt to exacerbate what misunderstandings and divisions, theological or otherwise, remain in the Chinese church. Instead we should draw a lesson from our own church histories about how long and arduous the path to unity and reconciliation can be.[10]

The Liberal Perspective

Missionaries and representatives from American mainline denominational mission boards that had been active in China gathered in 1951 to assess their experiences. Their evaluation was based upon replies to questionnaires received from 152 missionaries who had returned from China as well as discussion in a three-day consultation. The thirty-page mimeographed report that summarizes their findings indicates the basic problem with the liberal approach to China in the 1950s: a failure to even consider the Chinese revolution or the revolutionary movement that brought it into being, and thus a failure to think anew about the role of Christianity and the mission of the church.[11] Don MacInnis, who charges that new missionaries appointed to China as late as 1948 were not even briefed about the social issues raised by the revolution, says of this report:

> Nowhere do these missionaries, recently living in the midst of the greatest revolutionary upheaval in modern history, refer to the cataclysmic event, or to the social forces which brought it about; nor do they point to the need to understand and relate to such events in the future. Their concerns are parochial, institutional, introverted, subjective, focused on themselves, the mission, the church, and the institution they served.[12]

In the 1950s and early 1960s the liberal perspective on China was most forcefully represented by three men: Wallace Merwin, who was director of the NCCUSA China Committee throughout the 1950s; Francis Price Jones, who was editor of that committee's *China Bulletin* and a historian-translator concerned with Christianity in China; and Frank Price, director of the Missionary Research Library and a research secretary of the Division of Foreign Missions of the NCCUSA. All three had been China missionaries, and Price was especially well known for his work with the Chinese rural church, the NCC and Nanking Theological Seminary. Their opinions reflected those of many other mainline executives, missionaries and theologians in the United States and overseas.[13] This same perspective still shapes the understanding of many Christians who are concerned with developments in the church in China.

Because they did not take seriously the forces behind the Chinese revolutionary movement, American liberals could only see the excesses and injustices of the early years of the People's Republic. When United States troops began fighting in China in a war by proxy on the Korean peninsula, the difficulty in coming to terms with the Chinese revolution became even greater. Thus Wallace Merwin was vehement in this attack against Communist China and highly insulting to Protestant leaders there in an article entitled "Can the Church Survive in China?" published in 1953. Although he admits there was no government policy of religious persecution, Chinese Christians in his view were being "manipulated," "indoctrinated," "subjugated" and in other ways forced into all sorts of things by the Communists. One gets no sense in this article that some Christians might have been discovering what it meant to be patriotic Chinese who supported the People's Government, but only that they were compromising their faith and in other ways reacting to what Merwin calls the "terror" of the times.[14] The early 1950s were difficult times for many Chinese Protestants, but we shall see that Christians were also discovering a sense of hopefulness in the changes the revolution was bringing to Chinese society. This, however, was something that, at least at that time, former missionaries like Wallace Merwin could not understand.[15]

More than most other American churchmen, Frank Price did try to understand the challenge of Marxism and the Chinese revolution. His *Marx Meets Christ* is a thoughtful and personal reflection on the Communist challenge, emphasizing the encounter between two persons, two ideas, two systems, two faiths.[16] This work presents an interpretation of Marxist theory set against the background of Price's personal encounter with Marxist-Leninist practice in the Chinese revolution. Frank Price readily acknowledges the positive content of the Communists' revolutionary message, the achievements of the CPC program in China, and the problems with Western capitalism and Christian complacency. He is also aware of the difficulties with the theory and practice of Marxism-Leninism, and he forcefully presents the challenge that Christian faith poses to all systems.

For a missionary with his background, one who had been so involved with the rural church, one would expect Frank Price to have been able to accept the Chinese revolution and to understand the type of relationship Protestants were trying to establish in the TSM. But he could do neither. It is in part because of his position of ecclesiastical and social influence in pre-1949 China that Price could not accept the radical restructuring which came with the Chinese revolution. As late as 1948 he was still contemplating the possibility of a "Christian China" whose twilight or dawn would decide that country's future.[17] This would be a China forged on liberal-democratic principles and led by Chiang Kai-shek, who Price should have realized was neither liberal nor democratic. "The Christian World," wrote Price, "should rejoice that China in her crisis has had such a leader, and pray that he may be given wisdom, grace and strength to guide his nation aright through the years of rebuilding."[18]

It is not surprising that the author of those words would have difficulty in understanding the possibility of Christian cooperation with a Communist government. According to Price, "True Christians today would cooperate in the search for intermediate forms of government that lie between capitalist democracy and totalitarian socialism,"[19] but Christians could not work with the Communists. This is because of what Price termed the inner moral weaknesses of any Communist system:

> My own experience in Communist China revealed what seemed to me four serious moral weaknesses in the Communist system: deceitful propaganda and false accusations; hatred and an almost demonic brutality toward those who are considered "enemies of socialism"; tyranny over the mind and spirit of men; and idolatry—not so much the official atheism as the worship of false, man-made gods and the absolutizing of human power.[20]

Depending upon one's outlook, a similar set of accusations could be levelled against almost any political system. The problem was that for Price, communism was first and foremost a moral encounter and thus a religious temptation. This is always part of the Communist challenge, but it was not for Chinese Christians, even for those whom he puts in the "radical wing," the whole story. For such individuals there was always the matter of reserved differences within the common ground.

Francis Price Jones was more moderate and restrained in his approach than either Merwin or Price. His *The Church in Communist China* still remains a useful account of Protestantism in the 1950s. It must be said to his credit that Jones never questioned the sincerity or Christian commitment of TSM leaders in his published work. However, throughout the pages of his book and the *China Bulletin*, which he edited, the reader again and again confronts Jones' hostility toward the readjustments Chinese Christians were making under communism. He writes, for example, that Y. T. Wu "allowed the church to become a 'captive church' doing nothing but parrot the Communist line." This compromise was necessary to preserve a *modus vivendi* under communism.[21] Elsewhere Jones writes that his own analysis is substantially similar to that of the fundamentalist missionary Samuel Boyle.[22] Francis Price Jones tried very hard to be fair and objective, but he could not come to terms with a Christianity that supported socialism, affirmed the PRC, and rejected the foreign missionary presence.

The liberal perspective on China and the TSM suffered from an ideological bias against communism no less than that of the conservative. This resulted in an inability to understand that Christians could affirm the Chinese revolution and still maintain their sense of integrity. For Frank Price it was always a question of Marxian ideology versus Christian ethics.[23] And yet, as we have seen, Price had his own vision of the political order with its own liberal underpinnings. There was thus a tendency to confuse the struggle between communism and liberalism in China with a Communist struggle against the Christian church. It is true that the Communists themselves contributed to such confusion in the excesses of their revolutionary programs and their hurried attempts at social reorganization. But this should not have prevented American liberals from understanding that Chinese Protestants found good reason to support a revolution that was also bringing many positive changes to China.

A second problem with the liberal perspective was its consistent indifference to the question of patriotism. This is related to a theological difficulty that took for granted the incarnation in Western cultural and intellectual terms. As we shall see below, liberal missionaries were prepared to sacrifice the national rootedness of the Chinese church for a Western dominated ecumenical relatedness. But by so doing, they would alienate the church from the society of which it should have been a part.

Both conservative and liberal perspectives on the TSM tended to draw a sharp line between church and society in China. The relationship between faith and politics was always viewed from the standpoint of the missionary past or in terms of theological understandings that prevailed elsewhere. Conservative and liberal lines of interpretation very quickly hardened and became rigid and fixed. As a result, an "us and them" approach came to characterize the way in which their adherents looked at China, thus preventing the possibility of any breakthrough in ecumenical understanding.

Conservatives and liberals always maintained a very genuine concern for friends and former colleagues in China, and they never lost hope that the church would survive. It is precisely because of this that they should have rejoiced over whatever Christian contacts could have been established with the Chinese church. In time, some of them did. Walter Freytag, whose position is termed "extreme" by Francis Price Jones, understood very well what was required of Christians overseas in their relationships with the Chinese church. First, "we must keep our fellowship with Christianity in China free from our political interests. The more we might wish that China was not Communist, the more false it is to look at Christianity in China only from the one point of view of discovering how far it corresponds to that wish." Second, Christians in other places must "refrain from setting (themselves) up as judges out of zeal for the Gospel . . . (they) should also refrain from conveying to the Chinese Christians what (they) expect them to do. . . ." Finally, Christians overseas should not isolate their brothers and sisters in China.[24] On each and every point the words and actions of a Leslie Lyall or a Frank Price fell short of what was required to maintain the fellowship with Christians in China.

Shortly before his death, Searle Bates, the doyen of China mission historians and one who understood what Freytag meant, expressed a wise and farsighted opinion.

Our prime concern now and for the long pull should be: first, the well-being of the Chinese people, one-fourth of the persons in the world; second, the relationships between that near billion and the rest, especially the North Americans among whom we carry direct responsibility. . . . Beneath and above all differences of ideology and of systems, Chinese men, women and children are one with us in the family of God.[25]

It was from a similar understanding that some Christians had already begun to develop a more positive appreciation of the Chinese revolution, thus allowing them to view the changes that were taking place in a more dynamic way.

The Challenge of China: Emerging Perspectives, 1949–1979

The "debacle" of Christian missions in China had far-reaching implications, not only for the church in China, but for an understanding of mission in the rest of the world as well. Commenting on the changing view of mission after the founding of the WCC in 1948, Lesslie Newbigin assigns a prominent place to the end of foreign missionary activity in China and the questions it posed for the church:

It helped to produce a sense of crisis, though it is to be doubted whether the rethinking was sufficiently profound. Perhaps the most searching of questions arise from the fact—generally accepted—that the Communist government has been able to accomplish many of the reforms of which missions were the early advocates but which they were not strong enough to complete. The end of missions in China has therefore raised very profound questions regarding the relation of the Christian world mission to the whole world-wide process of secularization, and the exercise of political power.[26]

There were individual missionaries who realized the challenge that Marxism raised before the Chinese church and the missionary enterprise, and who understood that Chinese Christianity would have to go through a radical process of change in order to adapt to the new situation. Among Protestant missionaries from the English-speaking world, one thinks of such people as R. O. Hall, formerly Anglican bishop of Hong Kong and Macao, who as early as 1942 had contemplated the possibility of a Communist China and the role of the church there. Another British Anglican is David Paton, whose prophetic ideas on the implications of the Chinese revolution for the church we will consider shortly. The name of Randolph Sailer, a Presbyterian who taught for twenty-seven years at Yenching University, stands out among American missionaries. A lifelong friend of the Chinese people, Christians as well as Communists, Sailer understood their aspirations and believed that Christianity in China would have to go through a period of death and rebirth. There were a number of Canadian missionaries, including Edward Johnson, former Presbyterian missionary and one of the initiators of the Canada China Programme, and, of course, James Endicott.[27]

More than anyone else, the Rev. James G. Endicott stood at the center of controversies surrounding the North American understanding of the Chinese revolution in the 1950s. He has often been compared to his British counterpart, Hewlett Johnson, the "red" dean of Canterbury Cathedral. Both of them travelled to the PRC several times in the 1950s in order to put China's case before the Christians of the West. Endicott, who had worked as a United Church of Canada missionary in Sichuan for twenty-two years, was forced to resign his ministry for supporting the Chinese revolution, and he was subsequently vilified in the Western press. He continued to press his case through his writing about China in revolution on the pages of the *Canadian Far Eastern Newsletter*.

Endicott and Hewlett Johnson stand in the tradition of Christian-communism, which has never been part of the Christian mainstream. But it is necessary neither to adopt their theology nor endorse their political line in order to understand their importance for Chinese Christians. Jim Endicott and Hewlett Johnson tried to present matters as the Chinese saw them, affirming Christian fellowship and solidarity with a struggling Chinese church increasingly isolated by the rhetoric of the Cold War. At great personal risk they helped to keep lines of communication open with the Chinese church in the 1950s.

In his introduction to Endicott's biography, K. H. Ting wrote:

Today, thirty years since liberation, there is in China a Christianity to which revolution is no longer a stranger, and a revolution to which Christianity is not such a stranger either. Jim Endicott contributed much to the evolvement of both.[28]

Thirty-six years after his forced resignation, the United Church of Canada apologized to Endicott, recognizing that events of the past thirty years had borne out many of his predictions and actions, and affirming "the faithful and courageous contribution he made to the cause of peace and global justice."[29]

David Paton, who worked for more than ten years with the YMCA and the Christian movement in China, also understood the issues of justice that were involved in the Chinese revolution. But he was more immediately concerned with its impact on the theology and mission of the church. In *Christian Missions and the Judgment of God* Paton's thesis was "that God's judgment today is being executed upon His Church by political movements which are anti-Christian." Rather than offer advice to Christians living in the PRC, Paton argued that Western churches must discover what the Chinese experience had to say to their own situations. His own answer was unequivocal: Christian missions in China were a part of the total imperialist aggression of the West, and this jeopardized the future of the missionary enterprise.[30] Paton also understood the Communist challenge to the church in China. "Why did we fail? The Communist answer will be, 'Because of your bourgeois capitalist background.' "[31] At the time of his writing, however, the ideas of David Paton, like those of Roland Allen before him, could not even begin to be discussed, much less implemented, in the the life of the church.

It was not until the 1960s that the challenge posed by the Christian experience in China was to have any kind of significant impact upon the churches of Europe and North America. This was in large measure due to the fundamental shift in moral and religious values that came to be associated with that turbulent decade. In America this shift was characterized by a growing secularism, an increasing awareness of the glaring social contradictions in American life and a doubt about the capacity of existing institutions to rectify the contradictions.[32] The consciousness of urban problems, racial injustice, American interventionism and social and technological change spawned increasingly militant movements of blacks and minorities, students and women. It also brought together a broad coalition led by young people to end United States involvement in the Vietnam War.

These social changes also had their impact upon theology and the church. The 1960s marked the end of a theological era, which could be characterized in Protestant thought by Barth and Tillich in dialogue. The rediscovery of Bonhoeffer, "death of God" theology, secular theology and the theology of hope were significant theological responses to the experience of Christians from Europe and North America. Despite the ephemeral nature of much of what was called theology in the 1960s, men and women were trying to grapple theologically with questions for which existing institutions had no convincing answers.

What in the long run would be more important for an understanding of Christian faith and the Chinese experience was the challenge of Christians from the Third World. This challenge was put before the church at the World Conference on Church and Society called by the WCC in Geneva in 1966. Meeting to discuss and debate the theme "Christians in the Technical and Social Revolutions of Our Time," the conference was designed to speak *to* and not *for* the churches. It was the first ecumenical gathering in which the majority of participants were laypeople, and in which more than half of the delegates came from the Third World. Discussions centered around issues that were challenging the church from the outside, questions of economic development, technology and revolution. It is this last emphasis that needs to be underlined, for the message of the conference called upon Christians to recognize the radical or revolutionary position as a legitimate Christian option which "should have its rightful place in the life of the Church and in ongoing discussion of social responsibility."[33]

Revolution in general, and the Chinese revolution in particular, was also the concern of a new generation of students. China's Cultural Revolution came at the time of student uprisings in Paris, Berkeley and New York, and it led many to reinterpret revolutionary China in a more positive light. Some of this China interest was naive and overly enthusiastic. It was in part a reaction against the negative picture of China that had been painted in the 1950s, and in part a misunderstanding of China in light of the students' own needs and interests. Many young people began to read the works of Mao Zedong, and they studied the writings of Edgar Snow and others who were sympathetic to the Chinese revolution. In 1971 the first group of American China scholars visited the PRC, and it included two theologians.[34] More important, Nixon's visit to China in 1972 and the signing of the Shanghai Communique marked the end of China's isolation and a new opening to the outside world.

In the church the earliest attempt to develop a new perspective on the changes taking place in China and their significance for the world also came from the students. Meeting at almost the same time as the Geneva conference on church and society, the World Student Christian Federation (WSCF) initiated a study project on "The Rise of China and the Future of International Affairs" headed by Ross Terrill and divided into three regional groups. The aim of the study project was not theological reflection, but the interpretation of the Chinese revolution and its implications for Christians throughout the world.[35]

The Båstad and Louvain consultations organized by the Lutheran World Federation (LWF) and Pro Mundi Vita (PMV) in 1974 signaled the first attempt by European and North American churches to reconsider Christianity in light of the Chinese experience since the 1950s. Recognizing that a new phase in thinking about China had in part been occasioned by the global ferment in Christianity the world over, the two consultations set themselves the task of discussing five themes:

—The New Man in China and in Christianity
—Faith and Ideology in the Context of New China
—Revolutionary Antagonism and Christian Love
—The New China and the History of Salvation
—Implications of the New China for the Self-Understanding of the Church.[36]

One can see that when the ninety men and women gathered at Louvain to consider these themes, they were dealing with questions that were confronting churches around the world in a variety of different forms.

If one theological question stands out from the Båstad-Louvain consultations, a question that had been part of all ecumenical discussions on church and society since Geneva, and one that had polarized Christians who stood on different sides of the issue, it was the question of the relationship between salvation and humanization. This issue was related to the differing views of the "new man" in China, the "Christian" values implicit in the Chinese revolution, the usefulness of speaking in terms of religious analogies and alternatives, and the relationship between Christianity and Marxism. The salvation-humanization question as it was raised during and after Louvain led many people to a more positive understanding of the changes taking place in China, while it led others to reject the possibility of any kind of Christian-Marxist rapprochement.

At Båstad, C. S. Song's paper, "The New China and Salvation History," was a careful Protestant attempt to deal with the question. Song was concerned to establish a link between New China and Judeo-Christian salvation history. "Salvation history, in the sense of God's acts in history is intensely acted out in the transition of the old China to the New China and in the continuing effort of the Chinese Communist Party to transform man and his society." For Song, the acts of God are implicit in the revolutionary movements of humanization and liberation. Salvation in this context becomes "the freedom to be human," but it cannot be achieved without the freedom of the Spirit in China or anywhere else. Nevertheless, this understanding calls into question the claim of Western Christianity to represent the whole of salvation history, and it compels Christians to accept China as a legitimate concern for theological reflection.[37]

Song here represents both the strength and the weakness of the theological thinking that emerged from Louvain. At its best, such thinking was able to take the ideological challenge of China seriously, in a way that was neither defensive nor doctrinaire. It argued that China was important for the church, but that it could not be understood theologically within traditional Western frameworks. This was a significant departure on Christianity and China, representing a perspective that liberals and conservatives could not accept in the 1950s and cannot accept today. Theologically, it underscored the *continuity* between humanization and salvation in any movement for justice.

The weakness of the theological rethinking, which began in Louvain, was that it de-emphasized the uniqueness of the Christian message for China. Some Louvain participants, including C.S. Song, seemed to be baptizing the Chinese revolution using Christian categories and Christian analogies; for example, comparing the Long March to the Exodus. Others tended to overemphasize the "spirituality" of Mao Zedong Thought in much the same way that the ultra-leftists were doing in China. Still others attempted to bring Christian categories into harmony with Maoism. Writing in 1979 Ray Whitehead observed, "In the Maoist revolution to a significant extent justice is done and the broken are healed. Insofar as this is true, what Christians call God's saving power is there."[38] This comes dangerously close to identifying Christian salvation with the achievements of the Chinese revolution, going a great deal further in this direction than Chinese Christians ever would themselves.

Speaking in 1976, K. H. Ting cautioned against the tendency, which he saw in some of the Båstad-Louvain papers, to "politicize religious theological convictions and make them into a substitute sort of Marxism."[39] Although they firmly support the achievements of the Chinese Revolution, Chinese theologians have also understood the uniqueness of the Christian message for their own situation. The *discontinuity* between salvation in Jesus Christ and the humanization implicit in the Chinese revolution must continue to be affirmed. In this sense, the theological thinking that began in Louvain went too far in the direction of *continuity* and humanization.

Yet in another sense the redirection that started with Louvain did not go far enough. It is understandable that whatever insights came out of ecumenical consultations on China in the 1970s would be limited because of the absence of Chinese participation. What is not as easily understood is the manner in which ecumenical gatherings of Christians organized in Europe and North America tried to set the agenda for understanding and relating to China. Christians from China, as well as other Asian Christians, have indicated that this was a major weakness of the church in China studies in the 1970s. It is not surprising, therefore, that the theological directions that emerged from such consultations did not become the basis for new relationships with the Chinese church. For that to happen, Chinese Christians would have to help set the terms for the encounter.

However much progress was made toward understanding China in the 1970s, the effort faltered on the very point that had clouded perceptions in the 1950s. A new beginning could only come with a renewal of fellowship with Chinese Christians and a willingness to first listen to things from their point of view. As relationships began to develop after 1979, a perspective on church and society in China began to emerge that shed new light on our own understanding of faith and witness as well. This was decisive.

Writing about ten years after his own exit from China, David Paton indicated what was needed for an understanding of Christianity in the Chinese experience and what was to a large extent missing at Louvain:

> I know that I have never ceased to belong in some way to the Chinese Church, have never been able to speak or write in complete unawareness of what they might have to say if they heard me; have tried to think more in terms of "us" and less in terms of "them"; and have all the time been also aware that I might be doing the job so badly that the day might come when the Chinese Church would disown me, if in fact it has not already done so.[40]

It is only out of such conviction that an understanding of Christianity in the Chinese experience is possible at all.

2

Christianity, Marxism, and the Chinese Context

Implicit throughout the discussion in the previous chapter has been the question of Marxism and its relationship to Christianity. For Christians from the West, the Three-Self Movement put Marxism and Christianity in China right into the center of theological concern. However, dialogue about Marxism and Christianity in China or anywhere else was hardly possible for Europeans and North Americans in the 1950s. In the 1960s and 1970s we have seen that there were attempts to understand Mao Zedong Thought and Chinese socialism, but whatever discussion there was remained one-sided and without insight into the realities of the Christian-Marxist relationship in China. As we now try to come to terms with the Protestant experience in the PRC, the need to understand the theory and practice of Chinese Marxism in relationship to Chinese Christianity has become more important than ever.

Christianity and Marxism

The encounter between Christians and Marxists in China has developed differently from that in either Europe or Latin America. This reflects the different historical conditions of the Chinese revolution as well as the different experience of Christianity within the revolutionary process. However informative the insights from the European experience of Christian-Marxist dialogue and the Latin American liberation theology may be, it is important to demonstrate why neither approach is applicable to the Chinese situation.

It is necessary here to say something about the nature of Marxism, which has shaped the relationship with Christianity in China. This will set the stage for the discussion of the united front and religious policy in the next two chapters.

The European Experience of Christian-Marxist Dialogue

The history of Christian-Marxist interaction in Europe extends back before the possibility of dialogue ever existed. From the writings of the young Marx

17

on religion to the triumph of the October Revolution to the growth of communism as a worldwide revolutionary force, Marxism has exerted a profound and lasting impact on European Christianity. In this encounter the possibility of what Roger Garaudy has termed a movement from "anathema to dialogue" has been a relatively recent phenomenon.[1] Although there were some Christians who developed a positive interest in Communism in the 1920s, it was not until the early 1960s that a genuine *dialogue* emerged between Christian theologians and Marxist philosophers in Europe. This was related to such factors as the de-Stalinization campaign after the 20th Party Congress in the USSR, the easing of the Cold War tensions, changes in the Roman Catholic world following Vatican II, and increased Eastern European participation in the ecumenical movement.[2] Intellectually, the reawakened interest in the writings of the young Marx among Christians and Marxists alike created the possibility for fruitful exchange and mutual questioning. However, this stage in the Christian-Marxist encounter was short lived. Following events in Czechoslovakia in 1968, there was a decline in interest in the dialogue and a decreasing possibility for the open exchange of ideas. It remains to be seen how the *glasnost* of the 1980s will shape relationships between Christians and Marxists in the USSR and Eastern Europe in the years to come.

Although the Christian-Marxist dialogue was but a small episode in the European encounter, it made a significant contribution toward mutual understanding.[3] Paul Mojzes, who has perhaps had more contacts with the Christian-Marxist dialogue in Eastern Europe than anyone else, understands dialogue to be the primary category for defining and interpreting the Christian-Marxist relationship in that area. On this basis he has offered five different approaches to dialogue in Eastern Europe, which have varied from time to time and from country to country:

1. The total absence of dialogue, involving the annihilation of churches by the Communist government, as in Albania;

2. The avoidance of dialogue, coexistence and political cooperation leading to limited cooperation, which Mojzes understands to be the situation in the USSR, Bulgaria and Rumania;

3. Practical dialogue despite official disclaimers, in the case of East Germany;

4. Carefully managed dialogue in order to facilitate cooperation recognizing each other's strength, in Hungary and Poland;

5. Critical involvement in dialogue, pluralism of expectations and attitudes, which Mojzes finds in Czechoslovakia and Yugoslavia.[4]

In each typology the issue of whether or not to dialogue has become central to the position of Christian and Marxist alike. In Eastern European church-state relations there has been a movement between dialogue and confrontation, cooperation and accommodation, discretion and valor, which has influenced every aspect of Christian existence.[5] The whole character of the relationship has emerged from an understanding of Christianity and Communism as competing forces. This has shaped both Christian and Marxist perspectives as they have emerged within the context of Western civilization, and it suggests why the same set of typologies cannot be applied *mutatis mutandis* to China.

The Christian-Marxist dialogue developed within Christendom where communism has been viewed as alternative and challenge, judgment and hope, enemy and friend, at least since the time of the First International (1864–1876). The Christian's view of communism has been intimately related to his or her view of Western civilization. The Czech theologian Josef Hromadka, for example, associated the rise of communism with the spiritual and cultural decadence of Christendom. For him, in the years after the revolution in Czechoslovakia, communism was both a judgment and a hope, as these terms have been understood theologically.[6] Alternatively, Emil Brunner and Reinhold Niebuhr saw communism as a spiritual, cultural and social challenge to be resisted and opposed. Although the Christian-Marxist dialogue has developed considerably since the 1950s, the tendency to understand Christianity and Marxism as two *different* roads to the future of civilization has persisted. In this view their relationship has commonly been understood as an encounter between rival movements.

The history of the encounter in China, however, has been vastly different. Both Christianity and Marxism entered China as foreign doctrines at the height of Western expansionism. Yet each had different purposes and functions. Although Protestant and Catholic missions played a role in the foreign penetration of China, Christianity itself was more commonly understood in relation to questions of personal salvation, social service and gradual change. In contrast, Marxism entered China much later and became powerful as an ideology of revolution. Although initially supported by outside Commintern "missionaries," the CPC was for all intents and purposes an independent party at the time of its creation in 1921. While Western missionaries and Chinese church leaders were still talking about indigenization and operating from an urban base in the 1930s, the CPC was establishing itself in the countryside as a broadly based mass movement. The difference in these two histories means that Christianity and communism in China cannot in any realistic sense be understood as rival movements.

There was some discussion of the "choice" between Christianity and communism before 1949, but this was largely confined to a small circle of missionaries, students and intellectuals, most of whom had no direct experience with the CPC.[7] Whatever vision there had ever been of a specifically *Christian* program for social reconstruction in China had, by the end of the 1930s, given out.[8] Christians themselves were never more than a tiny fraction of the Chinese population, and they did not represent an alternative road to the political future of China. Although the theological challenge of Christianity is present whenever and wherever the gospel is confessed, this did not have the same social implications in China as it did in Europe.

For its part, the CPC did not have to face the task of confronting a powerful institutional church after 1949. Nor did it have to relate to a people whose whole outlook had been molded by Judeo-Christian tradition. The difference between this situation and that of the USSR and Eastern Europe cannot be stressed too strongly. In China the major problem from the Communist side after 1949 was to separate the churches from reactionary foreign influences. This also became the major task of the TSM in its effort to identify with the Chinese people. It was a posture that facilitated Christian cooperation with the CPC on important social and political issues, while at the same time preserving the Christians' identity as religious believers. In this situation Protestants of whatever persuasion have not tended to view communism as a theological problem, nor have they seen Christianity and Marxism confronting one another as enemies. There have been significant exceptions to this position from the Christian as well as the Communist sides, but at its best it has made the Christian-Marxist relationship in China a much more cooperative enterprise than it has been in any Eastern European situation, at least insofar as the united front has been a function of Chinese religious policy.

This suggests a second major difference between the European and Chinese situations. The European Christian-Marxist dialogue of the 1960s was by its very nature theological and philosophical. Although in practice the concerns of Christians living in Eastern Europe were more concrete, the very fact that Christians and Marxists could argue their differences in the world of ideas represented a significant achievement. Thus papers were written and conferences held to discuss and debate various aspects of the encounter. In contrast, there has been no popular movement in China. Chinese theologians have for the most part avoided theoretical discussions with Marxists on the nature of religion or the existence of God in the belief that there is little to be gained in exploring such questions. As they began a process of theological reorientation in the 1950s, a philosophical dialogue was implicit, but it was a discussion among Christians and was cast in the language of the Bible.

It is correct to say that Christians in China operate from a position of weakness. They do not have a strong institutional base, nor do they have an established tradition. Moreover, the activity of the church in Chinese society is circumscribed within well-defined limits. Yet in such weakness there is also strength. Unburdened by a history to perpetuate or an orthodoxy to uphold, Chinese Christians may be freer than their European counterparts to venture into new directions. The proliferation of home worship gatherings, new directions in theology and the Chinese experience of Christian unity are notable expressions of Chinese Protestant initiatives. Throughout church history Christians have been responding to movements and events out of necessity, and if the experience of Christianity in China is any indication, they will continue to do so. Yet even in necessity the Holy Spirit may still be at work, redirecting the church to its original and proper object.

The Latin American Experience and Liberation Theology

There are some obvious parallels between the situation of Chinese Christianity and modern political theologies, especially liberation theology. Chinese Protestant thinking after 1949 was characterized by a rediscovery of the political realm, an emphasis on the particularity of its own context, and a rejection of "universal" (Western) theological norms. In this regard Gustavo Gutiérrez' understanding of liberation theology is especially relevant for the Chinese situation,

> Liberation theology as we understand it here involves a direct and specific relationship with historical praxis; and historical praxis is a liberation praxis. It implies identification with oppressed human beings and social classes and solidarity with their interest and struggles. It involves immersion in the political process of revolution, so that from there we may proclaim and live Christ's gratuitous and liberation love. That love goes to the very root of all exploitation and injustice. That love enables human beings to see themselves as children of their Father and brothers and sisters of each other.[9]

This definition would be fully accepted by Chinese Protestant thinkers as a theological definition they would affirm and support, but not necessarily as one they would call their own. This is the point. There are many areas of contact between Chinese and Latin American theologies, but one should by no means attempt to understand one in terms of the other. The reasons for this should be clear, especially for the liberation theologians who have never sought to universalize their own theology.

For one thing, the historical contexts are vastly different. Latin America in the 1980s is a continent torn by social contradictions and controlled by ruling groups and capitalist interests which are, by and large, opposed to fundamental change. It is a continent in which Roman Catholicism is dominant, and in which an increasing number of Christians are turning to opposition and resistance to established power. When they succeed, Latin American Christians will have had a share in the struggle for revolutionary change. This is already evident in Nicaragua, where Christians are involved at all levels in the political process. In contrast, Chinese Christians played very little role in their country's revolution. When Protestants began rethinking their theological position in the 1950s, China had already been through one phase of its struggle for liberation and the immediate task had become socialist reconstruction. In this situation the Protestant church, a tiny fraction of the entire population and associated in most people's minds with foreign interests, increasingly sought to identify itself with the people's movement under the leadership of the CPC.[10]

A second difference is theological backgrounds. Liberation theology is largely Catholic, and it emerged in active dialogue with theologies in other parts of the world. The most creative theology to come from China has been Protestant, and until very recently it developed without the stimulus of theological conversation from other countries. Chinese thinkers rejected the fundamentalist, liberal and neo-orthodox theology of the 1930s and 1940s, but they were to a large extent cut off from later theological developments. In contrast, it would be hard to imagine the rapid development of liberation theology without Vatican II, the Christian-Marxist dialogue and the secular theologies that preceded it.

The approach to Marxism in Latin American and Chinese theology is also different. In both situations, theologians would agree that there is a mediation of faith by politics, that Christians should be involved in liberation movements, and that Marxism represents the most useful tool for social analysis. In Latin America Marxism tends to be viewed as an ideological option, and part of the theological task is to seek cooperative and critical rapprochement between Marxism and Christianity. In China, however, Marxism is the historical context. Protestant theologians have not found it desirable, therefore, to "mix theology and politics in the same pot," as they put it. Moreover, many of the things now being emphasized by liberation theologians about the nature of society became clear to the Chinese only after they had had their revolution. It may be said that for Chinese Christianity Marxism is a historical option forced upon the church by necessity, while in Latin America it is an ideological option forced on the church by history.[11]

Because of the above, Chinese Protestant thought tends to be focused on questions of a more traditional theological nature, although many of the traditional questions have been recast in a Chinese way. Protestant theologians in China are interested in such questions as the nature of God in Christ and the relationship between nature and grace, taking for granted the Marxist context in which they find themselves. There seems to be little urgency in appropriating the tools of the social sciences, and the eschatological element, which has been so prominent in the political theologies, is almost entirely absent from Chinese Christian thought. Chinese theology remains fairly conservative, and in a sense pre-critical.[12] This has been both a weakness and a strength for the Chinese church, as we shall see below.

On the relationship between Chinese and liberation theologies, K. H. Ting has observed:

> We are humbled and feel inspired by Christians in other countries who give themselves to the cause of the people's social and political liberation. We have great admiration and respect for the epistemology and hermeneutics of praxis and for the Christological insights they out of their struggle offer us. In their upholding of the Egypt/Exodus motif and in their stand against developmentalism and reformism and for efficacious love and basic structural change of society, we gratefully and penitently see something of what we Christians in China ought to have been like in our pre-liberation days. It would be a bad oversimplification to depict Chinese Christians as standing in opposition to the liberation theology of our fellow-Christians of Latin America. But from our situation we have to say that socio-political liberation is not good enough a description of our theology. The message we have received from God and have to transmit centers on reconciliation in Jesus Christ between God and man. We think it is a message just as valid in our post-liberation stage of history

as it is anywhere else. . . . The contradiction between rich and poor is an utterly important one which a Christian can ignore in the name of unity and reconciliation only to the deadening of ethical conscience, but to make that the focus of the good news or the theme of Christian theology seems to us a relativization of the Biblical revelation and a departure from the totality of the historical tradition of the church. There is also the danger of absolutizing the revolutionary justice of the poor just on account of their being poor, which we know something of from the ultra-leftism of the cultural revolution in China.[13]

It is clear that there exists the possibility for a creative dialogue between the Christians of Latin America and of China, and they have only in the last few years begun to get to know one another. But it is best not to prejudice such a dialogue at the beginning by suggesting that Chinese and Latin American Christians are speaking about the same things.

Marxism in the Chinese Experience

Chinese communism is based on a synthesis of Marxism-Leninism and Mao Zedong Thought. Mao Zedong Thought is said to have integrated the universal principles of Marxism-Leninism with the concrete practice of the Chinese revolution. Today it is officially termed an expression of "socialism with Chinese characteristics."[14] As Marxism-Leninism developed in China, it has functioned as both a means of knowing and a method for changing reality. Concerned with everything from the philosophy of history to the nature of economic development, from military strategy to cultural and religious policy, Marxism-Leninism Mao Zedong Thought has been a critical tool for the Chinese revolution, a guiding principle for socialist reconstruction and a "scientific interpretation" of the historical process. No less than sixteenth-century Calvinism, Marxism-Leninism Mao Zedong Thought is a total ideology.

Marxism in the Chinese experience may be interpreted on at least three different levels. At the most basic level it may be understood as *an expression of Chinese nationalism* or patriotism. Patriotism was an important concern for all Chinese in the 1950s, no less than it has been in the 1970s and 1980s. To make China strong, to build up a modern nation, meant that everyone would have to pull together to work for social reconstruction under the leadership of the unifying ideology of the CPC. For patriotic Chinese this meant that Marxism also became *a strategy for modernization*. The political, economic and social experiments of the last thirty-five years have all pertained to the question of modernization, and the policies associated with Mao Zedong, Liu Shaoqi and Deng Xiaoping are, in this respect, merely different strategies for achieving a common end. For the overwhelming majority of Chinese, modernization is the rationale for patriotism and unity under the CPC. Chinese Marxism has also had a third no less important but less easily defined function as *a philosophy of human transformation*. This is especially important when one asks the question, Modernization how and to what end? The emphasis here is on Marxism-

Leninism Mao Zedong Thought as a vision of human destiny with distinct philosophical implications about the nature of human society.

It would be difficult to overestimate the patriotic appeal that Marxism has exerted in the history of modern China. For Li Dazhao, China's "first Marxist," Marxism was primarily a way of speaking about the need for national salvation and the method to achieve it.[15] For Mao himself, to be a *Chinese* revolutionary meant that he had to become a Marxist, but to become a Marxist he first had to make Marxism Chinese.[16] This was what was important about his early work in the Hunan countryside. It has even been argued that the successful mobilization of the Chinese peasants after 1937 was primarily due to the identification of nationalism with communism in the war against Japan.[17]

In the 1950s, and especially after the outbreak of the Korean War, the CPC was able to generate a high tide of patriotic feeling among all strata of the Chinese population. It is impossible to understand the early years of the TSM without recognizing this. The repeated references to patriotism among Chinese Christians over the last few years are little more than reaffirmations of what they have been saying since the 1950s. It is also clear that this patriotism is associated with the program and achievements of the CPC. "For us, patriotism is not just the love of an abstract and ancient country with a long history. It is first and foremost a love for New China."[18] This understanding of patriotism will become especially important when we turn to a consideration of Chinese Christians within the united front.

The patriotic appeal of the CPC after 1949 was based largely on its program for socialist reconstruction. Since the nineteenth century China has been a country "in search of wealth and power." In 1949 the CPC succeeded in creating a unified and fully sovereign nation, without which modernization could not even begin. The Communist social programs for land reform, industrialization, national health care and education in the 1950s were, despite all of the problems in their execution, generally successful and popular with the people. These early efforts were interrupted by the more adventurous reforms beginning with the Great Leap Forward, and a "path for socialist modernization suited to China's conditions," in the language of the 1981 resolution on party history, was not fully reimplemented until the Third Plenum of the 11th CPC in 1978. Since then the emphasis has been on resolving the contradiction "between the growing material and cultural needs of the people and the backwardness of social production" based upon a step-by-step program of modernization, a de-emphasis on class struggle, and an experimental approach to the development of the social relations of production.[19]

Today in China there are many questions about how to proceed with modernization. To what extent should market mechanisms and capitalist innovations be adapted to an overall socialist economy? What should be the relationship between collective and state ownership, and how far should experimentation in the responsibility system go? What trade-offs are necessary between the goal of increased production and that of equal distribution? How is it possible to "break the iron rice bowl" and eliminate permanent job tenure yet preserve the social benefits that are open to all? The context of all this questioning is an acceptance of the socialist framework and a recognition of the positive changes it has brought to China, especially in the areas of economic redistribution and social welfare. Chinese Christians have been involved in the ongoing process of modernization, and their efforts in that regard have also shaped their participation within the united front. They too share in China's achievements, and at the same time they are pressing some of the unresolved questions.

To speak of Marxism-Leninism Mao Zedong Thought as a philosophy of human transformation is to enter a realm of thought somewhere beyond political economics. Mao himself seemed to do this at times when he speculated about the future of humankind in almost eschatological fashion. Any historical movement is in some sense concerned with its own transcendence, and this presents a danger to be both risked and avoided. In light of the extensive damage caused by ultra-leftism in China over the last forty years, the dangers of self-transcendence would have been better avoided. The question, which lingers in many people's minds, is whether or not, in fact, the dangers could have been avoided.

Marxism came to China, and to Mao, "as an instrumentality rather than a revelation."[20] Although there has been a strong emphasis on ethics and the concept of man in Chinese Marxism, these have generally been understood as corollaries of a more general understanding of reality based upon historical materialism. It is when the ethical or transcendent dimension of Mao Zedong Thought is isolated from historical materialism that ultra-leftism emerges as an extreme solution to the problem of social transformation. In attempting to overcome a given stage of historical development (to "catch up with England in fifteen years" as the CPC asserted in the late 1950s), Marxism overcomes itself and is transformed into its opposite. This is what happened during the Cultural Revolution.[21]

This suggests a need for caution in any understanding of Marxism as a vision of human destiny. And yet, it is still important to take seriously the capacity of Chinese Marxism to move people and provide them with a vision of human destiny, however differently this has been understood. The strategies for modernization represented by Mao after 1957 and by Deng after 1978 also entail different understandings of social transformation and the human capacity for change. It may be said that Deng's view of transformation is circumscribed by a sense of the limitations inherent in any situation, and the impossibility of changing everything all at once, once and for all. Mao, on the other hand, had tremendous faith in the spontaneity of the people, the "boundless creative energy of the masses," and at times he seemed to believe that this would lead them naturally to Marxism-Leninism.[22] Foreshadowing one of the central issues of the Cultural Revolution, Mao came increasingly to believe that it was not the people who were subject to corruption and embourgeoisiement, as Lenin had imagined, but the Party itself.[23] The problem was to curb capitalist tendencies within the Party, attack bureaucratization, and thus insure a continuing revolution.

It is precisely such ideas that have been under attack since 1978 as mistaken and erroneous ultra-leftist views. The questions raised by the Cultural Revolution were quickly lost in the subsequent struggle for power and the spontaneous violence and factional strife. As Mao became more and more closed off from other leaders and divorced from the day-to-day affairs of state, the chairman became a law unto himself. This reinforced the autocratic tendencies, which had never really been eliminated by the CPC, and it left the door open for the manipulations by those who are now known as the Gang of Four.

Together with their followers, the Gang of Four was able to use Maoist dogma in order to consolidate their own positions of power.[24] It is to this end that they advocated the "two whatevers": "We firmly uphold whatever policy decisions Chairman Mao made, and we adhere to whatever instructions Chairman Mao gave." Behind many other more progressive and idealistic slogans of the Cultural Revolution lay some of the most autocratic remnants of what the Chinese term "feudal thinking": submission to dogma and authority, loyalty to a single ruler, ignorance or neglect of science and technology, distrust of intellectuals, rejection of foreign ideas. The policies of this period were also responsible for the rejection of the united front, the decimation of religious life and the persecution of Buddhist, Muslim and Christian believers. The Cultural Revolution, which quickly degenerated into a chaotic ten-year struggle for power, must therefore be regarded as one of the most destructive events of recent Chinese history.

After such a period of anarchy and turbulence, the slogans associated with the "smashing of the Gang of Four"—"seek truth from facts" and "practice is the only criterion of truth"—allowed fresh air to enter into the stagnation and dogmatism of Chinese society in the late 1970s.[25] The subsequent critique of ultra-leftism has been thorough, and it is one of the most important ideological developments to emerge out of a socialist state. Along with this critique has come a renewed emphasis on economic development and the responsibility system; efforts for socialist democracy and a legal system; increased attention to the role of intellectuals; a concern for "socialist spiritual civilization" or ethics; and the beginnings of a debate on Marxist humanism.[26] It is in this context too that religious institutions and the united front have reemerged, and that theological renewal has begun.

All of these developments have implications for a philosophy of social transformation and a vision of human destiny no less than the ideas of Mao. In the present situation political unity does not mean uniformity of thinking, nor does a stress on development mean a rejection of social transformation. Intellectual or cultural modernization, if it may be called that, is accompanying the "Four Modernizations" in other areas. Indeed, there is an intellectual ferment in China today that finds expression in virtually all aspects of human life. Artists are experimenting with new subjects, writers are venturing into what were once forbidden areas and intellectuals are exploring new areas of inquiry.

And yet, behind these explorations, uncertainties and lingering fears about the possibility of future irruptions of ultra-leftism continue. Too, it is widely recognized that many young men and women have lost faith in Marxism. In the China of the late 1980s many observers are questioning whether Marxism can provide a soil for intellectual and social experimentation, let alone a compelling vision. For some Marxism has become simply the orthodox ideology of the status quo. The vision is beyond reach and the sense of existing limitations is too strong to generate new commitment for social change. For such people the criticism of "spiritual pollution" in 1985 and the movement against "bourgeois liberalization" that began in 1987 serve as timely reminders that the process of change is fraught with many difficulties.

There are others, however, for whom a more realistic, "practice-oriented" Marxism provides firm grounding for the future of a nation that has survived the destructive turmoil of the Cultural Revolution. Their hope is based on the significant achievements made by socialist China in the last four decades, and especially in the years since 1978. Chinese Marxism may no longer be as intellectually exciting or as politically inspiring as it once was, but it continues to provide a practical context for reform and social progress. In this sense a "socialism with Chinese characteristics" has become a standard against which the problems and possibilities of the present may be evaluated in light of their meaning for human destiny.

Regardless of their perspective on Marxism, an increasing number of Chinese are saying that today China is in need of peace and stability more than anything else. In a eulogy to a close friend, Cao Yu, one of China's foremost playwrights, paused to reflect on his country's future:

> China is like a great ship bearing a heavy load on a turbulent sea. To make a great about face on the rolling sea requires calm and care, and it will be a fairly long process. But "to be careful" does not mean we needn't be bold and resolute, nor does "to be calm" mean that we should be slow and lax. It is difficult to run such a big country as China and it is all the more difficult to govern it after the ten years of turmoil. What we need is unity and resolve from top to bottom.[27]

In these few sentences Cao Yu has captured the dilemma of the present situation as it is seen by many Chinese intellectuals of his generation. After ten years of chaos and turmoil, followed by another ten years of experimentation and reform, China needs to pursue a careful program of modernization, while at the same time preserving or restoring the principles that have been undermined in China's recent past. In this situation "unity and stability" will set the terms for patriotism, modernization and social transformation on the road ahead. The question that remains unanswered is what will happen if the forces for stability and change come into serious conflict.

Christianity and the Chinese Context

Any understanding of the Christian experience in contemporary China requires an approach to the events of the last forty years from a historical perspective. It may be argued, for example, that the place of religion in contemporary China owes as much to the Chinese tradition as it does to Marxism. This is what the French sinologist Rene Etiemble had in mind in writing, "When you deplore the politics of Mao Zedong with regard to religion you display your entire ignorance of Chinese history."[28] It is equally important to develop an understanding of the involvement of the missionary movement in modern Chinese history, without which it would be impossible to comprehend the forces that gave rise to the TSM in the early 1950s. Chinese Christians have not merely been responding and reacting to the forces around them; they have at the same time been struggling with their faith, reinterpreting their history and seeking to create an authentic Chinese church. For this reason it is also necessary to deal with the Three-Self idea, which has been so important for Chinese Christians in this process.

Religion in Traditional Chinese Society

In any consideration of religion in traditional China it is essential to remember what Frederick Mote referred to as "the cosmological gulf between China and the West," the fact that the Chinese have had a very different set of presuppositions about the nature of human life, history and the universe than our own. The existence of such a gulf means that it may not be assumed that our own norms and categories, however widely shared, are universally part of human experience.[29] In traditional China, for example, the absence of a concept of sin or of a creator God stands in sharp contrast to what we might expect according to the Judaeo-Christian tradition.

This may also help to explain why Chinese intellectuals have not, as a rule, been terribly interested in religious questions.[30] The revised edition of *Cihai*, a standard Chinese reference dictionary first published in the 1930s, defines religion in the following way:

> Religion (*zongjiao*) means to take an inherited doctrine (*zong*) as a life teaching (*jiao*). There are different teachings regarding the origin of religion. Some say that it arose out of humankind's feeling of psychological terror. Others say that because ancient man was unable to distinguish living from inanimate beings, he worshipped them equally. Probably, ancient people yielded to natural phenomena out of fear, thus giving rise to feelings of psychological terror, imitation, estrangement and hope. These then constitute the essential ingredients of religion.[31]

The materialist perspective of this definition comes not from Marxism, but from the then-popular theories of primitive religion set against the background of the skeptical and agnostic tradition of the Chinese intelligencia.

The authority for this tradition was Confucius, whose own agnosticism and seeming disregard for the religious is well-documented in the *Analects* (cf. 1:9; 6:20; 7:20; 11:11 and passim). Confucian social thought came to be characterized by a conservative this-worldliness that subsumed the transcendent within the immanent. For the Confucianist, transcendent norms were embodied in secular rules of human conduct with the unity of heaven and earth presupposed. The significance of this is that it rendered "the workings of the social system moral inner rather than social outer," and thereby sanctified the secular realm.[32] Transcendence, in short, became incarnate within the traditional social system, making possible a "perfectly" rational and harmonious order in which all attention was focused on the here and now. While religion may have been appropriate for the uneducated peasant, the scholar-official could rely instead on his more refined knowledge of the workings of the universe.

The rational and ethical humanism of Confucianism was the attraction that China held for countless Western scholars since the Enlightenment. Marcel Granet, himself an anti-clerical freethinker, greatly admired the Chinese moral tradition with its emphasis on imminent religiosity. The Chinese, in his understanding, did not lack a religious spirit, but it was a spirit of another kind, "namely a profound conviction of the value of moral tradition." Thus,

> everybody conceives of (spiritual) power as basically immanent. There is no need at all to throw the case for religious things onto the shoulders of the clergy; there is no temptation at all to place a world of gods above the world of men.[33]

Although the absence of a well-articulated perspective on the religious-transcendent has led many scholars, Chinese as well as Western, to conclude that there is no Chinese religion at all, it is difficult to reconcile such a view with the observable reality of religion in Chinese society. Alongside the rational and agnostic tradition there was a vast array of gods, ghosts and ancestors in the folk-religious pantheon. Temples, monasteries and family altars; geomancers, shamans and spiritual mediums; feast days and religious observances prescribed by the lunar calendar—evidence of a lively folk tradition abounds, even in the towns and countryside of present day Taiwan, Hong Kong and China. Because there were no tendencies toward monotheism in the Chinese tradition, and in view of the Confucian acceptance of religion for the lower orders, a proliferation of gods and religious practices is not difficult to understand.

Several considerations will afford a better understanding of the role religion has played in traditional Chinese society. The first of these has already been alluded to, namely the *functional working relationship between Confucian thought and Chinese religion.*[34] In the realm of ideas, ethics and social life, there was a matrix of mutually supportive and interdependent relationships. The Confucianist did not see any conflict between his own lofty humanism and the popular faith of the masses, at least in most situations. But at the same time, he did not care to provide popular theistic tendencies with a higher level of rationalization.[35] This is a basic difference in the relationship between intellectual and religious traditions in China as opposed to the European Middle Ages.

Although the Confucianist was not afraid of ghosts or spirits, he also did not want to upset the cosmic or social orders. The peasant could sacrifice to the earth god, and the scholar-official to the town god. Both would be hoping to maintain peace and stability, although they would have different justifications for their actions. There was a double moral and religious standard, but in a very real sense, Confucian thought and folk religion were different versions of the same thing. In contemporary China, the rhetoric of atheism notwithstanding, a functional working relationship has also been established between Marxist thought and Chinese religion, including Christianity. Of course, it is a relationship of a very different order.

A second consideration for understanding religion in Chinese society is that *Chinese religion has traditionally been non-exclusive.* To the great frustration of generations of Christian missionaries, it was difficult for the Chinese to understand why one could not be Christian, Buddhist and Daoist all at the same time. James T. C. Liu has described the Chinese view as a "functional particularistic polytheism," meaning that "the popular belief held that no god could take care of everything and each deity had its particular function."[36] There were many gods, all with their own place and value, and for the Chinese it was unnecessary, if not impossible, to place one god above all the rest. Religion became confusing, at least for the outsider, and highly specialized, because the wide array of religious beliefs and practices were never fitted into one coherent system.

This non-exclusive character of Chinese religion was also reflected in a healthy spirit of religious tolerance. There have been times of persecution in pre-modern Chinese history, but these have been infrequent and relatively short-lived, especially in comparison with European history. The more general situation in China has been a pluralistic approach to the coexistence of different religious ideas.[37] Although this picture of religious tolerance has probably been exaggerated by Chinese intellectuals, and although such tolerance was as much due to Confucian indifference as anything else, it is still important to bear in mind as an ideal derived from the Chinese tradition.

The non-exclusive character of Chinese religion also prevented well-defined dichotomies from emerging in the world of religious ideas. This is related to the fact that there was no sharp break between the human and the divine. To the consternation of Chinese Communist theoreticians, the relationship between atheism and theism was not dichotomized in traditional China either. Because there were different orders of spiritual beings, one overriding atheistic idea could not easily be juxtaposed against many theisms. Just as there was no tendency toward monotheism, so there is little evidence for a single-minded atheism in traditional China. One can imagine that traditional Chinese atheists or theists would be more tolerant than their European counterparts for the simple reason that the Chinese would not demand absolute loyalty to either idea.

Structurally, it is important to understand that religion in traditional China tended to be diffuse and non-institutional.[38] Just as it was non-exclusive in the realm of belief, so Chinese religion has been loosely structured. Religious organizations were seldom able to attain dominance over other institutions in traditional China. There was neither a monolithic Chinese church, nor a rationalized hierarchy of religious orders and institutions. Partly for this reason, the concept of the separation of church and state never emerged in China.

This should help to explain why religion never occupied the central place in Chinese society as it did in Europe. Liang Shuming has argued that there is really no contradiction in saying that China has no religion and that China has many religions. It simply indicates that China was not unified by religions and that religious ideas did not spark the development of the political and cultural order as they did in the West. For Liang, this also accounts for the weakness of organized social life in traditional China.[39] If the watershed between Chinese and Western civilization is religion, then at the apex of the watershed stands the institutional church.

There were occasions, however, when religious ideas and institutions did threaten the established order. In times of peasant rebellions, *folk religion provided a convenient source of millenarian ideas and alternative structures,* and the functional relationship between Confucian thought and Chinese religion broke down. Increasingly in the seventeenth, eighteenth and nineteenth centuries, religious alternatives, including the Christianity of the Taiping Rebellion, became loci of social discontent and political opposition. In the form of sectarian Buddhism, secret societies and millenarian revolt, religion provided a fertile source of heterodox ideas for those who were seeking to challenge the status quo. Such ideas and movements were forcefully opposed by the ruling elites, but in times of social change and disintegration, they could not easily be controlled.[40]

The threat posed by heterodox movements from within and aggressive missionary religions from without in part accounts for the increasing intolerance of Qing authorities in the eighteenth and nineteenth centuries. Orthodoxy was vigorously reasserted in statements such as the *Sacred Edict* of the Kang Xi Emperor, as well as in the institution of more extensive forms of ideological supervision. There has never been a legal or constitutional tradition in China limiting the power of the state in religious affairs, and Chinese officials were generally on the lookout for religious organizations that could provide a haven for rebels, dissidents and bandits. For their part, neither the dissenting sects nor the nineteenth-century missionaries could possibly conceive of an harmonious working relationship with the Chinese government.

This situation did not improve after the fall of the Manchus in 1911. Freedom of religion was granted to recognized religious institutions, but all voluntary organizations continued to be regarded with suspicion. For Chinese Christians the situation was never stable. Searle Bates has demonstrated that throughout the Republican period, the Chinese state consistently failed "to provide a reasonable legal status for Chinese church bodies."[41] The problem was further complicated for Chinese Christians by virtue of their relationship with foreign missionaries.

If some semblance of religious harmony had been achieved in traditional China, it was primarily because the non-exclusive and institutionally diffuse nature of Chinese religion made formal religious structures weaker than those in India or the West. Also, because intellectuals had no desire to provide popular religious ideas with a higher level of rationalization, Chinese religion was intellectually vulnerable. It is in light of the Chinese religious tradition, and perhaps with an eye on present policies, that Bishop Zheng Jianye has spoken of the historical weakness of the Han religious sense.[42] Insofar as religion is defined in terms of transcendent other, he is in large measure correct.

Nevertheless, there was a community of Chinese religion, one in which transcendent and immanent, sacred and secular, cosmos and society were blended together in undiscordant harmony. This is what Maurice Freedman has called a civil religion achieved without a church:

> Chinese religion was in a sense a civil religion—not austere and cunningly calculated to serve political interests, but based upon a view of the interpenetration of society and the universe, and upon a conception of authority that in the last analysis would not allow the religious to separate off from the secular. Caesar was Pope, Pope Caesar. And if the sectaries were sometimes tempted by turning away from normally constituted society, to introduce sharp difference between the secular and the religious, they incurred a reaction from the state that, in killing and maiming them, should convince us that the power-holding elite was not prepared to tolerate a bifurcation of authority. The Chinese state has on the whole been very successful—and to this day—in muting religious authority. That is one aspect of the religious unity of China.[43]

Insofar as this is still true, it is an important aspect of China's political unity as well.

The Missionary Movement and Imperialism

It has already been suggested that the missionary movement was very much a factor in the problem of church-state relations in the late Qing and Republican periods. The question of the missionaries' involvement with imperialism is also related to earlier discussions in this chapter of perspectives on the Protestant church in the 1950s and the appeal which Marxism exerted for patriotic Chinese. There will be need to return to this question at a later point, but a preliminary overview of the subject is necessary insofar as it is concerned with the broader interpretive questions being raised here.

That Protestant and Catholic missions were part of the imperialist expansion of Europe and North America in modern times is no longer a question that is seriously disputed. The missionary movement was very much a factor in both the penetration of China by the Western powers and the Chinese response to the West. Historians and scholars are in general agreement on this point, although they approach the question from radically different perspectives and with a wide range of interests.

The key consideration has to do with the nature of the relationship between the foreign missionary movement and imperialism. How were the missionaries involved in Western expansion and what was their understanding of their own role in this process? Some scholars have argued that the missionaries were actually the political vanguard of foreign incursions into China. Others have stressed the cultural character of missionary imperialism, pointing out that foreign missionaries were imposing Western values and ideas upon Chinese civilization. Still others have claimed that the missionaries were involved in a historical movement, the political dimension of which they did not really understand. In this line of reasoning the missionary effort is contrasted with the more overt expressions of imperialism in the forms of power, politics and trade.

Today there is general agreement that although the missionaries were dependent upon the Western presence in China, direct Protestant and Catholic intervention in political affairs was less common than silent acquiescence to the activities of the foreign powers. Some missionaries *were* directly involved in the politics of imperialism, from the signing of the first unequal treaties right down to the victory of the CPC. There were also some missionaries who protested against the abuses of Western semi-colonialism in China, and even a precious few who supported the struggle for liberation in the 1940s. But the vast majority fell somewhere in between, on the side of the status quo, and thus against any movement for *fundamental social change*. The missionaries' attitude reflected either an ignorance of or an indifference to Chinese nationalist aspirations. In the years after 1949 it was this opposition and this attitude, more than anything else, that evoked the charges of the missionaries' complicity in aggression against China.

It should be clear that this was more than a question of motivation. The issue of the missionaries' involvement with imperialism should neither impugn the genuineness of their theological convictions nor denigrate the significance of their contributions. The missionaries were the bearers of the gospel of Jesus Christ to the Chinese people, and this must never be forgotten. Moreover, their efforts in areas ranging from education to medicine to translation work must be regarded as contributions to social reform in China.[44] Because the message of Jesus Christ is incorruptible, it will always be able to transcend the limitations of the individual, church or movement that proclaims Christianity but acts in ways which undercut the proclamation.

But this does not solve the problem. The question of missionary motivation must be seen in relationship to historical movements, and the missionary contribution needs to be understood in light of other things that were going on in China at that time. There is a direct connection between the missionary cases of the second half of the nineteenth century and the Boxer Rebellion, and the anti-Christian movement of the 1920s and the denunciation movement of the early 1950s. What was there about the missionaries that generated such hostile reactions? How is it that Tang Liangli, a member of the Guomindang (GMD) and not the CPC, could write in 1927:

> There is no group of foreigners who have done more harm to China than
> the modern missionaries, either directly or indirectly. It is in connection
> with their subversive activities that China has lost the greater part of her

dependencies. By their teachings they have denationalized hundreds of thousands of Chinese converts, and have thus been instrumental, to a great extent, in disintegrating not only the body but the spirit of the nation.[45]

This is not to be dismissed as an exaggerated account by a Chinese nationalist, for it reflects what was basically at issue in the case against the missionary from the Chinese side.

The case can be argued in either political or cultural terms, but it must also be approached theologically. The history of the missionary movement in China should be considered, in Christian perspective, in terms of the power, foreignness and universality of the message of Jesus Christ, and the way in which they may become confused with more worldly equivalents.

The power of the gospel should not be confused with political power, but this is what happened in the missionary movement. The clearest expression of this was the missionaries' collaboration and support in the institution of the unequal treaties that had the effect of reducing China to a semi-colonial status. After the signing of the treaties of Tianjin in 1858, which granted religious toleration, the protection of foreign missionaries and Chinese Christians, and the right of missionaries to enter the Chinese interior, the missionaries' legal status was secured. As late as 1924 Leighton Stuart could still admit that missionaries dominated the Chinese church only because "foreign missionaries have military power to maintain unequal treaties and the Chinese government can't do anything about it."[46] The "Christian occupation of China" began with forceful entry in opposition to existing precedents of international law.[47] Regardless of their ultimate motivation, the missionaries' power and position had been secured by the gunboat. This seriously compromised their position and detracted from the message they came to preach.

The foreignness of the gospel is best not compounded by the foreignness of its bearer, but this is what happened in the missionary movement. K. H. Ting has written:

> The gospel convicts man of sin and that makes it something foreign to human nature as it is. But this is a foreignness or a scandal, or a stumbling block, intrinsic to the Christian message which we simply cannot do away with without changing the gospel into something else. Thus, we have the responsibility to see to it that, in the course of transmitting the message, no man-made foreignness is added to it so as to make its acceptance by men and women even harder. . . . This is especially important in a country with a small national awakening on the part of the people to whom the evangelist is sent.[48]

The implications of this statement for the history of the missionary movement in China are clear.

Foreignness is a question not only of nationality, but of class and social standing. To the extent that missionaries brought a prepackaged understanding of Christian faith to China, they would always be foreign because there could be no genuine encounter or identification with the people around them. Nor would they be able to develop a point of view consistent with the realities of the situation. The problem was only increased when it also involved methods of education and social change, which are even more dependent upon assumptions drawn from one's own national and ideological background. It is in this regard that such varied efforts as the work of the YMCAs, the Christian colleges and medical missions in China have been criticized as expressions of cultural imperialism.

As Christians, we believe that our kingdom is not of this world. But this cannot serve to justify the foreignness of cross-cultural missions in which the scandal is not the cross but the unshaken class and ideological standpoint of the bearer of the message.

> The Churches strike the Sheffield steel-worker or the African nationalist as "foreign" not so much because they smell sweetly of heaven and in them resounds the music of Zion, nor yet because they have come from another culture with the mind in them that was in Jesus Christ to tabernacle among them, but because they stink of a class which he would condemn as bourgeois or of a nation he would classify as imperialist, and seem largely undisturbed about it.[49]

Finally, *the universality of the Gospel does not mean the universality of Christendom,* but this was taken for granted in the missionary movement. It is important to dwell on this point in particular, for it most clearly indicates the way in which political, cultural and spiritual aspects of the missionary enterprise were inseparable. What bound them together through the middle of the twentieth century was the idea of an intact *corpus christianum.*

Johannes van den Berg has presented an excellent critique of the problem by establishing the connection between the idea of the *corpus christianum* and the various factors that gave rise to the missionary movement from Britain.

> In the sphere of the *corpus christianum,* it is difficult to discern between political, cultural and purely spiritual missionary motives: political expansion is at the same time an extension of the sphere of influence of the Church, and transmission of cultural values simply could not be thought of apart from the transmission of the Christian faith.[50]

This indicates why any consideration of the genuineness of the missionary motivation apart from its particular historical expression is inadequate.

The *corpus christianum* developed in missionary Christianity from the conversion of the Germanic tribes, through the Crusades, the Renaissance and the Reformation. The same idea is also present in the missionary movement from Europe and North America in the nineteenth century. To proclaim the universality of Jesus Christ in this historical process has always carried a double meaning. Positively it has meant that God is the Lord of history and creation, that God is known through Jesus Christ and the activity of the Holy Spirit. Negatively it has been interpreted as the missionary involvement with Western imperialism. These two understandings of universality have been so intimately interwoven that it is almost impossible to separate them. It has resulted in a confusing ambiguity in missionary preaching, but one which was seldom acknowledged. For van den Berg the recognition of the positive and negative aspects of such ambiguity could only be understood in terms of the brokenness of the world. But the missionary response, from the very beginning, was not to bear this brokenness but attempt to overcome it "by anticipating a form of life that cannot be realized within the dimensions of the world today."[51]

That missionaries did not take seriously the ambiguity of their message meant that they did not recognize the relationship between theological and political categories. Thus, their self-understanding became too self-confident, self-assured and at times self-centered. In the process the contrast between present reality and future promise was obscured, even to the extent that the idea of the coming of the kingdom was lost in the desire to expand the church. In the case of China, the universality of the church triumphant swallowed up the particularity of a church that first had to be rooted in the Chinese soil. It is in this regard that a former missionary could write in 1951, "We have intended to exalt ecumenical fellowship as a (possibly unconscious) cover for continued elements of control from London or New York."[52]

The idea of the *corpus christianum* has now been broken, making possible a new self-understanding that the church exists in this world only under the shadow of the cross.[53] Time and again the church has had to wander the earth as a stranger, suffering with Christ crucified and bearing witness to his resurrection.

For the Chinese church in the 1950s this also had a double meaning. The church, which had claimed to be universal, had discovered that she was a stranger among the people to whom she would bear witness. Chinese Christians needed first to learn the meaning of incarnation, so that the power, foreignness and universality of the Christian message would not be compromised by their association with worldly imperialism.

The Three-Self Idea

In both the theory and practice of the Protestant missionary movement there were always tendencies that mitigated against the extension and triumphalism of the *corpus christianum*. Time and again in the nineteenth and twentieth centuries individual missionaries and an increasing number of Christians from the Third World rose up to challenge the paternalism and imperialistic pretensions of the missionary enterprise. Although distinctions between "older" sending churches and "younger" churches or mission fields were not abandoned until the Whitby Assembly of the International Missionary Council in 1947, the idea of establishing independent churches, which would somehow be partners in mission, was almost as old as the missionary movement itself. This idea had come to be known as the "Three-Self formula," and it originated with two nineteenth-century missionary administrators, neither of whom had ever served in a "mission field."

Henry Venn (1796-1873) was a Church Mission Society (CMS) secretary for thirty-two years, but his influence on Anglican mission policy extends far beyond that. According to M. A. C. Warren, the key to understanding Venn's policies regarding "the native church was his concern that it should potentially be a church of the country, a church that could become self-governing, self-supporting and self-extending."[54] The purpose of the missionary, according to Venn, was to work to establish churches with such potential and not to extend his own influence over the population to which he had been sent. In this way, the church would be planted by the missionary, but would grow and flourish on its own:

> If the elementary principles of self-support and self-government and self-extension be thus sown with the seed of the Gospel, we may hope to see the healthy growth and expansion of the Native Church, when the Spirit is poured down from on high, as the flowers of a fertile field multiply under the showers and warmth of summer.[55]

Venn envisioned the eventual euthanasia, not of mission work in general, but of the stage in the life of the new church in which the foreigner exercised authority.[56] Neither he nor his immediate successors established a timetable for this, but the concern was to create truly independent and responsible churches modelled after the Church of England.

On the other side of the Atlantic, and almost at the same time, Rufus Anderson (1796-1880) was initiating an idea of Three-Self that was more along the lines of his own congregational tradition. More than forty years in the home office of the American Board of Commissioners for Foreign Missions (ABCFM), Anderson was referred to as "the most original, the most constructive and the most courageous student of mission policy whom this country has produced" by none other than Robert Speer.[57] Anderson's advocacy of self-supporting, self-governing and self-propagating churches was grounded in his opposition to both ecclesiastical colonialism and an individual-pietistic approach to salvation.[58] The purpose of missionary work was to proclaim the faith of the Bible, not to extend Western civilization. By recovering the faith of the apostles, by demonstrating that the church did not live in and for itself, Anderson believed that American Christians would rediscover Paul's intention of establishing independent local churches in mission fields:

> When (Paul) had formed local churches, he did not hesitate to ordain presbyters over them, the best he could find; and then to throw upon the churches thus officered, the responsibilities of self-government, self-support and self-propagation.[59]

If this apostolic Three-Self idea had not been lost in the early church, he continued, "not to be fully regained until modern times, how very different . . . the history of Christendom and of the world (would have been)!''[60] For Anderson, one difference would have been the proliferation, after an interim period, of local self-supporting congregations, somehow related to one another in brotherly and sisterly harmony.

Venn and Anderson were busy mission administrators, and they had neither the time nor the inclination to give their understandings of Three-Self a systematic expression. The similarity between their ideas, it should be added, was more than coincidental, for they were in correspondence with one another. Although their perspectives were informed by theological convictions, neither of them was concerned to subject his proposals to careful examination.[61] More important, neither man had ever been involved in the *practice* of establishing self-governing, self-supporting and self-propagating churches, yet they assumed that churches so established would resemble those from their own denominational backgrounds. Moreover, neither Venn nor Anderson was fully conscious of the ways in which the missionary movement was mixed up with the extension of the *corpus christianum* or of the non-biblical foreignness of the missions they were administering. Yet despite all of these shortcomings, Henry Venn and Rufus Anderson had introduced an idea that was revolutionary in its implications. They had redirected attention to a church-centered mission which looked to a day of true ecumenism and full partnership.

For Roland Allen (1868–1947), the problem of imperialism and the task of establishing independent and indigenous churches was far more urgent than it had been for Venn, Anderson, or any missionary before him. Allen was an Anglican missionary to China who had witnessed the Boxer Rebellion and understood the charge that Christianity was a foreign religion. Commenting on the difficulties of church work in north China, he wrote in the summer of 1902,

> At present the Chinese commonly look upon the missionary as a political agent, sent out to buy the hearts of the people, and so to prepare the way for a foreign dominion, and this suspicion has been greatly strengthened by the fact that Western nations have . . . used outrages upon missionaries as a pretext for territorial aggression.

After noting other sectarian and evangelistic difficulties, Allen concludes "that a Church which, whilst Catholic in principle, was yet obviously Chinese for the Chinese, would hold the real hope for church unity in China.''[62]

The next year Allen left China and spent much of the rest of his life writing on the need to reform missionary principles and practices. In books such as *Missionary Methods: St. Paul's or Ours?* (1912) and *The Spontaneous Expansion of the Church* (1927), and through his association with the World Dominion Movement, he argued that distrusting the ability of new Christians to run their own churches was tantamount to a denial of the power of the Holy Spirit. Allen believed very strongly in the power of Christian faith to shape its own context. For the missionary the task was not to do things *for* the convert, and thus foster dependency and paternalism, but to turn the convert's mind to Christ with the liberty to go his or her own way.[63]

Allen realized that you cannot establish a foreign church and then by some miraculous process of devolution make it indigenous. Instead, churches had to become self-governing, self-supporting and self-propagating right at the beginning of the process.

> Many years ago my experience in China taught me that if our object was to establish in that country a church which might spread over six provinces which then formed the diocese of North China, that object would only be attained if the first Christians who were converted by our labors understood clearly that they could by themselves, without any further assistance from us, not only convert their neighbors, but establish churches.[64]

It was not that churches had to be nurtured and cultivated to grow, for according to Allen, that would take place in God's own time as a more or less "spontaneous" process. What hindered such expansion was the meddling and control exercised by missionaries over the church.[65] In this regard Allen laid strong emphasis on the financial question, a subject that was to become paramount for the Chinese church in later years.[66] But more important than finances or self-support, Roland Allen believed that an indigenous church was, in the words of Harry Boer, "a Church that had the gift of the Holy Spirit and knew what this gift meant for its own life."[67]

Some would claim that Allen's concept of mission was unrealistic and that it exaggerated the role of the Spirit. Those from the Reformed traditions would find in Allen little emphasis on their concern for confessionalism and Christian doctrine. Too, he emphasized the ecclesiological role of mission to the exclusion of all others. Nevertheless, Allen's work called forth a rethinking of mission, although as he predicted this did not really begin in his lifetime. His creativity and insight have since informed thinking on mission in churches all over the world. It is not without significance that he is the one non-Chinese thinker whose theological understanding of Three-Self Chinese Protestants refer to again and again.

Church autonomy and the Three-Self idea are not explicitly biblical concepts. Yet through their reading of the Bible, and especially the letters of Paul, Venn, Anderson and Allen came to believe that this was a sound New Testament basis for establishing churches. Theologically Three-Self means that the church exists by the grace of God, through the power of the Holy Spirit and under the Lordship of Jesus Christ—and for no other external reason. Its selfhood is guaranteed not by human efforts but by grace. Peter Beyerhaus and Henry Lefever have pointed out that when Jesus says, "If anyone wishes to be a follower of mine, he must leave self behind, but if a man let himself be lost for my sake he will find his true self" (Matt. 16:24ff., *NEB*), he is indicating the "true self" that is found not in autonomy but in Christonomy, the rule of Christ.[68] This "true selfhood" makes possible a responsible church which is at the same time ecumenically related. It always comes as a *gift*.

But Three-Self is also a *task*. The church is continually called to responsible selfhood at every moment of its existence. For Beyerhaus and Lefever, "the truly responsible nature of the church and the development towards it are nothing but an expression in the life of the church of the relation between justification and sanctification."[69] It is in the interaction between selfhood as a gift and selfhood as a task, between justification and sanctification, that the church discovers what it means to be rooted and related in its own situation. To be rooted and not related means that one part of the Body has cut itself off from all the rest. To be related without being rooted means that the vine will wither and die.

Rootedness (selfhood) and relatedness (ecumenicity) are both important, but rootedness must come first. Peter urges Christians to be "like living stones by yourselves built into a spiritual house," (1 Pet. 2:5), because life requires roots. Similarly, Paul laid great emphasis on the particularity of individual churches (for example, 1 Cor. 4:2), the rootedness of which was the *sine qua non* for relatedness (Eph. 4:16).

His whole discussion of offering in 2 Corinthians 8 and 9 is based upon an interdependence and spiritual equality of churches that are themselves responsibly independent. This is crucial for an understanding of Three-Self, but its message is often lost in the hurry to be ecumenically related or "responsible" in mission.

The question that China poses for all of this is how does Three-Self happen in an actual situation? Does rootedness require the temporary suspension of relatedness? If the true selfhood of the church is a gift, and it always is, then what is involved in the struggle for Three-Self as a task? These questions must be dealt with in any understanding of the TSM, and they will be treated historically in subsequent chapters of this book. It may be said at this point that the response of Chinese Christians falls somewhere between the faith of Moses, who "refused to be called the son of Pharaoh's daughter" (Heb. 11:24ff.), and the faith of Paul, who asked, "Who shall separate us from the love of Christ?" (Rom. 8:35)[70]

There were efforts for indigenization in the Chinese churches before 1949, but they were too often cast in patterns that were familiar to the missionaries who were, if not directing the process, at least controlling access to funds.[71] The beginnings of the NCC in 1922 and the Church of Christ in China in 1927 are often cited as examples of Chinese ecumenism and Three-Self. But the NCC existed largely from the patronage of overseas mainline churches, and the Church of Christ in China achieved only limited success in its efforts for self-support.[72] Chinese Christianity remained like the "tail of an elephant," often related ecumenically, but lacking national roots.[73]

Indigenous Chinese churches such as the True Jesus Church, the Little Flock and the Jesus Family are sometimes also cited as examples of Three-Self before the TSM.[74] As we shall see in chapter 6, some of these sects posed serious problems for the comprehensive type of movement the TSM was trying to establish in the 1950s. The indigenous churches did not sacrifice rootedness for relatedness, but because they self-consciously tried to hold themselves aloof from society, they were never rooted among the people in the sense that the TSM was striving for. The question may also be raised as to the extent to which any sect that seeks to separate itself from the world can ever be rooted in a particular context. Despite these objections, the theological understanding and political function of the Chinese independent churches remains a problem that must be treated more extensively in a later chapter.

In an unpublished paper by Shen Yifan and Cao Shengjie, both prominent leaders in the TSM, the origin of the Three-Self idea in Chinese Protestantism has been traced to a source other than that of the mainline and indigenous churches before 1949. In the patriotic activities of Chinese Protestants who *both* opposed imperialism *and* worked to establish independent self-governing, self-supporting and self-propagating churches, the authors see the beginnings of an ''independence movement,'' which has been a part of the Protestant experience in China since the nineteenth century.[75] According to Shen and Cao, the first Chinese Protestant to advocate independence was Chen Mengnan, a Baptist who established an independent church in Guangzhou in 1872. There were similar but unrelated efforts in northeast China throughout the nineteenth century. In 1906 Yu Guozhen established the ''Chinese Jesus Independent Church'' in Shanghai, issuing a call to all Chinese Christians to,

> Give up the unequal treaties which protect the church . . . awaken churches in all areas and Christians with lofty ideals to plan for independence, self-support and self-propagation . . . absolutely refuse the jurisdiction of Western churches.

Yu thus became the first Chinese to speak of Three-Self by combining a love of his country with a love of his church.[76]

After the May Fourth Movement (1919), Shen and Cao argue that a patriotic ''movement'' among Chinese Protestants became more mass-based. It took the form of opposition to the unequal treaties, and especially the article on missionaries. In this way Chinese Christians became more conscious of the connection between the missionary movement and imperialism, and of the need to recover church sovereignty and independence from the mission boards. This ''movement,'' if it can really be called that, was as much concerned with nationalism as it was with indigenization, and the authors wish to distinguish it from the activities of the NCC. However, there was no way of fully realizing such an independence movement before 1949, the patriotic efforts of an increasing number of Chinese Protestants from the 1920s through the 1940s notwithstanding. Because of the control exercised over the Chinese church by the missionaries, and because the whole society was in a ''semi-feudal and semi-colonial'' situation, Three-Self could not really become a nationwide movement until the victory of the CPC.[77]

The paper by Shen and Cao represents one view on the origin of Three-Self current among Chinese Protestants today. It is a perspective that stresses the *continuity* between the Three-Self idea and the Three-Self Movement, between the expressions of Three-Self before 1949 and Three-Self as a movement national in scope after Liberation. This perspective emphasizes the consciousness of Chinese Christians before the revolution who were struggling to create an authentic Chinese Christianity, but who were frustrated in their efforts by the "semi-feudal and semi-imperialist" context of church and society.

There is another point of view in China that stresses the *discontinuity* between Three-Self as an idea and the Three-Self Movement in Chinese Protestantism. In this view Three-Self could not have been implemented until after 1949, for it was only then that the majority of Protestants came to a full realization of the need for church independence and Three-Self. In other words, the Chinese revolution itself made the difference in the consciousness of Chinese Christians before and after 1949. In this second view the *political* point of departure for Three-Self is emphasized more strongly than in the former view.

The difference in these two perspectives is more a matter of emphasis than it is of substance. Both accept the need for political mediation, because *the politics of the Chinese revolution was most certainly the point of departure for Three-Self in China.* This does not diminish the need for a theological understanding of Three-Self, but it places any such understanding in a broader context. Political assumptions informed by theological understanding were implicit in the ideas of Venn, Anderson and Allen, yet this does not give anyone the right to reduce their theology to politics. Nor should it be suggested that theology is subservient to the political realm, although time and again this has happened. If the contemporary situation is any indication, theological reflection can assume a variety of different roles in a changing world. The point is that theology should at the same time seek to point beyond its own context, even as it is shaped by it.

That a "non-theological" factor should initiate a new direction for the church should not come as a surprise to anyone who is familiar with church history. From the conversion of Constantine to the Great Schism to Luther's appeal to the princes of the German nation to the Protestant missionary movement, the political realm has shaped the context of the church's life in and for the world. This is no more and no less true for the Protestant Church in China than it was for the Church of England after the public politics and personal preferences of Henry VIII made necessary its separation from Rome. But in the case of China the politics involved were much more deserving of Christian support than those of Henry VIII, and yet the Chinese church as a whole was farther from them.

Once there has been a political shift as momentous as that of the Chinese revolution, a church that merely struggles to hold onto its religious identity will have little to offer in the long run. Nor are Christians in a position to provide a theological critique of a revolution in which they have had little or no share. Instead, the revolution should provide an opportunity for thinking anew. For Chinese Protestants who discovered the meaning of Three-Self after 1949, this meant that they had to change the standpoint of the church. To do so it was imperative to find some way of coming to terms with the CPC.

PART TWO

THE UNITED FRONT

3

Ideology and Organization

The united front, armed struggle and Party building are the three fundamental questions for our Party in the Chinese revolution.[1]
—Mao Zedong, October 4, 1939

We have no way of predicting the future. Will all the countries of the world eventually become socialist? If so, what would be the relationship between the workers, peasants, intellectuals and other groups? How will socialism and communism develop in China? We don't know the answers to these questions, but we can say this: no matter what happens, the Communist Party will always be in a minority, even here in China. There will be changes and progress, but there will always be certain problems between those who belong to the Party and those who do not. Thus, there will be the need to develop unity and to handle relationships between those inside and outside the Party. In this way, the united front will always have a role to play.[2]
—as recorded in an interview with the former deputy-director
of the UFWD,
Jiangsu Province, 1981

The united front is important for the CPC as strategy, ideology and symbol that continues to be applied to a wide range of problems related to modernization and national unity.[3] Before 1949 the united front served as a strategy for defeating first the Japanese and then the Chiang Kai-shek government's GMD party (Guomindang, KMT) under the banner of patriotism and national salvation led by the Communist party. Since 1949 the CPC has sought to develop support and enthusiasm for socialist reconstruction in the 1950s and for the "Four Modernizations" in the 1970s and 1980s on the basis of its united front ideology. In overtures to "compatriots" from Hong Kong and Macao, as well as in the calls for reunification with Taiwan, which have been made with greater frequency since 1949, the united front has become symbolic of the long-cherished dream of national unity. It is no wonder that in the major reassessment of CPC history that was adopted in 1981, the significance of the united front for the future as well as the past of the Chinese revolution was reaffirmed: "We must unswervingly unite all forces which can be united and consolidate and expand the patriotic united front."[4]

The ideology and organization of the united front are not self-sustaining, for they are dependent upon other factors. One of these is the composition of the united front—the classes, groups and organizations that make up the united front at any given period in its history. As the situation changes, so does the nature of friends and enemies. The GMD was part of the united front during the War of Resistance against Japan, but became isolated as its main enemy in the post-war years. To view matters from this perspective already accepts the context the united front sets for itself. However important this may be, it fails to take account of the fact that the united front is a function of something else.

This something else is the broader Communist ideology, which shapes the united front, or the ways in which Marxism-Leninism Mao Zedong Thought has been understood as an expression of nationalism, a strategy for modernization and a philosophy of human transformation. If, as was suggested in the last chapter, communism in China has been represented by *one* party but *two* lines, then there can be no doubt that the united front has only been practiced and understood by one of them. There is all the difference in the world between the ideas and ideologies of Liu Shaoqi, Zhou Enlai, Chen Yi and Deng Xiaoping, on the one hand, and Lin Piao, Jiang Qing, Chen Boda and Kang Sheng on the other. Mao Zedong, the man and the institution, was the mediator between the two lines, and the theoretical authority for both of them. This means that we will be interested in his ideas as interpreted, developed, and put into practice by the Liu-Zhou-Deng wing of the party, if it may be called that.[5]

The united front is here referred to as an ideology, in the positive sense that the term began to assume in Marxist thought after Marx's death.[6] As the united front developed from strategy to theory, it came to represent a form of political consciousness linked to the interests of those whom Mao refers to as "the broad masses of the Chinese people." The ideology of the united front could withstand no rigid class analysis, which helps to explain why it has so often been criticized as a revisionist concession to the bourgeoisie. Yet it will be argued here that the united front was and remains a distinctively Chinese departure in Communist thought, linking Mao's theory of contradictions and the mass line in the service of both reform and revolution.

It is the thesis of this chapter and the next that the united front is the key to understanding religious policy in contemporary China. In this chapter we will present a general consideration of united front theory and organization. In the chapter that follows we will see how this has been applied to the understanding of religion and religious policy in the PRC.

Historical Background

The ideal of a unified and harmonious society has been a recurring theme in Chinese thinking for more than twenty-five hundred years. The image used to describe such a society is that of *datong*, meaning universal harmony or great community, whose *locus classicus* is the section on the evolution of rites in the *Li Ji*:

> When the Great Way was in practice, a public and common spirit ruled everything under Heaven; men of talent, virtue and ability were selected; sincerity was emphasized and harmonious relationships were cultivated. Thus, men did not love only their own parents, nor did they treat as children only their own children. A competent provision was secured for the aged till their death, employment was given to the able-bodied, and a means was provided for the upbringing of the young. Kindness and compassion were shown to widows, orphans, childless men, and those who were disabled by disease, so that they were all sufficiently maintained. Men had their proper work and women had their homes. They hated to see the wealth of natural resources unused (so they developed it, but) not for their own use. They hated not to exert themselves (so they worked, but) not for their own profit. In this way selfish schemings were thwarted and did not develop. Bandits and thieves, rebels and troublemakers did not show themselves. Hence the outer door of houses never had to be closed. This was called the Great Community.[7]

Although universal harmony has been envisioned in different forms, the ideal has inspired philosophers and motivated peasant rebels throughout Chinese history. In modern times it has been important for Hong Xiuquan, who sought to establish a Heavenly Kingdom of Great Peace; for Kang Yuwei, whose book on the subject is a description of a contemporary utopia; as well as for Sun Yat-sen's principle of people's livelihood. Behind contemporary Chinese aspirations for "unity and stability" may lie a collective recollection of that which was once represented as universal harmony. Hou Wailu goes so far as to define universal harmony as an ideal "society in which comradely relationships prevail," the need for which, he argues, has been surpassed by the historical accomplishments of the CPC.[8] The united front may not be directly related to the traditional ideal of universal, but it is against this background that Marxism took root in China.

The united front has been present in Marxism whenever Communists have sought to enlist the support of non-Communists. Already in *The Communist Manifesto* Marx and Engels suggested this: "Communists everywhere support every revolutionary movement against the existing social and political order of things. . . . They labor everywhere for the union and agreement of the democratic parties of all countries."[9] Efforts for "principled participation" and infiltration, solidarity and support, organization and control, both national and international in scope, may be understood as implicit or explicit expressions of the united front in the subsequent history of the international Communist movement.

As it emerged from within original Marxism-Leninism, the united front was a strategy to promote national and anti-colonial movements, on the one hand, and to work toward the ultimate victory of the Communist party on the other. In theory, the Communist party gains its victory not apart from that of the whole movement. The ultimate victory is won only when the stage is reached when there are no classes, no military forces, and no parties, including the Communist party. This, however, will occur only in some distant future.

The united front strategy was adopted by the Third Communist International (Comintern) and applied to Third World countries, including China, in the 1920s and 1930s. The role of the local Communist party and of Comintern representatives was that of a "bloc within," joining in an alliance with the bourgeois revolutionary forces and at the same time deepening the contradictions in ways that would hopefully work toward the Communists' advantage. Such tactics tended to generate a good deal of mistrust on the part of non-Communist democrats in places where Comintern was active. The Communists were seen to play a subversive and manipulative role, which created suspicions on all sides. Questions over the Communists' ultimate goals, their trustworthiness and their manipulation of power have been raised by non-Communists about the united front from the beginning. They are questions that, from the perspective of the outsider, can never be answered once and for all, insofar as alliances are always temporary and the terms of struggle are never fixed. As we shall see in the next chapter, similar questions have been raised about Chinese religious policy within the united front.

The most significant non-Chinese statement of the united front was that of Georgi Dimitroff, leader of the Bulgarian Communist Party in the 1930s and general secretary of the Third Communist International. At the Seventh World Congress of the Communist International in 1935, Dimitroff issued a report calling for a united front of progressive forces against fascism. The choice was no longer viewed as one between proletarian and bourgeois democracies, but between bourgeois democracy and bourgeois dictatorship, or fascism. Dimitroff understood the united front as a transitional stage toward communism, one that renders "the working class capable not only of a successful defense, but also of a successful counter attack against fascism, against the class enemy."[10] This strategy helped to inspire Popular Fronts between Communists and other progressive forces in Western Europe, and it also generated international support in the struggle against Franco during the Spanish Civil War.[11]

In his most important surviving work of the May Fourth period, Mao Zedong reveals an early and abiding interest in the themes of unity and organization which were to become crucial for the united front in the Chinese revolution. Entitled "The Great Union of the Popular Masses," Mao gives the idea of unity an almost universal character:

> If we look at the course of history as a whole, we find that all the movements which have occurred throughout history, of whatever type they may be, have all without exception resulted from the union of a certain number of people. . . . In all hitherto existing cases of reform and resis-

tance in religion, science, politics and society, the politics of both sides necessarily had their great union. Victory or defeat are decided by the solidity or fragility of the unions on each side, and by whether the ideologies which serve as their foundation are new or old, true or ill-founded.[12]

History, therefore, moves forward through the union of peoples, and the success of any movement is determined by the nature of the unity that is achieved. In the final section of this three-part essay Mao concludes that "The great union of the Chinese people will be achieved earlier than any other people."[13]

The united front became important for the CPC almost from the very beginning. In 1923 the Third Party Congress, encouraged by Comintern, ratified participation with the GMD in an effort to become a "bloc within" or a united front "from above." This "First United Front" ended in failure with the White Terror and Chiang Kai-shek's campaigns of annihilation in 1927. The subsequent attempt to create a united front "from below" through long-range, low-key organizing in the cities was also unsuccessful.[14] It was primarily through Mao's work in Hunan, resulting in a shift in emphasis to the peasants in the countryside, that the Communist efforts to establish a revolutionary base achieved some measure of success. With the Long March and the consolidation of Mao's leadership at the Zunyi Conference in 1935, the stage was set for a new Communist initiative, this time from a relatively stronger position.

The Second United Front (1937–1945) involved CPC-GMD cooperation in the War of Resistance against Japan according to the Three People's Principles. Having rejected ultra-leftism and "closed door tactics," which opposed any alliance with the GMD, Mao argued that a new united front was a practical necessity for China:

> Communism will be put into practice at a future stage of the development of the revolution; at the present stage the Communists harbor no illusions about being able to realize it, but will carry out the national and democratic revolution as required by history.[15]

The period following the Xi'an Incident (December 1936) was most important for the development of united front strategy, articulated in theory and tested in practice by the CPC in Yanan and throughout northwest China. During this time the united front emerged from the practical needs and concrete realities of the Chinese situation as a particularly *Chinese* innovation in Communist theory.

Already in Yanan Mao was thinking in terms of a "new democracy" as the direction China should take after the war. His ideas were further articulated in the report to the Seventh Party Congress in 1945. There he wrote that feudal, national bourgeois and socialist states were all out of the question for China. What was needed, he wrote, was a new democratic state, "a united front democratic alliance based on the overwhelming majority of the people, under the leadership of the working class."[16]

It soon became clear that any form of coalition government would be impossible. As the CPC grew in strength Mao proclaimed that the Chiang Kai-shek government was "besieged by the whole people," and he declared that the Communists would lead a patriotic united front to victory over "feudalism and imperialism":

> The strata of the Chinese people oppressed by the reactionary policies of the Chiang Kai-shek government and united for their own salvation include the workers, peasants, urban petty bourgeoisie, enlightened gentry and other patriotic elements, the minority nationalities and Overseas Chinese. This is a very broad united front.[17]

Very broad indeed! The Communists were willing to open up the united front to include almost every group except those who were directly associated with imperialism, Chiang Kai-shek or bureaucratic capitalism. In this way the CPC hoped to generate wide appeal to the diverse groups whose support was necessary to win and consolidate the revolution.

On the eve of the CPC triumph, Mao delivered a speech that was to set the tone for the tasks of government in the years ahead. It begins philosophically, looking forward to the time when all classes and parties will die out and "mankind will enter the realm of Great Harmony."[18] Having said this, he immediately adds that this is "the long range perspective of human progress," which has been mentioned "in passing" as a preface to the more concrete and practical things which are about to be discussed. While reaffirming the party's commitment to socialist goals, Mao makes them secondary to the strengthening of government (and thus party power) and the priority of economic construction.[19]

The people's democratic dictatorship, which Mao goes on to describe, is in effect a united front state. Invoking the legacy of Sun Yat-sen, he speaks of the "principle and fundamental experience of the Chinese people" in terms of the united front. There is a domestic united front, consisting of those groups mentioned above, as well as an international united front "with those nations of the world which treat us as equals . . . and with the peoples of all countries." The united front will "lean to one side," drawing a clear distinction between friends and enemies, a lesson that Mao had learned in 1926.[20]

The people's democratic dictatorship is led by the working class and the CPC. "Democracy is practiced *within* the ranks of the people," and *over* the reactionaries, who must be eliminated as a class, but remolded and reeducated as individuals. The purpose of the united front after 1949 would be to *integrate* the people under CPC leadership and *isolate* those who continued to side with the "imperialists, feudalists . . . and Kuomintang reactionaries." In this regard the national bourgeoisie is singled out for special attention. Although they could not be counted upon to lead the revolution, their expertise was of vital importance.

Toward the end of the essay Mao again speaks of the "three main weapons" of party building, armed struggle and the united front. "Whenever we have made mistakes in these matters, the revolution has suffered setbacks.''[21] Recalling the "tortuous road" of the revolution up to that point, he acknowledges the right and left deviations and the setbacks they had caused. The task for the present was to avoid such extremes and to get on with economic construction and the consolidation of national unity.

A united front state was the goal of unity under the CPC in 1949. In the five major campaigns for land reform, Resist-America–Aid-Korea, *sanfan* and *wufan*, and thought reform, the united front was practiced with varying degrees of success. The scope of unity was sometimes broadened, as in the Resist-America–Aid-Korea movement, and sometimes contracted through struggle, as during the *wufan* campaign.[22] The united front was turned aside during the antirightist movement, reaffirmed for the Great Leap Forward, and following the struggle between left and right in the early 1960s, totally discarded after 1966. A new era of united front politics began after the Third Plenum of the CPC in 1978, once again setting the terms for Christian participation in Chinese society. It is the theory, application and organizational framework of the united front that now claim our attention.

Theory and Ideology

Marxists have been more conscious than most that there is no thinking without presuppositions. In China, theory is not discussed apart from its application in practice, and there is no consideration of policy implementation apart from the question of ideology. Behind what Chinese Marxists refer to as the "unity of theory and practice," however, there are philosophical presuppositions. In the case of the united front, two of these are important. One is theoretical, having to do with the nature of "man."[23] The other is ideological, concerned with political leadership in the contemporary situation.

For the Confucianist as well as the Chinese Marxist, man has always been first and foremost a social category. There is sound sociological theory that tends to confirm the Chinese assumption. Louis Dumont is among those who are concerned with a more holistic understanding of "man" and society than that afforded by modern Western individualism. The whole (society), he suggests, is more than the sum of its parts. It does no good to "atomize it into simple elements just to gratify our logic," for "it is the whole which governs the parts, and this whole is very rigorously conceived as based on an opposition. Moreover, there is no other way of defining a whole as distinct from a simple collection, and if we have to a large extent forgotten this it is because of the predominant tendency to replace reference to the simple, the independent, the self-sufficient, that is to say, the individual or substance."[24]

There is no concept of the private self or of natural rights in the Chinese tradition. Because the self is social, Chinese have generally emphasized the importance of the environment and of society in shaping (or remolding) the individual. As such, the study of man in China has been more a matter of functional or behavioral interest than of ontological or philosophical concern. Donald Munro has observed that in considering a theory of man, "the nature of predicted manifestations is more important to the Chinese than any empirical or logical arguments in favor of or against the theory.''[25]

The significance of this for united front theory should be obvious. It has to do with what Munro terms the malleability of man, the time frame for which in Chinese Marxism has been telescoped considerably from what it had been in Marx. Munro cites several factors that account for Chinese optimism over the possibility of changing human beings. One is the separation of human nature into biological and social elements, with little concern for the former except as they impinge upon the latter. Also, there is the conviction that ''correct ideas'' come from social practice, which makes the nature and extent of such practice crucial. Third, a belief in human malleability ''makes people optimistic about changing their undesirable personality traits and acquiring the technical skills needed for modernization.'' Finally, malleability is undergirded by the theory of contradictions (see below), which can be applied to human nature as well as to society.[26] Within the united front all of these factors assume an importance that is of practical significance for creating unity and transforming people.

The political presupposition for the united front is the leadership of the CPC. If society is so significant for fostering ''correct ideas'' among the people, then the government and party that control the society are of utmost importance. The primary function of government as the Chinese understand it is not the protection of people's rights, but the fostering of their social nature.[27] Insofar as the CPC is the only party that truly represents the interests of the ''vast majority'' of the Chinese people—and this is the party's assumption—then it is only natural that it should be in control of the reins of government.

This assumption became more problematic for the united front after 1949 than before. As long as the Communists were not in power, they had to continually relegitimate themselves as the rightful heirs of Sun Yat-sen and the leading party of the revolution. Once in power, however, the legitimacy and authentication of party leadership was no longer subject to open verification. The mass line (see below) provided some guarantee for verification, but in light of the criticisms that are now being made against the Cultural Revolution, it was obviously insufficient. Before 1949, and to an extent through the 1950s, the CPC could say that its ideology was true because it worked; however, it was ''true'' during the Cultural Revolution era because it was the only ideology there was. Since the Third Plenum the power of the party has been grounded upon the ''Four Fundamental Principles'': the socialist road; Marxism-Leninism Mao Zedong Thought; the leadership of the CPC; and the dictatorship of the proletariat. The legitimacy of these principles is not open to question, and they have provided the leadership framework for the united front in the period since 1978.

Dynamics of Unity

The Mass Line. The idea that correct leadership flows ''from the masses to the masses'' is central for Mao Zedong Thought. It represents an effort to encourage popular participation and democratic thinking from below in a society where peasants have traditionally had very little to say about the nature of government. The mass line means that the CPC derives its authority from the people. It must continually try to represent the masses by taking their ideas, concentrating them in systematic form, and then returning to the masses to propagate, explain and test the ideas in practice.[28] In this way the mass line stood for a challenge to bureaucratic and elitist forms of leadership. At the same time it was a way of resolving the tension between popular action and the need for party discipline. The mass line has therefore been regarded as one of the major innovations of Chinese Marxism.[29]

This mass line was important for the united front as a means of integrating intellectuals and the national bourgeoisie with the peasantry, as well as a way of providing them with political training. The students and intellectuals who went to Yanan in the years after 1937 had little in common with the veteran cadres of the Long March or the peasants they came to serve, other than a desire for national salvation and some sense of the Communists' credentials. Specific policies associated with the mass line, especially the *xia-xiang* movement in which city intellectuals went to learn and work in the countryside, served to make full use of the intellectuals' "positive factors"—that which they had to contribute from their background and learning—and at the same time helped integrate them into the life of rural China. In this way they became part of the united front under CPC leadership. The same principle was involved in the land reform movement after liberation and in the creation of mass organizations representing various groups and interests.

It was also necessary to provide intellectuals with political training and instill in them a sense of discipline. Learning from the peasants in the countryside was important, but it was not sufficient to effect a qualitative change in the thinking or practice of progressive intellectuals. Systematic and institutionalized political training had to be introduced so that Marxism could help in the remolding of peasants and intellectuals alike. Exhortations to study and the organization of study groups became permanent features of united front work after 1949, and they too had grown out of the early experience in Yanan.

Political training and integration with the peasantry were concrete ways of implementing the ideas that Mao first articulated in "On Practice" in 1937. Practice and participation take precedence over theory in Maoist epistemology, but they must, in a dialectical twist, be refined and transformed through reflection. Knowledge originates in experience, but experience must be systematized in order to assume objective significance. Through reflection on experience guided by Marxism, material existence is subjected to a dialectical critique which deepens and transforms knowledge. In the mass line one begins with the experience of the peasants, reflects upon that experience using Marxism, and then returns to the peasants to test the reflection, regenerate practice and discern new experiences.

It is this same epistemology that is reflected in participation in the united front. Illustrating the importance of direct experience, Mao once quoted an old

Chinese proverb: "How can you catch tiger cubs without entering the tiger's lair?"[30] United Front workers say, in effect, "How can you seek the common ground without entering into the united front with the masses?"

The Theory of Contradictions. The united front could never have developed within the framework of what Mao Zedong termed a "metaphysical world-view," which sees things "as eternally isolated from one another and immutable." In contrast, materialist dialectics "holds that in order to understand the development of a thing we should study it internally and in relation to other things." This, in turn, "teaches us primarily how to observe and analyze the movement of opposites in different things, and on the basis of such analysis, to indicate the methods for resolving contradictions."[31]

Mao believed that in the movement between practice and reflection there were myriad contradictions, which had to be studied, acted upon and resolved. Contradictions were the "stuff" of history for without them nothing would exist. In each situation there is a particular configuration of contradictions affecting individual, class, social and national relationships. Different kinds of contradictions had to be resolved or dealt with in different ways. What is important in each situation is the determination of the "principal contradiction," for example, Japanese aggression during the late '30s; and the "principal aspect of the principal contradiction," the need for a united front against Japan in this period. Contradictions are continually changing, making it necessary to distinguish between old and new aspects of contradictions, and to understand the movement from principal to secondary contradictions and back again.

All contradictory things are interconnected and can be transformed into their opposites: "The unity or identity of opposites in objective things is not dead or rigid, but is living, conditional, mobile, temporary or relative."[32] Unity is always conditional and transitory, but change and the struggle of opposites is absolute and eternal. Nothing ever stays still, including people. He who is an enemy today may become a friend tomorrow, and vice versa. It is therefore continually necessary to look at relationships and the types of contradictions they entail, gearing one's response accordingly. Although change is unceasing, there are different ways of responding to it and of seeking unity from it.

In Yanan Mao had indicated that "qualitatively different contradictions can only be resolved by qualitatively different methods."[33] In what became his most important theoretical essay after 1949, "On the Correct Handling of Contradictions Among the People" (1957), Mao took this idea a step further. There are, he argued, two types of contradictions, and each is dealt with in a different way. *Antagonistic contradictions* separate the people from the enemy, and they must be handled using coercion or even armed struggle. This was the type of contradiction or division that prevailed between the Japanese and the Chinese during the War of Resistance, or between the CPC and the GMD, or between the people and counter-revolutionaries. Antagonistic contradictions necessitate "drawing a clear distinction" between the people and the enemy.

On the other hand, *nonantagonistic contradictions* are conflicts and problems that arise among the people. They may involve differences between the government and the people, between Han Chinese and minority nationalities, or between state and individual interests, all of which are differences among "the classes, strata and social groups which favor, support and work for the cause of socialism." Nonantagonistic contradictions cannot be resolved by force or "administrative orders" from above, but must be handled using education and "ideological" means. Contradictions among the people are concerned with differences in worldview as well as what Mao refers to as "distinctions between right and wrong."

> Coercive measures should (not) be taken to settle ideological questions or questions involving the distinction between right and wrong among the people. All attempts to use administrative orders or coercive measures to settle ideological questions or questions of right and wrong are not only ineffective but harmful. We cannot abolish religion by administrative order or force people not to believe in it. We cannot compel people to give up idealism, any more than we can force them to embrace Marxism. The only way to settle questions of an ideological nature or controversial issues among the people is by the democratic method, the method of discussion, criticism, persuasion and education, and not by the method of coercion or repression.[34]

The method for resolving contradictions among the people is that of *unity-struggle-unity*. The cadre should begin with a desire for unity rather than a policy of "ruthless struggle and merciless blows." The intention of the struggle that follows—and it may take the form of criticism/self-criticism or denunciation/reeducation—is ideological remolding in order to seek unity on the basis of a common ground. Such unity is still conditional and relative, but it is a transformation of that unity which it preceded, and on a higher level.

"On the Correct Handling of Contradictions Among the People" was written in part to encourage participation by inviting criticism of the CPC by non-party intellectuals. During the five or six weeks of the Hundred Flowers movement such criticism was directed largely against the heavy hand of CPC control. It came to an end and was followed by a new movement to struggle against "rightists." This is now widely believed to have been an improper way of handling contradictions among the people; in China most of those who were labelled "rightists" in the years after 1957 have been rehabilitated, in some cases posthumously. It serves as an important reminder that what we are dealing with here is united front *theory* and not its successful implementation in *practice*.[35]

Unless nonantagonistic contradictions are properly handled, they may become antagonistic.[36] This means, in the first place, that they cannot simply be dismissed as unimportant, but must be dealt with forthrightly using the method of unity-struggle-unity. For mistakes among the people, the policy should be one of "learning from past mistakes to avoid future ones and curing the sickness to save the patient," allowing people to correct their own mistakes and continue taking part in the revolution.[37] Education is also needed to win those from the democratic parties and religious circles away from the enemy. As Mao wrote in 1952,

> Take Buddhism, for example. It has not had much contact with imperialism and its ties are chiefly with feudalism. As the struggle against feudalism involves the land problem, it affects the monks, and those who come under attack are the abbots and elders of the monasteries. Once this small number is overthrown, ordinary monks like Lu Chih-shen will be emancipated. Though no believer in Buddhism, I am not against forming an association of Buddhists to get them united and enable them to distinguish between the people and the enemy. Will the united front be abolished someday? I for one am not for its abolition. We should be united with everyone provided he truly makes a distinction between the people and the enemy and serves the people.[38]

Nonantagonistic contradictions may also be improperly handled if methods of force are employed. This approach not only fails to draw a proper distinction between the "people" and the "enemy," but it magnifies the nature of the contradiction among the people and exaggerates the role of the struggle. The result may be a stiffened resolve on the part of those who are the "objects" of united front work, even to the extent of driving some of them underground or into the hands of the enemy. If coercive measures are used to handle nonantagonistic contradictions, there can be neither a common ground nor reserved differences of opinion and world view.

Enemies and Friends. The goal of the united front is not uniformity of opinion but the establishment of a community of interest around a common political stance.[39] The theory of contradictions not only encourages, but even requires non-uniformity. The important thing is the distinction between enemies and friends, and the realization that criticism and free discussion apply only to relationships with the latter.

The united front is shaped by alliances formed through the differentiation of friends, enemies and those in the middle. Friends generally included those from all groups and classes that supported the same goals as the Communist party. Enemies were those closely connected with the imperialists and reactionaries, including the "anti-Communist die-hards." For the CPC, the key group in any situation is the middle forces (left-leaning, centrist and right-leaning) who had to be persuaded and won over to the Communist cause.

The basic consideration is how to isolate and eliminate the die-hards: "In the struggle against the anti-Communist die-hards, our policy is to make use of contradictions, win over the many, oppose the few and crush our enemies one by one, and to wage struggles on just grounds, to our advantage and with restraint."[40] As united front moves from theory to strategy, Mao's debt to traditional Chinese thinking on the art of war becomes increasingly obvious.

Winning over the many and opposing the few was a familiar tactic for Chinese strategists ever since Sunzi. So were many of the Communists' tactics in making use of alliances, taking advantage of splits within the enemy and guerrilla warfare.

After 1949, however, eliminating the enemy became more a matter of identifying and isolating those who were opposed to the revolution than it was of waging war. The last part of the above quotation, "to wage struggles on just grounds, to our advantage and with restraint," became more and more necessary, especially in relation to the bourgeoisie in the cities. The political movements and efforts to work through newly created people's organizations were intended to "unify all who could be unified" around the cause of patriotism under Communist leadership. Those who could not be unified were isolated, criticized, arrested and struggled against in part to try to change them and in part as an example to other would-be opponents. In this connection it was frequently reported that only a "small fraction of people" were real enemies, while the "vast majority" stood on the side of the CPC. The desire for unity meant that one would want to stand with the majority.

The vast majority were those in the middle. Within this group the united front approach had to be most carefully applied: "The middle forces tend to vacillate and are bound to break up, and we should educate and criticize them appropriately, with special reference to their vacillating attitude."[41] The "waverers" in the middle were inconsistent and could never really be counted upon. Nor were they able to distinguish between questions of principle and the flexible application of principle.[42] Yet it was the ability to appeal to this group and thus "seize the middle ground" that was crucial. Extremist approaches to revolutionary change or the dogmatic insistence upon Marxist principles could only be self-defeating with regard to the middle forces. A better approach was to listen to them, consult with them about questions of mutual concern, seek the common ground, and try to win them over. Viewed in this light, the united front approach was just as much a matter of Communists uniting with non-Communists as it was the other way around. In order to transform the intellectuals, the Communists first had to be united with them.[43]

The flexible application of principles meant that the united front worker had to understand the principal aspect of the principal contradiction in any situation. He or she had to know what could be subject to compromise and what involved questions of principle. He or she had to be able to differentiate friends from enemies, true progressives from waverers, primary matters from secondary considerations, and to relate to people on the basis of what he or she understood to be the situation. Should a person be criticized or encouraged? Is this mistake conscious or unconscious? Does it involve a question of principle?[44] These were the important questions to be faced in any situation in which the united front was to be applied.

With the CPC in power, the definition of the situation for the nation as a whole became the prerogative of the Central Committee. Different levels of party and state leadership would in turn set general and specific policy guidelines. A most important consideration for the application of the united front in the 1950s was whether its purpose was "loosening up" or "drawing in." In the former situation, criticism and discussion was encouraged as a means of opening up the united front; in the latter case, the purpose was to tighten discipline and thus consolidate leadership and unity.

Writing in early 1957, Li Weihan noted that there were periods of loosening up and drawing in, which varied depending upon the historical period. Methods such as that of unity-struggle-unity could represent a loosening up in one situation and a drawing in in another.[45] What Li does not explain is the way in which a particular approach is decided upon in practice. Without a frame of reference, it is not difficult to see how friends could be mistaken for enemies within a few months after Li Weihan was speaking of the subtleties of dialectics.

Left and Right Deviations. In attempting to seize the middle ground, the united front has to chart a course between left and right extremes. A stress on unity to the exclusion of struggle—too much loosening up—was considered to be a rightist deviation. An overemphasis on struggle and rigid adherence to principles—too much drawing in—was a leftist mistake. The united front is an effort to avoid both of these by combining reform and revolution without ultimate compromise.[46]

Throughout their writings on the subject Chinese leaders have gone to great lengths to differentiate the correct understanding of the united front from left and right deviations. (See Table 1.)

The common element in both left and right deviations is the failure to adequately differentiate. The leftist does not understand the distinctions within the middle forces, nor see that different kinds of contradictions require different approaches. The rightist cannot differentiate between enemy and friend, and does not realize that differences do matter. According to Zhou Enlai, this mistake is due to his or her bourgeois background: "When (the big bourgeoisie) is being polite and invite us to tea or dinner, we cease to make distinctions, and we put forward the proposals of the big bourgeoisie or the big landlords as if they were our own."[47] The reason that neither leftists nor rightists differentiate is either that they fail to take adequate account of the dynamics of unity in a changing situation, or that they do not proceed according to the concrete realities of a given situation.

Although there have been left and right deviations in the practice of the united front since 1949, they have not been in equal measure. The idea that a leftist mistake resulting from excessive zeal is somehow less culpable than a rightist mistake of lukewarm enthusiasm has persisted in Chinese Communist thinking, although this view has been attacked in recent years. In the early 1940s Mao realized that the ultra-leftist viewpoint was the major danger to the party, and the experience over the past forty years has certainly borne this out.[48]

Since 1978 there has been an outpouring of self-criticism about the dangers that leftist influences have inflicted upon the party in an effort to reinvigorate

Table I
Deviations in United Front Work[49]

	Left Deviation	*Right Deviation*
The mass line	"Blind proletarian class hatred"	"Disbelief in the power of the masses"
	Fails to unite with the bourgeoisie	Fails to understand the leading role of the workers and peasants
	Opposes common action	Ignores differences with others
Contradictions	Outstrips the given stage of historical development by straining to "realize in the present an ideal which can only be realized in the future." (Thus, the tendency for a nonantagonistic contradiction to become antagonistic.)	Fails to advance as contradictions change
		Tends to view all contradictions as nonantagonistic
Enemies and friends	Mistakes friends for enemies, not realizing that yesterday's enemy may be today's friend	Mistakes enemies for friends, not realizing that yesterday's friend may be today's enemy
	Can see only the "reactionary nature of the enemy"	Forgets the "reactionary nature" of the enemy
Working style	Tends to be adventurous, impetuous, dogmatic, factionalist and to become "dizzy with success"	Tends to be timid, pessimistic, revisionist, capitulationist and to "fear a new situation"
	Insists on the dogmatic application of principles	Overemphasizes the flexibility of principles
	Purist	Compromiser

the united front approach.[50] More than simple mistakes, however, the leftist alternative is a challenge to the basic idea of the united front. This challenge cannot be met without some kind of institutionalized guarantees that are more substantive than assurances that it will not happen again. This is why the promotion of socialist democracy and the rule of law in China is so very important, especially for minorities, intellectuals and religious believers.

Working Style

Mao Zedong was the major theoretician of the united front, but Zhou Enlai, more than any other party leader, understood its significance and knew how to apply it in relating to others. Affable and urbane, Zhou was especially effective in dealing with middle-of-the-roaders as well as in building relationships with "foreign friends." In China today Zhou is remembered for his faithfulness to the Chinese people, his concern for people's individual needs, and his warm personality, characteristics that are well-suited to the united front approach. The party newspaper has held up Zhou as a model for united front work and has called upon people to learn from his example.

> Without doubt, Comrade Zhou Enlai is the primary model for those en-
> gaged in united front work since the founding of our Party. He has won
> over, united and educated group upon group of non-Party friends for our
> Party and for China's revolutionary enterprise. He has attained high pres-
> tige in the minds and hearts of friends at home and abroad.[51]

A number of considerations that are important for the application and working style of the united front have already been touched upon: the necessity of study for reeducation, differentiation, and the flexible application of principles. Because united front theory is so closely bound up with united front strategy, working style is more important here than in other areas of Communist ideology. Also, because the united front is concerned with relationships between party members and non-party people, the question of the application of the theory is central for the implementation of all social and political programs in the PRC. This is why Zhou Enlai's example is so important.

Anyone who has the least familiarity with China understands the central place of friendships and relationships in the lives of the Chinese people. Human relationships and the moral obligations they entail are arguably more important for the Chinese than for any other civilization. It is part of the reason why Chinese philosophy has been preeminently social philosophy, and why networks of relationships have played such a significant role in Chinese politics. "To be out of relation is to be a non-entity."[52] This statement is just as true today as it was in traditional China. Drawing upon the traditional Chinese insight into the priority of human relationships, the united front approach has sought to transform political relationships and encourage popular participation.

Three emphases stand out in the working style of the united front and are important for understanding its application in the PRC. Each of these has been stressed repeatedly in Communist writings, but here we can only attempt a brief summary.

1. *Learning from Others* means that Communists should try to set an example by their own actions and behavior (so that others can learn from them), but it also means that they should be open to learning from others.

The importance of models (such as Zhou Enlai for united front work) and their significance for education and discipline in China has been widely investigated.[53] Certain kinds of behavior are especially prominent in discussions of the united front. Cadres should recognize situations in which they lack the requisite experience or expertise. They must also be aware of their own shortcomings and mistakes. Leadership should be exercised as if it were a collective enterprise, lest the cadre be accused of "commandism." If misunderstanding occurs, cadres should not bear grudges, for personal animosity is just as harmful to the society as is favoritism. Humility is an important personal quality, and cadres should not take all the credit for or exaggerate their own accomplishments and achievements. United front workers must be disciplined, but at the same time flexible, understanding and sympathetic for others. The one cardinal virtue crucial to the united front is *prudence*. Prudence is needed for the patient and thoughtful action the united front approach requires, and stands in sharp contrast to governance by across-the-board interference through ill-conceived "administrative measures."[54]

Learning from non-Communists implies that the cadre may himself or herself be changed through participation in the united front. Although the major initiative for united front work lies with the CPC, it is wrong for party members to take this as an excuse for imposing their opinions on others. In 1938 Mao wrote that there were only a small number of Communists in China, but a large number of progressives outside the party with whom they could work. Communists should not separate themselves from those outside, but they should try to learn from them: "It is entirely wrong to think that we alone are good and no one else is any good."[55]

In the early 1950s Li Weihan was quite outspoken in urging party members to learn from those outside. If cadres thought they had nothing to learn from non-party people, then they would become arrogant and conceited.[56] A newspaper article goes further in urging party members to learn from non-party members, especially when the latter are in situations of leadership and authority:

> If the non-Party comrade has primary responsibility and the party member occupies the secondary position, he should first of all recognize that the non-Party man is in charge, and that he is to assist him. . . . Should there arise a difference of opinion in principle between the non-Party and Party men, the responsible member should earnestly set forth his own opinion so that both sides can arrive at complete unanimity. If his opinion is not accepted by the other side, he can only reserve his opinion, waiting for the appropriate time to bring it up again, or bring it up in other ways. He cannot constrain others to accept his own opinion.[57]

The fact that the CPC has continued to stress this issue suggests that it is a continuing problem for the realization of unity in what was intended to be a united front state.

2. *Consultation*. The united front is a consensus-building approach that seeks

to create a unified political standpoint. The importance of "democratic consultation" in the day-to-day workings of this process should not be underestimated. At its worst it has merely been a technique for convincing others of a pre-arranged program which has already been decided upon. At its best it serves as a method of bringing about people's democracy in a society that has never enjoyed the material conditions for a political system not subject to the manipulations of special interests. Luo Hanxian, a deputy secretary general of the CPPCC, explained that people's democracy in China is an attempt to encompass a variety of opinions and interests under a single, unified program. Thus, the unanimous votes on most issues in the National People's Congress (NPC) are the result of a process of consultation, solicitation of opinion and revision, which goes on before the vote is taken.[58] In actual practice, democratic consultation in the united front is probably some combination of control exercised from above and people's democracy from below. It is a reflection of the "from the people to the people" approach in the Chinese political process.

Political consultation also helps to adjust the internal relationships and nonantagonistic contradictions that emerge in the united front. It is a way of ferreting out problems through the regular exchange of ideas. Consensus and unity become a means of clarifying issues and identifying new problems. In a people's democracy the interests of the majority are foremost, but the interests of minority groups cannot be glossed over and ignored. According to Li Weihan, democratic consultation is an effort to realize the political power of the majority while respecting the position of the minority, so that every opinion can be gathered together, summed up and "unified."[59]

The nonantagonistic contradictions that continue to come to the fore must be resolved using democratic methods. For example, the method of "playing the devil's advocate" may be employed to encourage the free and open expression of opinions.[60] Both sides should speak their minds openly and honestly, criticizing one another, and arguing back and forth. Although unanimity and a common ground are sought, it is permissible in the end to "reserve one's opinion" when there is disagreement. The "reserving of one's opinion," or "reserving differences," may be regarded as an expression of dissent from within the united front. It is an important, and often neglected, concession to pluralism within overall uniformity, and is often a privatized and individual phenomenon. Playing the devil's advocate necessitates both the free exchange of ideas (democracy) and a unified conclusion (centralism). For Li Weihan, therefore, there is no contradiction in this process between developing people's democracy and strengthening the party's leadership.[61]

Criticism and self-criticism is a sharpened expression of consultation for the resolution of contradictions. Criticism, in the Communist lexicon, is a way of distinguishing right from wrong and of consolidating unity. It must be straightforward and honest, involving the recognition of one's own mistakes as well as the mistakes of others. Within small groups, the cadres should try to reduce individual disputes and concentrate energies on bringing the group together.[62] The power of the cadre—or official—should not be used as a way of forcing the issue. Therefore, officials must observe the "three don'ts": don't take advantage of another's shortcomings; don't use a big stick, that is, excessive force; don't put false labels on people.[63] Criticism was designed to be a method of education and an adjunct to the process of democratic consultation.

3. *Concern for the people's well-being* is an attribute of the Communists' social ethic. In order to win friends and particularize its concern for the society as a whole, the CPC has been consistently interested in the problems voiced by the people themselves. The problems could be as little as the price of cooking oil or a family's need for more fuel, or as far-ranging as the educational program for the countryside or the policy of religious freedom. Insofar as the CPC has tried to unify all the Chinese people, it has had to be able to demonstrate that it had their interests at heart.[64]

Lyman van Slyke has noted that before 1949 the community of interest, which the Communists hoped to establish through the united front, had to be patiently cultivated.

> The Party had to give sustained attention to the specific interests and needs of the particular groups from which allies were to be recruited. This undramatic, routine work (best done face-to-face) has frequently been underestimated, perhaps because of its prosaic and pervasive nature. Yet care for the "pressing needs" of potential friends probably won as much support for the CPC as any element of doctrine, including nationalism.[65]

A similar effort has been made since 1949, especially with regard to those groups that have been objects of united front work. The repeated calls to pay attention to the needs of intellectuals and national minorities in recent years suggests that united front policy has had only limited success in dealing with these two groups. The harsh treatment of intellectuals during the Cultural Revolution era has been well-documented, but by almost everyone's account, their situation is improving. In contrast, the situation of ethnic Tibetans stands out as a glaring example of the failure of united front work in one particular region, as the demonstrations in Lhasa over the last year show so clearly.[66]

There are, however, also positive examples of concern for people's well-being within the united front. Special considerations have been granted to many organizations and individuals outside the party. Too, attempts have been made to maintain the living standards of former national capitalists and non-party leaders, whose lifestyle was and is significantly higher than that of the average Chinese. This is a concession that has helped to win them over.[67] Religious groups within the united front have also been given special consideration, with regard to the reopening of places of worship, the setting up of seminary programs and provision for the printing of scriptures and other literature.

The lavish reception often accorded to foreign guests and visiting dignitaries is also an expression of the concern implicit in the united front approach. This use of traditional Chinese hospitality should be understood as an open effort to make friends and, where appropriate, to expand the united front, rather than as a devious political maneuver to beguile naive foreigners as some reporters have claimed. But it also illustrates another way in which Marxism may be blended with elements from the Chinese tradition to create the working style of the united front.

The most frequent criticism that has been levelled against the united front approach is that it is a cunning strategy to deceive people into cooperation with the Communists. The united front is seen as a trap that, when sprung, will ensnare the unsuspecting victim. From Taiwan and Hong Kong have come frequent warnings of Communist manipulations and urgings to be on guard against any new initiatives for friendship, peace and cooperation. Even the use of the word "front" in the English translation has caused alarm among those who suspect Communist devilry behind every false front of friendship. Such suspicions have also been fed by the familiar racial stereotypes of the "inscrutable Oriental" and the "tricky Chinese."

People within the PRC have also had suspicions about the united front. Some have offered criticisms similar to those mentioned above. Others have said that the united front is merely a showpiece with no lasting significance. But the most dangerous and damaging criticism of the united front has come not from outside but from within the CPC. For at least ten years the united front was not even operative, and for a longer time than that it was (and in some cases still is) plagued by leftist mistakes. During the Cultural Revolution era the united front was said to be a capitulationist and revisionist approach, which watered down communism and delayed the revolution. Such ultra-leftist criticism of the united front is in some ways similar to the fundamentalist Christian critique of interreligious dialogue: any cooperation or dialogue between faiths and ideologies is wrong.

The major content of the criticism, from the left and the right, is that the united front is pure instrumentality. From the right, it is assumed that once the united front reaches its final goal, it will be dispensed with as no longer necessary. From the left, the instrumentality of the united front is understood as a reformist diversion from the goal of true communism. Even in the early years of the PRC this was a problem:

> With the victory of the revolution, there has developed a feeling of pride among some comrades within the Party who wrongly feel that we have conquered rivers and mountains, what further need do we have for the united front? Some even express serious aversion to the participation of some patriotic commanders of the former KMT army and many patriotic democrats in the CPPCC. They put forward strange theories such as, "Coming early to the revolution is not so good as coming late, not coming is better than coming late, and being counter-revolutionary is better than not joining the revolution."[68]

The real question being raised here is whether or not the united front is necessary. Communists evaluate things according to their understanding of material needs and interests, and their evaluation of the united front has followed the same criteria. In favor of the united front approach, leaders such as Zhou Enlai, Liu Shaoqi and Li Weihan have argued that the united front was necessary to win the revolution, it was necessary for socialist reconstruction in the 1950s and it will be necessary for a long time to come. The CPC requires the assistance and participation of as many people as possible in building up Chinese society. It cannot afford to go it alone, nor will it be useful to try to coerce people using "administrative measures." Because nation-building cannot take place overnight, there is the necessity of a policy of "long-term coexistence" between the CPC and the democratic parties. So runs the argument in favor of the united front.

In the passage just cited, Li Weihan continues in the same vein.

At the general membership meeting of the Party called following the CPPCC, Liu Shaoqi persuasively countered the wrong thinking saying, "We do not decide whether or not we need the united front by whether or not we have achieved victory, but on the basis of China's national conditions. The working class is at present very small in China. . . . The country is not industrially well-developed and productivity is low. *These conditions dictate that the Party must carry out the united front policy*, must unite with the peasants, with every democratic class, with all who desire to work with us and follow us, which includes those who waged war with us in the past but have had a change of consciousness and have left the counter-revolutionary camp."[69]

This line of reasoning, which emphasizes the necessity of the united front for the CPC as well as for China as a whole, has been convincing for the large number of those who now take part in united front related organizations in the PRC. K. H. Ting has gone so far as to describe China as as much a united front country as it is a Communist country. Because Christians are just as interested in China's prosperity as anyone else, there should, therefore, be a willingness on their part to take part in the united front.[70] For the TSM and other minority groups in China, the united front has become just as necessary for them as it has been for the CPC.

For Chinese from Hong Kong, Macao and Taiwan, the same line of reasoning has not been equally convincing. National unity—the reincorporation of Hong Kong and Macao and the reunification of Taiwan with the mainland—is still an unfinished task of the united front. If this effort is to be successful, then the burden of proof lies with the CPC to demonstrate how reunification will be in the best interests of the people from those areas not yet under Communist sovereignty.

Organizational Framework

The people's democratic dictatorship set up in the PRC was intended to be a united front state. It was designed to mobilize the energies of all Chinese people for the task of nation building. The preamble to the "Common Program," which provided the legal structure for the new government from its adoption by the CPPCC on September 30, 1949, to the passage of the Constitution in 1954, states:

> The Chinese People's Democratic Dictatorship is the state power of the people's democratic united front of the Chinese working class, peasantry, petty bourgeoisie, national bourgeoisie, and patriotic elements based on the alliance of workers and peasants led by the working class. The Chinese People's Political Consultative Conference, composed of the representatives of the Communist Party of China, all democratic parties and groups, people's organizations, all areas of the People's Liberation Army; all national minorities, overseas Chinese and patriotic democratic elements, is the form of organization of the people's democratic united front.[71]

In addition to the CPPCC, other national, provincial and local organizations began to be set up or reorganized after 1949 to provide a framework for the united front. Prior to 1954 the CPPCC was both a governmental and united front organization, but other organizations had less powerful and more specific functions. The most important of these was the United Front Work Department (UFWD), a *party* organization designed to implement and promote political policy. For religious believers, the Religious Affairs Bureau (RAB), a *state* organization concerned with religion and religious policy, has been important as that bureaucracy with which religious groups relate on a day-to-day basis. Although not specifically a united front organization, its purpose and function often overlaps with that of the UFWD, especially at the local level.

The mass organizations that were set up after 1949 were voluntary expressions of the united front approach on the part of specific groups. Some of these had already been established in Yanan, but others, including the Three-Self Movement, the Catholic Patriotic Association (CPA) and the Chinese Buddhist Association (CBA), were new. Mass organizations had the dual function of relating to groups such as the CPPCC, the UFWD and the RAB, and of encouraging participation and promoting government policies among their members.

The organizational framework of the united front was designed to create national unity and political solidarity for socialist reconstruction and modernization. The question of the extent to which this framework had been appropriate for or successful in achieving its broad goals is debatable, and beyond the scope of this study.[72] That the organizations were crucial in establishing intermediate vertical and horizontal linkages between the people and the government is unquestionable. This makes a consideration of their purpose and function essential for understanding the place of religion in the PRC.

The Chinese People's Political Consultative Conference

The idea for a CPPCC arose during the Second United Front of CPC-GMD cooperation. A Consultative Conference was actually held in 1946, although it had little impact in light of the all-out Civil War which followed. In 1948 the CPC proposed a new *people's* consultative conference for those groups and individuals represented in the democratic united front. Held in September of the next year, the First CPPCC proclaimed the establishment of the PRC and ratified the ''Organic Law'' and the ''Common Program.'' The CPPCC was the highest governmental body until it was superseded by the NPC in 1954, after which only the united front and consultative functions of the CPPCC were retained. Dismantled during the Cultural Revolution, the Fifth CPPCC, chaired by Deng Xiaoping, did not meet until 1978, and the first plenum of the Sixth CPPCC was held in June of 1983.

Besides exercising state power the CPPCC had one important united front function prior to December 1954. At various levels, and working through both individual members and mass organizations, the CPPCC played a major role in the promotion, organization and mobilization of various sectors of the population to participate in the campaigns and mass movements designed to encourage patriotism, isolate ''bad elements'' and unify the people around CPC leadership.[73] Activities included the promotion of the ''Common Program,'' propaganda work for the various campaigns, the organization of study groups, and the preparation and distribution of educational materials. The working style of the united front encouraged voluntarism and active enthusiasm on the part of members of the different organizations related to the united front, and those who had most potential were brought to the fore to assist the CPPCC in its work. Delegates to the CPPCC, it should be pointed out, were not elected but appointed as part of the consultative process between the CPC and ''patriotic personages,'' democratic parties and those mass organizations that were recognized as representatives of the people.

After 1954 the CPPCC was in many ways turned into the political framework of the former bourgeoisie. Significantly, because it was no longer the highest organ of state power, chairmanship was passed from Mao Zedong to Zhou Enlai. Beginning with the Second CPPCC the large majority of delegates has been drawn from parties and organizations whose leadership is overwhelmingly urban (there are no people's congresses below the county level) and intellectual. This would include most of the delegates from the eight democratic parties, as well as those from the culture and arts, science and technology, social sciences, medical and hygiene circles, and also those representing overseas Chinese and compatriots from Hong Kong and Macao.[74] It would also include virtually all of the Protestant and Catholic delegates to each of the six CPPCCs. The function of all these groups since 1954 has been that of bridge-building between their constituencies, the party and the government.

Zhang Zhiyi noted five continuing functions that the CPPCC would continue to have after 1954:

—Consultation on national and international issues.

—Participation in international activities, including peace meetings, friendship associations and visits with foreign guests.

—Investigation of particular problems as they arise.

—Organization of voluntary study programs.

—Organization of symposia in specific fields.[75]

We shall see that the TSM was active as a mass organization in all of these CPPCC-related areas of work.

The revival of the CPPCC after 1978 under a new constitution has strengthened the organization as a forum for its two major functions of democratic consultation and mutual supervision. The Sixth CPPCC is bigger than ever before, and in addition there are eighteen hundred people's congresses at local and provincial levels which involve more than twenty thousand voting delegates.[76] Today the work of the CPPCC includes:

—*Business meetings*, national and local, meetings of the standing committee four times a year, etc.;

—*Conduction of Inspections*, of special projects and in problem areas;

—*Coordination of fifteen working groups*, dealing with economic construction, democracy and law, education, culture, public health, physical culture, science and technology, national minorities, religion, women, international affairs, overseas Chinese, industry and commerce, city planning and agriculture, each of which is concerned with the dual functions of consultation and supervision;

—*Investigation and research*, for proposals on a national scale;

—*Correspondence*, with people who offer suggestions and complaints;

—*Propaganda work*, the CPPCC has its own weekly newspaper;

—*Compilation of "Resources on History and Literature"* (see introduction);

—*Promotion of unification*, with Taiwan, Hong Kong and Macao;

—*Organization of study*;

—*Maintenance of relationships*, with organizations and groups that make up the CPPCC.

All of these activities are concerned with the coordination and implementation of policy at a step lower than that of the NPC.

Religious believers have been involved in the CPPCC since the beginning, though at first not as representatives of recognized mass organizations. There were eight Christian, Muslim and Buddhist delegates in the First CPPCC (1949-54); twelve in the Second CPPCC (1954-59); eighteen in the Third CPPCC (1959-64); sixteen in the Fourth CPPCC (1964-?); twenty in the Fifth CPPCC (1978-83) and forty-five at the Sixth CPPCC.[77] This only includes those who were designated as delegates from religious circles, and so the total number is actually somewhat higher. For example, Holmes Welch calculates that there were at least fourteen Buddhists at the First CPPCC, although only three of these were delegates assigned to the working group on religion.[78] The percentage of religious delegates as a fraction of the total has doubled from the First to the Sixth CPPCC (1 percent to 2 percent), and the percentage of Protestants has always far exceeded their representation in society as a whole.

The United Front Work Department

The UFWD, which falls under the jurisdiction of the General Committee of the CPC, was organized in the 1940s. It was headed by Li Weihan through the

1950s and today is directed by Yan Mingfu.[79] In his mid-fifties, and well-educated, Yan is held in high regard by religious believers in China. His father was formerly on the staff of the YMCA in Chongqing, giving Yan Mingfu some understanding of and support for the position of Chinese Christians.

Active through the early 1960s, the UFWD began to be seriously criticized in 1962. In 1964 "A Report on Comrade Li Weihan" officially labelled him a "capitulationist."[80] The UFWD ceased to function beginning in 1966, but it was revived after the Third Plenum in March of 1979 and Li Weihan was rehabilitated. The UFWD has played a highly visible national and international role in the China of the 1980s.

The primary function of the different levels of the UFWD is to implement policy in relationship to the various groups under the CPPCC. "The major responsibility of the UFWD," wrote Li Weihan in 1950, "is to understand the situation, grasp the policy, make arrangements for personnel matters, and adjust relationships."[81] What sounds like a rather vague portfolio in fact covers a multitude of initiatives based upon the application of the theory presented earlier in this chapter. The UFWD assisted in carrying out the study programs associated with the campaigns of the 1950s, is active in propaganda work and encourages participation in other united front activity. Whereas the CPPCC is more of a forum for the coordination and discussion of policy, the UFWD is the working group involved in its implementation.

A significant feature of the work of the UFWD is surveillance. In the slogan representing the relationship between the CPC and the democratic parties, "Long term coexistence, mutual supervision," the Chinese word for supervision may also be translated surveillance or control. Given the leading role of the CPC and the tremendous disparity in size and power between the CPC and the democratic parties, it is hard to imagine how surveillance could really be mutual. Surveillance is, in effect, an important mechanism of control in China's collective society.

In the UFWD dossiers are compiled on individuals and organizations, and a united front security structure has been set up to keep tabs on the activities and thinking of those who are objects of united front work.[82] There is nothing particularly unique about this kind of activity. Chinese Communist society is built on the interconnection between democracy and centralism, voluntarism and control, freedom and security. What would be remarkable is if the UFWD had no control function, for that would represent an abrogation of its responsibility as a representative of the people in the dictatorship of the proletariat.

Nevertheless, it is correct to say that the UFWD has too often paid more attention to centralism, control and security, and not enough to democracy, voluntarism and freedom. There is a great deal of variation in the ways in which UFWDs implement policy, especially at the local level. This has often meant that the UFWD has been responsible for subverting the very unity it has tried to create.

A united front slogan, which often accompanies the one quoted above, is "utter devotion to our friends, sharing honor and disgrace together." Taken together, the two slogans suggest the relationship that should exist between control and voluntarism. Although it in no way does away with the criticism of the tendency toward oversurveillance on the part of UFWD cadres, "sharing honor and disgrace" acquires a special meaning in light of the experience of the Cultural Revolution era. High-ranking cadres such as Li Weihan and Zhang Zhiyi were subjected to greater punishment, disgrace and humiliation than those whom they related to outside the Party, including religious leaders. This shared history may help to create better cooperation between the UFWD and mass organizations in the years ahead.

The Religious Affairs Bureau

There was no CPC office for dealing with religious affairs before 1949, and so the earliest contacts between religious believers and Communists were on the basis of the united front. This is significant because a Communist religious policy was also slow to emerge, and even the explanations of the article on religious freedom in the "Common Program" provided few concrete guidelines. The earliest statements to Christians by party leaders such as Dong Biwu and Zhou Enlai after a CPC victory was assured stressed the united front rather than the Marxist-Leninist theory of religion.[83] Historically, therefore, the united front has set the terms for PRC religious policy.

The religious affairs group attached to the CPPCC probably began to assume some policy functions before the Religious Affairs Division (RAD) was established in January 1951. This RAD was under the Committee on Cultural and Educational Affairs of the Government Administrative Council.[84] Among those who were involved with religious affairs during this period were Chen Qiyuan, at that time a deputy minister of Internal Affairs, and Pu Huaren, a former Protestant who joined the CPC in the 1940s.[85] The Religious Affairs Bureau was established along with nineteen other government departments under the State Council in November of 1954, in accordance with the new Constitution.[86]

The RAB was headed by He Chengxiang until 1961, when he was succeeded by Xiao Xianfa. National, provincial and local bureaus were all shut down during the Cultural Revolution. They were revived along with the UFWD and other state agencies after the Third Plenum. Xiao Xianfa died in August 1981, and he was succeeded by Qiao Liansheng.[87] Ren Wuzhi, the present director, assumed his responsibilities in 1985.

The purpose of the RAB is to represent the government in the implementation of religious policy. Because their functions overlap, it is important to understand the relationship of the RAB to the UFWD. Party members in all Chinese organizations are organized into party committees. In the case of the RAB, the party committee is under the discipline of the UFWD. The director of the RAB is in this sense accountable to the director of the UFWD, whose area of responsibility is much broader. This means that the RAB at whatever level is subordinate to the UFWD to which it relates.

The work of the RAB is more specific and concrete than that of the UFWD. It is involved with religious groups on a day-to-day basis, acting as the intermediary between Muslims, Buddhists and Christians, and various government or collective bodies. Given the importance of making connections in contemporary China, the RAB sometimes performs a crucial function on behalf of religious organizations by negotiating with appropriate units as the need arises. For example, in 1980 the RAB helped the TSM to arrange for the purchase of eighty-two tons of bible paper, a not insignificant achievement for a society plagued by shortages.[88] Also, the RAB has assisted the TSM in the early 1980s by making representations on its behalf for the return of properties confiscated during the Cultural Revolution era and the reopening of church buildings.

Christians may also appeal to the RAB in cases where they believe their religious freedom has been violated. This is most effectively done on an organization-to-organization basis, with the local TSM contacting the local RAB. It should be understood that when Chinese Christians say that they wish to assist the government in the implementation of the policy of religious freedom, they are not simply "mouthing the Party line." On the contrary, they are exercising their rights in relationship to the RAB and other government bodies in an active way.

The RAB is also concerned with the resolution of more sharpened forms of "nonantagonistic contradictions" that emerge among the people. These include the differentiation between religion and superstition, and the discrimination against non-believers that has been reported in some Muslim and minority areas. The RAB has also been involved in isolating those responsible or suspected to be responsible for "antagonistic contradictions." This occurs in situations where religions are said to be used as a cloak for politics, illegal activities or foreign infiltration. There certainly have been cases in which Christianity was used as a cover for clandestine political activity against the CPC, in the 1950s as well as in some well-publicized cases since then. But more often RAB cadres like their counterparts in the UFWD, have until very recently tended to confuse the nature of contradictions among religious people, mistake friends for enemies and rely on an excess of force.

Speaking before the Fourth Assembly of the CBA in 1980, Xiao Xianfa confessed that religious affairs work had suffered from serious leftist mistakes since the late 1950s. At the same time he admitted his own personal responsibility for unjustly criticizing no less a personage than Shirob Jaltso, the former head of the CBA.[89] Xiao is to be commended for his forthrightness. But leftist influences continue to be a problem for the implementation of religious policy in many areas.

One difficulty is that some RAB cadres have little or no understanding of religion and its practice, and therefore tend to view all religious believers with suspicion. They may also have an inadequate understanding of Marxism-Leninism Mao Zedong Thought, leaving them with little grasp of the subtleties of the united front approach. Until *all* RAB cadres at whatever level can be educated to understand the importance of the rule of law for socialist society, there will continue to be problems in the implementation of religious policy. In the meantime it is important for those at the highest levels of the RAB bureaucracy to seek to establish a working relationship with religious leaders that is conducive to seeking the common ground while reserving differences.

Mass Organizations

Mass organizations include groups such as the democratic parties, labor unions, youth leagues, the All China Women's Federation, the various circles of professionals, and the individual associations of Protestants, Catholics, Buddhists and Muslims. They are voluntary associations, but not interest groups as such. The influence and appeal of the CPC is extended through the mass organizations into all areas of social life. Jean Chesneaux refers to them as "transmission belts," organized outward from the center to the grass roots. In the 1950s,

> They were very active and in close touch with the concrete problems found in each social category; at the same time, they attempted to explain and win approval for the line and decisions that came from above.[90]

The mass organizations are, simply put, organizational expressions of the mass line in the united front.

In his New Year's message for 1949, Mao put the question before all such organizations of whether they intended to "carry the revolution through to the end or abandon it halfway." Every party and group "must choose its road and clarify its stand." For Mao and the CPC the question was one of unifying the political stance, "not the setting up of any 'opposition faction' or the pursuit of any 'middle road.'" Only by completely destroying the enemy, he went on, could China truly gain independence, democracy and peace. To accomplish this task, the CPC needed friends and allies, but it had also to be aware of its enemies.[91]

This set the tone for the campaigns and movements among the mass organizations in the early years after liberation. In this regard the Korean War became the context for clarifying the stand of urban-based groups such as the TSM. In the cities the Communists' major political appeal was nationalistic or patriotic, not socialist.

> For a few years after 1949 it could remain so, because the Korean War gave the CPC many opportunities to make demands on noncommunist but patriotic urban groups, that, without the war, would have been far less inclined to accept the reforms implicit in these claims. Previously foreign influenced institutions, including many universities and large enterprises, could be easily reorganized on grounds of the war, as they could not have been without it.[92]

The bridge-building function of the mass organizations has already been noted. It was necessary to have leaders and activists in groups such as the TSM to "reflect and report" the problems and opinions of their members upward, and the policies of the government downward. In some cases, it also became desir-

able for mass organizations to better integrate their membership into the socialist society that was evolving and thereby build bridges horizontally with the
rest of the people. This meant, for example, that the TSM needed to change
the image of Christianity in the eyes of the Chinese people so that it was no
longer viewed as something foreign and, in many cases, elitist.[93]

An especially important activity for mass organizations in the 1950s was
providing leadership for small and large study groups for reeducation and ideological remolding. We will be considering some of these which were organized by the TSM in a later chapter. For now, it should be pointed out that
through group study, the individual was encouraged to develop the feeling that
he or she was doing something for him or herself, the group and society as a
whole. Martin Whyte, who has studied the role of small groups in China in
some detail, observes,

> Through the process of organized group discussions people can learn to
> constantly analyze the world around them. They can begin to look at
> themselves and those around them and ask what the consequences (for
> individuals, the organization and the entire society) would be if one course
> of action were followed rather than another. Behavior will then be the
> result of more careful reflection and analysis than of impulse or habit. If
> *xiaozu* (small group) discussion can successfully support this kind of an-
> alytical thinking, they can contribute to the members' feeling that they
> understand the world around them and are active and intelligent actors
> within it, rather than drifters in a sea of unpredictably changing circum-
> stances.

Whyte concludes that although this may sound authoritarian by Western standards, the small group study process was designed to reduce not enforce coercion, and to encourage enthusiasm for the project at hand.[94]

On a larger scale, the same was true of the mass movements and political
campaigns in society as a whole. A distinctively Chinese phenomenon, movements represented attempts "to link the masses to the important decisions of
the moment, to give them an active role, and to consolidate new ideological
values through campaigns of spontaneously written posters, through discussion
meetings, and through enormous marches."[95]

Using such movements, the Chinese were trying to create a people's democracy that was appropriate for all strata of the population and not just the educated intellectuals. Yet for the intellectuals, and the bourgeoisie particularly,
the movements became increasingly difficult and hard to bear. In one respect
they did help to integrate these groups into the society of socialist China, at
least superficially. But at the same time, by attempting to do too much in too
short a time, the mass movements of the fifties and sixties slowed up the very
process of social change they were supposed to encourage.

Mass organizations continue to be a prominent feature of Chinese society,
although their role may no longer be as emphatic as it was in the past. As is

true for the society as a whole, the leadership of the mass organizations is older now, and they are often less capable of generating popular enthusiasm. Many of the leaders have gotten to know one another through the regular meetings of the CPPCC and other government functions. In this way they still take part in the united front, representing their constituencies as they gather at the cross-roads where ideology and organization meet.

4

Religion and Religious Policy

The goal must be to respect the people's freedom of religious belief, abide by the Constitution and mobilize the positive factors of religionists. Dogmatism, brutal methods and the use of administrative methods regarding questions of faith must be resolutely corrected; but we must also prevent and correct opportunism. . . . If there are mistakes in our work, then we must call them mistakes. If there are omissions, then we must call them omissions. If we do not act in this way, then we are not thoroughgoing materialists. We cannot indiscriminately follow others in shouting this and that without checking into things first. We must affirm that our work is fundamentally correct. If we fear gods and spirits, then we are not thoroughgoing materialists, but we cannot unconsciously or blindly arrange for their removal either.[1]

—Li Weihan
September 25, 1956

Marxism is incompatible with any theism regarding worldview. But in terms of political action, Marxists and patriotic believers can, indeed must, form a united front in the common effort for socialist modernization. This united front should become an important constitutive element of the broad patriotic united front led by the Party during the socialist period.[2]

—The Central Committee of the CPC
March 31, 1982

The "religious question" has been a particular focus of united front work since the founding of the CPC. It includes the theoretical approach to religion, religious policy and its implementation, and the role of religious institutions and religious believers in society. In each of these areas the united front has had a decisive impact. It has been responsible for a distinctively Chinese contribution to Communist religious theory. It has functioned as the positive rationale for Chinese Communist religious policy. And the united front has provided the framework for the participation of religious believers in Chinese society.

Without an understanding of the united front, it is difficult to reconcile religious theory with policy and practice in contemporary China. On the basis of the Marxist-Leninist view of religion, it is easy, for example, to understand the context and limits of religious toleration in China. What is not as easily understood is why Christians, Muslims and Buddhists should be encouraged to play any kind of role at all in Chinese social and political life. The question may be asked, Why did the Chinese adopt a relatively moderate approach to the religious question after 1949, when just as easily they could have adopted a more forceful line similar to the one that Bukharin outlined for the Soviet Union after 1917? Why did the CPC not launch an anti-religious movement similar to the one that it advocated in the 1920s? Some of the answers to these questions may be derived from the particular understanding of religion in Chinese society. But even more important is the way in which the united front approach was applied to matters affecting religion and religious policy in China. In comparison to other possible options open to the CPC, the united front has provided a flexible and relatively positive framework for religion in the PRC.

Any consideration of the Three-Self Movement is either superficial or incomplete without an understanding of the united front. Yet this has been the most egregious omission in most of the standard works on Christianity in China that have been published in the West.[3] It is in part for this reason that there has been the tendency to misread the reemergence of religion since 1978 and to misunderstand what the TSM was trying to do in the 1950s. The united front distinguishes the Christian-Marxist relationship in China from that of other socialist countries. Despite its many practical and theoretical weaknesses, it continues to provide space for the development of religion in the PRC.

The Chinese Communist View of Religion

Religion in China is viewed within the Marxist-Leninist framework against the background of the traditional religious skepticism of Chinese intellectuals. It would be misleading and overly idealistic to approach the Chinese view of religion in terms of the humanistic concerns of the young Marx, just as it would be overly pessimistic to suppose that the united front oriented Marxist-Leninist interpretation is a direct function of the religious policies of Lenin and Stalin. Nevertheless, when religion has been criticized in the press for being unscientific, a form of false consciousness or an expression of class or imperialistic interests, Chinese theoreticians are following the line that was laid down by Marx, Engels and Lenin.

In this view the religious question is bound up with the question of oppression. For Marx, religion was understood to be a distorted expression of human consciousness that prevented men and women from realizing who they were and from dealing effectively with the world around them. In what has become his most celebrated passage on the subject, Marx wrote in ''The Critique of Hegel's Philosophy of Right,''

Religious suffering is the expression of real suffering and at the same time the protest against real suffering. Religion is the sigh of the oppressed creature, the heart of the heartless world, as it is the spirit of spiritless society. It is the opium of the people.[4]

Religion in this sense is a form of opium and thus an expression of alienation that masks the real human problem. It can be dangerous because it diverts attention from the struggle for social change.

Later Marxists came to believe that the role of religion was more direct in obstructing fundamental change. It was argued that this was especially true in class society, where religion helped to perpetuate exploitation by serving the interests of the ruling class. Engels developed his views on the class character of religion on the basis of European history since the sixteenth century. Although he saw religion primarily as a weapon used by the ruling classes to control the proletariat, he also held open the possibility that religious ideas could play some positive role as a cloak for the material interests and political struggles of the oppressed.[5]

Lenin, however, saw little possibility of religion serving such a progressive function. "The roots of modern religion," he argued, "are deeply embedded in the social oppression of the working masses."[6] Religion, for Lenin, was a tool used in modern capitalist countries to mystify the working class. The opium of the people had been transformed into an *opiate for* the people.

The question was how religion could be overcome. For Marx, religion was only a symptom, not the cause of the social problem. What was needed was an active human effort to change the historical conditions that gave rise to suffering and religion in the first place. This undertaking begins with criticism, but moves on to a praxis aimed at the transformation of society and thus the removal of the social sources of oppression. This explains why Marx argued at the first congress of the First International not for an attack on religion but for a struggle to bring about an end to human exploitation.[7] Religion would not disappear until society had reached its communist stage.

Lenin chose to confront the problem more directly. As with so many other questions in Marxism-Leninism, his own views on the subject are often contradictory, and the hermeneutic depends on the perspective of the interpreter. Before the revolution he argued that there should be no "war on religion" and that religious questions should not be pushed to the foreground:

> We must not allow the forces waging a genuinely revolutionary economic and political struggle to be broken up for the sake of opinions and dreams that are of third-rate importance, which are rapidly losing all political significance, and which are being steadily relegated to the rubbish heap by the normal course of economic development.[8]

After the revolution, anti-religious propaganda against the "opinions and dreams of third-rate importance" became necessary. However, echoing the criticism Engels had made of the Blanquists, Lenin also urged restraint.

The Party strives for the complete dissolution of the ties between the exploiting classes and the organization of religious propaganda, facilitates the real emancipation of the working masses from religious prejudices and organizes the widest possible scientific, educational and anti-religious propaganda. At the same time, it is necessary carefully to avoid giving offence to the religious sentiments of believers, as it only leads to the strengthening of religious fanaticism.[9]

The "ideal" was for religion to become a "purely private matter," without the benefit of the state support and social compulsion Lenin had found so oppressive in Imperial Russia. But although the Communist party insisted that religion be declared a private matter, Lenin never intended the fight against the "opium of the people" to become one.[10] The anti-religious effort had to continue.

The contradiction between not "giving offence to the religious sentiments of believers" and "real emancipation" through the organization of anti-religious propaganda describes the tension for religion and religious policy in all socialist countries, China included. On the one hand, religion is understood to be a form of social oppression, and it must therefore be *actively* resisted using whatever means are deemed necessary by the party in power. On the other hand, religion is a problem "of third-rate importance," and it will eventually die a natural death. Religion should therefore be *passively* tolerated in the meantime. The former view is more concerned with the negative impact of religion in the immediate future, while the latter takes a longer view of things from the perspective of historical materialism. In either case the question is whether it is more important to struggle against religion itself, or to struggle against the forces that give rise to religion.

In China this question was argued in a debate over atheism, religion and superstition in the early 1960s. The debate illustrates the ways in which the Marxist-Leninist view of religion was interpreted by Chinese theoreticians, and it is of more than passing interest insofar as the same questions are being raised today.

Atheism, Religion and Superstition

The debate on religion and religious policy was carried in the Chinese press between early 1963 and late 1965, before the outbreak of the Cultural Revolution. What was at issue was not the validity of the Marxist-Leninist theory of religion, but the way in which that theory should be interpreted and translated into policy in light of the Chinese experience. The debate has been subjected to extensive analysis and interpretation elsewhere, and here we need only recapitulate the central issues in order to illustrate their continuing significance for Chinese religious theory.[11]

In one camp there was Ya Hanzhang (who reemerged in 1978 to continue writing on Chinese atheist theory). Ya's articles in 1963 initiated the debate by centering on the need to differentiate between theism, religion and superstition. *Theism* was simply the belief in gods and the supernatural, as well as the ideas and philosophical constructs behind the beliefs. *Religion*, on the other hand, was theism plus organization, rituals and religious practices. As religion is distinguished from theism by the presence of organization and activity, so *superstition* is distinguished from religion by the absence of organization and a higher level of rationalization. "All religious activities are superstitious activities," wrote Ya Hanzhang, ". . . but not all superstitions are religious activities."[12] Included in the former are both the "spontaneous" superstitious activities of the believing masses, as well as the "professionalized" activities of fortune-tellers, geomancers and physiognomists. Both of these are different from the organized "world religions" of Buddhists, Muslims and Christians.

While superstition, according to Ya, must be eliminated and destroyed, religion should be allowed to continue to exist as long as it does not interfere with society and politics. Religion should be combatted using the ideological weapons of persuasion and education, but it would be both incorrect and counterproductive to oppose religion with force. For this reason religious activities should be tolerated. Ya's reasoning is based partly on what he sees as a Chinese religious and social situation which is different from the West, but more specifically on his understanding of the "correct" Marxist-Leninist interpretation.[13] His debt to both Lenin and the religious ideas of the Confucian intelligentsia should be obvious. With the Confucianists Ya shares the intellectuals' disdain for the religion of the "lower orders," and he does not believe that their beliefs pose a serious threat to society.

The major articles in the opposing camp were written by Yu Xiang and Liu Junwang, although they were joined by others as the debate progressed. They regarded theism, religion and superstition as equally harmful forms of idealism, which represented essentially the same thing. Thus there was no need to differentiate between them on the basis of Marxist-Leninist theory. They criticized Ya for being "unscientific" in turning his back on the materialist base of all religion. Moreover, Yu and Liu argued that class struggle was still "reflected in religion," suggesting that religion should be opposed in a more forceful way than that suggested by Ya. Struggle must be combined with unity, they urged, for peaceful coexistence between the CPC and religious believers would always be an impossibility.

> In the struggle against religion, the opposition to the use of administrative orders by a Marxist-Leninist political party definitely does not imply that in actual work we can disregard the struggle to promote the extinction of religion, and adopt an attitude of waiting for the extinction of religion, and even permitting the uninterrupted expansion of religious influences.[14]

Two latecomers to the debate, Liang Hao and Yang Zhen, adopted essentially the same position as Yu and Liu, but they were more direct in criticizing the systemic nature of Ya Hanzhang's errors. Ya was basically a "revisionist," they claimed, who had attempted "to remove the theoretical cornerstone of Marxism" by saying that religion did not always "function as an opiate."[15]

The question of whether Ya had ever intended to say any such thing is moot, and the debate itself ended abruptly. Liang Hao and Yang Zhen had had the last word.

The first article on religion to appear after the end of the Cultural Revolution era did not pick up where the earlier debate had left off, but it did signal that religious subjects could once again be discussed.[16] In March 1979, however, there appeared an editorial in *People's Daily* that hearkened back to the words and ideas of Ya Hanzhang: "All religion is superstition, but not all superstition is religion."[17] This editorial clearly reflected the views that were subsequently articulated in the Third Plenum. A moderate view, associated in the debate of the early 1960s with Ya Hanzhang, was reaffirmed, not only in terms of the definitions of religion and superstition, but also with regard to the clear differentiation that must be made between antagonistic and nonantagonistic contradictions.

Since then there have been numerous articles on religion and religious policy in the Chinese press.[18] An Institute for the Study of World Religions (ISWR) has been reactivated in Beijing as an affiliate of the Chinese Academy of Social Sciences, and other institutes have been set up elsewhere. The ISWR has its own journals and publications, and other presses are also coming out with material on religion, religious philosophy and subjects of a related nature. Although the revival of religious studies in China reflects a variety of interests and concerns, the purpose of the ISWR has been to develop a "Marxist science of religion." This means that the investigation of religion will go hand in hand with the criticism of theology and religious belief.[19]

The reemergence of religious studies in China has profound implications for religion and religious policy. The very fact that religious subjects are again being discussed is a positive sign, as is the reaffirmation of the moderate position that was associated with people like Ya Hanzhang in the past. But leaving aside the practical implications of the "Marxist science of religion" and focusing on the actual study which is going on, one encounters a fundamental problem. The difficulty is not that religious studies in China has been critical of theology—that has been the situation in the West for at least the last hundred years—but that it has not been critical of itself.

From the 1950s and 1960s to the 1970s and 1980s, regardless of the different interest and emphases, the academic study of religion and atheism in China has been barren and arid territory. Theoreticians have generally been more concerned with the degree to which their definitions and concepts have corresponded with some ideal interpretation of Marxism-Leninism than they have with their appropriateness for the concrete realities of religion in history and in contemporary society. As a result, they have rejected what is supposed to be a critical precept for Marxism-Leninism Mao Zedong Thought: the unity of theory and practice. The problem is all the more serious given the implications of religious studies for religious policy, because a unity between theory and practice is presupposed that does not in fact exist.

Ya Hanzhang is a case in point. He is known as a moderate and is relatively sympathetic to religion, as even a cursory reading of his essays in comparison with others from the early 1960s will show. Moreover, his article in the first issue of *Research on World Religions* is perhaps the most informative essay in the journal. Entitled "A Preliminary Survey of the History of Chinese Atheism," it is a lengthy overview of the social and intellectual characteristics of atheism in Chinese history from the Spring and Autumn period to the twentieth century. Ya stresses the need to go more deeply into the particularity of the *Chinese* atheist experience, which means that he comes closer than any other contributor to "unifying" theory and practice. But at the same time he ignores his own best evidence by suggesting that classical atheist thinkers were persecuted throughout Chinese history. In fact, the people he considers were all somewhat loosely associated with the Confucian tradition and many were high officials, making them unlikely candidates for persecution. Putting aside the question of whether they should really be called atheists at all, Ya Hanzhang bases his formulation on a perspective that is entirely too European, and nineteenth-century European at that. Atheism in Christian Europe meant something entirely different than it ever did in Confucian China.

This is not to suggest that Chinese religious studies should deal exclusively with Chinese subjects. Sun Ruogong's essay in the same issue, "On Feuerbach's Humanistic Atheism," provides an excellent exposition of Feuerbach's approach. The author surveys the German social and intellectual background against which Feuerbach wrote and sheds some light on a neglected area in his all too brief discussion of Feuerbach's *political* perspective (the identification of God with the monarch in interpreting one aspect of his atheism). The problem is that Sun's criticisms of Feuerbach are the same as those of Marx and Engels: he did not understand the need for practice; he eliminated the social from his understanding of humanity; he spoke too much of the natural order and not enough of human society. As a result, the article does not suggest any *new* way in which the criticism of Feuerbach might be pursued from a *Chinese* perspective on Marxism.[20] If the limitations of a method that concludes with the same answers as those discovered by Marx are not overcome, then the theory which results will neither be materialistic nor dialectical.

The examples could continue. Yang Zhen's academic work on Christian history and theology ranges between the doctrinaire and the propagandistic.[21] The debate over whether Jesus of Nazareth ever existed has been more repetitive than constructive, and entirely without the benefit of original research.[22] This question is, for some reason, still important in China, although the debate consists mainly in restating past positions. This is also the case with most essays in *Research on World Religions* that deal with the view of religion in Marx, Engels and Lenin. The sad irony is that little religious research of a creative nature is being conducted at the institute in Beijing which was specifically designed for this purpose.

The practical implications of this absence of creativity are even more disturbing. It concerns the way in which religious data are manipulated to fit the theory. When the actual facts of the material world are misrepresented or even ignored, when Marxist theory takes precedence over socialist practice, the result is devastating for research and policy alike. During the Cultural Revolution era it was this very problem that brought all cultural life in China to a standstill. Although a great deal has changed in China since the Third Plenum, lingering fears over dogmatism and ultra-leftism in the academic world of religion continue to hamper new initiatives in research, policy and planning. Moreover, there is little evidence that the "Marxist science of religion" has done anything to promote the "Four Modernizations" as was one of its original intentions.[23]

Ninian Smart has argued that part of the problem is that it is not scientific to say with Ren Jiyu, the first director of the ISWR, "Only the Marxist study of religion is scientific."[24] Not only does this statement preclude the possibility of progress through the encounter with other theories, but it prevents the theory from being tested in practice. It is *theoretically* possible that the "Marxist science of religion" is indeed scientific, although given all the evidence to the contrary, this possibility seems unlikely in the extreme. Yet if one chooses to begin with this premise, then it becomes necessary to proceed to the actual situation of religion in China and "seek truth from facts."

In Chinese Marxism today, beginning with "facts," "practice" and "reality" have become code words for combatting dogmatic thinking and ultra-leftism. Mao's argument that "social practice alone is the criterion of the truth of the knowledge of the external world" is put forth as an authoritative source for this point of view.[25] The opposite of proceeding from "reality" is to begin with theory or definitions. "In discussing a problem we should start from reality and not from definitions."[26] As always, Mao is being selectively quoted and used to promote a certain point of view. In the situation under discussion, this viewpoint is more realistic and open-ended than that which prevailed in the past. Today, beginning with "facts" is considered to be concrete, open-minded and pragmatic, whereas "proceeding from definitions" is said to be abstract, dogmatic and ultra-leftist. It is sound practice and good advice to accept the epistemology implicit in the slogan "practice is the only criterion of truth," at least insofar as the religious question is concerned. At the very least, it would provide motivation for testing the "Marxist science of religion."

At the ISWR, however, this is not being done. The intention to "seek truth from facts" has been violated time and again by those who have been entrusted to guide religious research. Consider the following two examples taken from the writings of Ren Jiyu:

Religious theology advocates obscurantism, deprecating man's rational faculty to the extreme. It hates science, hates culture, hates all civilization and progress of mankind.[27]

One of the basic differences between religion-superstition and Marxism is that the former seeks the protection of God or some supernatural power, while the latter relies on its own force to transform the world.[28]

Statements such as these are not even definitions, but rather emotional blasts that are caricatures of religion and theology. The first statement is at best a characterization of one particular kind of theology that no longer poses a serious challenge to science in most parts of the world. The second statement, which appears in the context of a more general discussion of religion in contemporary China, confuses the very distinction which Ya Hanzhang was trying to make in the early 1960s and thus misrepresents the actual situation of Chinese Buddhists, Muslims and Christians. Both statements are entirely too simplistic and at odds with the religious policies that have been reimplemented since the Third Plenum. As such they are detrimental to a united front with religious believers in China today.

The "Five Characteristics of Religion"

The "Marxist science of religion" has been one source for the formulation of religious policy in China, but it has not been the only source. Nor was it the first. The idea for conducting advanced research in the area of Marxist religious studies was not proposed to Ren Jiyu until 1959, and although the ISWR was established in 1963, its work did not begin until after the Third Plenum.[29] In the 1950s the formulation of Chinese religious policy was based on other considerations.

The theoretical framework that was used to describe this other approach came to be known as the "five characteristics of religion." In this understanding, religion is described as being 1) complex; 2) mass-based; 3) long-lasting in character; with both 4) national-ethnic and 5) international implications.

First introduced by Li Weihan in the early or mid-1950s, the "five characteristics of religion" has been completely overlooked in Western scholarship on religion and religious policy in China. The reason for this oversight may be that there has not been a full articulation of the theory in published form, and when it has been mentioned by scholars or cadres, it has generally been referred to in passing as something taken for granted. The "five characteristics of religion" is, in fact, better understood as a *working hypothesis about the nature and function of religion in China today*, rather than a systematic analysis or conceptual definition of religion in the abstract.

Developed by a senior cadre in charge of a party department, and not by an academic or religious scholar, the "five characteristics of religion" is the best expression of the religious viewpoint of the united front. It is based on the ideas of Marx and Engels as described in the first part of this chapter, but is more concerned with the function of religion than with its essence or truth. The framework around which the five characteristics revolves is well-suited for the CPC approach to unity with Christians, Muslims and Buddhists; passive toleration; and not "giving offence to the religious sentiments of believers." Although any theory of religion based on Marxism-Leninism misses what is really central to the faith and belief of the Christian, the "five characteristics of religion" at least allows for a Christianity which can be interpreted as a legitimate expression of social existence. At the same time, it encourages an approach to religious research which is more open-ended than that of the "Marxist science of religion."

In a speech before the Seventh National Conference on United Front Work, Li Weihan presented a lengthy analysis of the "religious contradiction." Because this represents the most comprehensive statement of the rationale behind the "five characteristics of religion" available, it is translated here in full.

> Religion, or theism, is the people's ignorant and impotent response to the inevitability of nature and society, and is the most negative form of this ignorant and impotent response. Therefore, Marx says that religion is the "opiate of the people." Religion has its history of development and change. In class society, every type of religious development and change is determined by the changes in the class relations of society. Historically, the ruling classes all have made use of a religion suitable for their own class to achieve control. The major religions of the present are: Christianity (Roman Catholicism is a branch of Christianity), Buddhism, Islam, and Daoism, which is peculiar to China, all of which have been used by the ruling classes over a long period of time.
>
> However, as for the phrase "religion is the tool of the oppressor classes and reactionary rule," we must differentiate things historically.* We cannot take a sweeping view, because historically religion has also served as "an ideological cloak for certain progressive classes" (Engels said this on the basis of Feuerbach's theory), and has provided the unifying link of resistance for certain oppressed classes or peoples. We must look at this aspect. We must further differentiate between the mass of pious believers and the minority of reactionary religious degenerates. This kind of differentiation exists objectively in any nation and in any society. All religious believers cannot be reactionary. From a political perspective, this is an extremely important differentiation.
>
> Historically, there have been two types of situations with regard to China's several religions: (1) In varying degrees, oppressor classes and Chinese and foreign reactionary cliques have dominated religions using them as covers to achieve their reactionary political goals. But it has been, after all, only a minority of religionists who have willingly played this role. The majority have been simple, honest and patriotic. (2) Religion has served as the unifying link of resistance for some minorities and oppressed peoples. Numerous examples can be found in the modern history of national (ethnic) and democratic movements, for example, the Boxers, the Taipings, the White Lotus Sect and so on. Religion also played a role in the historical struggle of the Tibetans to oppose British imperialism. How much revolutionary nature is there here? That is an-

---

*This sentence is the turning point in Li's presentation. He moves from the popular Marxist view, repeated in the first paragraph of this translation, to a stress on differentiation. This may be regarded as the point of departure for the "five characteristics of religion,"and it represents an attempt to move from "definitions" to "facts."

other question, and it is not to say that there have not been reactionary elements in those struggles. All in all, the situation in religious circles is exceedingly *complex*, and we should have a detailed understanding of each religion, analyzing and not treating it simplistically.

In the past several years, the people's government has applied a policy of differentiation to the religious contradiction based upon the nature of belief, circumstances, time and locale. This is in accordance with objective conditions. Now, due to the victory of the democratic revolution and the socialist transformation, there has already been a fundamental change in the class background of the religious contradiction, with the exception of some individual minority regions. Religion has already basically cast off the domination of the oppressor classes and the Chinese and foreign reactionary cliques, and it is progressively distancing itself from their influence. Step by step it is returning to its place as a private matter of individual citizens. With regard to the nation, religion is a private matter of individual citizens. This is what Engels said it should be. Therefore the Constitution stipulates the freedom of religious belief.

This is to say, except for individual regions, the religious contradiction has already been transformed from being both a nonantagonistic and antagonistic class contradiction into what is basically a nonantagonistic contradiction among the people. It is basically not an antagonistic contradiction. It has become an internal contradiction between those who do and do not believe in religion, between those who believe in this rather than that religion, or between those who believe in this rather than that sect. Even though in the near future religion will to a certain extent reflect class contradictions, even though the class stamp of religion has not yet been eradicated, and even though enemies at home and abroad may yet try to use religion for destructive purposes—which means that we cannot relax our vigilance—the primary contradiction is now between theism and atheism, between religionists and non-believers. Non-believers stand in the absolute majority of the Chinese people (ordinary superstitionists are not regarded as religionists), which means that they should take the initiative and be in the leading position in dealing with the religious contradiction. This is the religious reality which we face.

The people's knowledge of and ability to deal with the inevitability of nature and society follows the development and gradual increase of human praxis in history. The elimination of social oppression, the thoroughgoing liberation and advanced development of productive forces, and the advanced development and widespread dissemination of science and culture will finally result in the masses freeing themselves from the fetters of theism and religious belief. But this is a question which can only be resolved gradually over a long period of time. This indicates the *mass character* and *protracted character* of religion. In our nation, some religions also have an *ethnic character* and an *international character*.

Within a definite scope, the influence of religion is wide and deep. It influences relationships among national minorities, and some religions influence international relationships. Therefore, we conduct united front work in religious circles. Some people do not understand this. They do not see the mass character, nor the ethnic character, nor the international character nor the protracted character of religion. They only see religion as superstition, as opium. Therefore, they do not permit the people to exercise their freedom of religious belief. They use administrative measures to prohibit this spiritual opium, even to the point of applying brutal force. What they do not understand is this: freedom of religion is granted in order to unite politically with religious believers, to strive for the unification of the masses under the influence of religion with the great masses of the people, in order to free and develop productive forces so that over a long period of time the sources of religion will gradually be eliminated. To arrive at this positive goal, a passive freedom is tolerated. These questions must be fully explained on the level of principle and appropriately dealt with on the level of policy.[30]

Several things are remarkable about this statement of Li Weihan. It reveals that first and foremost he is interested in the specific religious situation of China rather than in the Marxist theory of religion in the abstract. In this regard he notes that in China there has already been a fundamental change in the nature of the "religious contradiction." Religion, says Li, has "basically cast off" its class character because it has been transformed by socialism. This means that religion is primarily a nonantagonistic contradiction and has assumed what for Lenin was its "ideal" place as a "private matter of individual citizens." Li assumes that religion will be around for some time, or until the masses "free themselves" from its fetters. Therefore he criticizes those who would use coercive measures in dealing with religion. The problem, instead, is to struggle against the forces that gave rise to religion in the first place. This means that the passive toleration of religion is absolutely necessary until that time when the forces of production are sufficiently advanced.

Both the substance and the tone of Li Weihan's remarks are vastly different from the theoretical debate over atheism and religion in the early 1960s or the "Marxist science of religion" of today. Li's views are more characteristic of the prudence and patience of the united front approach, in comparison with those of someone like Ren Jiyu. They have had a more positive impact on the development of Chinese Communist religious policy, both in the 1950s and since the Third Plenum. More recently, they have helped to generate a new approach to religious studies.

The *protracted* or long-lasting nature of religion is especially important for understanding the Chinese Communist viewpoint. It is on this basis that theoreticians arrived at the "law of development of religion" in the 1950s. According to this "law," religion has its own process of origin, development and decay, a process that is retarded or speeded up by more general phenomena such as the social relations of production, the advancement of science and culture, and the development of material society. Because it is considered to be an "objective law" of social existence, religion should not be tampered with in the short term, for that would only exacerbate the religious contradiction. Cadres are cautioned to be "clearheaded" and "realistic" about the continuing existence of religion in socialist society and are warned not to try to hasten the process of religion's demise.[31]

One of Mao Zedong's earliest references to religion is related to the question of its protracted nature. Commenting on the situation in the Hunan countryside, he wrote that because the peasants had made the idols of religion, it was up to them to cast them aside and destroy them with their own hands. "There is no need for anyone else to do it for them prematurely." Rather, Mao said that the policy of the CPC in such situations should be to "draw the bow without shooting," indicating the motions but taking no action against religious belief.[32] This served to reaffirm the contention that religion was an "ideological problem" which had to be handled with patience, care and understanding.

To say that the "religious contradiction" is *complex* means that it cannot be considered in isolation from history and society. This is why a certain sophistication is needed for dealing with religious questions. Religious complexity makes it especially important to treat the subject in its concrete manifestations, beginning with facts and realities rather than with definitions and abstractions. The complex character of religion is revealed in the relationship between religion and other areas of social life including politics, education and economics, as well as in its relationship to the other four characteristics of religion. In policy and planning, this is overlooked in left and right deviations, both of which ignore the existence of complexity by over-emphasizing one aspect of the religious situation to the exclusion of all others.

The class basis for the existence of religion in contemporary China has been eliminated, but "because people's consciousness lags behind social realities" religion continues to exert considerable influence as a *mass* phenomenon.[33] This is a significant theoretical concession to religious believers, because it implies that religion is something the masses still want. Thus, in the contemporary situation religion is no longer seen to be subject to the manipulations of an exploiting class, a foreign power or a "reactionary clique." Rather, it is understood to be an historical phenomenon which has a definite social base among *Chinese* religious believers themselves. Therefore, religious believers need to be involved in the process of democratic consultation about religion and policy. Although the Chinese Communist idea of religion's "mass character" developed indigenously, it is in some ways similar to the power of popular Catholicism which Gramsci observed among the Italian peasantry.[34]

The *ethnic* character of religion in China is especially relevant for the nationalities question. Although China's more than fifty ethnic minorities number only about five percent of the entire population, many of them have long religious traditions. The Tibetans are almost entirely Buddhist or Lamaist. Ten minority nationalities, including the Hui, have Islam as their religion. For the minority nationalities, the religious question is considered to be especially "complex" insofar as it relates to almost every area of social and cultural life. In the CPC viewpoint the "religious contradiction" of the minorities before 1949 was under the influence of "feudalism" and tribal politics, not imperial-

ism or international issues, the existence of a similar minorities question in the
U.S.S.R. being the primary exception. For the Han Chinese, the ethnic char-
acter of religion is not really an issue. Nor is ethnicity especially important for
Christianity in China, although Koreans and some tribal groups in southwest
China do have sizeable Christian populations.

Because Buddhism, Islam and Christianity are all world religions, the fifth
characteristic is concerned with religion's *international* ramifications. In this
respect it has been important to differentiate between friendly relationships with
foreign religious groups and continuing vigilance over the possibility of "foreign infiltration." Since the Third Plenum, all religious groups in China have
been developing friendly exchanges with their overseas counterparts, exchanges
that began with the Third World Conference on Religion and Peace in 1979.[35]
The CAB has probably had more exchanges with overseas religious groups,
especially with Japanese Buddhists, than have other Chinese organizations.
Protestants have exchanged visits with Christians from North America, Asia,
Australia and Europe, including highly publicized visits to China by the Arch-
bishop of Canterbury, Bishop Desmund Tutu and Billy Graham. At the same
time, the concern over the "infiltration" of overseas religious groups has been
a recurring theme in the Chinese press. This has been of greater concern for
Chinese Christians than for Buddhists or Muslims, and for Catholics more than
for Protestants.[36] Whether viewed positively or negatively the international
character of religion takes the whole question of faith and belief beyond China's borders and into the whole *oikumene*.

The fullest embodiment of the "five characteristics of religion" on the level
of policy is the 1982 CPC directive known as "Document 19", which is quoted
at the beginning of this chapter. It is the most important statement on religious
policy since the founding of the People's Republic, and a significant expression
of the united front approach to religion. In contrast to previous Chinese and
Soviet documents on religion, the approach of "Document 19" is realistic,
flexible and understanding of the needs and aspirations of religious believers.
Although it still draws too heavily on the theoretical approach discussed in the
last section, and despite the major weakness noted below, this statement represents a new departure for Chinese religious policy in the 1980s.

If viewed as a social scientific theory, the "five characteristics of religion"
is clearly inadequate. It offers no rationale for why religion in China should
have these particular characteristics and only these, nor does it fully explain
why the situation in China should be different from that which prevails elsewhere. Even in interpreting the Chinese reality, it leaves many questions unanswered; for example, given its functional and phenomenological concern,
one would expect some consideration of religion in its relationship to kinship
and village authority. It would be hard to imagine popular religion in China
which did not touch on these areas of life.[37] Yet in these and other areas of
folk religious practice, such as death and funeral rituals, the "five characteristics of religion" offers little guidance.

But the "five characteristics of religion" was never proposed as a comprehensive religious theory. As a working hypothesis it provides a framework for the articulation of religious policy in China, one which is preferable to the more rigid orthodoxy of the ISWR. Perhaps because it has never had to defend itself as a theory, the "five characteristics of religion" has played an important role in practice. Its analytical framework can be easily mastered by cadres at the grassroots who have not done advanced work in religious studies. Also, it provides a way of relating the religious question to other areas of life; this is important for religious believers and administrators alike. Finally, it has generated a new approach to religious studies in China that offers creative possibilities for the future.

A New Departure in Chinese Religious Studies

For almost four decades social scientists in the PRC have tended to limit their understanding of religion to the definitions and theoretical constructs proposed by Marx and Engels in the mid-nineteenth century. As we have seen, this perspective still informs the "Marxist science of religion" at the ISWR in Beijing. Its journals carry discussions of religion that are similar to those which were popular among certain sections of the European intelligentsia in the last century. It has been clear for some time that this understanding is totally inadequate in explaining the existence of religion in contemporary China. To continue with this approach represents a failure to take advantage of the one possibility that was never open to Marx or Engels: the transformation of religion in a socialist society.

It is precisely this possibility that today marks a new point of departure for Chinese religious studies. Using the practical and analytic approach of the "five characteristics of religion," an increasing number of Chinese social scientists are proposing a new perspective on religious studies. It is one that presupposes an open-ended Marxist orientation and is consistent with "seeking truth from facts." As applied to religious studies, this understanding began to emerge in the early 1980s, especially at the Institute for Religious Studies at Nanjing University, where most of the faculty are Christians, and at the Institute for Religious Studies of the Shanghai Academy of Social Sciences, where most researchers are Marxists.

One thoughtful expression of this new approach is contained in Zhao Fusan's widely publicized speech on religion at a meeting of the CPPCC in April 1985. Zhao, deputy director of the Chinese Academy of Social Sciences and a vice-chairperson of the Chinese Christian Three-Self Patriotic Movement Committee, argued that religion is an important aspect of the spiritual culture of every nation. It is therefore of value for China's development. To say that religion can only function as "a fantasy of human subjective consciousness" or as "a political tool of reactionary classes" or as "opium fumes"—all terms widely used in the "Marxist science of religion"—is erroneous and should be rejected.[38]

Opposition to the view of religion as opium has been central to the argument of those urging a more empirical approach to religious studies. In an essay published shortly after his CPPCC speech, Zhao Fusan delved into the origin of Marx's words on "religion as the opium of the people," and he concluded that they in no way represent the realities of contemporary socialist society:

(It) is hard to understand why some people today, with a socialist perspective, continue to stress that "religion is the opium of the people . . . that serves . . . to befuddle the working class" without looking into the context of Marx's words. Doesn't this amount to declaring that socialist society is no different from the old societies with their classes and class exploitation, so much so that millions of people among our ethnic groups remain "oppressed creatures," sighing in the form of religion? Doesn't this amount to regarding socialist society as a "heartless world" under whose "spiritless conditions" millions of people have no place to go for emotional and spiritual support other than religion?[39]

Many Chinese intellectuals, Marxists as well as Christians, were making the same case. As a result of their efforts, the understanding of religion as opium has now been almost thoroughly discredited in China. This represents an important and very practical victory for a more open approach to religious studies. The term *opium* does not even appear in "Document 19," thus indicating that this perspective has been gaining ground for some years.

In turning away from the definition of religion as opium, religious scholars have focused attention on the actual situation of religion in China today. Their question is not, "What is the correct Marxist understanding of religion?" but rather, "What is the meaning of religion in a society in which there is no longer exploitation of one class by another (i.e., under socialism)?" The answer to this question lies not in the study of classical Marxist texts, but in the investigation of religious practice in contemporary Chinese society.

Such investigations reveal the transformation which Chinese religions have undergone since 1949. Religious believers today are found to be good citizens who support socialism and actively participate in socialist construction. As such, they cannot be regarded as "backward elements" or "feudal remnants" or "imperialist running dogs." Because people's religious outlook has changed, religion itself can be "synchronized" or "brought into harmony" with socialism. Religious values may even help to promote social progress.

In this connection one writer has argued that the social function of religious values has changed with the realignment of political power:

In the old society, the Christians' stress on love, hard work, honesty, patience, service, selflessness and other virtues could be used to serve reactionary class rule. Therefore, the reactionary classes welcomed their propagation as an opiate to befuddle the people. But today, there has been a fundamental change, for political power is in the hands of the people themselves. The political and social function of these Christian "virtues" has changed, and they now serve to promote and not obstruct unity, stability, and increase production.[40]

This opens up new possibilities for religious participation in Chinese society. If religious values can play a positive role, then people may also come to a better understanding of religious belief.

The most thorough presentation of this new approach to the study of religion in China is contained in a 268-page volume entitled *The Religious Question During China's Socialist Period*. Under the general editorship of Luo Zhufeng, who chairs the Shanghai Federation of Philosophy and Social Sciences, this study is based on research conducted by the Shanghai Academy of Social Sciences. It moves from a discussion of the historical experience of religion in China since 1949 to empirical studies conducted in various parts of China in the early 1980s, the results of which are contained in nine individual appendices.

In his introduction Luo offers a useful summary of the ways in which the new approach to religious studies represents something of a "theoretical breakthrough" for the social sciences in China. It begins with the traditional ethical and this-worldly emphasis of religion in Chinese culture. This has meant that in Chinese history, religion was always related to the political order, and sometimes subject to political controls. Unlike religion in the West, therefore, religious life should not be seen as something that is inherently threatening to society.

Moreover, the new approach concentrates on the actual situation of religion in China since 1949, not social scientific theory. Over the last forty years Chinese religious groups have undergone a fundamental change. In the process, religious organizations have become fully Chinese and religious belief has become, for Chinese citizens, a "private matter." Unlike religion in class society, religion in China's socialist period may have a creative role to play. Therefore its process of development and evolution must be respected.

A third point is the recognition that religion is a historical phenomenon which has not and will not disappear with the elimination of social classes. Religious belief has "its own internal laws of development," which embody the "five characteristics" discussed above. This means that any discussion that centers on the elimination of religious belief represents an ultra-leftist deviation and is counterproductive for society.

The objective existence of religion in China's socialist period means that patriotic religious believers can make a positive contribution to society on the basis of "seeking the common ground, while reserving differences." Luo sees religious belief and socialism reaching the same destination by different paths. He continues, "For believers, religious regulations and religious ethics basically involve a discipline which encourages resistance to evil and adherence to the good. Whoever does what is beneficial for the country and for the people, regardless of his/her starting point or motivation, has a place in socialist modernization. In this perspective, religion and socialist society may be synchronized.''

"Synchronization," however, is a two-way street. Luo's final point, therefore, is that the government must continue to affirm the policy of religious freedom. Only in this way can unity and stability among believers and nonbelievers be maintained and developed.[41]

This empirical turn in Chinese religious studies obviously has positive implications for religious existence in China today. As a development from the "five characteristics of religion," it has been said to represent a "truly Chinese contribution to the development of the Marxist understanding of religion."[42] The fact that it remains underdeveloped on the level of theory should not bother us, for its significance lies in the practical contribution it can make to a more open society.

In contrast to an approach that would continue to stress religion as the opium of the people, the need for aggressive atheist propaganda, and the rejection of a united front with religious believers, the new departure in religious studies offers a promising approach to the development of religious policy in China today. It is already clear that this approach is gaining wider recognition among those who are entrusted with policy implementation. Viewed in a broader context, it also represents a significant point of departure for religious policy and practice in the socialist world.

The United Front and Religious Policy

We have seen that the Chinese Communist view of religion is inseparable from its implications for religious policy. This is consistent with an epistemology that emphasizes the unity of theory and practice and with a social philosophy that stresses the nature of predicted manifestations over logical consistency. At the same time, religious policy considerations are also a function of something else. They are in part derived from a certain view of religion, but are more generally related to the guiding principles that are the basis of a particular CPC political line. The line that has been conducive to the development of a relatively positive approach to religious questions after 1949 is that which is associated with the united front. Because the "five characteristics of religion" is itself a product of the united front, the relationship between the view of religion, religious policy and guiding principles is brought full circle.

Such a circular interpretation is more significant for our understanding than might at first seem apparent. It suggests that a general understanding of the politics of the CPC is as important for interpreting religion in China as the specific articulation of religious policy. The context and conditions, in other words, are more important than legal or constitutional guarantees. This was certainly true for religion in traditional and republican China, but it is also true for Marxists who believe that law is no more than a reflection of society and class interests at a given stage of historical development. In the China of the 1950s the context and conditions for religion and religious policy emphasized patriotism—the common ground—first, and the freedom of religious belief—reserved differences—second.

Other than one short sentence in Article 5 of the Common Program which guaranteed the freedom of religious belief, there was nothing published in the national press which dealt specifically with religious policy until September 1950.[43] The new government was involved in a number of more pressing issues, most of which, like the question of religious policy, they had had little experience with. In the absence of a more comprehensive policy statement, however, there were indications of what the attitude of the people's government would be. Especially for those Christians who had been active in the united front, it was possible to deduce implications from more general pronouncements, view documents that had not been openly distributed, and converse with CPC leaders on the nature of future policy. By virtue of their understanding of and relationships within the united front, individuals such as Y. T. Wu, Cora Deng, Chen Sisheng, Liu Liangmo and Shen Tilan—all of whom had been present at the first CPPCC—were able to interpret the religious policies of the PRC to the Christian community.

The earliest full presentation of the new government's approach was outlined in an article by Y. T. Wu entitled, "Christianity under the People's Democratic Dictatorship."[44] Based upon conversations with CPC leaders in February and March of 1949, Wu delivered his "personal reflections" in an address before the NCC in Shanghai on June 28. They represent a summary of the prospects for religious policy within the united front prior to the outbreak of the Korean War. Wu begins by saying that the CPC advocacy of the policy of religious freedom is genuine because it is based on two concrete considerations. First, Communists are historical materialists, which means they recognize the fact of religion's existence. They believe that there is no need to use coercive measures to attack belief, for it will eventually wither away as society develops. Second, the Communists recognize that all people are needed to work for socialist construction within the united front, including religious believers. To encourage such participation, they have put forward the policy of religious freedom.

Although the CPC is sincere about this policy, Wu notes it does have certain conditions. The use of religion for "reactionary purposes" will not be tolerated, nor will the practice of "superstitious" beliefs that are detrimental to the people's well-being. After going into some detail about what this means, Wu urges Chinese Protestants to try to understand the "special conditions" of China's liberation and to realize that Christianity was facing a situation which demanded "a new consciousness, a new awakening and a new viewpoint."

The demands that this new consciousness imposed upon Chinese Protestants will be considered in the following chapter. What concerns us here are the "special conditions" of China's liberation as these were interpreted for religious policy. Most important was the meaning that patriotism came to assume for the Protestant churches as the common ground of the united front. The functional significance of patriotism was fully developed by the end of the Korean War, and it has set the terms for religious policy in China ever since.

Religion and Patriotism

From a political point of view, the CPC saw itself facing two separate problems with regard to Chinese religions in 1949. On the one hand, there were the indigenzied Han or minority religions—Buddhism, Daoism and Islam. They were pervasive in the cities and countryside all over China and, with the exception of Islam, were non-exclusive and institutionally diffuse. They were regarded by the Communists as negative expressions of the old society, susceptible to the manipulation and control of "feudal land owners, feudal lords and reactionary warlords as well as the bureaucratic capitalist class."[45] Although they represented ideological obstructions to land reform and socialist reconstruction, these were internal problems.[46] This put them in a different situation from Christianity, for there was never a question of ties between Buddhism or Daoism and foreign powers. Significantly, when they finally formed their own mass organizations, Buddhists, Daoists and Muslims organized associations, not "patriotic" associations.

The problem for Protestants and Catholics, however, was whether or not they could really be regarded as "patriotic." Patriotism, or the "love of the motherland," had a very particular meaning for Chinese in the 1950s. More than the love of an old civilization, more than simple nationalism, patriotism meant the love for New China, and with it, loyalty to the People's Government under the leadership of the CPC.[47] While most Muslims, Buddhists and Daoists knew as little about socialism or New China as the Christians, the problem for Protestants and Catholics was complicated by their association with "foreign colonial and imperialist forces."[48] Chinese Christians were viewed as semi-foreign by many Chinese, as one popular saying in the China of the 1940s so clearly shows: "One more Christian means one less Chinese." Although such an accusation was not really fair, it does reveal the nature of the problem Christians faced. This was further complicated by the mutual suspicions of those who regarded Christianity and Communism as rival faiths. As a result, Chinese Christians may have been seen by the CPC to be a potential fifth column, and therefore a threat to social stability and political unity.

The Communists approached their "Christian problem" from the point of view of institutional linkages and material interests. They believed that the churches were dominated by foreigners because they supplied the financial support and thus exercised the power of the purse. For this reason the social base of Christianity was not judged to be really Chinese. Moreover, the material interests of the Protestants and Catholics seemed to lay with the perpetuation of a situation in which the bulk of their financial support came from overseas. Neither one of these assumptions was unreasonable. Many Chinese Protestants had been arguing for some time that their churches were too foreign, and although the question of the churches' self-support was understood to be a matter of crucial concern, little progress toward financial independence had been made by the mainline denominations prior to 1949.[49]

The solution from the CPC was twofold: first, to sever the institutional and ideological linkages between Christianity and imperialism; and second, to encourage and endorse the formation of a patriotic mass organization of Chinese Protestants that would be a bridge between Christians at the grass roots and the Chinese leadership. Both of these points were presented in the now famous series of conversations between Zhou Enlai and Chinese Protestant leaders in 1950.

In late April Y. T. Wu, Cora Deng, T. C. Chao, Zhang Xueyan, Liu Liangmo, Wu Yifang, Shen Tilan and Chen Sisheng, all of whom, with the exception of Liu Liangmo, were delegates at the First CPPCC, went to Beijing to request a meeting with government leaders to discuss problems associated with the implementation of religious policy in the Chinese countryside. There they were joined by Z. T. Kaung, Y.C. Tu, H. H. Tsui, N.S. Ai, and seven other Protestant leaders from North China representing a variety of denominational traditions. They met with Premier Zhou and other government and party officials on May 2, 6, 13 and 20. Each meeting lasted three to four hours, during which the Protestants presented their questions on religious policy, and Zhou Enlai elaborated his own views on the subject.[50]

Zhou's primary interest was in the social function of Christianity in China, and particularly the relationship between the missionary movement and Western imperialism. While acknowledging the positive contributions that Chinese Christians made to the Chinese revolution, Zhou speaks in no uncertain terms about the conscious and unconscious association between the Christian churches and foreign aggression. His point is that the churches must sever their linkages with imperialism if they are to continue to exist in China.

And yet nowhere in these conversations or, for that matter, in any of his writings on religious policy, does he advance a theoretical view of religion. There is no mention of religion being the opium of the people, and he is quite specific about not wanting to open up a debate on theism and atheism. It is very clear that Zhou Enlai was trying to downplay the theoretical differences between Christians and Communists in China, because these could only lead to polemics harmful to cooperation and social reconstruction.

Zhou Enlai tends to be subtle, and the nuances implicit in his words about Christianity and imperialism must not be missed. Toward the end of his conversation of May 13th he summarized his understanding of imperialism as it relates to the churches:

> Let me say once again that we see the question of the manipulation of religious organizations by imperialism in terms of the distinction between the subjective and objective perception of imperialism on the one hand, and its impact on the minority and the majority of religious believers on the other. Objectively speaking, imperialism has manipulated religious

organizations, but in fact, the number of religious believers who are reactionaries is extremely small. Religious groups should have their own internal self-criticism, in order to examine themselves and straighten out their organizations. What is involved is a question of principle. If we are clear about the principles and do the work well, imperialism will never again be able to manipulate religious organizations. This is also a means of self-protection for religious organizations.[51]

Zhou is not suggesting that Chinese Christians willingly allowed themselves to be used for imperialist purposes. Nor, for that matter, is he saying that foreign missionaries were involved in conspiratorial plotting with their governments. Imperialism is a question of political, cultural and economic forces operating in the international arena. Its primary impact is social and organizational (objective), not personal (subjective). For this reason Zhou emphasizes that the number of political reactionaries in the Christian community is extremely small. The key issue is the future political line of Christian organizations, and not self-recriminations about the extent of one's personal responsibility for the past.

It must be emphasized that even before the outbreak of the Korean War Chinese Christians were being told to eradicate imperialistic influences from their churches. The subject of American imperialism received major attention in the Chinese press in the late 1940s and early 1950s, and this could not but have an impact on Christianity in China. Early in the 1940s Mao had already spoken of the connection between imperialism and missionary work.[52] In Shanghai an article written by Xiao Qian provoked a great deal of discussion in the churches because he accused Christianity of being part of "compradore" culture.[53] The subject of missionaries and mission boards in China, however, became a much more urgent question for Christians and Communists alike after North Korean troops moved across the 38th parallel on June 25, 1950.

China did not want the Korean War, nor at the beginning did the government anticipate its own involvement.[54] Nevertheless, Chinese People's Volunteers entered the conflict on October 26, and for the next two and one half years the war colored just about everything that went on in China, including religious policy. It has been mentioned that the Korean War precipitated an outpouring of patriotic fervor among the Chinese people. This provided an opportunity for the CPC to further consolidate its own leadership and to intensify initiatives aimed at socialist transformation. As far as religious policy was concerned, these efforts ultimately led to the end of foreign involvement in the Chinese Church.

On December 16 President Truman announced the United States' decision to freeze all PRC assets held in American banks. The Chinese responded in kind, and on December 29 the 65th session of the State Administrative Council (SAC) took up the question of organizations that received financial assistance from the United States. In the major report at this meeting, Guo Moro began by charging that Americans, who were responsible for fifty percent of the funding of churches and other religious institutions, had all along used religion to "enslave the Chinese people." He went on to argue for the "complete autonomy" of churches and related institutions that were working toward autonomy; the differentiation between Chinese organizations that were self-supporting and those that were not; and an end to American "cultural imperialism" in China. Guo's recommendations were endorsed by the SAC and embodied in a ten-point document entitled "Regulations Governing the Registration of All Cultural, Educational, Relief and Religious Organizations Receiving Foreign Financial Assistance and Managed with Foreign Funds."[55]

A second meeting called by the SAC in April of the next year went even further. This time 151 Protestant leaders were invited to Beijing, and besides dealing with the question of financial relationships and control, the conference also became the organizational meeting of the TSM. Regarding the financial support given to religious organizations by foreign mission boards, Lu Dingyi, then vice-chairperson of the Cultural and Educational Committee of the SAC, noted three reasons why it had to cease: such support allowed foreigners to control religious organizations in China; these organizations could then help spread American influence and propaganda; and, the severing of support was in response to the prior move made by the American government in freezing Chinese assets.[56] Lu's speech continued with a lengthy diatribe on patriotism, American imperialism and the government's hope for Chinese Christians.

The new regulations that came out at this meeting, entitled "Methods for Dealing with Christian Organizations Receiving Financial Assistance from America," were much stronger than the earlier ones. They called for the immediate severing of relationships between Chinese organizations and American mission boards; the end of all missionary activity in China conducted by these boards; and the prohibition of foreigners from holding administrative positions in Chinese churches. They allowed mission boards to turn over their assets, excluding land, to Chinese churches, provided that such gifts were unconditional and without strings attached.[57]

Originally intended for American mission boards alone, the "Methods" were in time applied to all foreign mission agencies in China. These actions effectively brought an end to foreign participation within and financial control over the Chinese church.

It has been an unchanging principle of PRC religious policy for the last forty years that there should be no foreign interference in the Chinese church. This is one of the few similarities between the united front oriented religious policy and the anti-religious policy of the Cultural Revolution era. Such a policy is related to a more general principle of "self-reliance" in Chinese socialist development and "mutual non-interference" in international relations. It is also a product of the traditional fear and suspicion of things foreign, exacerbated in the case of Christianity by the long experience of "semi-colonialism" at the hands of the very powers whose missionaries brought the gospel to China. The last clause in the article on religious freedom in the 1982 Constitution states: "Religious bodies and religious affairs are not subject to any foreign domination."[58] Although the reference was not as explicit in earlier constitutions, it has always been implied. This is one way that the CPC has sought to safeguard Chinese national sovereignty and at the same time insure no bifurcation of authority that could threaten the political unity of the Chinese people.

A second way has been the CPC's encouragement and endorsement of the formation of a patriotic mass organization of Chinese Christians. It is significant to remember, in this regard, that the five Protestants who attended the first CPPCC as religious delegates went as "specially invited delegates" and not as institutional representatives. The CPPCC Preparatory Committee did not recognize the churches as organizations that had a democratic character, in which case they could have selected their own representatives, and so it chose those Christians who had been associated with the united front for some time. The delegates themselves never claimed to represent all Protestants, but only those who would welcome the New Democracy and a New China under the leadership of the CPC.[59]

The encouragement of patriotic activity by Chinese Christians was part of an overall approach to popular mobilization through mass organizations. For this to be effective, it had to be actively supported by the leaders, if not the general membership of the mass organizations themselves. It is therefore mistaken to think that the Three-Self Movement was initiated by the CPC. Rather, it was organized and supported by Chinese Protestants who understood and supported the united front under CPC leadership, and by the early 1950s they included a rather broad spectrum of Chinese church leaders and prominent Christians. This is not to say that popular mobilization did not rely on the CPC, or that patriotic activity was meant to be spontaneous. A combination of democracy and centralism is what was intended. Thus the "Resist-America–Aid-Korea" campaign, although based on popular expressions of patriotism, was organized and orchestrated from the center.[60] Protestants were informed of their "primary responsibility" in this movement in a speech delivered by Pu Huaren.[61] In subsequent movements through the 1950s Christians were reminded of their patriotic duties time and time again by local and national representatives of the UFWD, the RAB and other government bodies.[62] In this way the encouragement of popular participation went hand in hand with a clear indication of what such participation should entail.

For the churches and the TSM there was a more positive and concrete expression of government support. With the sudden cut off of all foreign funds it was obvious that churches and religious organizations would be placed in serious financial difficulties. There was no longer the possibility of the churches' running schools, hospitals and welfare organizations. Besides being the province of the socialist government, such institutions no longer had any way of supporting themselves. But although schools and hospitals could be turned over to the state to administer and fund, churches and groups such as the YM and YWCA were a different matter. They could not very well be run by a party which disavowed theism and religious belief.

The government, therefore, had to find another way to provide for the material needs of the churches. This would be in line with its responsibility to show care and concern for all the people, including Chinese Christians. The solution, contained in the "Methods," was twofold. First, taxes on buildings used for religious or YM/YWCA work were to be remitted (Article 5). Second, Chinese Christian organizations would be allowed to rent out buildings which they no longer needed (Article 6). The second provision was especially important. In Shanghai, for example, a system of "fixed rental under government rental" was developed. Some former church buildings, including the building which housed the NCC offices on Yuanmingyuan Road, were turned over to the government to manage and rent out. Sixty percent of the rents collected by the government was retained for upkeep and management fees, and forty percent was turned over to the local Three-Self committee.[63] In Nanjing, where there were more than thirty church buildings before 1949, rent was eventually paid on all except those actually in use by Chinese Christians.

Along with support for the patriotic activities of Chinese Protestants, efforts were made to isolate those individuals who were regarded as sympathetic to "reactionary" (GMD) or "imperialist" causes. In these situations Christians were told to "clearly distinguish" between China and "the enemy." What was at stake was a political matter or an antagonistic contradiction over which there could be no "reserved differences."[64] In the early and mid-1950s the minority was said to be extremely small. Insofar as patriotic Christians were regarded as part of the people, the problem was to limit the potential involvement of the minority who would use the "cloak of religion" to carry out counter-revolutionary activity.

After 1958 the tendency to confuse the relationship between friends and enemies increased, thus transforming a non-antagonistic contradiction, which is settled by education and persuasion, into an antagonistic contradiction, which must be resolved through struggle. Zhang Zhiyi, then deputy director of the UFWD, later admitted that he himself had at times confused the two, saying pointedly, "We have made these mistakes which cannot all be vaguely ascribed to the ten year catastrophe."[65] He meant that the problem of ultra-leftism in religious policy predates the Cultural Revolution era. In fact, it has been injurious to the implementation of religious policy since the very beginning. While it may be understandable that the question of counter-revolutionaries received a good deal of attention in the early 1950s, it was disastrous for China that this continued to dominate the thinking of many officials as they sought to relate to religious believers in the years since.

By cutting off foreign involvement in the churches and by encouraging the patriotic activity and self support of Chinese Christians, the CPC hoped to establish a common ground so that religious believers could become part of the united front. Once Chinese Christian institutions had freed themselves from imperialistic influences—and before the outbreak of the Korean War this process was envisaged to take some time—once they were regarded as independent and patriotic, they could establish a positive and cooperative relationship with the Chinese government. Cooperation was not interpreted as a lofty philosophical concept, but as a practical working relationship based upon the guiding principles of "The Common Program," China's first constitution. From the government's point of view, the purpose of this working relationship was to encourage the Christians' involvement in social reconstruction and service to the Chinese people. By emphasizing cooperation based upon a "common responsibility" to uphold "The Common Program," Zhou Enlai was suggesting in his conversations with Chinese Christians that they should play an active role in Chinese society.

Because they believed that the political and material interests of all Chinese should, under socialism, be basically the same, the CPC wished to encourage Christian involvement in society. However the whole question of religious orientation was secondary to patriotism and national unity. For the Communist there is neither God nor the transcendent. The possibility that a religious difference could become the pretext for cutting oneself off from the rest of the people does not exist. Any such attempt, therefore, is by definition political. As in traditional China, the government has sought to mute the political significance of religious authority and to establish undiscordant harmony.

This approach is not without parallel in Western church history. Although there has not always been a similar stress on political unity, loyalty to the government in power and harmonious relations between church and state have, since the time of Constantine, been the rule rather than the exception. In China, harmony and unity are based upon an understanding of the rightful "place" of religion in society. In contrast to the West, churches in China have never been in a position to set limits on the absolutist tendencies in Chinese governments. In contemporary China the "ideal," from the government's point of view, is for religion to become a "private matter" and for the churches to become patriotic.

There is a serious objection to the Chinese synthesis which comes from within. It concerns the way in which patriotism has been defined by the CPC. The question has been raised by Chinese intellectuals as to whether it is legitimate to identify the "love of the motherland" with support for the CPC. The playwright Bai Hua was perhaps hinting at this problem when he had a character in one of his plays say, "I love my motherland, but my motherland doesn't love me."[66] For this, he was severely criticized in the Chinese press in 1981.

Lyman van Slyke has maintained that the party's identification of patriotism with support for the CPC has been a way to "reinforce its claim that only through serving socialism can people exhibit their patriotism." This has put many intellectuals in a dilemma in cases in which they did not agree with the CPC, but loved their country just the same. Van Slyke quotes one of these who eventually left China as saying, "Many intellectuals serve patriotism under a penalty. The Communists want patriotism for the sake of Communism, but these are patriots in spite of Communism."[67] This has been a problem for many Chinese intellectuals from the beginning. In the 1940s and 1950s liberal intellectuals opposed the GMD and sympathized with the CPC social program.

But sympathy did not always mean support, for Chinese intellectuals remained critical of Communist methods and took a more independent line on questions involving individual freedom.[68]

The question for the 1980s is whether there is the possibility of a form of patriotic political involvement that questions the leading role of the CPC in the formulation of policy. The answer, in light of the "four fundamental principles," is that there is not. This is one of the limitations of the patriotic context defined by the united front, and it continues to be troublesome for Chinese intellectuals.

For Christians the question of patriotism and political involvement has been difficult since the nineteenth century. As members of voluntary organizations associated with foreign interests, "Christians were condemned for political activity as wrongful interference; for political inactivity as denial of patriotism."[69] The question after 1949 was, Did the People's Republic of China represent anything different? The answer for an increasing number of Protestants was that it did. For Chinese Christians who were attempting to chart the future course of the TSM, support for the CPC was based on its program for modernization and human transformation. Patriotism became identified with the CPC in the 1950s, because Christians believed that the Communists would help to bring an end to poverty, injustice and human misery, goals which the missionary movement had been trying to accomplish for more than one hundred years. In return for their support, patriotic Christians were given "the opportunity for a continued existence" by the government's policy of religious freedom.

The Policy of Religious Freedom

In light of the foregoing discussion it should be clear that the policy of religious freedom cannot be isolated from the more general treatment of patriotism and the united front. There is no concept of natural law or the inviolability of conscience in Chinese thinking, and so religious freedom cannot be based on these considerations. Nor are there absolute rights apart from social responsibilities. For example, there is no absolute right of dissent. When dissent or open social criticism have been tolerated in China, they have generally been justified in terms of the mass line and not the "rights of man."[70] In other words, individual freedom and the so-called "bourgeois" rights are less important than social significance and political function. The whole takes precedence over any individual part. So it is with the religious question. Religious freedom in China is understood by the CPC to be something less encompassing and therefore less important than the more basic concern for political unity and social progress. The latter is the concern of *all* the Chinese people, whereas the former will directly affect only a relatively small number.

Nevertheless, religious freedom has been included as a citizen's right in every PRC Constitution since the Common Program.[71] Already by the mid-1940s Mao was saying that religious freedom should be the party's policy in the Liberated Areas:

All religions are permitted in China's Liberated Areas, in accordance with the principle of freedom of religious belief. All believers in Protestantism, Catholicism, Islamism, Buddhism and other faiths enjoy the protection of the people's government so long as they are abiding by its laws. Everyone is free to believe or not to believe; neither compulsion nor discrimination is permitted.[72]

The similarity between the thoughts expressed here and the wording and rationale of subsequent constitutions is striking.

Constitutionalism has had an uncertain history in China, where law has never been understood to be impartial. In the Marxist understanding, a constitution is not a fundamental law of state as much as it is a reflection of power relationships between classes, and therefore an instrument of class struggle.[73] In the PRC constitutions have been based upon different interpretations of people's democracy under the leadership of the CPC. Thus the constitutions of 1954, 1975, 1978 and 1982 are reflections of the ways in which class struggle, people's democracy and party leadership have been understood in each of those years. The policy of religious freedom is but one aspect of these interpretations.

In general terms the constitutions of 1954 and 1982 may be grouped together over against the constitutions of 1975 and 1978. From the point of view of the policy of religious freedom, the former are united front oriented constitutions, while the latter are ultra-leftist in orientation. The wording of the clause on religion in the 1975 Constitution is identical to the separate article on religion in the 1978 version. The reference to religious freedom is expressed most simply in the 1954 Constitution, and it is considerably amplified in the constitution passed in 1982. The basic difference between the 1975/1978 and 1954/1982 articles on religious freedom is the inclusion of the "freedom not to believe in religion and to propagate atheism" in the former.

Efforts were underway to remove this offensive clause within a year and a half after the passage of the 1978 Constitution, and they probably began soon after the closing of the Third Plenum.[74] Prominent religious leaders, such as K. H. Ting and Zhao Puchu, were active in the movement to change the wording, because they believed that the reference to the freedom to propagate atheism reflected ultra-leftist thinking. As Ting later commented,

> The wording of the present old constitution is not satisfactory to us because of its ultraleftist content. It says that all citizens of the PRC enjoy the freedom to believe in religion and the freedom not to believe in religion and to propagate atheism. It says nothing about the propagation of theism. And this sort of wording can give the constitutional ground for the ultra-leftists in dealing with religion. Leaders of various religions have done a great deal of work in the last year or two to ask for a revision of this article. . . . We think that religious freedom *includes* the freedom not to believe in any religion. . . . When we say people have the freedom of speech, we don't say at the same time they have the freedom to be

silent. When we say that people have the freedom to write letters, we don't say that they have the freedom not to write letters. Because the negative freedoms are implied.[75]

When the 1982 Constitution was finally passed, it was regarded as a return to the spirit of the 1954 version.[76] Yet at the same time it reflected a development and refinement of religious policy. Although the new wording undoubtedly reflects compromises and give-and-take on different sides of the issue, the three additional clauses deal with specific concerns or emphases which were deemed necessary to amplify the simpler wording. Although this makes the article more difficult to interpret, it also provides insight into the united front understanding of religious freedom and its translation into law.

The first clause of the new Article 36 is identical to the entire article on religious freedom in the 1954 Constitution:

Citizens of the People's Republic of China enjoy the freedom of religious belief.

Zhao Puchu wrote a somewhat enigmatic poem on this article in 1954, which said in the last stanza:

Freedom of religious belief,
So much in one sentence,
Nothing can be added
To say more would be to leave something out.[77]

Nothing may have been added, but a great deal more was implied. Yet what was implied was consistent with the united front approach to religious policy. Religious believers were expected to be patriotic and support socialism and the CPC. Along with the right of religious freedom went the obligations implicit in good citizenship. Moreover, as Liu Shaoqi reported in 1954, the article on religious freedom would not protect those who would don the "cloak of religion" to carry out counter-revolutionary activities. Peng Zhen's comments on Article 36 of the 1982 Constitution are similar, but more moderate in tone.[78]

CPC members do not enjoy the freedom of religious belief. Because they belong to a Marxist political party, they have the duty to uphold the party program which is consistently materialistic. This principle has been flexibly applied for party members from national minorities "who cannot completely shake off all religious influence." Such members, who are mainly Muslim, should be "patiently educated" but not dismissed if they are doing good work.[79] Members of the People's Liberation Army and the Communist Youth League are also discouraged from religious belief, apparently for similar reasons.[80] In these cases also, it may be safely assumed that the principle is flexibly applied.

The major ambiguity in interpreting this clause is the question of its applicability to young people under the age of 18. Article 34 of the 1982 Constitution stipulates that the legal age for voting and standing for election is 18.[81] It is unclear whether this means that minors below the age of 18 do or do not enjoy the freedom of belief and other freedoms guaranteed by the constitution. This ambiguity suggests that the clause may be flexibly applied—or poorly implemented—depending on the attitude of the local official. To interpret Article 36 in terms of Article 34 is a manifestation of lingering ultra-leftism on the part of some cadres. Whatever the policy, it has not prevented young people from joining religious groups in large numbers.

The second clause of Article 36 states:

> No state organ, public organization or individual may compel citizens to believe in, or not to believe in, any religion; nor may they discriminate against citizens who believe in, or do not believe in any religion.

On one level, this clause follows an understanding of religion as an "ideological problem," which cannot be resolved using coercive measures. This has been part of the united front approach to religion all along, but it is given new force by being included in the constitution. An even more explicit provision is contained in Article 147 of the new Penal Code, which states that any government official who attempts to restrict the religious belief of any citizen be subject to up to two years of imprisonment.[82] Insofar as this represents an attempt to ground the policy of religious freedom more firmly in law, it is a most significant effort.

The clause also refers to public organizations and individuals that compel persons to believe in religion. This would seem to include religious organizations, clergy and other influential religious believers, including parents. It is especially applicable to areas of China where Muslims are in the majority. The emphasis throughout is on the word *compel*. The practice of sending young people to temples or monasteries was common in the countryside before 1949. In some cases parents wanted their children to become priests, monks or nuns as an expression of their own piety, while in other cases children were sent off as a matter of economic necessity. In any event this practice, which is still common in some countries, is now forbidden in the new constitution.

However, there is still a definite and perhaps unavoidable ambiguity in the new clause. Is infant baptism or the religious instruction of minors a form of compulsion? Religious instruction of children is routinely carried on in Chinese families, and children are commonly seen in churches and temples. There are also minors preparing for religious work in professional schools—the youngest student entering Nanjing Union Seminary in 1981 was only 17. The point centers on the clarity and adequacy of the constitutional provision, and the way in which it will be developed in law. As it stands, this clause, like the first, is subject to a variety of interpretations. Implementation and interpretation are left to the discretion of the administering official.

There is the same problem with the third clause:

The state protects normal religious activities. No one may make use of religion to engage in activities that disrupt public order, impair the health of citizens or interfere with the educational system of the state.

Again, two levels of interpretation are possible. One can emphasize the protection and explicit sanction of religious activities. The reference to "counter-revolutionary activities" which appeared in the draft of this article and was circulated for public discussion has been deleted. This revision helps to depoliticize the whole religious question.[83] In the second sentence, "superstitious activities" that are detrimental to human well-being are clearly implied in the reference to the health of citizens. In the same sentence, interference with the educational system probably refers to illegal Muslim schools in some minority areas. All of these provisions are well within the united front understanding of religious freedom.

However, the interpretation of the entire clause hinges on the word *normal* in the first sentence. Who is to decide what is a normal religious activity? A home worship gathering, for example, may appear to be a perfectly normal activity in one area, but it may be decided that such a gathering is disruptive to public order in another. Writing in 1961, Zhou Enlai spoke of "normal" religious activities that were disturbing to some party members.

Belief in God means going to church or praying silently before meals. Some comrades are startled by these things. They are not used to them and this creates needless tension and disruption in society.[84]

The disruption to which Zhou here refers is caused by the party official, but the clause under discussion concerns disruptive activity on the part of religious believers. If Zhou Enlai were doing the interpreting, it would be one thing. But few local officials have Zhou's insight into the workings of religion in the united front. The ambiguity of the constitutional provision makes understanding and flexible application less likely, therefore, than poor implementation at the local level.

The final clause of Article 36 prohibits foreign domination of Chinese religious bodies and religious affairs. This is, of course, implicit in the whole understanding of the relationship of religion to patriotism. In recent years this provision has been more of a problem for the relationships between patriotic Catholics and the Vatican than it has for any other Chinese religious group. Commenting on this clause, Peng Zhen linked his interpretation to the self-propagation, self-administration and self-support of Chinese religious believers.[85]

There are other areas of concern for Chinese Christians that are not specifically dealt with in the new constitution. The question of home worship gatherings, which became increasingly important for Chinese Protestants after 1958, has already been referred to. It would have been good if the constitution had made some reference to the place of worship, because this represents a particularly "complex" issue for the implementation of religious policy, especially in the countryside where the number of church buildings is inadequate. The government would probably prefer religious activities to be carried out in recognized places of worship, for it would help to minimize the administrative problems which arise. The fact that Christians gather for worship in their homes all over China gives the lie to the charge that such activities are forbidden. But from the point of view of law, a certain ambiguity remains.

This is true even in "Document 19." In the very same paragraph of this comprehensive statement, religious activities that take place in the home seem to be both sanctioned and protected, yet disallowed in principle. Some writers have protested against this wording, calling attention to the inconsistency. It has been rumored that the government has subsequently taken steps to correct the problem in order to make the protection of home worship gatherings more explicit.[86]

Another area of concern is that of evangelism or religious propagation. During the Land Reform Movement in the late 1940s and early 1950s, Christian activity outside of church buildings was expressly forbidden in the countryside. In some areas churches had to be closed for a time because they might "affect the sequence of reform work."[87] When they reopened, and ever since then, the understanding has been that religious propagation could not be conducted *outside* of religious institutions, nor could anti-religious propaganda be carried on *inside* churches, temples and mosques.[88] Holmes Welch has wryly noted that "this division of space gave advantage to the latter."[89] As we shall see, Protestants have been able to make adjustments, and their evangelical outreach has continued. But the contradiction between religious policy and the freedom of religious propagation remains.

Other problems with the content of religious policy are more specific, and in most cases less urgent. For Protestants these include: the return of church properties confiscated during the Cultural Revolution era; the return of church buildings for religious use; and the securing of various materials and facilities needed by the churches for their day-to-day activity. In all of these areas the problems are little-by-little being resolved. However, as it has been repeated throughout this chapter, the major problem for religious policy within the united front is not its content but its implementation.

Conclusion

From the CPC point of view the purpose of religious policy is to "correctly" handle the religious contradiction among the people, while at the same time developing a common political ground with religious believers. The formula for this is "seeking the common ground, while reserving differences." On the *political* level, patriotism as defined by the Chinese Communist Party is the basic requirement, on which point no basic differences can be tolerated. What differences exist must be overcome and transformed. This has been the reason behind the struggle against imperialism and foreign influence in the churches;

the encouragement and endorsement of the patriotic activities of Chinese Christians; and socialist education for people in religious circles.[90] While the third and fourth clauses of the 1982 Constitution indicate that there may still be a good deal of concern in some quarters over the social and political interests of Chinese religious groups, the TSM began to establish a common ground between the CPC and Chinese Protestants in the early 1950s.

In contrast to the political level, on the *ideological* level there can be both reserved differences and established or protracted differences.[91] This is the *sine qua non* for the cooperation between theists and atheists, between Christians and Communists in the PRC. It provides the positive framework for religious policy within the united front. The reservation of differences is interpreted by the CPC in terms of the "five characteristics of religion" and the effort to encourage the participation of religious believers in Chinese society. Just as the differences between Han Chinese and ethnic minorities cannot be overcome, neither can those between atheists and religious believers. The *protracted* nature of the "religious question" means that the CPC is prepared to wait for religion to die a natural death. The *complex* nature of religion means that, in policy matters, one should proceed from facts and social realities. The "five characteristics of religion" implies that there can be differentiation between *religious belief* in Communist theory and *religious institutions* in policy and practice.[92] Or, as the late Jiang Wenhan once put it, "Communists are not interested in Christianity, but they are interested in Chinese Christians."[93] From the perspective of the united front, the point is to minimize the potential conflicts, problems and contradictions of a social and political nature between atheists and religious believers, so that Christians, Buddhists and Muslims can become a part of society rather than a threat to unity and stability.

All of this takes a long-term view of Christianity in Chinese society. Zhou Enlai believed that religion would continue to exist for some time to come. This understanding was quite different from that of other Chinese Communists who predicted the early demise of religious belief. His words on this subject in 1957, therefore, have just as much relevance today as they did then:

> Some friends in religious circles fear that reform in our economic base will have an ideological impact, and that this will in turn have an impact on religion. Reform of the economic base will inevitably have an impact on ideology. But ideological changes do not develop in the same way as reforms in the political system, for the process is much slower. There are now religious believers in socialist countries. Can we say that eventually, when we enter a communist society, there will be no religious believers? No, religion will not die off so easily. Now we can only affirm that religious belief is a question involving people's faith and ideology, one which does not involve political questions. It doesn't matter whether one is an atheist or a theist, a materialist or an idealist—everyone is able to support the socialist system just the same. . . . Religion will continue to exist for a long time, and its future development will depend upon future

conditions. But as long as there are questions which people are not able to explain and resolve on an ideological level, the phenomenon of religion will be unavoidable. Some expressions of faith have a religious form, while others do not. Friends in religious circles should not worry about whether or not religion will survive. According to the materialist perspective, religion will continue to exist until society has developed to the point where the conditions which give rise to religion disappear. At present the question to be concerned with is not whether religion can survive, but whether the people can prosper.[94]

It is a similar perspective which has guided the formulation of Chinese religious policy since the Third Plenum.

And yet, there is a basic problem with this formulation. Within the united front the religious question is understood to be, at the same time, *less important than unity, but important for unity*. This is the dilemma of religious policy in China today. On the one hand, the religious difference is secondary, but on the other hand, unity with religious believers is essential. The first involves a question of worldview, while the second is a matter of political policy. The two have been confused over and over again in the last forty years, primarily because of the ongoing struggle between ultra-leftist and united front oriented lines within the CPC. In other words, the dilemma for religious policy is a dilemma over the way in which the CPC has chosen to interpret Marxism-Leninism Mao Zedong Thought. Thus the question for religion in China is not simply a difficulty over policy implementation, but a question of whether the united front is being practiced at all.

This raises an ever more basic problem for religious policy. In the absence of institutionalized structural or legal guarantees, what is there to insure that the united front will be practiced in the future? Has it not been the case that the policy has been turned on and off at the discretion of the people in power? As we have seen, one Communist answer, based upon the viewpoint of historical materialism and favoring the united front approach, is that the united front must be practiced because it is absolutely necessary for modernization and unity and stability.

But there is also another Communist answer, that of the leftist who denies the necessity of the united front. This may be a wrong answer, but it underscores the fact that the "correct" understanding of the united front is not absolute. Nor could it ever be. The united front is something more than tactic or expedient, but it is also a good deal less than an ironclad guarantee. The realization of absolutes cannot be hoped for in this world, and in China change and unpredictability have been the rule rather than the exception. A religious policy based upon the united front may be a relatively hopeful solution to the "religious contradiction" under the CPC, but it is one which requires a stronger basis in law.

The constitutional guarantee of religious freedom is therefore of the greatest importance for religious believers, despite all the ambiguities surrounding its context. However its implementation remains a very serious problem for policy and practice within the united front. If the ambiguities of the 1982 Constitution are any indication, it is not likely that the difficulties will go away. Chinese religious policy has not necessarily followed legislation, however, nor has law been as important as political principle. For the immediate future this means that the sensitivity and understanding of RAB, UFWD and other officials concerned with religious policy is crucial. Li Weihan's statement cited at the head of this chapter bears repeating to cadres at all levels of state and party structure, but especially to local officials. The difficulty is with the religious understanding and "cultural level" of such cadres, many of whom do not even possess a rudimentary grasp of the beliefs of the people they are dealing with, much less an understanding of the subtleties of the working style of the united front.

The education of local officials and the difficulties which exist over the development of a working legal system are much more than a problem of religious policy. They concern the modernization and improvement of society as a whole. Because of this the future of religious policy in China is related to such diverse areas as economic planning and educational reform, socialist democracy and foreign policy. Religious believers have just as much stake in these questions as anybody else. Their concern cannot be limited to the "religious question" in any kind of narrow and parochial way, but must be related to the interests and the future of the Chinese people. The participation of Buddhists, Muslims and Christians within the united front, therefore, must be regarded as something more than a return or *quid pro quo* on the policy of religious freedom. Rather, it is an expression of the Chinese version of people's democracy in which religious believers have taken their share of responsibility for the future of the nation.

PART THREE

THREE-SELF AS
A CHINESE MOVEMENT

5

Seeking the Common Ground

The historic tragedy of Christianity is this, that in its history of the past hundred years it has unconsciously changed to become a conservative force. And now at the present stage it has become a reactionary force. Christianity feels warm and comfortable within the circle of the present system, because its doctrines and its spirit have been brought to birth by this system. So it clings to its special position in the false liberty which it has received from this system. Still, this is not enough to be called a tragedy. The tragedy lies in the fact that the capitalist nations not only regard as gospel their own plans for resisting the course of history, but use their financial and military power to bolster up the reactionary forces in other countries. . . . In the course of this tragedy of history, Christianity has not only not shown the insight of a prophet in opposing the forces of reaction, but it has almost made itself one with those forces.[1]

—Y. T. Wu
March 31, 1948

Heretofore, the Chinese church has been keeping itself aloof from the political torrents that surged around it. The new philosophy considers that all phases of life must necessarily come under the influence of politics in contradistinction to the traditional Protestant view of the separation between church and state. In a world where political influences play such an important part and affect our lives and work so extensively, it is a challenge how the church as an institution and how Christians as citizens in society can perform their Christian functions and discharge their duties to society at the same time. In areas of social service and education we shall have to accept the leadership of the government and conform with the general patterns of service, organization and administration. Just how these new adjustments are to be made, is for the Chinese churches to determine. We have our privileges as Christian believers. We also have our duties to perform as Chinese citizens and Chinese social organizations.[2]

—"Message from Chinese Christians to Mission Boards Abroad"
December 1949

113

With this chapter our attention shifts from religious policy and the united front, as these have been understood and articulated by the CPC, to the ways in which Chinese Protestants responded to the Chinese Revolution and initiated the Three-Self Movement. As we have seen, a united front oriented religious policy did not begin all at once in China. Instead, it evolved slowly, was interpreted inconsistently and developed with many twists and turns. The same can be said for the history of the TSM. Its organization and development have been bound up with the vicissitudes of the Chinese social and political climate. Chinese Protestants came to identify with the TSM at different times with different understandings and with varying degrees of enthusiasm. Regardless of the many differences, however, they came together as a patriotic movement of Chinese Christians, a mass organization which joined in the political movements of the 1950s as part of the united front.

But the Three-Self Movement was never just another mass organization alongside all the rest. It was also a movement of Christian men and women concerned with the future of their church. By the late 1940s Christians all over China were raising questions about faith, politics and repentance, and some of them had come to believe that radical change was necessary. "The ax is laid to the root of the trees," as Zheng Jianye quoted from Matthew's gospel. He went on to argue that the church needed to identify with the "revolutionary tide" if it were to play any kind of role in the new society at all. Huang Peiyong, a Methodist pastor and former YMCA student secretary, noted a few weeks later that the church had become an orphan in society, because it had been too much like a spoiled child while it was still under the patronage of the missionaries.[3] Others posed the question less sharply and in more conventional ways, but practically everyone understood that some kind of change was both necessary and inevitable.

There are thus two ways in which the Three-Self Movement may be understood. On one level, the national or political, the TSM may be regarded as a *Chinese mass organization*, similar in nature and function to groups such as the All China Women's Federation and the Young Pioneers. On another level, Three-Self has been a *Christian movement* concerned with indigenization and ecclesiastical renewal. The two levels of interpretation are by no means mutually exclusive, and any division between political and religious concerns would be both artificial and misleading. Nevertheless, a consideration of the TSM from these two different perspectives may serve to clarify our understanding using an interpretation which is suggested in the Chinese sources themselves.

Since the 1950s Chinese Protestants have been speaking of the need to emphasize patriotism, or the love of the motherland (*aiguo*), alongside the love of the church (*aijiao*).[4] The slogan "Love-Country–Love-Church," in Chinese *"aiguo-aijiao,"* summarizes these two levels of understanding. Patriotism is concerned with the political dimension of the TSM, or Three-Self as a *Chinese* movement. It came to include the efforts for the eradication of imperialistic influences from the Chinese churches, intellectual remolding and the organization of a patriotic mass movement. Love for the church refers to Three-Self as a *Christian* movement, particularly the undertaking to create a self-governing, self-supporting and self-propagating Chinese church. This has included such specific concerns as pastoral care, Christian nurture, theological education and evangelism.

"Love-Country–Love-Church" represents the goals that the more independent elements in the Chinese church had been struggling for since the nineteenth century—a Christianity that would be *both* anti-imperialist *and* responsibly independent. The TSM was urging the constructive participation of Protestants in the Chinese Revolution within the framework of a united front oriented religious policy. While Chinese Christians did not necessarily accept the self-understanding of that policy as it came to be more fully articulated, it was an approach that they could work with. But it all depended upon the extent to which Protestant Christianity as a whole could be convinced that "Love-Country–Love-Church" was a legitimate expression of Christian existence in a socialist society. The crucial question revolved around the relationship between religious and political realms in the new situation.

This relationship was never a static one, and the differentiation was more a matter of emphasis than it was a strict separation. Severing the links between Christianity and imperialism was a manifestation of love for the church as well as patriotism, because it helped to purify the church from corrupt and non-Christian influences. Likewise self-propagation came to be understood as a political as well as a theological concern, at least to the extent that it touched upon the ever-present question of imperialism in the early 1950s. The emphasis in patriotism is on seeking the common ground, while love for the church is an expression of the reserved differences. Within the TSM there are also theological sources for differences within the common ground, but these need not concern us initially. As different emphases, the two understandings assumed different degrees of importance at different times in the history of the TSM. Generally speaking, patriotism was more important in the early fifties when Christians began to identify themselves as part of a broader patriotic movement. Love for the church became relatively more important in the mid-fifties when the TSM started to concentrate on church renewal.

As the "Message from Chinese Christians to Mission Boards Abroad" clearly indicates, "Love-Country–Love-Church" represents a radical departure from the traditional Protestant understanding of the separation between church and state. This should already be apparent from the foregoing discussion of religion and patriotism as interpreted by the CPC. More important, Chinese Christians began to develop a theological understanding after 1949 in which church and state were no longer regarded as alternative or opposing loyalties.[5] As they read the Bible in their new situation, Chinese Protestants from a variety of theological backgrounds began to see that patriotism was a good word. Love for the motherland was the context of the faith of biblical personages ranging from Abraham to Daniel, from Jesus to Paul. Moses revealed his patriotism when he led his people out of Egypt, and Jesus his when he wept for Jerusalem. Chinese Christians came to see that they did not have to reject their people or their country in order to become good Christians. Moreover, they increasingly saw that they could work within a socialist framework.

For Jiang Peifen the rediscovery of patriotism, separation from the missionaries and the purification of faith went together:

> The Bible does not teach against communism, nor does it say that we must separate ourselves from our fellow citizens in order to be good Christians. Our separation from the missionaries was a way of returning to the Bible and purifying the faith. It enabled us to speak from our hearts, and in the process, the Bible gained new meaning.[6]

If these words sound prosaic, we should remember that Sister Jiang comes from a strong separatist and anti-communist background. As we shall see, her acceptance of the Three-Self Movement was based largely on her desire to witness more effectively to her people.

Although radically different from traditional Protestant notions, "Love-Country–Love-Church" bears some similarity to the theological understanding of the state in other Christian traditions, including Anglicanism. Anglicanism has no conception of church and state as two rival societies in conflict.[7] It is based upon an understanding of the interpenetration between religious and political realms, although the context has been vastly different from that of China. The Anglican principle of "nationalism in religion," however, is in fact quite similar to the Chinese approach, at least on the surface. It stood for the rejection of foreign domination in religious matters, religious freedom made manifest in national identity and mutual support between church and nation. When the young William Temple wrote,

> The Church must recognize the nation as having a certain function in divine providence with reference to man's spiritual life. It must not try to usurp the State's, for if it does it will perform them badly, and it will also—which is far more serious—be deserting the work for which it alone is competent.[8]

he was speaking a language which Chinese Christians would have understood.

Beyond the apparent similarities to Anglicanism, the self-understanding of the Three-Self Movement is perhaps even better understood in relationship to the political theologies of the present day. Both are interested in discovering a way in which Christians may play a liberating and constructive political role. Moreover, in their rejection of Christendom, their emphasis on the relationship between theory and praxis, and their committed participation in a new kind of politics, Chinese Protestantism of the 1950s was remarkably similar to contemporary political theologies.[9] Despite the differences with liberation theology noted above, Chinese Christianity is also concerned with providing a positive rationale for Christian participation in a revolution for which Marxist analysis sets the terms. In 1957 Jiang Wenhan tried to show how the Chinese Christian acceptance of the People's Government was linked to an evaluation of its liberating potential interpreted in light of biblical faith. Twenty-five years later, in one of the first meetings between Chinese Christians and other Christians from the Third World, Jiang participated in a "new beginning," a dialogue over some of the very same questions which China had been struggling with since the 1950s.[10]

Such comparisons with Anglicanism and the political theologies can at this point only be suggested. Their relevance to the Chinese situation will have to be judged on the basis of what the TSM has said of itself. In the meantime, the question raised earlier still stands: How were patriotism and love for the church related in the TSM? What did love for the motherland mean in the struggle to realize the selfhood of Chinese Christianity as a task, and how was it related to the true selfhood of the church which is a gift of God's grace? This question is fundamental for any consideration of Three-Self as a *Christian* movement. But it can also be raised in another way: How did Chinese Protestants relate themselves to the united front, and what did this mean in terms of their Christian faith? On this basis the question may be addressed with reference to the Protestant response to the government initiatives outlined in the previous chapter. It is the first question which must be asked in any treatment of Three-Self as a *Chinese* movement, the discussion of which will precede our interpretation of Three-Self as a Christian movement in the final two chapters of this book.

In this chapter and the next the TSM will be analyzed as a mass organization of Protestant Christians in China. Especially important will be the way in which Three-Self came to play a bridge-building role between Chinese Protestants and the CPC in an attempt to establish a common ground within the united front. This will be discussed in three overlapping but roughly chronological stages. The first was from 1949 until the outbreak of the Korean War and the launching of the "Christian Manifesto." This was a period of questioning and searching preceding the entry of Chinese Protestants into the united front. The second stage was more or less coterminal with the Korean War, and it was the most difficult time for Chinese Christians in the early 1950s. Through the denunciation and study movements Chinese Protestants severed their links with imperialism and identified themselves with the united front. The third period was that of the organization of the TSM. Although a Preparatory Committee was set up as early as April 1951, the TSM was not formally constituted until the First National Christian Conference in 1954. An overview of organizational developments in the TSM will set the stage for the discussion of the rejection and renewal of Three-Self in the chapter which follows.

Protestants and the Chinese Revolution

In 1949 there were close to one million Protestant Christians in China, who accounted for less than one-half of one-percent of the total population. They were related to twenty-three major denominational groups, representing both indigenous organizations and foreign mission boards. Including those working in Christian institutions, there were about ten thousand professional Chinese church workers and almost four thousand foreign missionaries. Shanghai, which had always been the center of Chinese Protestantism, had 141 places of worship in 1950. Throughout China there were 322 Christian hospitals, more than 240 schools, 13 Christian colleges and 210 seminaries and Bible colleges.[11]

The situation of Protestant Christianity, which is represented by these figures, was an exceedingly complex one. For one thing, the small number of Christians and missionaries belied their real social influence. Chinese church leaders, Christian intellectuals and foreign missionaries were involved in almost every area of society, from education to health and social welfare, from rural development to publications. Moreover, to speak of the church situation, it is necessary to clarify which situation one is referring to, for there were important differences among the mainline denominations, the foreign mission boards and the indigenous churches and sects. The last were largely fundamentalist and pre-millenarian in theological orientation. Within the mainline churches there were the wide-ranging theological divisions between liberals and conservatives, differences which are still problematic in churches all over the world. Even the students were not exempt, divided as they were between the Student Christian Movement, a Christian student movement open to all, and the more rigidly evangelical Inter Varsity Fellowship.[12] Perhaps the most important difference, however, at least from a sociological perspective, was that between the churches in the cities and those in the countryside.

China has always been an agricultural society. The evangelization of the Chinese countryside had been an important emphasis in Protestant mission work since the nineteenth century. By 1937, two-thirds of the fifteen thousand places of worship in China were in the countryside, and although many of these were damaged or destroyed during the War of Resistance Against Japan, the Protestant population was still overwhelmingly rural in 1949.[13] Christians in the countryside were men and women of simple beliefs, and their churches, though small and generally poor, were often vital centers of faith and fellowship.

The problems faced by rural churches were different from those in the cities. Christian communities in the countryside were perpetually understaffed, and what pastors there were tended to lack the education and experience of those who settled in the cities. In 1922 two-thirds of the foreign missionaries and one-third of the Chinese church workers were in urban areas which accounted for less than six percent of the population at large and twenty percent of the Protestant communicants.[14] The city congregations had more contacts with other denominations and more access to Christian institutions than those in the countryside. In contrast, rural churches were isolated, less ecumenical and fertile territory for the proliferation of sects and "heterodox" beliefs.[15] This last problem is related to the educational and economic level of rural Christians, and this is something which continues to be problematic in China. It is part of an overall picture of a rural church which was and is numerically stronger, but structurally, financially and intellectually weaker than its urban counterpart.

As the Communist armies marched toward victory in the late 1940s, rural churches faced a more difficult situation than those in the cities. This was especially true in north China, where the CPC had achieved almost total control of the countryside by 1948. Several reasons have been put forward to account for the difficulties that the rural churches encountered.[16] In some villages the church was the most prominent institution, and a source of friction and resentment for the local populace. This meant that it could become a focal point for factional disputes within the village. Resentment was exacerbated by the presence or history of foreign missionaries, and also in cases in which the church was patronized by a local landlord or owned a great deal of property. The sectarianism and anti-communism of some rural Christian leaders was another source of friction, especially in areas where they had been used by GMD sympathizers to attack the CPC. On the Communist side, difficulties were often caused by local cadres who viewed all religious activities as superstitious or foreign-controlled. Also, the Communists' program of land reform obstructed the religious activities of rural churches, although it improved the material situation of the Christian peasants.

Despite all of these problems, it is difficult to make generalizations about the situation of rural Christians in the first months and years of the Communist victory, especially when regional variations in the pattern of liberation are taken into account. For example, in large parts of East China, the rural churches adjusted rather smoothly to the Communist victory. Searle Bates reported that some Christians even became leaders of newly formed organizations because of their experience, education and good reputations in local villages.[17] Perhaps all that can be said is that the CPC attitudes toward the church in the countryside oscillated between hostility and tolerance, supporting the conclusion of fifteen "knowledgeable missionaries" that

> Responsible Communist leadership since the beginning of the Sino-Japanese War has been disposed to judge the Church on the basis of its performance in the actual situation and not on the basis of any systematic and determined opposition to Christianity as such.[18]

In part because of the relative strength and influence of urban churches and Christian institutions, and in part because of the more consistent implementation of the Common Program, the situation of the churches in the cities was more favorable than in the countryside after 1949. It should be remembered that as we take up the attitudes of Chinese Protestants toward the new situation, we will be drawing almost entirely on the views of urban and educated church leaders. This is true regardless of whether one is speaking of mainline church executives, Christian intellectuals, prominent leaders of indigenous sects or the originators of the TSM. There can be no question that they represented, to a greater or lesser degree, the views of Christians in the countryside. However, as with society as a whole, one of the special characteristics of Protestantism and the TSM is the contradiction which persists between the cities and the countryside.

Although their political and theological perspectives varied, Chinese Protestant leaders increasingly came to believe that the fundamental problem which the church faced in 1949 was its identification as a foreign-oriented institution. The problem did not come as an entirely new realization. Protestants had been caught up in the emerging sense of nationalism among the Chinese people since the May Fourth Movement.[19] But with the victory of the CPC and the growing understanding that radical changes were absolutely necessary, the problem of the churches' identification became a much more urgent one. This new sense of urgency was reflected in statements such as the "Message from Chinese Christians to Mission Boards Abroad" cited at the head of this chapter.

The same concern was voiced in statements, speeches and articles of individual Christians. Speaking to students in the spring of 1949, T. C. Chao is reported to have said,

> Christianity as represented by the churches often appears as a twisted thing, a thing connected with foreign imperialism, bourgeois idiosyncrasies, and the corrupt and dying status quo; a thing that is the opiate of the people, an escape from reality, a high-sounding idealism that is nowhere effective. . . . No wonder so many Christians go over to the Communists. Yet the churches have not awakened.[20]

This is an extremely sharp statement coming from a world renowned Protestant theologian who did not accept the program of the CPC.

For those who did, the problem for Christians centered on the question of imperialism and the missionary movement. But it did not follow that all Christians who welcomed the New Democracy and the united front accepted the CPC's understanding of imperialism. In contrast to Mao's view that imperialism had been a form of aggression against China,[21] one writer argued that the missionary movement had been an expression of sincere goodwill which had failed. It had failed because the missionaries had never really understood the Chinese point of view, and therefore they could not preach a Christianity which could really take hold in China. The missionaries proclaimed brotherhood, the kingdom of God and a more abundant life.

> Throughout the missionary movement, however, there has never been a clearly defined theory, practice or experiment by and for Chinese Christians as to what a better and more abundant life, the brotherhood of man or the Kingdom of God would mean in China. To, by, and for the Chinese, the Christian message was one of personal salvation. There was no clearly defined socio-personal preaching that one could be saved in relation to the society in which he lives. The result has been that the Christian convert in China might become a better parent or child, but not a new man in the world as St. Paul exemplified, nor a new citizen of his community.

The writer continues in the same vein,

> To tell a Chinese to be a Christian, to instruct him to read the Bible, to counsel him to love God and to follow Jesus—all this is not enough. He has to learn how to act upon Christian principles in the problems that confront a Christian living every day in this common world. Positively, he has to know what he can do and learn how he may do it, and understand why he must do it so that there may come a new world in which he can enjoy a better, more abundant life and real brotherhood of man.[22]

This was something which could never have happened under foreign missionary tutelage, despite the best of intentions.

Although his essay reveals considerable insight into the problem of the churches' foreign orientation, the views of C. H. Lee were not widely shared by the Protestant leadership in 1949. They tended to be more moderate or conservative in their positions, more sympathetic to the foreign missionaries, and in varying degrees suspicious of the Communists' intentions. At the risk of oversimplification, it is possible to identify three different positions which Chinese Protestants maintained *outside* of the united front. The three positions should be viewed neither as fixed categories nor as organized groups. Rather, they represent commitments based upon theological conviction, political orientation and institutional linkages relative to the united front.

(1) On the extreme right there were those who were associated with the four "big families" (Jiang, Kong, Song and Chen), many of whom had already fled to Taiwan or the United States in 1949. Chiang Kai-shek was himself a Christian, as were many of the high-ranking ministers and prominent individuals associated with the GMD. Although they were small in religious influence, they had had enormous political power. In America they were supported by some highly vocal China missionaries including Walter Judd, who became a moving force behind the China Lobby. It was said of these Chinese Christians, "They used Protestant Christianity to build up their prestige abroad, while certain Protestant leaders used them to build up the prestige and influence of Protestant missions in China."[23] Such Christians were also ambiguous about the foreign identity of the Chinese church, because they often chose to exploit it. There was no way that they could accommodate themselves to a Communist society or work within the united front.

(2) A second group of theologically conservative Christians were not as political in their orientation. They included many of those from indigenous churches and sects, as well as conservatives and fundamentalists from the mainline denominations. They represented the majority of Chinese Protestants in 1949, and even today they are the most numerous. Conservative and fundamentalist leaders were unalterably opposed to any compromise with either Communism or liberalism on religious questions, but they were divided over how they should respond to the new situation. Some viewed the CPC victory as an apocalyptic event, while others believed that they could accommodate themselves to the

new order and still maintain their loyalty to the New Testament. They wanted the church to be Chinese, although many tended to think that they should remain aloof from society and politics. However there were also conservatives such as Marcus Chen (Chen Chonggui), Xie Yongqin and Zhu Guishen who played leading roles in the early years of the TSM.

(3) The third position was that of a large majority of the leadership of Protestant organizations and mainline denominations. They tended toward the moderate or liberal in their theology as well as their politics, were concerned about the foreign identity of the Chinese church but cautious in their approach to the CPC. Like their more conservative counterparts, they had a deep pastoral concern for the church as it faced the many challenges of the new situation, a concern poignantly expressed in the NCC's three messages to Chinese Christians.[24] Most denominations were dissatisfied with the corruption of the GMD, but they were not pro-communist. In the language of the united front, they comprised the "vacillating middle." Other leaders were politically more progressive, but they had not developed close linkages with the Communists. Among these were many denominational leaders who played active roles in the early years of Three-Self, including H. H. Tsui, Robin Chen (Chen Jianzhen) and Z. T. Kuang (Jiang Changchuan).

Alongside these three positions there was that of the avowed progressives who had already identified themselves with the New Democracy. Without denying the importance of conservative and liberal church leaders, the contribution of this group was crucial for the creation of Three-Self as a mass movement of Chinese Christians. A consideration of these Protestants within the united front will afford an understanding of the reconciliation between Chinese Christians and the Chinese revolution which began to take place in the thinking and actions of those who accepted the political leadership of the CPC even before 1949.

Christians within the United Front

The problem of the church's identification as a foreign oriented institution was posed most sharply by Y. T. Wu. He brought the emerging conflict between Chinese Christians and missionary interests out into the open with the publication of "The Present Day Tragedy of Christianity" on Easter of 1948, and he was fired as editor of *Tian Feng* because of it. The essay was a shattering critique of the association between Protestantism and capitalism, which Wu analyzed in Marxist terms as "two expressions of the same society." As a result of this association, Christianity had become opposed to fundamental social change, and this represented a rejection of the gospel's original revolutionary nature. This was especially tragic in China, argued Wu, because the country was in the midst of the greatest period of change in its history.[25] Rereading the essay forty years later, its charges sound neither sharp nor unfamiliar, especially in light of the theological developments in the Third World since the 1960s. But in 1948 its impact was devastating, particularly because it came from what was then North America's largest mission field.

Y. T. Wu (1893–1979) became the leading figure in the TSM from its inauguration up to the Cultural Revolution. Theologically and politically he had been moving toward his position since the 1930s. Converted to Christianity in 1920, Wu became a YMCA secretary who was involved in publication work for most of his career. He studied at New York's Union Theological Seminary, where he was influenced by the ideas of Harry Ward and Reinhold Niebuhr in theology, and John Dewey and William James in philosophy. Wu's lifelong concern was the relevance of Christianity to social questions, and from the 1920s to the late 1930s he moved from pacifism, to the social gospel, to a limited synthesis between communism and Christianity. By the early 1940s he had more or less identified himself with the position of the CPC on China's social needs, and after the end of the war against Japan he became one of the prominent "democratic personages" within the united front.[26]

By then Wu believed that Christians must throw themselves fully into the movement for revolutionary change which was led by the CPC. His theological emphasis on God's immanence in history and nature corresponded with his political commitment to a social program which would bring fundamental change to China.[27] Although he understood that transcendence and immanence had to be kept in dialectical unity, the growing importance of God's immanence in Wu's theological position was designed to counter what he saw as the pessimism implicit in the prevailing tendency in Western theology to dwell on divine transcendence alone. As he later wrote to one of his missionary friends, this type of transcendence was debilitating.

> If we see God only in his transcendence, we are bound to arrive at a pessimistic view of man. . . . According to this one sided emphasis, man is sinful, miserable and utterly depraved; God and man are separated from each other by an absolute chasm. . . . The "salvation of the soul" takes the place of interest in social change since genuine social uplift is impossible with man's heart "at fault." . . . Thus we arrive at the "above politics" mentality par excellence. . . . Unfortunately, this is not "above politics" but a service to reactionary politics![28]

For Chinese Christians who were concerned about "national salvation," this understanding was both theologically and politically liberating. It allowed them to make the Christian concern for love, service and social change politically relevant. This was an important aspect of the faith for many Christian students and intellectuals, who were forever struggling with the way in which Christian "ideals" could have a social impact. Given a church which had discovered no real way of addressing China's social problems, Wu's perspective enabled Christians to enter into a political movement which was not expressly Christian. What should be Christianity's special contribution to this movement? This, according to Wu, was not the fundamental question.

> This is as if to say that Christians should do different things from the rest of the people, and if we throw ourselves into the new tide, we will be the same as everyone else. Jesus said we should be like yeast and salt;

he did not tell us to create another world, but in this world to play a reforming and transforming role.[29]

Wu was no longer arguing for an independent Christian social program, but for Christian participation in the united front. The churches as churches had no way of solving China's social problems, but Christians could enter into a broader social movement and respond to God's promise there. At this point Wu's theological and political concerns were brought together, but not unified. As K. H. Ting later wrote, Wu's thinking about God's immanence in relation to the Chinese political situation allowed "many Chinese Christians to take their place in the movement for national salvation with their faith intact, as well as for intellectuals mindful of the national fate to take their place among Christians."[30]

The problem was that a large majority of Christians did not want to throw themselves into the "new tide." Wu argued that this was because their political thinking was unclear. Because of their close relationship with the status quo, because of their lack of historical vision, because of their inadequate understanding of communism, Christians remained either suspicious of or aloof from the CPC.[31] This was all part of the present-day tragedy of Christianity, and it meant for Wu that Christianity had to change and be changed in order to recover its original and revolutionary nature.

> We still believe that reform within Christianity must come. Christianity has evolved from Roman Catholicism of the feudal age to Protestantism of the capitalist age. This was one stage of development. In today's world, capitalism is gradually developing towards socialism, which means that Christianity will also necessarily enter a new stage. We have said that Christianity has an inner life of its own. This inner life will naturally have different expressions in different times.[32]

Y. T. Wu's criticism of the missionary movement and the churches followed a Marxist line, but his theology was a product of his own wrestling with God and the Bible in light of the Chinese situation. His faith was a "reserved difference" within the common ground of the united front, but it was also his point of contact with all Chinese Christians and with the new form of Christianity which he hoped would emerge. Throughout his career Wu confronted Christianity with the question of political accountability. By so doing, he hoped to change the image of the church in the eyes of the Chinese people so that Christianity could take root in China on a new footing.

Although he was the acknowledged leader, Y. T. Wu was not the only Protestant of his generation who accepted the CPC position in the 1940s. Liu Liangmo, another YMCA secretary, had organized a "mass singing movement" during the war which helped to give a voice to the emerging sense of progressive patriotism among the Chinese people.[33] Wu Yifang (1893–1985) was another "Christian democrat" within the united front. A consistent proponent of women's liberation, she was the first woman college president in

China and represented China nationally and internationally before and after 1949.[34] Cora Deng, K. Z. Lo, Y. C. Tu and Shen Tilan were also early proponents of the united front, as were many other less widely-known Christian intellectuals.[35]

The SCM and the YM/YWCAs attracted a younger generation of Christian students who were committed to national salvation and the reform of the church. Kiang Wenhan (1908–1984) argued in 1947 that the SCM had all along been trying to make Christianity socially effective. Especially after the Japanese invasion of China, the SCM helped Christian students understand and confront China's social problems.[36] Although its sense of identification with the Chinese revolution was never complete, the SCM did constitute a progressive influence on the campuses of many Christian universities in the 1940s. By the autumn of 1950 at least one SCM could report that it had arrived at a "clear political standpoint" along the lines which were then being drafted into the "Christian Manifesto."[37]

Much of the leadership of the TSM came from those who had been involved with the YM/YWCAs, and especially with the student relief committee. A list of those with Y experience among the senior leadership of the TSM and China Christian Council reads like a "Who's Who" of Christianity in contemporary China. They include K. H. Ting, Kiang Wenhan, Cora Deng, Liu Liangmo, Li Shoubao, Phoebe Shi, Zhao Fusan, Zheng Jianye, Shen Derong, Lo Guanzong and Han Wenzao. The Ys attracted Christian young people who were interested in social reform, many of whom would have been opposed by Chinese leaders and foreign missionaries in the more conservative denominations. This is not to say that the YMCA encouraged a radical approach to social change, but that Christians who accepted the Communist challenge often entered the YMCA or YWCA because no other organization would have them.

In 1951 Zhao Fusan evaluated the role of the YMCA in this way.

We should in all fairness point out that certain YMCAs have in certain periods done work that benefits the people, especially like the work of the Shanghai YMCA during the last ten years. But we should also point out that this work can never be separated from the support of some progressive secretaries and the impetus given by progressive young people. Moreover, this work has never been that which was stipulated by the guiding principles of the YMCA. Following Liberation, there were also some fellow workers who contentedly believed that every sort of pre-Liberation YMCA activity produced numerous revolutionary youths. But I must honestly say that these revolutionary youths were in no way consciously produced by the YMCA. Their revolutionary nature was not taught them by the YMCA; quite the opposite, it was due to their rejection of the bourgeois reformism taught by the YMCA and their acceptance of the people's democratic revolution taught by the revolutionary movement.[38]

This analysis supports the conclusion that it was not the YMCA experience per se, but the acceptance of the New Democracy which made the difference for the young Y secretaries who assumed a place within the united front.

David Paton has emphasized the significance of what he calls the "Christian Movement" for understanding the changes which some Chinese Protestants were going through in the 1940s.

> It was the phrase used by a good many educated Christians in the circle of the YMCA and YWCA and the universities to describe what they belonged to; and its significance seemed to be mainly negative—in rejection of the Church as foreign, and of its orthodox faith as incredible and, because apparently indifferent to the tragic frustrations of China, reactionary. Those who sought a positive point of view found it in the "Social Gospel," which facilitated a combination of religious concern for politics and society with detachment from the institutional Churches and from, in particular, orthodox Christology. The men and women of the Christian Movement were passionately concerned with national affairs and national politics, especially as these were focused in successive student movements, and were on the whole politically very left wing.[39]

These were the men and women about whom we have been speaking, those who identified with the united front at a relatively early stage. Some of them began to develop personal contacts with Chinese Communists in the early or mid-1940s, and they were challenged by the dedication and spirit of self-sacrifice which they encountered. The type of theology which was being discussed in relation to the "missionary Christian world" was irrelevant, abstract and boring to the Christian movement. However, as they deepened their commitment to the Chinese revolution, theological questions again became important for those who were also concerned about the future of the church. Paton is therefore correct when he says "that it is precisely where Christians are most preoccupied with the role of the church in the service of the Chinese people that they are most concerned with theology."[40]

This observation is important because it emphasizes the changes which had to come if the church were to be truly Chinese. That church might have little role to play in social change, but it was still important theologically. Those who were associated with the Christian movement also loved the church, even though they were alienated and disappointed by the foreignness of the Protestant denominations in China. They argued that the church itself was out of touch with society, and that it had to be reformed, but they never attempted to substitute their own movement for the church, nor did they try to impose their own theology upon the churches as a new form of orthodoxy.

The men and women who were associated with the Christian movement were accused of being naive and overly optimistic about communism. This critique often came from individuals who rejected any possibility of Christian-Communist cooperation. Nevertheless, there is a certain amount of truth in the criticism, especially in light of the ultra-left tendencies which have beset the Communist movement in China. Some of the essays published in *Tian Feng* in the late 1940s and early 1950s reveal the buoyant optimism of those who championed a brilliant future which could be realized in a few short years. Was such optimism a product of the times? or an overly idealized perspective on what could be accomplished in a short period of time? or an inadequate grounding in the Bible? Probably something of all of these was involved. But the question is, Does the criticism invalidate the perspective which was adopted at the time, or does it instead call for its modification? Was the enthusiasm misguided or simply overdone?

Reflecting on the situation in China in light of a trip he had just made to Hungary and Czechoslovakia in 1949, K. H. Ting commented,

> Upon entering the new situation of Communist control, if we must err, I would prefer to err on the side of naivety rather than cynicism. The cynic bangs the door of opportunity himself and lands himself in nothing but spiritual frustration and greater cynicism. But the naive Christian worker sticks to his job. Doors banged against him will eventually give him the needed corrective to make him a true realist. There seem to be some redeeming possibilities in naivety which cynicism lacks.[41]

Christians who commit themselves to progressive social movements have tended more toward the innocence of the dove than the wisdom of the serpent. This is as true today as it was in 1949. The absence of sufficient wisdom has been both costly and dangerous. But, as K. H. Ting reminds us, there is a sense of hopefulness and openness to the future that can redeem naive innocence and put it on firmer footing. The men and women who were associated with the Christian movement in China before 1949 learned a great deal about the problems and pitfalls of revolutionary change over the next forty years. But this did not lead them to reject the position that they had adopted in the first place or to deny the possibility of Christian-Communist cooperation. Instead, what they learned served to strengthen their faith, reorient their theology and deepen their political understanding. This process began with the writing of the "Christian Manifesto."

The "Christian Manifesto"

After the close of the First CPPCC, the four Protestant delegates and three other Protestants who were delegates representing other areas returned to Shanghai to report to the churches on the Conference.[42] There it was decided that church visitation teams would be organized to report on the experience and accomplishments of the CPPCC; to explain and promote the policy of religious freedom; and to deepen the cooperation and understanding between church and government leaders in local areas. The teams set out in late November of 1949, and originally intended to visit eighteen cities in the next two-and-a-half months, beginning with those in the older Liberated Areas of North China. In attempting to establish connections between local church leaders and government authorities, the visitation teams, which included the CPPCC delegates and representatives chosen by the NCC, YMCA and YWCA, marked a first step toward bringing Chinese Protestants into the united front.[43]

George Wu, who was then General Secretary of the NCC, commented on his experience on one of those teams.

> We met with government leaders in all of the places we visited. In Wuhan, we saw Li Xiannian, who welcomed us. We were very warmly received, and even feasted and entertained by him. In Kaifeng we saw Wu Zipu, and in Jiangxi, Shao Shiping (all high ranking officials), and we discussed the local situation with them. We also visited churches and met with church leaders in each area. . . . All of our experiences (in Wuhan, Kaifeng and Jiangxi) were very good. . . . However, in Shandong the situation was different. Not only did the top official not see us, but even local officials refused to meet with us. That was in Jinan, where we were not even allowed to go into the countryside. This illustrates that there were places where there were problems with the policy of religious freedom.[44]

The difficulties faced by the churches in the countryside were related to the churches' own attitude toward the CPC and the local populace, the attitudes of local officials and the experiences which the local peasantry had had with the church. Some churches were occupied by poor peasants or PLA soldiers; church articles were confiscated for daily use in different places; local church work was subject to various restrictions; and, in some cases, church workers were detained. Local peasants broke into churches and did a great deal of damage in certain parts of the countryside, resulting in the cessation of all worship activities by government order during the period of Land Reform. A revolution was in progress, and there was a great movement for change and reform taking place in the Chinese countryside. Violence had never been unusual for Chinese peasants used to domineering landlords, warlords and corrupt officials, but now the situation was being turned around. The churches were either caught in the middle or identified with the landlords, and it is therefore no wonder that they became the objects of attack in some areas. The countryside around Jinan was one such area, and it made the visitation teams aware that something had to be done.

While it was true that there were serious problems with the implementation of religious policy in some parts of the countryside, this was not the only difficulty which the churches faced. As Y. T. Wu and others had been arguing for years, the more basic problem was the churches' identification as foreign-oriented institutions, and specifically their dependence on the foreign mission boards.[45] This became a question of how the churches had situated themselves in the struggle for liberation, and whether or not they were now prepared to change. According to one author, such change was necessary from the Christian perspective because the church had to stand with the poor and oppressed. However, four impasses had to be overcome before it could do this. There was first of all the economic impasse, or the dependence of the churches on foreign funding. Next was the faith impasse, or the opposition which prevailed between Christianity and communism. The third difficulty was that of policy implementation on the part of local CPC officials. Finally, there was the impasse from the Christians' point of view of accepting China's decision to "lean to one side" in favor of the Soviet Union. Christians could eventually find a place in New China, argued Zhu Chensheng, if they would take an active part in socialist reconstruction. Using the traditional Chinese saying that many years later would make Deng Xiaoping famous, he justified his position by noting, "It doesn't matter whether a cat is black or white as long as it catches mice."[46] In other words, Christians would be accepted in the New Democracy as long as they made a contribution. While not everyone would agree with Zhu's assessment of the situation, he did identify four related problems which the Chinese church would have to resolve.

Probably all four were discussed in the meetings with Zhou Enlai, but it was the third impasse which led Chinese church leaders to request the meeting in the first place. The nineteen Protestant leaders who met with Zhou Enlai had originally prepared a statement about the difficulties which the churches faced in the new situation, but after these meetings they decided to withdraw it. Instead, they drew up a new statement to address the question of the churches' political standpoint. It is this document which came to be known as "The Christian Manifesto."[47]

The actual process of drawing up the "Christian Manifesto" was as painstaking as it was controversial.[48] Some of the Protestant leaders who met with Zhou probably believed that they had to do something in order to placate the Communist authorities and save the church. Others saw more clearly how the churches had become isolated from the society around them, and they now wanted to identify with the New Democracy. Still others had an analysis of the situation which, from a political standpoint, was substantially the same as the CPC position.

The document itself went through numerous drafts and revisions, beginning with the one which was presented to Zhou Enlai at the last meeting with him. Subsequently it was discussed with Christian leaders in Shanghai and in other cities in North and East China. Many leaders were reluctant to subscribe to such a statement as coming from the churches, and the wording of an early draft was rejected outright by some Protestants in Shanghai.[49] The writing continued with periodic consultation with CPC leaders in Beijing as part of the united front process. Y. T. Wu was the leading force behind the "Christian Manifesto," but when it was finally issued, a covering letter bore the names of forty prominent Christians.[50] With publication, subsequent endorsement on the front page of *People's Daily*, and the movement to gather signatures and support, the effort of Chinese Protestants to identify with the People's Government and assume a place within the united front had begun in earnest.

In the early 1950s there were people in China and overseas who charged that Zhou Enlai wrote "The Christian Manifesto" and created the Three-Self Movement. The recently published notes of his conversations with Chinese Protestants should close the book on these charges. In a talk presented to the United Front Work Department in January 1951, he again referred to the drafting of "The Christian Manifesto."

> Of course, if I had drafted the manifesto and brought it out for them to sign, they would have agreed to it. But what use would there have been in that, for everyone would have said that so-and-so had drafted the statement for them? It is better for them to speak about reform on their own. As long as they are close to our national policy and correct in their general orientation, there is no need to interfere. It is much better if they are a little bit different from us than if they say things exactly the same as we do. We cannot require them to be faultless in every respect. Our cooperation with people from outside the Party is based upon a common premise. We accept their good suggestions because they enrich our own position. As long as there is commonality on things of major importance, differences on lesser matters may be permitted.[51]

Both here and in his conversations with Protestant leaders, Zhou's tone is at times patronizing. He speaks about what is best for the churches in an almost imperial manner. Indeed, there can be no doubt that Zhou Enlai expected his advice to be accepted, for he was not about to have government policies challenged by a small minority in the formative period of socialist China. Yet his principle throughout is that of "seeking the common ground while reserving differences." Shortly after his conversations with the Chinese Protestant leadership, the Korean War broke out, and this made the possibility of further dialogue on the subject moot.

According to the covering letter which was sent out with the "Christian Manifesto," the statement was published for the benefit of people *outside* the church so that they might know "the standpoint of Christianity in the New Age." It begins with the historical connection between Christianity and imperialism in China, a problematic relationship which now sets the terms for the Christians' "basic task":

> Christian churches and organizations give thoroughgoing support to the "Common Program," and under the leadership of the government oppose imperialism, feudalism, and bureaucratic capitalism, and take part in the effort to build an independent, democratic, peaceable, unified, prosperous and powerful New China.[52]

On this basis, the churches were called both to acknowledge the problem of imperialism and work for the promotion of selfhood in the churches. Concretely, this would mean: (1) the termination of overseas financial assistance "within the shortest possible time"; and (2) an emphasis on a "deeper understanding of the nature of Christianity'' in religious work, combined with an understanding of the "New Age" in the "more general work" of the churches. In a short statement of less than 1,000 Chinese characters, the "Christian Manifesto" summarizes the task which Christians would face in the years ahead. It combines what was important for resolving the question of religion and patriotism from the CPC viewpoint with an insistence on the necessity of "Love-Country–Love-Church" in Chinese Christianity.

By the end of August more than fifteen hundred individuals had signed the "Manifesto." They included the original sponsors, a large number of denominational leaders and YMCA and YWCA secretaries, as well as outstanding Christian educators and other lay leaders. The largest number of signatories (381) was from the various branches of the indigenous Jesus Family in Shandong.[53] The movement to gather signatures assumed increasing importance over the next few months. Although initially reluctant to do so, the Fourteenth Biennial Meeting of the NCC endorsed the "Manifesto" in October.[54] This was the very first all-Chinese gathering in the history of the Protestant Church in China, and its endorsement of the "Manifesto" marked a significant turning point for that organization. It helped to open the way for changes which were coming with the TSM, and it encouraged Christians in local congregations to put their signatures to the "Manifesto." Within six months 180,000 people had signed, and by the time its circulation was complete, the "Christian Manifesto" bore the names of 417,389 Chinese Protestants.[55]

Although there was intense social pressure for the endorsement of the "Christian Manifesto," not everyone did sign. The most notable exception was the standing committee of the Anglican House of Bishops. The Anglican bishops especially objected to the statement that Christianity had "consciously or unconsciously . . . become related with imperialism." In response, they issued their own pastoral letter, which had a more explicit theological purpose, to Anglican communicants. It affirmed that "the Church not only cannot compromise with imperialism, feudalism or bureaucratic capitalism, but also that these are fundamentally against the faith of the Church.[56] The pastoral letter was not a refutation of the "Manifesto," but an alternative document issued by a particular church. Some of the bishops who refused at first to sign the "Manifesto," including Robin Chen, later took an active part in the TSM.

Many Chinese Christians agonized over the "Christian Manifesto." It raised for them questions about political loyalty, Christian faith and personal relationships with missionary friends. In so doing, the "Manifesto" was performing the function which its authors had intended: putting the question of political accountability before the church, and the standpoint of the church before the Chinese people. In the words of Wang Zizhong, a Congregationalist leader from North China and one of the original forty sponsors, the "Manifesto" clarified the political standpoint of the Chinese church and outlined the path for the future. He added,

As Christians, we should not say that all politics is of the devil, for such an attitude is just other-worldly and escapist. Nor should we say that any political system is entirely of God, for this smacks of confusing one thing with another and is not in the Christian spirit. The spirit of the genuine Christian is to act according to the blessings, intelligence and experience bestowed on us by God and do what is required by the age in which we live. God is the final authority for whatever success or failure we encounter. We can do no more than follow where He leads in doing what we should do in this age.[57]

Wang Zizhong's interpretation is a good example of the type of theological reorientation that was going on among many Protestants.

It must be emphasized that the "Christian Manifesto" was a *political statement* about the situation of the churches, and not a *theological statement* about the claims of Jesus Christ. The former can never preclude the latter, but the point is that Christians were issuing this particular statement as patriotic Chinese citizens. If instead they had issued a theological statement, then they never would have been able to make themselves understood before the Chinese people. Throughout the document, and especially in the final paragraph, the interrelationship between "Love-Country–Love-Church" is clearly stated. But the accent in the "Christian Manifesto" is on patriotism, making it a contractual expression of Protestant participation within the united front. This is what helped to establish a common ground between Chinese inside and outside the church.

It should be obvious that the political program of the "Manifesto" would coincide with the CPC understanding of patriotism as the basis for religious freedom in China. Severing the relationship with foreign mission boards and expressing loyalty to the People's Government were the preconditions for the existence of the church in the PRC. What was important about the "Manifesto" was that this action was taken on *Protestant initiative* and not by government fiat. The difference may appear to be a fine line, especially in light of the mixed motivations of some of those who sponsored the "Manifesto," but it is significant nonetheless. In contrast, there was not yet a similar movement among Chinese Catholics, and Zhao Puchu was telling Buddhists to follow the example of the Protestants and take the initiative for reform without waiting for government approval.[58] What is involved here is an understanding of independence and initiative within the united front.

In issuing the "Christian Manifesto" a very diverse group of Chinese Protestants were saying that they wished to join the Chinese revolution. This is why the wording of the document was so important. It was not first drafted in English, nor was it refined by the theological medium of the Chinese Protestant leadership. Rather, the "Christian Manifesto" was an expression of the new political language that was developing out of the Chinese revolutionary movement. Every revolution creates its own language, and the adoption of that language implies an acceptance of the political goals and values of the new movement. This has been especially true in China, where the widespread use of overtly propagandistic wording often means little more than a general affirmation of national identity and the values of the Chinese revolution.[59] The authors of the "Christian Manifesto" consciously took over the language of the united front, and this implied an acceptance of its political goals.

Precisely because of this, the "Manifesto" was criticized by some as a "betrayal" of the missionary past.[60] It certainly was, in the words of one missionary, "the self-assertion of Chinese Christians over against their missionary origins."[61] But this was by no means a bad thing. In China, it would eventually mean the rediscovery of the church's self-identity as well as Chinese Christians' national identity. Both of these were at the heart of the TSM, and similar efforts have been underway among Christians from many parts of the Third World over the last forty years. It is understandable that most missionaries could not accept the political judgment of the "Christian Manifesto." This was difficult even for many Chinese Christians. But it was the height of missionary arrogance to suggest, as some did, that the "Manifesto" represented the failure of Christian conscience in China. On the contrary, it meant for many Chinese Christians the discovery of a new understanding of Christian social conscience. They were struggling with the relationship between faith and politics in order to find their way as a church and as a mass organization. That missionaries could not be part of the latter is one reason why they could no longer have a place in the future of the Chinese church.

It is important to remember that the "Christian Manifesto" was published just after the outbreak of the Korean War, and that the movement to gather signatures did not get into full swing until the entry of Chinese troops into the conflict. Initially the movement toward self-administration, self-support and self-propagation was envisioned as a gradual process, taking place over a period of several years.[62] But the Korean War and related events changed all that, just as it hastened the process of church independence. By the end of 1950 missionaries were departing from China in large numbers, and their exodus was virtually complete by 1951.[63] A number of individual missionaries were imprisoned during this period, casualties of the Chinese revolution and victims of the politics of the Cold War. For Chinese Christians, however, the process of "severing the links with imperialism" had only started, as the movement which began in April of the following year was to indicate so clearly.

Severing the Links with Imperialism: Denunciation and Reeducation

The denunciation movement is probably the most controversial and least understood episode of the early years of Protestant Christianity in the PRC. It was different from the other political movements of the time insofar as its main arena was within the churches and other Christian institutions. The denunciation movement was related to the program of political study and ideological remolding, which also became important in the early 1950s, and they need to be understood as two aspects of the same process. Both denunciation and ideological remolding were, moreover, steps toward the formation of the TSM as a mass organization. As such, they illustrate the demands which the revolution and the united front were imposing on Chinese Christians, and the ways in which Christians were responding.

The Denunciation Movement

The denunciation movement began on April 19, 1951, at the meeting called by the SAC in Beijing. It was not so much an independent movement alongside Three-Self as it was a method within the broader patriotic movement of and for Chinese Christians to deepen their criticism of American imperialism. At the April meeting, particular American missionaries and Chinese church leaders were singled out for criticism and attack in speeches by former colleagues and associates.[64] The general approach was for the speaker to identify the individual being criticized as an agent or "running dog" of American imperialism; substantiate the charge with particular examples or evidence; and provide a self-criticism for one's own complicity in the relationship. The speeches were made before a large meeting of the 150 odd Protestant leaders who had gathered in Beijing. They were followed by study and discussion in small groups designed to deepen the analysis of imperialism, foster individual change and force a break with the past. This set the pattern for the denunciation movement in cities across China over the next fifteen months.[65]

Major denunciation meetings were held to criticize the NCC, the YMCA and YWCA, and the Christian Literature Society (CLS). There were also denunciation meetings for individual denominations, including the Anglicans, the Little Flock, the Seventh Day Adventists, the Methodists and the Church of Christ in China. City-wide meetings were called in many places; the largest, in Shanghai on June 10, drew an estimated crowd of more than twelve thousand people. Although denunciation meetings would continue to be held in some places in 1953, the movement was no longer being promoted after the middle of 1952. In his report on the second anniversary of the TSM, Y. T. Wu stated that there had been 169 "rather large scale" denunciation meetings in 124 towns and cities around the country.[66]

The denunciation movement began before the Chinese revolution had been firmly consolidated, and when there were still serious internal and external threats to Chinese security. It was a period of open trials, mass arrests and public executions, during which the state started to set up its extensive public security apparatus. The continuing concern over the sabotage and espionage activities of GMD remnants and other disaffected elements was expressed in a series of draconian laws and new policies. The most important of these was the "Regulations for the Suppression of Counter-revolutionary Activities," published on February 20, which authorized action against individuals even suspected of dissident activity. There was a legitimate security concern for the newly established government, heightened by the tensions over the Korean War and by the avowed intention of Chiang Kai-shek to retake the mainland. But the campaign against counter-revolutionaries also became a pretext for terror and indiscriminate violence, political repression and the settling of old scores. This should be understood in the context of the violence and repression with which the bulk of the Chinese population was faced before 1949. The revolutionary violence of the early 1950s was part of the process which brought an end to the pervasive institutionalized violence that had characterized China's "semi-feudal and semi-colonial" past.

The party's understanding of the purpose and goals of the denunciation movement was clear. According to an editorial published in *People's Daily* shortly after the close of the April meeting, it was to "draw a clear line" between patriotic Chinese Christians and American imperialism:

> The Protestants' denunciation movement is a movement of self-education based on facts personally experienced by Christians of American imperialist crimes against the Chinese people. This is the most important method by which the Three-Self Reform Movement may spread among and penetrate the masses of Christians, and it is also at their urgent request.[67]

The editorial goes on to catalogue the ways in which Christianity had been used by American imperialism and urges Chinese Christians to support the denunciation movement as Chinese who love their motherland and as Christians who love their church.

For the Three-Self leadership, the denunciation meetings became an intensification of the process which began with the launching of the "Christian Manifesto." The recently organized TSM Preparatory Committee called upon Protestants to prepare for denunciation meetings in cooperation with the local authorities by starting with a thorough investigation into foreign missionary activity in each area. This would help to uncover "counter-revolutionaries" hidden in the churches, expose the relationship between Christianity and imperialism, and "purify the temple."[68] In one stroke the Three-Self leadership was attempting to sever the relationships, personal as well as institutional, between Chinese Christians and foreign interests and initiate a process of criticism–self-criticism without which a new mass organization would be unthinkable. Within this process no individual or institution was immune from criticism.

Many Chinese Christians agonized over their participation in the denunciation movement. They were called upon to criticize former missionary colleagues and Chinese co-workers, as well as present confessions about their own complicity in imperialism. What was being attacked was the systemic nature of the relationship between Christianity and imperialism in China, and this meant that everyone had been affected in some way. However, many individuals did not see the issue in systemic terms, and they believed that denunciation was against the whole spirit of Christian faith. Some church leaders believed in the goals of Three-Self and anti-imperialism, but thought that denunciation was the wrong way to go about achieving them. Judging from the repeated calls for "deepening" the movement and different analyses of its problems, there must have been considerable resistance in the churches.[69] Some church leaders simply refused on principle to attend a denunciation meeting. There were probably a number of others who felt forced by the situation into presenting a denunciation, with the result that what they said was either superficial or excessive.

Probably many people felt that if they did not make a speech, they themselves would be denounced.

Yet there were also Chinese Protestants who came to a definite change in political standpoint as a result of this movement. Evidence for this may be found in numerous personal statements which appeared in *Tian Feng* and *Xie Jin* in the second half of 1951. In one of these H. H. Tsui describes his own personal struggle over the denunciation at the April meeting, but goes on to tell of what he learned from the experience.

I have had over 30 years of experience as a pastor of the Church and in administrative work in the denomination. In the past, I always took the attitude of "standing aloof from the world" and "covering up others' bad deeds while praising their virtues." After the study sessions at the Beijing meeting and following the reports of Vice-chairman Lu and others, I discovered the error of that kind of thinking, which is that it is in no way beneficial to the nation. Leniency towards enemies is cruelty to oneself. I first undertook serious criticism and struggle with my own thinking. God has bestowed a special blessing upon me, that I have always been able to sleep well no matter where I have been. But on the night before I was scheduled to do this denunciation, I couldn't close my eyes all night even though others in the room slept soundly. During that night I experienced numerous emotions. I came to a deep awareness of the pain and ideological struggle, and the joy which follows. From the Christian perspective, I can say that from that day on, I found new life.[70]

This was part of the process through which Chinese Christians came to understand the problem of imperialism and identify with the united front.

The particular object of H. H. Tsui's denunciation was the Southern Presbyterian missionary Frank Price. Price was criticized more than any other single missionary in the course of the next seven months, and no less than five major speeches about him were published in *Tian Feng*.[71] He had been one of the most knowledgeable missionaries on the China scene and must have been deeply resented by many Chinese Christians who took the opportunity afforded by the denunciation movement to vent their inner feelings about him. If one clears the excessive language and obvious distortions away from the speeches attacking him, the criticism of Frank Price boils down to four primary charges: First, his close connection with the American government in China. This was true of many American missionaries at the time, but Price was especially suspect because of his position of influence and his intimate knowledge of the Chinese countryside. Second, his identification with the policies and the person of Chiang Kai-shek. Third, his leadership in the Chinese church, which many Chinese found to be intrusive. And finally, his clear anti-communism and antipathy toward the new order. All four of these assertions were true.[72]

In denouncing Frank Price the Chinese were rejecting the missionary and political order for which he stood. It is unfortunate that particular individuals became subject to such extreme criticism, and no amount of explanation can justify the excesses of the denunciation movement. But at the same time it is important to see the truth which was expressed in the critical process. Frank Price and Chinese church leaders such as Y. Y. Tsu (Zhu Youyu) represented an order which had to be changed. Neither of them could have assumed positions of leadership in the New Democracy, nor could they have accepted a united front oriented Christianity. By criticizing such individuals in the denunciation movement, Chinese Protestants were hoping to separate themselves from a system which no longer had a future.

Very few Chinese church leaders who were criticized were cut off from the TSM. The purpose of denunciation was to get people to change, for criticism was not seen to be an end in itself. Z. T. Kuang and Zhu Guisheng were both criticized, but they subsequently became members of the Preparatory Committee. Jia Yuming, a prominent fundamentalist leader, was also denounced, but he too became a supporter of the TSM. After the denunciation meetings local leaders would approach those who had been criticized and who indicated that they wanted to change and would say that what was done was now past.[73] In this way, individuals were encouraged to reform themselves.

If denunciation was the negation of the missionary past, it also meant the affirmation of new institutional forms which would prepare the way for the future. In the absence of a successful denunciation movement, however, the TSM Preparatory Committee warned that local Three-Self branches should not be set up. On August 6 the Preparatory Committee issued a statement which made denunciation the first priority for Chinese churches, without which "nothing else can be discussed and there can be no talk of setting up a local TSM branch." Only "when more activists have been discovered and trained within the movement" would it be possible to set up a local branch.[74] The denunciation movement was thus linked with the establishment of a locally recognized Christian organization with its own leadership.

One of the most successful examples of this process cited in *Tian Feng* was the Christian Reform Movement in Nanjing. In a lengthy report on the Nanjing experience Han Wenzao traces its development in three stages.[75] Beginning with the circulation of the "Christian Manifesto," the whole question of imperialism was discussed in a very general way. The second stage commenced with the city-wide denunciation meeting in May. Those whom Han Wenzao calls the Christian "masses"—ordinary laypeople and Christian students—were deepening their consciousness of imperialism. They pushed church leaders to a clearer sense of the differentiation which was now needed (from the masses), and the church leaders helped to educate their congregations on the relationship between imperialism and the missionary movement (to the masses). This made possible the organization of a municipal Three-Self Reform Assembly as a third stage. A branch TSM organization was set up at this meeting, study groups were organized and the movement penetrated more deeply into the churches.

Although the Nanjing experience may not have been typical, it does illustrate one way in which the denunciation movement was envisioned as part of a broader program of change and reorganization.

This wider picture is also evident in a later report on the experience of denunciation as a prelude to reform in Kaifeng.[76] In both instances the sensitivity of the leadership is emphasized, as is the need to involve the Christian "masses." Both were needed in order to make the move from a missionary-oriented to a united front oriented Christianity. Local leadership was an important variable in the progress of the denunciation movement in towns and cities. A patient and discerning leadership which was at the same time committed to the united front could help put the movement in perspective. But this could happen only if leaders were able to relate themselves to the ordinary believers. Franz Schurmann has observed that the CPC encouraged denunciations from below as a way of promoting direct control by the masses and the activation of public opinion.[77] Through the denunciation movement Chinese Christians were trying to lay the foundation for the creation of a mass organization which would take its place alongside other groups in the New Democracy.

Before moving on to the programs for political study and ideological remolding, it is necessary to offer an assessment of the denunciation movement. One of the major areas of reevaluation in the interviews which I conducted with Chinese Protestant leaders in 1981–1983 was the period which has here been under discussion. The major point on this subject made in all of the interviews was that the denunciation movement was necessary in the effort to come to a clearer understanding of the missionary past, but that it was too one-sided and tended to go to extremes. Two such evaluations are cited here.

> The denunciation movement was necessary. Without it, we never could have come to a new understanding of our situation. But we didn't have a lot of experience with this kind of thing. In looking back, I realize that we were a bit too one-sided in our criticisms of missionaries. Of course, there were some who were actively involved in imperialist politics, but there were others who were on our side. Most missionaries, however, came to China with a sincere religious purpose, and were simply a part of an imperialist system which they could not change. They were involved in imperialism without realizing it. At the same time, the religious message which they preached in China could not really take root, because they transferred American or other Western ideas to Chinese soil. . . . All of this is true. Yet we still exaggerated our criticism of them.[78]

> Some people overseas thought that we were out to persecute fellow Christians or accuse them in a court of law. This was never our intention. At the time, our slogan was, "Strengthen communication, strengthen denunciation." This helps to indicate the educational purpose of the denunciation movement. . . . It was designed to point out mistakes, not condemn. This is why it was linked to the study programs. . . . There were,

of course, excesses in the movement. But it should be remembered that the denunciation movement was directed against a system, not individuals. We were not saying that the missionaries had been immoral, but that the system under which they operated was bad.[79]

Similar statements have been made by many other Chinese Christians over the last few years. The criticism is directed against their own errors and exaggerated responses in a period of their history which is now past. In light of the Korean War and the China of 1951, it is difficult to see how the extremes could have been avoided. They may be part of the price which Chinese Christians had to pay in the process of their identification with the Chinese people. It should be added that one need only turn to the pages of *The Christian Century* or any number of other North American Christian publications which were reporting on the church in China to see that verbal excesses were not confined to the Chinese side.

The denunciation movement as a whole is much easier to interpret in terms of Three-Self as a mass organization of patriotic Chinese than it is as a movement within the Protestant church. As an expression of nationalistic feeling, the outpouring of resentment against the foreign missionaries is not very difficult to understand. Missionary power and influence had been criticized in the churches for some time, but now Chinese Christians were being encouraged to air their feelings in public. Other aspects of the denunciation movement—the beginnings of ideological remolding, the emergence of activist leaders and institutional reorganization—were common features of all urban-based mass organizations in the early 1950s. Even the excesses of the times are understandable, for they have been present in the formative stages of most religious and political movements. Severing the linkages with the past is aptly summarized by the Chinese expression, "breaking the caldron and sinking the boat," that is, cutting off all possible means of retreat. This is what the Chinese Protestants were attempting to do in the denunciation movement. All Chinese mass organizations had a similar purpose, but in light of their history, it was the Christians who had a special responsibility to "draw a line" between themselves and imperialism.

The same history also meant that a Christian movement could not become a movement among all the others, even if it did have identical political goals. At the very least it must interpret those goals at a different level. There were attempts to provide a theological rationale for the denunciation movement. Y. T. Wu argued that denunciation did not mean sitting in eternal judgment on others (Luke 6:37), but pointing out evil and identifying sin. In Wu's understanding, Jesus' criticism of the Pharisees (Matt. 23:13ff) was the deepest kind of denunciation.[80] Others saw the denunciation movement as a path of pain and humiliation they would have to endure if they were to be able to identify with the people and continue to witness in the new society.

Caught up in the denunciation process, however, it is doubtful that most Christians could understand any theological interpretation of the movement at all. Some of the explanations that were offered at the time seem, in retrospect, to be more in the nature of the self-justification of a patriotic movement than they do of justification by faith. Yet there can be no doubt that the denunciation movement did help to cleanse the Chinese churches from their alienating foreignness. To fail to see this is to ignore the difficulties which Protestants faced in trying to root the Christian church in Chinese soil. The denunciation movement was part of the process of transplantation, a violent uprooting which preceded replanting. If there had only been uprooting, then the church would have died. But without it, the church could not have taken root in a radically new situation.

That which is absolute in the Christian message is always expressed in a relative and tentative way through institutions and movements, people and ideas which point beyond themselves. The absolute is clearer at some times than it is at others. This has been true of the Three-Self Movement no less than it was of the missionary enterprise. Despite all the errors and excesses, the denunciation movement was pointing beyond itself to the possibility of a Christian existence which would no longer be disfigured by imperialism. Even though its proponents did not and could not realize that the future they were trying to create would be limited in other ways, they were setting in motion a movement that would eventually achieve a life of its own.

God judges and speaks the Word of grace to all human movements, and in God's own time they are brought to their rightful conclusion. In the story of the woman caught in adultery, Jesus neither condemned nor offered excuses but pointed the way to the future (John 7:53-8:11). Ultimately the theological meaning of the denunciation movement does not lie in its excesses or mistakes any more than it does in its educational or cleansing functions. If it is discernible at all, it is to be discovered in the movement between judgment and grace which has characterized Christian existence through all of its history. God acts, in spite of the best of human intentions and because of the worst. The truth of the denunciation movement lies somewhere in between, caught amidst all the ambiguities inherent in any movement for change and renewal.

Ideological Remolding

The denunciation movement was itself part of a process of reeducation and ideological remolding. But whereas denunciation was primarily a *negative* dynamic of exposure and renunciation, ideological remolding had a more positive purpose in the formation of men and women for socialist construction. Denunciation was an intensely emotional experience for all who were involved. The individual exposed himself or herself before a large group, speeches were made, often in the heat of the moment, and the debate that followed sometimes reached a fever pitch. In contrast, ideological remolding was a more carefully thought out and well-reasoned process. It encouraged a deepening of one's understanding so as to foster a changed way of life. For Communist and non-Communist alike, reeducation involved a lifelong process of study for the raising of one's political consciousness. This is the reason why study, and especially small-group study, has long been an important part of the program for intellectuals within the united front.

The Chinese term which we have been using for ideological remolding has also been rendered as "reeducation" or "thought reform." It is related to the more emotive and value-laden term "brainwashing," which came into our lexicon around the time of the Korean War. The social and psychological implications of ideological remolding have been subjected to extensive analysis in the West. Many studies have created the impression that ideological remolding is primarily a Communist technique for indoctrinating the unsuspecting or the unwilling, with the ultimate purpose of total regimentation and the control—or even destruction—of the human spirit.[81] This has often been viewed as part of a manipulative and totalitarian program which the CPC has tried to impose on the Chinese people, just as it tried to "brainwash" American prisoners of war in Korea.

While the coercive nature of ideological remolding should not be minimized, the study programs need to be understood within the framework of a very different set of cultural values and presuppositions derived from the Chinese tradition as well as from socialism. A number of these have already been alluded to: the social and functional interest in humanity; a belief in human malleability; and the role of government in fostering "correct ideas." On the basis of such presuppositions, ideological remolding was encouraged primarily by indirect social pressure, persuasion and exhortation, so that change and cooperation would follow from conviction and not coercion. A participatory understanding of reality was implicit in this process, and all individuals were both actors and acted upon. Even the more sharpened expressions of social reinforcement, such as criticism–self-criticism, were ultimately aimed at the voluntary participation of the individual in the social process. They also entailed a lifelong struggle for personal renewal. In the words of an American who was imprisoned for four years after 1949:

Having one's innermost self brought out and dissected under the glaring light of self-criticism was a shattering experience, but the resulting recognition of myself made me determined to overcome the weaknesses of my own character which had been the cause of those former mistakes. Thus began the struggle with myself which was to last throughout the rest of my stay in prison, and, indeed, goes on even today.[82]

A similar process has been involved in every movement for revolutionary change since the Protestant Reformation. What was different about China was the fervent and didactic sense of purpose with which the task was approached.

In actual practice ideological remolding assumed a variety of forms. The case histories of imprisoned foreigners and emigrant Chinese intellectuals are extreme examples of a process that, for the citizenry as a whole, was both less severe and more constructive. Although it may be misleading to compare the China of the early 1950s to Calvin's Geneva or Puritan New England, the intention in each case was to promote a world-transforming ideology which would guide both individual and society in the effort for revolutionary change. In each case the program resulted in a decisive shift in the way in which men and women came to perceive the world, but not the total transformation that was anticipated by the movement's visionary leaders. People cannot change their ways of thinking overnight. The most egregious error of the movement for ideological remolding in China was the assumption that new men and women could be created in a relatively short time.

Very early on, Chinese Protestants were encouraged to study the Common Program so that they could begin to prepare themselves for the New Democracy. Some churches set up regular classes to study current affairs as early as 1949.[83] On a very different level the Land Reform Movement became important for the ideological remolding of intellectuals who took part either as participants or observers. It was designed to enable them to understand and identify with the problems of the peasantry, in order to assist in the transformation of their own political consciousness.[84] Before the outbreak of the Korean War, church leaders also attended lectures on current affairs and religious policy given by government officials. This too was part of the resocialization process which had been going on since the establishment of the PRC.

With China's entry into the Korean War and the beginning of the denunciation movement, the importance of ideological remolding was raised to a new level. Speaking before the Third Session of the CPPCC, Mao said that "great victories" had been achieved in the Resist-America–Aid-Korea Movement, Land Reform and the Suppression of Counter-revolutionaries. He continued, "Ideological remolding, primarily of all types of intellectuals, is an important condition for the completion of democratic reforms in all fields and the gradual industrialization."[85] Tu Yuqing (Y. C. Tu), who attended the CPPCC as a Protestant delegate, cited this sentence as particularly important for Christians who were interested in creating a truly Chinese church.[86] At about the same time the first training class for new Christian leaders was organized in Shanghai, and subsequently similar classes were held in Fuzhou, Tianjin and other major cities. These involved intensive political study over a period of several months, and they were conducted by Chinese Protestants and local Religious Affairs organizations.[87]

The leadership training classes are most important for understanding the history of Three-Self as a patriotic movement. They were classes for political and patriotic consciousness-raising, not for modernizing or criticizing Christian faith.[88] Although remolding could not but have an impact on theology and faith in the Chinese Protestant experience, political change and the search for a common ground did not necessarily mean theological transformation. The relationship between Christianity and communism expressed in Y. T. Wu's "How the Communist Party Has Educated Me" represents a position he had been moving toward for some time.[89] In this essay Wu reveals very clearly how the Marxist perspective had forced him to reconsider and reorient his theological beliefs. But alongside this essay consider the very different statement written by fundamentalist preacher Marcus Chen. Entitled "How My Political Thinking Has Changed," this essay is strictly limited to a discussion of Chen's changing political orientation.[90] Like many conservative Christian leaders in China today, Marcus Chen never believed that ideological remolding should alter or improve upon his theology, nor did he use Marxist categories to redefine his understanding of faith. Although this at times resulted in a sharp dichotomy between the religious and political realms, it also provided a way for conservative Christians to adapt themselves to the new order. The strengths and weaknesses of this approach will be developed more fully in succeeding chapters, but it must be stressed that ideological remolding did not mean theological uniformity.

What it did involve was the cultivation of a new generation of leaders who would fully understand and be strongly committed to Three-Self as a patriotic movement. Politically it was necessary for such leaders to leave behind the Liberalism which was implicit in the religious message that had been brought to China by the Western missionaries. This meant that the real ideological struggle in the early 1950s was between Liberalism and communism, and not between communism and Christian faith. Democratic liberalism had been the premise of Christian higher education and of a great deal of missionary practice in China, and it was this premise which now came under attack. An editorial from *Tian Feng* argued that Liberalism was confining, not only because of its anti-communism, but because it did not allow students to come to grips with the social contradictions of China:

American-style Liberalism requires of us that we take in everything from all points of view, resulting in extreme confusion in our thinking. This way of thinking is unsystematic, and without principle or standpoint. It is called "freedom" but is in fact never able to shake off the enslaving ideology of imperialism.[91]

A liberal education, the editorial continued, cut the students off from reality and made them oblivious to the need for change. Therefore a new type of study was now needed.

The political content of this new type of study was threefold. First, it provided a new methodology for study, emphasizing the "unity of theory and practice" and the establishment of concrete goals. Second, it introduced the domestic and international situations from the perspective of the CPC. This included an understanding of the two camps in world politics; the New Democracy; and the meaning of patriotism in the new situation. Finally, the study program dealt with the nature, development and purpose of Three-Self as a patriotic movement.[92] In each area study emphasized a united front approach to the problem at hand. It was to enable a new leadership to understand its place in society as part of the effort to unify the Chinese people around the political leadership of the CPC.

Judging from the reports published in *Tian Feng*, the leadership training program which was organized in Shanghai in 1953 was seen as a model for similar programs elsewhere. Lasting three months, it involved almost 100 participants of all ages, more than half of them clergy. This study program was jointly sponsored by Protestant leaders and the local RAB. In his summary report on the program, Robin Chen emphasized the ways in which participants had been changed through their study. Whether it meant coming to terms with the possibility of religious faith in a socialist society or developing a better understanding of the relationship between Christianity and imperialism, the students were undergoing a process of personal change and transformation. The extent of such change, however, was uneven. According to Chen, the decisive element was the way in which students approached their study.

> Three months' time is very precious to every church worker. . . . Each person pondered and studied, studied and pondered, individually and then again collectively, enlightening each other, helping each other, raising each other's level of consciousness. Along with meetings for the exchange of ideas, discussion groups, blackboard newspapers, cultural and recreational activities, individual study continually pushed the students forward. It led them to a personal sense of awareness that not only was this type of study helpful, but that without it, one would still be confused, not only backward in him or herself, but an obstacle to others' progress. Experience has shown that if students want to study well, each one must consciously and willingly study hard. Those sluggards who just want to get by, the lazy thinkers who are afraid of exercising their brains, and those who can only rely on a bunch of so-called theories to demonstrate that they have a "high level of political consciousness"—but who do seek to integrate their own authentic thinking and indulge in exaggeration instead—such students have not resolved internal contradictions either ideologically or emotionally, and have achieved heartfelt happiness even less.[93]

How many people actually changed through their experience in this and other study classes, and to what extent? In the absence of sufficient data on the participants, these questions are impossible to answer. But it is possible to indicate different types of responses the students might have to the study programs. Robert Lifton identifies three of these on the basis of his interviews with emigre intellectuals in Hong Kong in the 1950s. On either extreme were the "zealous converts" and the "stubborn resisters," those who became either true believers or irreconcilable opponents. Both of these are pure types, however, and therefore relatively rare. The more general response was that of the wide range of people in the middle. Lifton calls them the "adapters."

> An adapter is partially but not entirely convinced by the program; essentially he was concerned with the problems of coping with a stressful experience and finding a place in the new society. His feelings about

thought reform may have been similarly complicated; he may have experienced it as painful, perhaps even coercive, but at the same time possibly beneficial—like medicine which may do some good just because it tastes so bad.[94]

Although Mao never would have presented quite so sympathetic a picture of the adapters, Lifton's categories are not all that different from Mao's own. The adapters were the waverers in the middle, and in the former bourgeoisie, they would tend to be in the majority. While ideological remolding may have resulted in a decisive shift in the way in which they perceived the world, the change effected in any single individual could be neither instantaneous nor total. For Chinese Christians especially, the process of ideological remolding must forever be incomplete, at least in the terms in which it was understood by the CPC. If it were otherwise, ideological remolding would destroy the significance which reserved differences held within the common ground between Christians and Marxists.

Ideological remolding was never complete, but those who experienced a genuine change in the process did a great deal more than adapt. Some Christians developed a radically new perspective on things as a result of the study program. Jones cites the example of Shen Yifan, son of the Anglican bishop T. K. Shen.[95] A student at Nanking University in the late 1940s, he went on to study for the ministry in Shanghai after Liberation. He was also one of the participants in the study class which Robin Chen discusses above. A reading of Shen's final report reveals the way in which he came to a new understanding of communism, patriotism and imperialism because of the study program. More important, it identifies the way in which his whole approach to the possibility of Christian existence in a socialist society had changed.

> Until this study, I always thought that Three-Self was a way to cater to the Communist Party, the price we must pay for freedom of belief. So my participation was passive, I did it because I saw no other way. However, after this study, it became clear to me that the TSM was a spontaneous movement of Chinese Christians to oppose imperialism, express patriotism and purify the Church. Only through the TSM can we eliminate the distance and misunderstanding between Christianity and the masses, break the shackles of the past that have bound Christianity and develop the pure truth and innate vitality of the Church in this age. From now on, I must take the initiative in participating in this movement and work for a Chinese people's Church.[96]

Thirty years after he wrote these words, Shen Yifan challenged a gathering of Christians from around the world by saying:

> The Church must make a choice at all times and in all places. It must choose where it wishes to stand. Is it going to stand on the side of the

broad masses of the people? Or is it going to stand on the opposite side? There is an old saying in the Church: *Vox Populi, Vox Dei.* The voice of the people is the voice of God. Today may we all hear the voice and the call of God addressed to us through the broad masses of the people.[97]

Shen Yifan is now pastor of the Community Church in Shanghai, and an executive Vice-President of the China Christian Council. Along with so many others of his generation, Shen Yifan has been through the process of ideological remolding, as well as the difficult years of the Cultural Revolution era. His political consciousness and Christian faith have been strengthened in these experiences. It is among such individuals, those for whom ideological remolding meant a renewed understanding of Christian faith in a socialist context, that one must look for the positive influence which the study programs had on Chinese Christians. Neither zealots nor adapters, these were men and women who came to understand the ways in which socialism would benefit China, and who believed that their role was to bring the church into the process.

The Organization of Three-Self as a Patriotic Movement

As early as October 1949 Chinese Christian leaders began calling for a nationwide meeting of Protestants who would represent all churches, Christian institutions and denominational constituencies in China. The first CPPCC had not recognized the churches as institutions that had a democratic character. This meant that Chinese churches had an uncertain status in the first few months of the PRC. The call for a broadly-based national conference of Chinese Christians, therefore, was aimed at establishing a new national organizational framework. No single denomination or church could organize such a conference; memberships were not comprehensive enough. The proposed gathering would involve laypersons, young people and women, as well as established leaders from the mainline denominations and indigenous churches.[98] The idea attracted considerable interest among Chinese Christians, and the conference was finally scheduled for the following August.

Unfortunately the proposed conference was never held. In April *Tian Feng* announced that it had been postponed indefinitely, for three reasons. First, the desire had been to hold a "unified conference, not an argumentative one," but in light of the great diversity among Chinese Protestants this was not yet possible. Second, the conference was designed to discuss the reform of the churches, but many churches were not interested in reform. Finally, it was believed that such a conference would be hard-pressed to resolve the many problems confronting the churches, and that in all probability it would degenerate into "empty debating and empty speeches."[99] Because Chinese Protestants had not yet arrived at unity around the common ground of patriotism and anti-imperialism, the possibility of forming a new national organization was out of the question.

For a mass organization to be effective, both the leadership and the grass roots have to be in general agreement about matters of political principle, so that as problems and programs arise, there can be open avenues of communication. Moreover, there must be good relationships and close contact between the leadership and the grass roots, not only for the work of bridge-building between the party and the people, but also for the integration of the constituency into the society. In 1950 Chinese Protestants were neither unified politically, nor well-connected from bottom to top. To set up a new national organization under such circumstances would have been counterproductive. Its leadership would have been elitist and cut off from the grass roots. If the Three-Self Movement had been formally established in 1949 or 1950, it would have meant imposing the will of a progressive minority upon the majority of Chinese Christians. But that did not happen. When the First National Christian Conference was finally held in 1954—four years later than originally anticipated—a great deal more had been accomplished toward promoting the unity and relationships that would make the TSM a broadly based, representative and effective mass organization.

Many of the changes that made this possible were related to what was taking place in society at large. Christians studied the Common Program along with everyone else. They took part in Land Reform. During the Korean War Protestants were involved in the Resist-America–Aid-Korea movement together with all other citizens. Through the organization of patriotic activity during the Korean War, through involvement in other nationwide movements aimed at eradicating corruption and "counter-revolutionaries," and through study and endorsement of documents concerned with national and international policy, Protestants were showing that they too were patriotic Chinese, and they were coming to a new understanding of patriotism in the process.

The severing of institutional linkages with foreign mission boards and the gradual incorporation of Christian institutions into a socialist framework were part of the same process. With the cutting off of financial contributions from overseas, the departure of Western missionaries and the turning over of schools, hospitals and welfare organizations to the People's Government, Chinese Christians no longer represented an overbearing institutional presence allied with foreign interests. The organizations that remained, primarily the NCC, individual churches and denominations, the YMCA and YWCA and a few theological seminaries, were for all intents and purposes self-administering, self-supporting and self-propagating Chinese institutions by the end of 1951. Other organizations, such as those concerned with Christian publications, were well on their way toward developing a unified leadership that would support the goals of the New Democracy.[100] All of these changes tended to make Christianity in China more institutionally diffuse as well as more open and malleable politically.

The activities that Chinese Protestants organized for their own constituencies were no less essential in preparing the way for the organization of the TSM. The "Christian Manifesto," the denunciation movement, programs for study and ideological remolding helped to provide a new sense of identification of Chinese Christians within their own society. They helped to raise the political consciousness of Protestants at the grassroots and enabled a new generation of activist leaders to emerge who could staff the TSM at local and national levels. One general intention of all such movements in the 1950s was to involve the

Christian "masses" in the important decisions that were facing society, give them an active role to play, and thereby consolidate the ideological values and political principles of the New Democracy. Although there was as yet no mass organization which could formally direct the process, the Preparatory Committee of the Chinese Christian Resist-America–Aid-Korea Three-Self Reform Movement was set up in 1951, and over the next three years it provided what leadership and support was necessary.

Organized at the end of the April meeting called by the SAC, the Preparatory Committee initially had twenty-five members led by Y. T. Wu, Y. C. Tu, Robin Chen, Marcus Chen and Cora Deng.[101] Originally there was some talk of setting up two committees, one for church affairs and one for a patriotic Protestant movement, but for reasons which have already been mentioned, this was rejected as being premature. The stated purposes of the Preparatory Committee were threefold: to promote patriotic activities and education in Christian organizations among the Christian "masses"; to work for the eradication of the imperialist influences from the churches; and to carry out the responsibility for Three-Self reform in a planned and step by step way.[102]

The offices of the Preparatory Committee were located in Shanghai, and a small staff, all of whom served on a part-time basis, divided its duties into three general areas.[103] The Propaganda Division, headed by Liu Liangmo, was in charge of promoting study programs and patriotic activities. The Liaison Division, directed by Zheng Jianye, related to various churches and Christian organizations, while the General Affairs Division was entrusted with staff work and supervision under the leadership of Y. C. Tu. Both the membership of the Preparatory Committee and the work of its staff expanded over the next three years. More and more prominent church leaders were brought onto the Committee, thus helping to broaden its base and enhance its influence. As it moved closer to the possibility of holding a national conference, the Preparatory Committee became involved in a variety of activities relating to national policy, world peace, church affairs and reorganization.

For Three-Self to be a movement at all, it had to draw on the support of the Christian "masses" in large numbers. Organizationally this meant that the Preparatory Committee had to encourage the formation of local Three-Self committees in order to bring more people into the movement. In some places this did not prove to be a problem. In Shanghai, Guangzhou and Nanjing, for example, Resist-America–Aid-Korea committees or other Christian patriotic associations had been organized even before the Preparatory Committee.[104] In other areas, especially in small cities and towns in the countryside, there was a clear difficulty in establishing local organizations. For the Preparatory Committee this meant that the movement had not yet "penetrated deeply enough into the masses."[105]

In order to help the process along, as well as to strengthen the relationship between Christians at the grass roots and the Preparatory Committee, visitation teams were organized to go into the countryside. One of these, a high-level delegation including Y. T. Wu, H. H. Tsui and Xie Yongqin, spent a month in Zhejiang and Fujian in the spring of 1953.[106] They met with church leaders, laypeople and government officials in each place they visited, in order to look into problems faced by the local churches and to try to find ways of resolving them. They discovered problems ranging from difficulties over self-support to the implementation of religious policy. While these could not be resolved immediately, the visitation team reported its findings to relevant individuals and departments and thus initiated a process of reform.

Based upon ideas quite similar to that of "from the masses to the masses" in the united front, the visitation teams and local Three-Self organizations did help to strengthen communication between the Preparatory Committee and Christians at the grass roots. But there were also obstructions to communication caused by many local Three-Self leaders. Overly zealous proponents of Three-Self often tried to organize study programs, denunciation meetings and local groups administratively, from the top down. The political and patriotic emphasis in much of their work tended to lack a pastoral dimension. In his report to the First National Christian Conference, Y. T. Wu charged that some progressives in the TSM approached their work with too much of a "sectarian spirit."

> There have been varying degrees of "sectarianism" within the TSM and we have often looked on fellow Christians who do not take part in the movement as backward. We have not entered deeply enough into others' situations or understood their problems in order to seek those common points on which we could cooperate. We have frequently taken an impatient attitude towards those who have been slow in making progress and have not tried to help them with sympathy and patience. This sectarian tendency is an obstacle to unity, leading some Christians who have not yet taken part in the Three-Self Reform Movement to adopt a hesitant wait and see attitude or even to oppose the movement.[107]

As we shall see in the next chapter, this proved to be a continuing problem for the Three-Self Movement.

It was clear to the leaders of the TSM that their movement had many weaknesses. But by 1954 they could also look back on some significant achievements. A small and very weak Chinese Christian community had survived the traumatic experience of being cut off from the worldwide Christian fellowship and losing all the institutional and material privileges that had come with the patronage of the missionary movement. The Preparatory Committee interpreted this as a positive movement of identification with the Chinese people. As a result, Chinese Protestants were learning that they could develop a renewed sense of Christian purpose in a socialist society. Perhaps most important of all, they were developing a new sense of unity, theological as well as political.

Speaking of this newfound unity in the report just cited, Y. T. Wu linked it to the different goals which the TSM had set for itself.

The unity Christians throughout the nation have achieved on the basis of "Love-Country–Love-Church" is unprecedented in both scope and degree, and it is extremely precious. The broadly representative character of the Christians attending this conference is an excellent proof of this. At the same time, however, the experience of the last four years makes clear that imperialism is constantly trying to malign and destroy our unity. Therefore, with hearts full of love for the Church, we must cherish the unity of all Christians. We must endeavor to do whatever increases that unity, and we must point out and correct whatever threatens it.

For the sake of unity, we must be more humble than in the past, not thinking more highly of ourselves than we ought, ready to help our fellow Christians, our brothers and sisters, with love and patience. We should cast off Christian pride and impatience in order to think and work together.

For the sake of unity, we must recognize the differences among churches, sects and theological viewpoints and establish the principle of mutual respect.[108]

It was in the context of such unity that the First National Christian Conference was held in Beijing from July 22 to August 6, 1954. Two hundred and thirty-two representatives from sixty-two churches and Christian organizations gathered together for what was the largest meeting of Chinese Christians ever assembled. For sixteen days they worshipped together, listened to speeches and met for discussion in fourteen small groups. At the end of the Conference they passed resolutions on the new Constitution, the American presence in Taiwan and Korea, and the future work of Three-Self. In addition, a constitution for the Committee of the Chinese Christian Three-Self Patriotic Movement was approved, and 139 members were appointed to the Committee. The standing committee with forty-two members was chaired by Y. T. Wu, while Robin Chen, Wu Yifang, Marcus Chen, Z. T. Kaung, H. H. Tsui and Ting Yuzhang served as vice-chairpersons.[109]

This was the conference which had been so long in the making. Although we have now come to take for granted broad ecumenical representation at major Christian gatherings, the theological diversity of the men and women who attended the First National Christian Conference was unprecedented, not only for China, but for other countries of the world as well. Among the vice-chairpersons there was an Anglican bishop, a Methodist bishop, a Church of Christ in China executive, a very unorthodox university president and two well-known fundamentalists. At the conference itself leaders of the Little Flock met with Anglicans, preachers from the old C.I.M. were in discussion groups with YMCA secretaries, Protestants from almost every province and denominational background greeted one another and prayed together. It is true that not all Protestants endorsed the Conference—Wang Mingdao especially was noted by his absence. But under the circumstances, and in light of the difficult years which

Chinese Christians had been through, the unity which had been achieved by 1954 was remarkable by any standards.

To say that Chinese Protestants were increasingly unified meant, in 1954, that they were adopting a common political point of view. This was a prerequisite for being recognized as a mass organization, and it is what was missing in 1950. Political unity did not attempt to swallow up denominational diversity, and leaders of the TSM bent over backward to see that their intentions would not be misunderstood. For example, the Preparatory Committee had called itself a reform movement, which naturally left the impression in people's minds that the TSM was interested in changing Christian doctrine or transforming Protestant beliefs. Although there can be no doubt that Y. T. Wu and other progressive leaders did want theological reform, they did not prevail over the majority of leaders on the Preparatory Committee. At the National Christian Conference, therefore, the word *reform* was dropped from the name of the TSM, and it was clearly stated that the movement had no intention of changing Christian doctrine.[110] "Resist-America–Aid-Korea" was also dropped from the name, because the Korean War had ended.

The policy of "mutual respect" was affirmed at the 1954 gathering insofar as it related to self-government, self-support and self-propagation. The Conference document "Letter to Christians Throughout China" thus contrasts the common ground of unity with the need to respect differences.

> The purpose of the Three-Self Patriotic Movement is to unite Christians throughout the country in order to promote the thoroughgoing realization of self-government, self-support and self-propagation in the Chinese church, to take an active part in opposing imperialism, supporting patriotism and safeguarding world peace. We know that the goal of self-government is not the unification or modification of the organization of each church, but that each church cut off all relations with imperialism and to have Chinese Christians ourselves unite to govern the church. The goal of self-support is not to interfere in the finances of any church, but to have each church cut off all economic ties with imperialism and become a church which is entirely the responsibility of Chinese Christians. The goal of self-propagation is not the unification or modification of belief, but the thoroughgoing eradication of vestiges of imperialist thought, and the bringing of preaching into harmony with the true Gospel of Jesus Christ. We should have mutual respect for the differences that exist among the churches in creed, organization and ritual.[111]

The unity which was achieved at the First National Christian Conference was surpassed at the Second Enlarged Plenum held in March 1956. By all accounts this was the most significant gathering of Chinese Christians before the Cultural Revolution. There were even more participants than at the National Christian Conference (249), and they represented *all* churches and denominational groups in China. The emphasis at the Second Plenum was clearly on ecclesiastical matters and the local church; these were discussed in speech after speech from the floor. Of the 131 proposals dealt with at this meeting, the majority related to such matters as local Three-Self organizations, evangelism, Christian publication work, theological education and self-support. Although problems still remained in relationships with the World Council of Churches and foreign mission boards, Chinese Christians also began to reconsider the church's international role. Over the next year visitors from Australia, India and Eastern Europe were welcomed to China.

All of these developments were summarized in Y. T. Wu's call for the realization of the "Three Witnesses and the Ten Tasks." The "Witnesses" were: (1) the Three-Self in the Chinese church; (2) participation in socialist reconstruction; and (3) safeguarding world peace. The "Ten Tasks" facing the church were: (1) the consolidation and expansion of unity; (2) church reform and reorganization; (3) self-support of *all* churches; (4) self-propagation; (5) publication of Christian literature; (6) theological research; (7) the training of new leaders; (8) participation in socialist reconstruction; (9) promotion of peace and international goodwill; and (10) patriotic study.[112] The "Three Witnesses and the Ten Tasks" are important to bear in mind as we take up the question of church construction in the 1950s and since 1979.

Several factors account for the renewed emphasis on church affairs in the TSM between 1954 and 1957. The Korean War had ended, and the international atmosphere had definitely improved from China's point of view. Domestically, there was less disruption from major national campaigns and greater attention to the tasks of socialist construction. The new Constitution and the First Five-Year Plan provided for increased political stability and economic direction. Because Christians were no longer seen to represent a major social contradiction, the churches became freer to look after their own ecclesiastical concerns. As a result, more churches began to be opened and rebuilt, spiritual retreats and evangelistic meetings were held, and there were reports from some areas that the church had begun to grow.

A continuing function of the TSM was to represent its constituency before the government. As bridge-builders, Protestant leaders not only interpreted government policy to Chinese Christians, but they also presented Christians' grievances to appropriate government bodies. Many times this meant low key, informal and behind-the-scenes maneuvering as the best way to achieve significant results on specific problems. At other times the activity was more public. There were political structures set up for this purpose—various levels of the CPPCC and the people's congresses—where Christian representatives stated problems they were facing and, when appropriate, criticized government policy. A government based on "democratic consultation" and "mutual supervision" required criticism and self-criticism between the government and the people. Once Three-Self had been recognized as a legitimate mass organization, Christians could assume that they could bring the problems encountered by their churches to the attention of government officials. Supervising the policy of religious freedom, therefore, became a special concern for Christians within the united front.

In 1956, for example, Cora Deng and Y. T. Wu visited Anhui Province in their capacity as delegates to the NPC in order to investigate religious conditions and "assist the government in the implementation of the policy of religious freedom." This phrase, which appears often on the pages of *Tian Feng*, does not mean that Protestant leaders were policing the churches. Quite the contrary, it indicates in typically indirect fashion that they were concerned about the less-than-adequate implementation of religious policy. Their assistance was intended to prod local officials into action. In the report submitted from their trip to Anhui, for example, Wu and Deng laid special emphasis on particular problems which churches faced in the countryside and urged government assistance in the rectification of the situation.[113]

Marcus Chen's outspoken criticism of the implementation of government religious policy from the floor of the CPPCC has been widely cited as an example of the prophetic function of Chinese Protestants during the "100 Flowers" campaign.[114] What is not as widely known is that Chen was speaking in support of a statement which Y. T. Wu had made a few days earlier. By virtue of his leadership of the TSM and his importance as a national figure, Y. T. Wu was in a better position than anyone else to bring the problems which Chinese Christians were facing to the attention of government officials. Formally and informally he worked on behalf of the churches, particularly with regard to their problems with the full exercise of religious freedom. In the statement just mentioned, Wu not only criticized the poor implementation of religious policy, but also spoke out against the prejudices of those government officials who regarded religious belief as some sort of "defect." Citing numerous examples, he attacked the distortions in some recent anti-religious propaganda as well. Wu closed his four-page statement by urging greater care in policy implementation and suggesting that Article 88 of the Constitution be supplemented with specific provisions for the safeguarding of religious rights.[115] The statements of Marcus Chen, Y. T. Wu and many other Christian leaders serve to illustrate an important way in which "Love-Country–Love-Church" were combined in the activity of the TSM.

The relationship between patriotism and the churches helps to explain why Three-Self had to be both a mass organization and a Christian movement at the same time. After 1949 there could be no church without a new understanding of the Christian's role in society. As a mass organization the TSM made definite contributions to the united front in the 1950s. It encouraged patriotism, promoted Christian participation in socialist construction, helped to implement the policy of religious freedom, and took part in the movement for world peace. But Three-Self, the mass organization, also stimulated new developments in theology and Christian witness. Although it was rejected by the right and by the left in the 1950s, and completely turned aside during the Cultural Revolution era, Three-Self was reaffirmed after 1979 and assumed responsibility for a Christian future which no one had imagined was possible.

6

Rejection and Renewal

We will not unite in any way with these unbelievers, nor will we join in any of their organizations. And even with true believers and faithful servants of God we can enjoy only spiritual union. There should not be any kind of formal, organizational union, because we cannot find any teaching in the Bible to support it. Our attitude in matters of faith is this: all truths that are found in the Bible we accept and hold. Whatever teachings are not found in the Bible, we totally reject.[1]

—Wang Mingdao
June 1955

Some people have asked me: "In the past you were opposed to the Three-Self Movement and today you participate in it. Have you changed, or has the Three-Self Movement changed?" My answer is: "I have changed, and Three-Self is also in the midst of change. Nothing in the world remains static and unchanged. However, regarding my faith in the Bible and salvation in Christ, I have not changed one bit."[2]

—Wang Zhen
May 1983

At the heart of the understanding of unity in the TSM there has been a comprehensive approach to Christian faith combined with a strict adherence to political principles. Mutual respect and the reservation of differences were joined with the requirement of political unity for the good of the nation. A sense of yielding was implicit in the toleration of religious differences no less than in the acceptance of CPC leadership. Yet strength was at the same time revealed in an insistence upon belief in Jesus Christ and on adherence to political principles that had been established for all the people of China. The TSM could work within the framework of a united front oriented religious policy because it gave Christians a constructive role to play in the Chinese nation. Thus Three-Self became a united front oriented movement based upon the common ground of Christian faith and political participation. Had there been no TSM, patrio-

154

tism still would have set the terms for Christian existence in the PRC. But there would have been no recognized, institutional expression of Christian faith, and Christians would forever find themselves confronting a hostile world.

It was such a world that sectarian leaders believed they were facing all along. By their very nature many religious sects are hostile or indifferent to state and society. Commanding strict conformity and high moral standards from its own members through implicit and explicit methods of social control, the sect gains its identity by assuming a position over against the "world." Because they reject any appeal to authority beyond their own leadership, sectarians have been both praised and condemned as ideological protest groups and totalitarian minorities.[3] A key consideration for understanding sectarian groups in relationship to the TSM was the irreconcilability of many sectarian leaders. The militant separatism and theological exclusivism—often apocalyptic and pre-millenarian—of a number of indigenous Christian sects made it impossible for them to accept either Three-Self or the political leadership of the CPC. And because they would not be comprehended, they could not be indulged.

As we saw in part 1, the persecution of sectarian heterodoxy by the state is not new in China. To the extent that religious sects rejected integration and challenged social harmony, they were viewed as threatening to the traditional order and were suppressed by the authorities. De Groot's work on the subject has become a classic, providing hundreds of cases of sectarian persecution in late Imperial China in an attempt to prove that the Chinese state was "the most intolerant, the most persecuting of all earthly governments."[4] De Groot overstated his case, but he did understand that Christianity could not but be viewed as an alien form of heterodoxy. This view persisted into the Republican period, and it also helps to explain some of the difficulties faced by Chinese Protestants after 1949. The issue was not Christianity *per se*, but the threat which separatist religious sects, some with foreign connections, might pose to social unity.

It is against such a historical background that we must consider the CPC approach to the Chinese sects. The Communists viewed all separatist and secretive religious organizations with suspicion, whether they were Christian, Buddhist, Daoist or Muslim. Christian groups such as the Jesus Family and the Little Flock had similar suspicions about the Communist party. The TSM, which hoped to become a mass organization for *all* Chinese Protestants, argued against the separatist sects and in support of the People's Government on theological as well as political grounds. A variety of issues were usually involved, theological and non-theological. In the discussion which follows, therefore, it will be important to consider the different ways in which sectarian groups, indigenous churches and the TSM situated themselves with regard to questions of faith and politics.

In retrospect, the damage done to Christian and national unity by the religious sectarianism of the right was minimal in comparison to the harmful effects of the political sectarianism of the left. Marx and Engels had spoken of political sectarianism as a primitive phenomenon characteristic of radical movements prior to the advent of communism.[5] The subsequent history of the Communist movement has shown that it too can be fertile ground for the development of leftist-sectarian heterodoxy. Lenin addressed this problem in his "Left Wing Communism, an Infantile Disorder," but he still maintained that "doctrinarism" on the left was a "thousand times less dangerous and less significant" than that of the right.[6] For China, especially in light of the ten-year-long Cultural Revolution era, events have proven otherwise.

Ultra-leftism as a deviation from the principle of seeking the common ground within the united front preceded the Cultural Revolution era. It has, in fact, had an impact on all areas of Chinese social and cultural life since the 1940s. The TSM has itself been subject to a kind of leftist sectarianism since its founding. The leadership of the movement recognized this as a problem very early, and it tried to find ways of dealing with it. The problem, however, has persisted. In the second section of this chapter leftist tendencies *within* the TSM will be examined as an expression of the way in which theological differences were sometimes confused with political contradictions by Chinese Protestants themselves. The Tenth Meeting of the standing committee of the TSM provides a good illustration of how Three-Self comprehensiveness was rejected on the left in the late 1950s.

The derivative leftism of the TSM was of a vastly different order from the ultra-leftism *in power* which plagued the entire nation during the Cultural Revolution. In terms of both religion and religious policy the common ground of patriotism as the basis for the united front was all but totally rejected during the years between 1966 and 1976. This was a period of large scale repression, growing confusion and selective persecution in almost all areas of social and cultural life. For an understanding of the recent history of Christianity in China, it is essential to analyze the impact of the Cultural Revolution on the TSM, and to consider the ways in which Chinese Christians responded to their ordeal during this turbulent decade.

Although the churches were closed and the TSM dismantled, Christian faith did not disappear. Contrary to almost everyone's expectations, a renewed and strengthened Christianity began to emerge in China after 1978. The proliferation of home worship gatherings during the 1970s, the reopening of churches and the restructuring of the Three-Self Movement have generated a growing interest in Chinese Christianity all over the world.

The rejection and renewal of Three-Self must be seen in relationship to "Love-Country–Love-Church" in the Chinese Christian context. Both "Love-Country" and "Love-Church" were rejected from the right and the left, but they were brought back and rejoined after 1979. In the TSM there is a sense in which one can jump from the 1950s to the late 1970s, but only if one understands what happened in between. This middle period of rejection has had a significant impact on the way in which the heritage of the 1950s is being reappropriated in the 1980s. The pattern of rejection has informed the path of restoration in such a way that the restructuring of the TSM is accompanied by a renewed understanding of unity within the common ground. We can affirm with Wang Zhen that Three-Self is changing, but we must also ask why this is so.

It must be emphasized from the beginning that the following discussion does not and cannot represent a comprehensive analysis either of the events surrounding the criticism of Wang Mingdao or of the Tenth Meeting of the TSM standing committee. Any such analysis would be severely limited by the scarcity of documentary materials concerning both events. The history of Three-Self in the 1950s has been extremely controversial and subject to a wide range of interpretation. Our concern will be limited to a consideration of Three-Self in relation to the question of unity, in the hope that this will serve to clarify the issues involved.

Rejection from the Right

Protestant .sectarian groups became increasingly important for a large segment of the Chinese Christian population in the second half of the nineteenth century.[7] By the time of the May Fourth Movement, several indigenous churches and sects were already well organized. Most of these groups, including the True Jesus Church (founded in 1917), the Jesus Family (1921) and the "Little Flock" (1922), were headed by charismatic leaders who maintained strict standards of social control guided by theologies which were as idiosyncratic as they were fundamentalist. Their organizations set themselves apart not only from the "world" and the mainline denominations, but even from one another.

Nevertheless, in terms of both numbers and influence the indigenous churches and sects were, by 1949, a force to be reckoned with. It has been estimated that by that time they represented as much as one-fourth of the total number of Protestant communicants.[8] Independent evangelists such as John Sung, Leland Wang and Wang Mingdao were popular speakers at meetings and rallies which extended beyond narrow denominational divisions.[9] In this way, although they rejected ecumenical participation in any formal sense, the leaders of the indigenous churches and sects had begun to represent an evangelical challenge to the established denominations.

Several factors may account for the rapid growth and increasing influence of indigenous Chinese Christianity. The self-understanding of most conservative groups was that they had recovered true biblical teachings based upon apostolic principles which were untainted by modern perversions of the gospel.[10] Such a theology was apparently welcomed by a considerable number of Chinese people. Similar to fundamentalist Christians in other times and places, the leaders of the indigenous churches and sects jumped back two thousand years to biblical times, discarding much of what happened in between with the singular exception of the Protestant Reformation.

The indigenous churches also represented an incipient nationalism in Chinese Christianity. Rejecting missionary tutelage, foreign structures and modern Western values, many of the indigenous churches and sects believed that only they could serve the cause of Christ in China. Although the criticism would be made in later years that much of their theology and part of their funding actually did come from overseas, it may still be maintained that the Chinese origin of such groups accounted for a large measure of their appeal.[11]

From a sociological point of view the indigenous churches may be viewed as authoritarian religious responses to the uncertainties and chaos of the times. As such, they reflect a common religious reaction to periods of rapid social change—a reassertion of "nativist" culture combined with new religious values. Sociologists have analyzed similar religious phenomena using theories of "relative deprivation" and millenarian protest over the last thirty years.[12] Although a sociological approach to indigenous Christian communities tends to minimize the theological nature of their appeal, it also helps to balance the self-understanding which such groups have of themselves.

Alongside the positive appeal which their message had for group members, the indigenous churches and sects also created serious problems for other Chinese Christians. Growth in numbers was sometimes at the expense of the membership of established denominations, whose leaders criticized Christian groups which practiced "sheep stealing." Moreover, many groups were intentionally divisive. A report in the 1932-33 edition of the *China Christian Yearbook* expressed alarm over the goals of the "Little Flock," whose declared purpose was "the destruction of the present Church as moribund, corrupt and apostate."[13] A year later a second report commented on the view of church leaders in Peiping (Beijing) regarding the growing power and influence of various sects in that city.

> They are creating division and dissension in some of the churches and are drawing many members away from regular church organizations. There seems to be no limit to the number of smaller sects into which these movements divide themselves. The sect is generally dominated by one strong personality who commands the loyalty of his followers. It must be said, however, that these religious activities are putting new life into many dead church members, and while they are creating problems, they are also a challenge to the regular churches to be more energetic and to place greater stress upon the deeper spiritual needs of the people.[14]

Despite the optimism of the last sentence, the author continues to strike a note of warning in the remainder of the text over the individualism, other-worldliness and divisiveness of the indigenous sects. The message of many such groups was personal, not social, and they tended to divide more than unify.

It was also, in some cases, a message marked by extreme deviations from established Christian teachings. The Ling En-hui in Shandong, for example, elevated personal revelation to the point that biblical teachings became of secondary importance. According to one observer, the religious practice of this group seems to have been a form of extreme pentecostalism.

What started as a simultaneous prayer has in the same section of the country degenerated into a "ritual of chaos" and a liturgy of disorder. Dancing, jumping and unrestrained actions in church are practiced without check. The meetings are pandemonium. As if to break with the past and its quiet, dignified worship, the gatherings glorify noise, "cacaphonous praying" splits the ear, wild wailing and tears, worked up in a similar fashion to and reminding one of wailing at the graves, rob the services of all reverence. Carried on into the small hours of the morning, they degenerate into exhibitions of "emotional debauchery." . . . A few have died as a result of the emotional strain; not a few have lost their reason.[15]

Even allowing for the preference for worship conducted decently and in good order on the part of the Presbyterian missionary who wrote this passage, we can imagine that government authorities would have even more trouble than he understanding, much less relating to, groups such as the Ling En Hui. After 1949 the CPC would be forced to determine the line which separated religion from "superstition" in the practice of this and many similar groups.

Although there has been a continuing concern over "heterodox" Christian beliefs in the Chinese countryside, not all indigenous churches and sects could be so characterized. Moreover, their staunch fundamentalism did not necessarily mean that they would oppose the People's Government or reject the TSM. The Chinese Jesus Independent Church has already been mentioned as an example of an indigenous group which combined anti-imperialism with an independent expression of Christian faith. Its leader, Xie Yongqin, who presided over a membership of 30,000 in 1949, subsequently became a committed leader of the Three-Self Movement.[16] There were also a number of smaller independent churches in different parts of China which experienced no great difficulty in the early-1950s. Many based their interpretation of church-state relations on Romans 12 and 13 in such a way that they had little problem in accepting the political rationale of the CPC.

However, other indigenous churches and sects had a different perspective. Many of their leaders began preaching against the CPC in the late 1940s, and after 1949 some Christian groups actively opposed the government's new laws and social policies. In addition, their internal relationships and tightly disciplined church structures made such groups likely targets for CPC efforts aimed at social reorganization. The self-criticism of Isaac Wei, whose father was the founder of the fiercely independent True Jesus Church, should be read with this in mind. It emphasizes the structural connections between his church, the largest independent Protestant group in China, and the bureaucratic capitalists and landlords of the old order.[17] In any consideration of such churches and sects it is important to keep in mind the basic question about unity and the common ground being raised in this book: To what extent was each particular group willing to seek the common ground on political and social questions, and how far was the CPC willing to go in respecting reserved religious differences?

This question also has a bearing upon human rights abuses in China. There were a number of Chinese Protestants who were arrested and imprisoned during the 1950s. In some instances clear human rights violations were involved. The case of the Anglican Bishop Kimber Den may be cited as a classic example. Imprisoned for five years without trial, he was released in 1957; at that time one foreign reporter was told that it had all been a big mistake![18] Many more examples could be cited of a similar nature.

Serious questions must be raised about all such violations, especially the widespread attacks against Christians and other Chinese citizens beginning with the Anti-Rightist movement.[19] The fact that there were also Christians involved in subversive political activity in no way excuses the abrogation of human rights on the part of Chinese authorities. However, in light of the tremendous social, cultural and political differences which separate Christians in the West from the People's Republic of China, the imprisonment and arrests of Chinese Christians need to be differentiated on a case-by-case basis. Not all cases involving religious personages warranted imprisonment by the People's Government. But neither were they *ipso facto* cases of religious persecution.[20]

It also is important to remember that individuals who were arrested were charged with crimes by the People's Government, not the TSM. Mass organizations have never had a judicial function in the PRC. As a Chinese mass organization, the Three-Self Movement did support the government's decision in the cases which are here under discussion, but in none of these cases was the crime one of non-participation in the TSM. The rejection of Three-Self may have implied an anti-government stance, but it was not in and of itself grounds for arrest. Criticism of Three-Self, therefore, needs to be based on a full understanding of all the issues which were involved.

The Jesus Family

The Jesus Family, centered in Mazhuang, Shandong, was organized as a network of rural, self-supporting, Christian peasant communities. All of the communities were under the direction of the founder of the Jesus Family, Ching Tien-ying (Jing Tianying, 1890–?), who controlled all property and dictated religious and social policy for "family" members. Jones estimates that there were 141 communities in 1949, with 6,000 adherents in Shandong alone.

In the life of the Jesus Family, worship and labor were combined in a communal setting. One author has painted an idyllic picture of the way in which "family" life was integrated around the chapel.

> For some time now the local churches of the Chia-ting (*jia ting*) have emphasized the sanctity of labor. To them, work in the name of the Lord is worship. Their chapels are therefore used as workshops, where weaving, spinning, sewing of shoes and knitting are carried on. As soon as the service begins, all noisy work is stopped. The zest of singing and testimonies is if anything enhanced by such a method. "Music while you work," becomes a very pleasant fact.[21]

It will be remembered from the last chapter that the Jesus Family accounted for the largest number of initial signatories of the "Christian Manifesto." Ching and other leaders probably had decided that they were already a Chinese organization and that the "Manifesto" would not affect them very much. It must have been easy to get the membership to sign, because the Jesus Family was a small and highly centralized organization over which Ching and other pastors had virtually complete authority. Because of their support for the "Manifesto," and because the communal pattern of organization in the Jesus Family bore a superficial resemblance to primitive communism, many outside observers were predicting that this group would adjust rather smoothly to the new order. It seems that such predictions were based on the hopes of the observers as much as they were upon the realities of the situation, however, for very little was known about the Jesus Family outside of Shandong.

As it turned out, the Jesus Family was formally disbanded in the early 1950s. Ching Tien-ying was arrested in 1952, the rural communities were dissolved and the Jesus Family was slowly reorganized into "normal" churches. The details of this series of events are not known, but it is clear that the CPC viewed the group as a "feudal" expression of primitive socialism and therefore an obstacle to change in the Shandong countryside. Y. T. Wu criticized the exploitative and hierarchical character of the group's social organization, and he also noted that it served imperialist interests by setting itself up as an alternative form of socialism.[22] Ching's nephew subsequently attacked the "feudal" character and dictatorial style of his uncle's leadership. He charged that Ching Tien-ying's emphasis on high moral purity was contradicted by his own decadent lifestyle and the sexual manipulation of female group members.[23] Leslie Lyall has also commented on the erratic history and extreme views of the Jesus Family, including its "notorious lawsuits to obtain possession of church property not theirs (and) its spiritual 'love-ins.' "[24] This judgment would tend to substantiate the criticism of the group's "feudal" character made in *Tian Feng*.

It is extremely difficult to arrive at a reasoned assessment of the nature of the Jesus Family and its eventual fate. Marriages were arranged within the "family" and Land Reform was probably resisted, both of which contravened the law and policy of the People's Government. The story which is told by Ching's nephew, whose criticism reads like that of a former cult member who has been deprogrammed, is probably closer to the truth than the peaceful and idyllic picture which was painted by Vaughan Rees after a brief visit.

It is certain that the Jesus Family represented a form of social organization which the CPC was trying to destroy in its effort to modernize the Chinese countryside. This in itself raises all sorts of questions about the role of a Christian community in a situation of revolutionary change. How should such a group respond to the social program of the revolutionary movement? What theological factors should inform such a decision, and how are they to be mediated? Other questions need to be posed to the revolutionary movement. Does a small communitarian group really represent a serious threat to the program of revolutionary change? How can structural transformation be pursued in ways which do not alienate minority interests? In the absence of sufficient information, these questions cannot be answered insofar as they pertain to the experience of the Jesus Family. But they need to be thoughtfully considered by all who share a concern for understanding the purpose of Christian witness in the PRC.

The "Little Flock"

The history of the "Little Flock" is very different from that of the Jesus Family. An urban-based group founded in Fuzhou, it was led by Watchman Nee (1903–1972), a prolific author and powerful speaker, and an inner circle of trusted associates. The correct name of this group is the "Christian Assembly," derived from the understanding that Christians had a *place* where they worshipped God, but were without a *church* which was understood to be a human institution. "Little Flock" comes from Jesus' words to his disciple in Luke 12:32, and it is by this name that the group is more widely known in the West.

The "Little Flock" was originally opposed to any formal denominational structure. Nee's message was that the local "Christian assemblies" represented the form of Christian community mandated by the New Testament. All other forms of church structure were sinful and heretical, for the New Testament taught that only one church should exist in each geographical area. Nee's preaching on the necessity of a personal sense of salvation and his rejection of a professionalized clergy inspired a feeling of evangelical revivalism among his original followers. Local assemblies sprouted up all over East China in the 1920s and 1930s as the power and influence of the movement grew.

By the early 1940s, however, the situation began to change. The original spirit of the "Little Flock" began to wane, as Watchman Nee became embroiled in a number of personal controversies. He was increasingly preoccupied with managing the day-to-day affairs of his brother's pharmaceutical company. After a great deal of pressure from other leaders of the "Little Flock," Nee handed over the Shanghai factory to the local Christian Assembly in 1945. Nevertheless, many viewed this commercial venture as a significant departure from Nee's original teachings. Another change was that the "Little Flock" began to develop its own denominational structure. This was a response to the growing size of the movement—the "Little Flock" had a membership of more than 70,000 in 1949—over which the leadership wanted to maintain strict doctrinal standards and a centralized form of control. Although many aspects of its teachings remained distinctive, the increasingly hierarchical structure of the "Little Flock" was little different from that of rival denominations in 1949.[25]

Watchman Nee was arrested in April 1952 in connection with the *wufan* (five-anti's) movement directed against capitalists suspected of involvment in bribery, tax evasion, the theft of state property, cheating on government contracts and the theft of secret economic information. Although Nee and three others from the Fuzhou "Little Flock" had been criticized at the end of 1951

for trying to obstruct Land Reform, there is no evidence that his arrest in April
was directed against the "Little Flock" as a whole.[26] In Shanghai and elsewhere the local Christian assemblies continued to function without his leadership. Subsequently Nee was charged with selling to the state at inflated prices
and sentenced to fifteen years in prison.

In 1956 Nee was publicly criticized, and this time the "Little Flock" was
involved. The full indictment against Nee was published in *Tian Feng*; it charged
him with three counts of a political nature, the theft of state property and gross
indecency.[27] Four Shanghai leaders were also arrested and charged with "counter-
revolutionary" activity. Other leading members of the "Little Flock" were
invited to Nee's public trial, where his original fifteen-year sentence was reconfirmed. After the trial the Shanghai RAB called together some twenty-five hundred
Protestants to explain the circumstances surrounding Nee's arrest and imprisonment. Subsequently the TSM organized its own campaign of criticism against
Nee, and statements by prominent Protestant leaders were published denouncing Watchman Nee and urging other members of the "Little Flock" not to
follow his example.[28] With all this attention, and with so many of its leaders
under arrest or suspicion, the reorganization of the "Little Flock" proceeded
with little opposition in most major cities.

The political nature of three of the charges against Watchman Nee are not
only vague, but impossible to prove or disprove on the basis of independent
investigation. Why was so much publicity given to the case in 1956, when the
trial merely reconfirmed the sentence handed down four years earlier? Any
answer to this question would be based on speculation without the benefit of
Nee's own testimony surrounding the events of the case. We may surmise that
the government still believed some people in the "Little Flock" to be involved
in political activity that somehow threatened the leadership of the CPC. It was
not uncommon in the 1950s for leading government opponents to be accused
of "counter-revolutionary" activities. Some of these were involved in espionage, but a great many more were simply unenthusiastic about or opposed to
the socialist program. It is difficult to say where Nee belonged.

In the late 1940s Nee and other leaders of the "Little Flock" opposed the
CPC, and it is entirely possible that they may have also attempted to organize
an underground opposition movement. According to Tang Shoulin, who was
with Nee in Shanghai during much of this time and is now an adviser to the
China Christian Council,

Immediately prior to Liberation, Nee and Witness Lee (Li Changshou)
began to develop a secret plan to oppose the CPC. They felt that Liberation would be bad for the "Little Flock." Religious belief had grown
up among some young people during the uncertainties of the War, but
this situation would change with a Communist victory. At the same time,
we had our own internal slogan—"use the gospel to eliminate the revolution." Because of this, the "Little Flock" became very anti-communist
and anti-revolutionary.[29]

In any event, the organizational network of the "Little Flock" was thoroughly dismantled after 1956. But the local Christian assemblies did not disappear. The RAB was explicit in maintaining that the "Little Flock" was not itself a "counter-revolutionary organization," and that it had not been banned. In Tangshan, for example, the local Christian assembly never withdrew from the TSM Committee, and it continued to play an active role.[30]

Today, although there are no longer individual denominations in China, groups associated with the former "Little Flock" continue to meet. In the words of Tang Shoulin,

> We no longer call ourselves the Christian assembly. We simply say that we are Christians in Shanghai. This was the original way we spoke of ourselves in the 1920s and 1930s.[31]

At least one part of the heritage of the "Little Flock" has in this way been recovered.

Wang Mingdao

Of the Protestant leaders whom we have been discussing, Wang Mingdao (1900–) is probably the best-known outside China. He is also the one who can be most easily understood in traditional Protestant terms. Although belligerently fundamentalist and militantly independent, his theological views in no way represented a significant departure from established Christian teachings, as did those of Watchman Nee and Ching Tien-ying. He was also free from the political and commercial entanglements which plagued the True Jesus Church and the "Little Flock" after 1949. Wang Mingdao did have his own church, the Christian Tabernacle in Beijing, and he distributed *The Spiritual Food Quarterly*, which reflected his viewpoint. In the 1930s and 1940s his main activity seems to have been the extended speaking tours he made all around the country. Described as a spellbinding preacher who could keep a congregation's attention for hours on end, Wang Mingdao enjoyed a considerable influence among certain sections of the Chinese Protestant community.[32]

Although he was willing to preach in other churches, Wang Mingdao remained staunchly independent in matters of faith and order. He often cited 2 Corinthians 6:14 as the basis for his refusal to enter into any kind of relationship with either "modernist" Christians or secular authorities: "Be ye not unequally yoked together with unbelievers. For what fellowship hath righteousness with unrighteousness?" (*KJV*).

In the 1940s this attitude precipitated a minor confrontation with Japanese military authorities. Requested to participate in a pro-Japanese "Northern China United Christian Promotion Association," Wang refused on theological grounds. Although he was interrogated by the authorities and pressured to join, he remained adamant and the matter was eventually dropped.[33] In the 1950s, under a very different set of historical circumstances, Wang Mingdao rejected participation in the TSM on similar grounds. This time, however, his confrontation with the government was a far more serious one.

Initially Wang encountered little difficulty in the new situation, and although he spent most of his time in Beijing, his work went on much as before. His Christian Tabernacle was an independently organized church, with no institutionalized linkages to either the Western mission boards or the GMD. Although there were rumors circulated in the early 1950s that he had been arrested or even executed—rumors that Wang Mingdao never saw fit to deny—these turned out to be total fabrications.[34] Even during the Korean War and the denunciation movement Wang was not openly criticized for his lack of involvement.

All during this time he was approached by other Protestant leaders and asked to join the TSM, or at least refrain from attacking it, but he refused. In 1954 Wang Mingdao and Bi Yongqin, his top associate, were invited to attend the First National Christian Conference. Five older ministers went to call on them in Beijing, but Wang and Bi refused even to see them.[35] The Conference was held without their participation, but it was after this that the situation started to change.

In September of 1954 a special meeting was called by the TSM committee in Beijing to criticize Wang Mingdao. Wang himself was present as his views were denounced in speech after speech by other Protestant leaders.[36] The meeting apparently had little effect, however, and Wang continued his work. Over the next year veiled and open attacks were made against Wang Mingdao in *Tian Feng* and other periodicals. On August 8 he was arrested by the Public Security Bureau and charged with directing a "counter-revolutionary clique."[37] He was said to have organized a "Daniel Group" which promoted a "three-no's" policy of noncooperation with the government. After spending a little more than a year in prison, Wang was released and presented his confession at an open meeting in Beijing. Although he was under severe mental strain, Wang repudiated his confession a few months later. He was then returned to prison, on unspecified charges, where he remained for most of the next twenty years.

In light of the circumstances surrounding his arrest and imprisonment, a great deal of sympathy and support has been extended to Wang Mingdao in Christian churches the world over. Had there been an Amnesty International in 1955, he would undoubtedly have been adopted as a prisoner of conscience. The charges against Wang Mingdao were never very specific, and whatever the purpose of his "Daniel Group," it could not have represented a serious political challenge to the Chinese government.[38] The burden of proof lay with the Chinese government and the CPC, but they have never made their case in a convincing way. Although the TSM joined in the attack, no documentation of the *legal* case against Wang Mingdao has ever appeared on the pages of *Tian Feng*. Wang's arrest and imprisonment exemplify the inadequacy of legal safeguards for Chinese citizens in the early years of the People's Republic.

To say that Wang was unjustly imprisoned, however, is not to vindicate the cause for which he stood. In so many of the accounts of his life Wang Mingdao is portrayed as a "man of iron" whose trials and tribulations indicate the path which all Christians should follow in resisting communism.[39] Wang has become a symbol of Christian anti-communism for many Christians in Hong Kong and Taiwan. His is a faith which is opposed to any form of reconciliation with Christians who would hold a different point of view.

The witness of Wang Mingdao has been exaggerated out of all proportion by his supporters from overseas. It leaves the impression that even the fundamentalism of Marcus Chen, Jia Yuming or Wang Zhen has somehow been tainted through its association with the TSM. But it also raises the question of the way in which Christian faith should be lived out in a socialist society. Anyone who is familiar with the situation will admit that Wang Mingdao was opposed to the principles and policies of the People's Government, and this is the most likely reason for the action taken against him. Yet the theological issue was that of the Christian's relationship to a world in which the fundamentals of faith did not set the terms for human existence.[40] The question must therefore be raised as to the adequacy of Wang Mingdao's theological position in facing such a world.

His own answer would probably be that the very posing of such a question is indicative of the chasm which separates "modernists" from true believers. The Christian should never think that he or she could improve the world—that can only come *after* the return of Christ. Instead, Christians should separate themselves from the world, lead upright individual lives and lead others to Christ.

> After the Christians have received the grace of God, they must separate themselves from this sinful world. Yet at the same time they must go into the world, not to be tainted by the evil therein, but to call others to repentance and to receive the salvation of God so that they may escape the wrath which is to come. Nor should the Christians try to improve this corrupt and sinful world—this world cannot be improved but must be destroyed—they should only call others to separate themselves from it and enter into the safe refuge that God has prepared for us.

Commenting on this viewpoint, Ng has rightly observed that there is nothing unique about Wang's theological understanding, for his ideas are representative of a fundamentalism which has continued to exert an influence all through church history.[41] What is different, however, is the social context in which Wang Mingdao made his assault against the so-called modernists, and for this reason, it is important to examine his views more closely.

Wang Mingdao's position is argued in a long essay he wrote in 1955 entitled "We, Because of Faith." The essay sets out a theological rationale for his disagreement with the "modernists" and his refusal—because of faith—to participate in the TSM. A large part of his argument is devoted to a refutation of the ideas of Y. T. Wu, H. H. Tsui, K. H. Ting and Wang Weifan, then a student at Nanjing Theological Seminary. He points out that his objection to their positions is not on any political grounds but is strictly theological, and that the controversy is similar in nature to that of the modernist-fundamentalist debate that had been waged in other parts of the world since the last century. Wang contends that he cannot enter into a relationship with such people as he has named, because they are not even Christians!

> We should respect the beliefs of others, and others should respect our beliefs. But this applies only to religious beliefs different from ours. If someone believes another religion or in no religion, we should not attack him, just as believers in other religions or in no religion should not attack us. However, we cannot hold this same attitude toward the "party of unbelievers" inside the Church. These people have no faith; they do not believe in Jesus; they are not Christians. Masquerading as Christians, they mix with church people and spread some kind of ambiguous, false doctrine to lead astray true believers and corrupt their faith. They are thieves and robbers within the Church, they are wolves in sheep's clothing who get into the sheepfold. Every single Christian is under obligation to rise up and expose the real features of these false Christians, to resist them or make it impossible for them to injure God's flock. We cannot talk about respect for such people or union with them.[42]

In no uncertain terms, and in the strongest possible language, Wang rejected relationships with other Christians in the TSM and formal organizational union of any kind. Wang Mingdao was not interested in dialogue, and it is therefore not difficult to see why the arguments on both sides became increasingly vehement. Both Wang Mingdao's words about the faith of the Three-Self leadership and many of the essays published in *Tian Feng* were unnecessarily harsh. Putting the polemics aside, however, there were theological issues at stake. The Three-Self position was argued in *Tian Feng*, and it is in light of this *theological* critique that the adequacy of Wang's position must be assessed.

Three points stand out in the position which was put forth by representatives of the TSM. The first of these was developed as an exegesis of 2 Corinthians 6:14–18, the text which Wang Mingdao used to justify his rejection of relationships with non-believers, including all "modernists." Huang Peiyong's interpretation of this passage centers on the word *yoked* in verse 14. For him, the term carries two meanings—that Christians should not be yoked in sinful behavior with anyone, and that Christians should not be yoked in religious faith to the followers of other religions. Christians must hold to the principles of their faith in dealing with those outside the Christian community, and they must continue to bear witness to Jesus Christ. Christians should not, however, set themselves apart from other Christians or non-believers, for faith can only grow and develop in relationship to others.[43] Although Wang Mingdao is not criticized by name, his was clearly the position which Huang Peiyong had in mind when writing this essay.

A second essay by Huang Peiyong foreshadows the critique that would be made of Wang Mingdao after his arrest. The argument is that Wang's theological position in "We, Because of Faith" is indeed mediated by a political interpretation of the gospel. Huang reasons that a distinction must be drawn between the political term for unity (*tuanjie*) and the theological term for church union (*heyi*). It would have been an understandable and acceptable theological difference if Wang Mingdao had said that his faith did not permit confessional union. However, the TSM was not asking Christians to unite together doctrinally but to gather together as Christians who were at the same time patriotic Chinese. The policy of mutual respect, which had been inserted into the constitution of the TSM at the insistence of theological conservatives, was particularly designed to guard against such union.[44] Wang Mingdao's refusal to accept this policy therefore carries an implicit political message.

Simliar to the Liberation theologians of the present day, Huang Peiyong is underscoring the political implications of all faith decisions that have an impact on the broader society.[45] Wang was asking that he and his following be ignored, but this in itself involves a social and political understanding which was neither mandated by the Bible nor acceptable in a socialist context. In urging his followers to separate themselves from the world, Wang Mingdao seemed to be ignoring the fact that it was a world in which they had to go on living and working.

Responding to the criticism that Wang Mingdao made against him personally, K. H. Ting raises a third point. He questions the theological presuppositions of Wang's fundamentalism by focusing on the relationship of theology to ethics. Ting argues that the world can indeed be improved, and that China is changing for the better through the program of socialist reconstruction. This should be recognized as something of practical significance by all Christians, even though they may have different theological interpretations of such improvements. The TSM had been saying that Christians should understand and accept theological differences and relate to one another on the basis of mutual respect. This, according to Ting, is based not on the truth of doctrine but on the practice of love. Differences and divisions in the home, at work and in the church are due more to the lack of love than to the specifics of faith. Mutual respect, therefore, is not a path to church union but a challenge to Christian faith.

> The Holy Spirit is testing our love to see whether or not we are really servants of God. . . . Mutual respect not only requires us to see that others respect us, it also calls us to learn humility, the love of others and the value of other persons, and to see the other's good points. Learning to respect others means that we must acknowledge that they have points which are worthy of respect. It means that we must learn to see other people as Jesus saw them. If we are proud and arrogant, if we consider everyone and everything unworthy of our attention, if we reject another's faith as wretched, then we do not know how to respect others. Paul wanted us to "do nothing from selfishness or conceit, but in humility count others better than (our)selves" (Phil. 2:3). He wanted us not to think of (ourselves) more highly than we ought to, and to "live in harmony with

one another; not to be haughty, but associate with the lowly; never be conceited'' (Rom. 12:3,16). When others reviled him or levelled irresponsible criticism at him, Paul said, "Look at what is before your eyes. If anyone is confident that he is Christ's, let him remind himself that as he is Christ's, so are we."[46]

Neither K. H. Ting nor anyone else in the TSM had ever accused Wang Mingdao of having forsaken the Christian faith. Yet this was precisely the charge that Wang had been making against all who disagreed with his extremely narrow interpretation of the gospel. In this sense it was Wang Mingdao who raised the theological question of the Christian's role in society in the strongest and most strident terms imaginable.

Wang Mingdao's theological position presupposed a fallen world in which a small group of true believers was set against everyone else. Faith meant the withdrawal from any effort aimed at social improvement, and always implied that doctrinal rigidity was the true mark of the Christian. While the attacks made against Wang Mingdao in 1955 and 1956 were vastly out of proportion to the charges against him, sympathy for the underdog should not obscure the fact that it was Wang Mingdao who rejected the TSM and not the other way around. Ng's conclusion that "we interpret the persecution of Wang as the judgment of history on a theological point of view, and on a theology that did not allow for the betterment of a society of man" is relevant in this regard.[47] But there were also other issues involved.

Francis Price Jones has compared Wang Mingdao and Y. T. Wu to George Fox and Oliver Cromwell, a comparison which is instructive, but only partly accurate.[48] The real issue for Chinese Christians was not the freedom of conscience—Wang Mingdao would never have spoken in such secular terms—but the relationship between different understandings of Christian faith in a world in which Christians had to go on living. The TSM was insisting that there could be unity in terms of basic political principles without uniformity of belief. For a variety of theological, organizational and political reasons, the Protestants whom we have been discussing ruled out such a possibility. In so doing they also rejected Christian cooperation and theological comprehensiveness in any form.

It is at this point that Jones is helpful by turning our attention back to seventeenth-century England where a similar set of issues was involved. Unlike the Church of England, the TSM did not attempt to bring a broad spectrum of religious opinion within a single church. But it did strive for practical unity within a single patriotic movement of religious believers. The difficulty in both cases was that the idea of such unity, or comprehensiveness, was never one which could command heartfelt loyalty or religious fervor. Owen Chadwick has observed of the British situation,

Comprehension seemed to be a negative, an expedient, a political device. It were better that all men should agree upon the truth and accept it. If they were going to allow rival opinion, they would allow it because the state needed it, or because it was advantageous to unite the Protestants against the Papists, and not because it might be true. . . . The defense of a known and imperative truth elicits the highest decision of conscience. Comprehension was a charitable expediency; and expediency, however charitable, is a judgment of reason and cannot easily stand against the judgment of conscience.[49]

Viewed from the outside, comprehension can indeed be described as a "charitable expedient." But, concludes Chadwick, comprehension also "possesses a moral imperative comparable in degree with the moral duty of loyalty to the truth." Because of the intensity with which they held to their own positions, this was a moral imperative of which Wang Mingdao and other sectarian leaders could never be convinced.

Rejection from the Left

When Y. T. Wu criticized the "sectarian spirit" within the TSM at the First National Christian Conference, he was identifying a problem which had been with the movement from the start. Unlike the religious sectarianism of the right, the sectarianism of the left developed within the TSM as politicized Christian counterpart of the ultra-leftist tendency which has afflicted the Chinese Communist movement for much of its history. Before 1957 the sectarian spirit was not dominant in the Three-Self Movement, although Christian leftism did pose a persistent problem for Protestant leaders who were attempting to establish a broadly based mass organization. It was reflected in an over-zealousness in the pursuit of the patriotic goals of the TSM; an extreme politicization of the Christian message; an inadequate understanding of the concrete realities of Chinese Christianity at the grass roots; and a poor grasp of the united front approach. Both evangelical and liberal Protestants were criticized by Christian leftists for their backwardness and lack of political enthusiasm. Leftist sectarianism thus implied a rejection of the common ground in an effort to overcome or even eradicate reserved differences among Christians in matters of faith.

The earliest criticism of Christian leftism on the pages of *Tian Feng* was an article by Li Chuwen, an early proponent of the TSM.* Entitled, "Draw a Clear Line Between the People and Imperialism," Li criticized the editor of a church periodical in Chengdu for publishing an essay which apparently suggested that all Protestant evangelicals were agents of imperialism.[50] This, according to Li, was a serious mistake in principle, for imperialism—a political category—cannot be identified with a denominational or theological viewpoint within the Chinese church. Citing references from the Pauline epistles on theological diversity, Li reiterates the principle of mutual respect and argues that

*Li Chuwen returned to China from the United States at the time of Liberation and became pastor of Shanghai's Community Church. In the 1950s and early 1960s he was a key figure on the national Three-Self committee. During the Cultural Revolution Li Chuwen repudiated his relationship with the church. In 1981 he became the deputy director of the Xinhua News Agency in Hong Kong, China's *de facto* diplomatic presence in the territory.

the TSM should never try to get evangelicals to change their faith. The editor is called upon to issue a retraction and publish a self-criticism. Although we are not told how the matter was finally resolved, the essay does show that Three-Self leaders were aware of such problems within the ranks of Christian progressives at least as early as 1952.

Awareness of the problem, however, did not mean that it would go away. The following year the editor of an Anglican church paper wrote a self-criticism for publishing an essay by a young "activist" preacher which suggested that the TSM was an instrument of "revolutionary class struggle."[51] This too was a mistake in principle, for the TSM was never intended to be any such thing. Sectarians of the left tended to confuse religious and political categories in their zeal to relate Christian faith to the social situation. This was especially harmful in the early 1950s because it undermined unity and inhibited cooperation between evangelicals and progressives within the TSM.

It is difficult to make generalizations about Christian leftism in the early and mid-1950s, especially in light of the differences in Three-Self organizations at provincial and local levels. Christian leftists were certainly a factor in the denunciation movement and other nationwide political movements of the time. A number of preachers turned their pulpits into political platforms during these years, despite the objections of their congregations. At Nanjing Theological Seminary there were cases of activist students in the early 1950s who wanted to eradicate material of a "feudal" nature from the Bible. For example, the story of the prodigal son was objected to because it reinforced patriarchal family structures. Other examples could be cited in which the Christian community was little more than a reflection of the spirit of the times. Thus, although the attack against the Marxist literary critic Hu Feng had nothing to do with the church, the TSM joined in the chorus of those who were denouncing him.[52] It may be said that although overt expressions of leftist sectarianism were not uncommon in the 1950s, they were more a matter of style and attitude than of policy. As such, they could be effectively resisted by the responsible Three-Self leadership.

Beginning in 1957, however, the situation changed. During the Hundred Flowers movement Chinese Protestants were encouraged to air their grievances in public. At the Ninth Plenum of the TSM standing committee, Y. T. Wu urged those in attendance to fully "develop a democratic style of work, and allow everyone to express opinions and boldly voice their criticism." In small group discussions delegates spoke of their problems with the implementation of religious policy, anti-religious propaganda and pressures which were exerted on religious believers in schools and places of work. Even the Three-Self Movement was not exempt from criticism. It was pointed out that,

The work of the National Three-Self (Committee) had become separated from the masses, that the strength of all committee members had not been brought into full play, that many organizations exist in name only, that many people had jobs but no power, and that work was concentrated in the hands of a few. Assistance to local Three-Self (organizations) is insufficient and relationships are inadequately defined. Even today, the Three-Self Patriotic Movement has not extensively penetrated the countryside. Fellow Christians also brought up the fact that the government, in the implementation of religious policy, had previously only emphasized propaganda work among religious believers and had not universally propagandized the broad masses of the people (about the policy of religious freedom). As a result, there is still a kind of amorphous oppression and discrimination toward religious believers in certain organizations and schools, a linking of faith with backwardness and similar attitudes. There are areas where it is not permitted to have home worship gatherings and where children are not permitted in the churches.[53]

These observations were made during the so-called "blooming and contending" period of the Hundred Flowers movement (April–June 1957), an unprecedented time of relaxation of party control in literary and cultural fields.

In the wider arena non-Communist intellectuals stepped forward to speak out on matters ranging from literary affairs to state policy.[54] They included Christian intellectuals who were involved in the broader issues raised during the movement, as well as Protestant leaders who directed their criticism to the area of religious policy. The speeches of Y. T. Wu and Marcus Chen on the floor of the CPPCC have already been mentioned, but Christians in many other parts of China also voiced their complaints. Stephen Chang (Zhang Haisong), the Anglican bishop from Wuhan, encouraged this when he said, "Now is the time for the faithful to turn the tables." Other Protestants made sharper and more explicit attacks against the CPC. Liu Lingjiu, editor of *The Christian Farmer*, is reported to have said that it took the GMD twenty-two years to become corrupt, but that the CPC had done the same thing in only eight years. Fang Aishi, a Methodist pastor from Ningpo, attacked Russia for its suppression of the Hungarian uprising and reportedly demanded that the CPC give up its leadership.[55] Similar criticisms were being heard all over China in May and early June.

The Hundred Flowers movement came to an abrupt end with the publication on June 9 of an editorial in *People's Daily* which announced that a period of counter-criticism was now needed.[56] This signalled the beginning of the Anti-Rightist campaign, a movement from the relaxation to the tightening up of party supervision.

Chinese Christians were given an official interpretation of events two days later in a talk by Cheng Zhiming, then head of the Shanghai RAB. Simply stated, Cheng declared that "blooming and contending" had been intended not for religious believers, but for those in literary and scholarly circles. This was not to imply that there should be no criticism of government religious policy, but that the question of unity should take precedence for religious believers. Problems of a religious nature or difficulties within the TSM could be discussed, but the type of criticism which had been voiced over the previous months was not "appropriate" for the churches.[57] This interpretation came too late for those who had already spoken out. Encouraged in part by the publication of Marcus Chen's criticism of government policy in the official party newspaper, Chinese Protestants had freely aired their views. In a sharp reversal they were now being told by the RAB that the Hundred Flowers movement had never been meant for them!

In July Cheng Zhiming again spoke to Christians in Shanghai, this time warning that the ideological understanding of many individuals in the religious world was still "unclear." This left them open to manipulation by "imperialism, rightists, and reactionary classes."[58] The question of Chinese Christians' patriotism was again being raised, this time in relation to the criticisms which some Protestant leaders had been making over the previous months. More significantly, renewed attention was given to class struggle in CPC ideology, and the religious question was seen as one aspect of this struggle. This was a leftist error in the language of the united front, for it implied the necessity of struggle against religious belief. Patriotism as the basis of the common ground was thus rejected during the Anti-Rightist campaign in favor of a more rigid and ideological approach to national unity.

The leftist errors of this period are today generally acknowledged in China. Cheng Zhiming's speech would probably be criticized as an example of leftism in the religious work of the CPC. The "Resolution on Party History" admits that the scope of the Anti-Rightist movement was too broad, and that many patriotic Chinese "were unjustifiably labelled as 'Rightists' with unfortunate consequences."[59] Leftism also had a significant impact on the mass organizations whose duty it was to interpret government policy. For this reason the TSM must bear its share of responsibility for the way in which it undermined the very unity it was trying to achieve in the years after 1957. There is no better example of this than the Tenth Plenum of the standing committee of the Three-Self Movement.

If the Second Plenum of the TSM was the best meeting of Chinese Protestants in the 1950s, then the Tenth (Enlarged) Plenum may very well have been the worst. Lasting a full five weeks, from October 28 to December 4, 1957, the Tenth Plenum marks a decisive shift in the TSM toward an increasingly leftist and sectarian position. It came only five months after the Ninth Plenum, and brought together forty-three official delegates (twenty-six from Shanghai) and eighty-seven non-voting members. In his opening address, Y. T. Wu stated the purpose of the meeting as reaffirming the commitment of Chinese Protestants to the socialist road. In light of the events of the past few months, Wu argued, it had become clear that a new initiative in socialist education was needed in China, and that this was especially important for the churches. Protestants should understand that the churches should play a role in "raising (the people's) ideological consciousness."[60] What was distinctive about the Tenth Plenum, however, was not Y. T. Wu's call for more study and consciousness raising, but the intense criticism sessions directed against seven leaders who had been prominent in the TSM.

The seven were Marcus Chen, Liu Lingjiu and Fang Aishi, who have already been mentioned; Zhou Qingze, a pastor from Xiamen (Amoy); Zhou Fuqing and Dong Hongwen, both pastors in Shanghai; and Sun Pengxi, a pastor from Shenyang. The official report on the Tenth Plenum contains more than two hundred pages of criticism of these individuals, almost eighty percent of the entire volume. Because of his prominence as a national Christian leader, some of the most severe criticism is directed against Marcus Chen. He is charged with holding an anti-party line, examples of which are drawn from his speech at the CPPCC. Chen is also criticized for more specific things, ranging from his doubts about the denunciation movement to his unenthusiastic support for the *san fan* campaign. Some of the charges against him are extremely petty—he had referred to Song Meiling as Madame Chiang, and he had not taken any notes during one meeting at which he was criticized.[61]

After the Tenth Plenum criticism sessions were held in other cities against Three-Self leaders who had spoken out during the "blooming and contending" period. Other prominent Christians who were attacked included Jia Yuming in Shanghai, Bishop Chang in Wuhan, and dozens upon dozens of local Three-Self leaders. Many of those who were criticized, including the seven mentioned above, were labelled "rightists" and removed from positions of leadership.

The Tenth Plenum promoted struggle and division rather than unity around a common ground. Criticisms were directed against individual leaders who generally supported the Three-Self Movement, all of whom were patriotic Chinese who supported the leadership of the CPC. This meant the attacks made against them were doubly unjust. The Tenth Plenum exaggerated the threat which so-called rightists posed to Chinese socialism and politicized the quest for unity within the common ground. Since 1978 thousands of men and women who were cast as rightists, including those mentioned above, have been officially rehabilitated and some restitution has been made for the injustices they suffered. Although this cannot undo all the damage that was inflicted upon these individuals and their families, it does help. Other, more personal acts of reconciliation have gone a long way toward healing the wounds within the church and in the wider community.

After 1958, the work of the TSM increasingly assumed a leftist character. Greater attention was given to Christians involved in "illegal activity" ranging from preaching against the government to obstructing socialist production. There was also a renewed emphasis on the relationship between missionaries and imperialism. Historical materials on this subject were collected and analyzed by local Three-Self committees all over China. They produced short essays which were published in *Tian Feng* and in inexpensive local editions. It was as if Chinese Christians had no other function than to rewrite the history of the missionary incursion into China and ferret out illegal activity. Many if not most of the essays written during this period were little more than dogmatic renditions of the excesses of the missionary movement. Contrary to "seeking truth from facts," "facts" were found to fit the "truth" of the existing ideology.

More than one essay argued that *all* missionaries were imperialists, and none that I have seen suggested that they made any substantial contribution to China.[62]

A more serious concern was the apparent inability of the TSM to address in any meaningful way questions relating to the inner life of the church. This was in part related to developments in society as a whole as people from all walks of life became increasingly involved in agricultural and industrial production. The Great Leap Forward had a tremendous impact on the Chinese church, and it generated a renewed sense of commitment to socialist construction on the part of many Christians in the late 1950s. While it may be possible to make a virtue out of necessity, there is no question that the pastoral work of the church suffered from either deliberate or benign neglect. "The Three Witnesses and the Ten Tasks," which Y. T. Wu had outlined for the TSM, were put aside, and Christians were told that religious work should not interfere with socialist production. Between 1958 and 1966 the impression is that "Love-Country" became increasingly separated from "Love-Church" in the Three-Self Movement.

The Second National Christian Conference, held in Shanghai from November 12, 1960, to January 14, 1961, may have been an attempt to remedy the situation. If so, it did not get very far. Representation at the conference was quite broad—319 delegates from 25 provinces, including representatives from three national minorities—but most of the reports and speeches focused on the experience of the Great Leap, the political consciousness of Chinese Christians and the question of imperialism. There is little reference in the published conference documents, to the work of the church or to the principle of mutual respect. In fact, the major changes in the Constitution of the TSM approved by the Second National Christian Conference are the deletion of the article on mutual respect and the strengthening of the patriotic functions of the TSM (Article 2).[63] There is a similar problem with the conference "Resolution" which lists the future responsibilities of Chinese Christians as follows:

1. To continue to hold high the patriotic and anti-imperialist banner, to oppose U.S. imperialism in its seizure of the Chinese territory of Taiwan and its creation of a "two China" plot; to thoroughly sever relations between Chinese Christianity and imperialism, to continue with the eradication of lingering imperialist influences, to be on guard against and expose imperialist plots to use Chinese Christianity, and to work for the thoroughgoing realization of the Chinese Christian task of self-government, self-support and self-propagation.

2. To wholeheartedly accept the leadership of the CPC, to follow the path of socialism, to resolutely uphold the Three Red Banners of the General Line, the Great Leap Forward and the People's Communes, and to continue to promote active participation in all aspects of our country's socialist construction on the part of fellow Christians together with all people throughout the nation.

3. To continue to strengthen political study, to actively participate in productive labor and social practice, and to strengthen the transformation of the political stand and ideology of we Chinese Christians.

4. To assist the People's Government in the implementation of the policy of religious freedom, and to arrange religious activities under the prerequisites of serving production, the policies, laws and decrees of the nation, and socialist welfare.[64]

In sharp contrast to statements issued at Three-Self meetings before 1957, this resolution refers to the arrangement of religious activities almost in passing, further indication of the way in which leftism was leaving its mark upon the TSM.

It should not be imagined that from 1958 on there was a steady and linear progression toward leftism culminating in the outbreak of the Cultural Revolution. For both the CPC and mass organizations like the TSM, the situation was never so simple and clear-cut. One recent study has emphasized Mao's veer to the right after the Great Leap Forward, and another has stressed the tentative critique of ultra-leftism between 1958 and 1961.[65] There were continuing struggles between different ideological lines in the CPC during this period. However, the net result of these struggles was a leftward drift in Chinese society that lasted almost twenty years. In the words of the study which has just been cited,

> From 1957 on, the values of Chinese political culture became increasingly skewed to the Left. The cumulative effect of the anti-Rightist campaign, the Great Leap Forward, the Lushan Plenum, the ascendency of Lin Piao and the Gang of Four, and, more importantly, Mao's twenty-year-old battle against revisionism was to induce an ideological paralysis in the Chinese political system that effectively stifled those who might have spoken out against the spread of the ultra-Left trend.[66]

Despite all of the excesses of the times, the years between 1958 and 1966 also witnessed, indirectly, some positive trends in Chinese Christianity. The unification of worship services took place during this period, and it could not but have importance for ecumenical relationships between Christians. In 1961, Nanjing Theological Seminary reopened after having been closed for a period of years, indicating that some attention could still be given to the training of Christian leadership.[67] Consideration of these events will be reserved for the next two chapters.

By far the most significant and hopeful phenomenon in Chinese Christianity during this period was the growth of home worship gatherings. The movement of urban Christians to the countryside was an important factor in this regard. Living and working together through very difficult times helped to promote improved relationships between Christians and people at the grass roots in rural areas. It is for this reason that K. H. Ting has termed the growth of Christian home meetings the most positive development in Chinese Christianity in the years after 1957.

> It was a new phenomenon. There had been home gatherings before, but participants had all been church or family members. After 1957, many new Christians, as well as church members began to meet in homes. There were a number of reasons for this. In many places, especially in the countryside, there were too few church buildings. Also, some preferred such informal worship. Too, there were some church leaders who had grievances against the TSM. Some wished to sow alienation, but others had real grievances. There were some in Three-Self, for example, who thought Christians meeting in homes would be illegitimate. This was wrong, a result of the increasing ultra-leftism in society as a whole.[68]

We will have more to say about the home worship gatherings shortly. Their growth and development indicates that while leftism may have been on the rise, it could not prevent new expressions of communal faith and witness in the life of Chinese Christians.

Before concluding our discussion of leftism within the TSM, a word of caution is in order. In comparison to the information which is available about developments in the TSM between 1949 and 1957 and from 1979 to the present, very little is known about Chinese Christianity in the years under consideration. *Tian Feng*, which was the only Christian periodical in China during this period, became a monthly in 1961, and for several months during 1960 it was not published at all. Overall, there was little news about the inner life of the churches from any source, including the reports from occasional overseas visitors. An NCCUSA paper published in 1960 confirms that "information about the Church is scarce and growing steadily scarcer."[69] While the NCCUSA tended to draw a consistently negative picture despite this lack of information, the Conference of British Missionary Societies was more prudent when it observed that not only were the facts not known, but that "it is not easy to be sure of the right interpretation of the facts which are known."[70] That caveat is still in order.

How, then, are we to interpret the problem of leftism as it relates to Three-Self? The most obvious answer also has the most truth to it: ultra-leftism within the TSM was a reflection of developments within the wider arena, and especially within the CPC leadership. That this was the case should not be very difficult to understand. In a collective society what happens at one level is bound to have an impact on every other level as well, and the higher one ascends in the power structures—or the closer one gets to the center—the truer this becomes. As leftism increasingly set the terms for decisions made at the center, it was reflected in policy and practice in the provinces, cities and towns around the country. Mass organizations, by virtue of their role as bridges or transmission belts between the masses and the government, would be hard pressed to respond in ways which ran counter to the political recognition which they had worked so hard to achieve.

The Three-Self leadership must have been under increasing pressure in the years after 1957 to guide its constituencies further and further toward the left. Overwhelmed by much larger events, it could do little in terms of resistance, even if that were a possible option, which it was not. A similar observation could be made about all of the mass organizations in China, most of which were much larger and more influential than the TSM. If mass organizations are to have a more positive role to play in guarding against the reemergence of leftism in Chinese society, then the whole question of their independence and initiative needs to be reconsidered. In light of the discussions of democratization and political reform at the 13th Party Congress in 1987, this rethinking may have already begun.

The role of mass organizations in contemporary China is related to the much broader question of the origin of leftism in the Chinese revolution. This has been a subject of considerable interest to Chinese scholars in recent years. Although this question cannot be analyzed within the framework of the present study, the reader is referred to earlier discussions in this book on Chinese Marxism and on left and right deviations in united front work.

One aspect of the larger debate may offer guidance in understanding the attraction which Marxism in its ultra-leftist manifestation has had for intellectuals, including Christian intellectuals, in China and elsewhere. An essay which was published as part of a volume entitled *The Ideological and Theoretical Contributions of Zhou Enlai* describes ultra-leftism as a "stubborn illness" of the revolutionary. Because of its high-sounding idealism and radical egalitarianism, it has helped to inspire "petit-bourgeois" progressive intellectuals to work for social change. The problem is that this sort of leftist, steeped in the world of ideas, proposes goals and ideals which cannot possibly be fulfilled all at once. He or she lacks patience and perseverance, and has an overly abstract and "metaphysical" understanding of social practice and revolutionary change. The authors of the essay identify such a perspective with petit-bourgeois intellectuals because they tend to be inexperienced with concrete social realities.[71] Marx, Engels and Lenin also spoke of this kind of middle-class radicalism, which has been a recurring phenomenon in movements for revolutionary change during most of this century.

This analysis may help to explain why progressive Christians have sometimes adopted an ultra-leftist stance that in certain ways seems contrary to the spirit of Christian faith. It is not the association between Marxism and Christianity which is at issue here, but the relationship between a particular variety of Christian leftism and an ultra-leftist version of Marxism. Christian leftists who become caught up in movements of revolution and change expend a good deal of time and energy trying to prove to the revolutionaries that they belong there. They may exaggerate how far they are willing or able to change, telescope the time it will take to achieve their goals, and underestimate the difference between the gospel message and the revolutionary promise, all in a very sincere attempt to make good the place of Jesus Christ in the movement of history.

The position of the Christian leftist is very different from that of the naive Christian spoken of in the last chapter. Instead of being open to be changed and to witness within the revolutionary movement, the Christian leftist is determined to interpret faith in terms of social justice, radical liberation and eschatological hope, and these alone. He or she presupposes a closer correlation between theory and practice—with an overemphasis on the former—than can reasonably be hoped for in a world which is bracketed by the realities of sin and human finitude. It is just this perspective that a more practically minded Marxist could criticize for its revolutionary impetuosity and petit-bourgeois impatience. The Christian leftist overextends himself or herself in revolutionary commitment and loses touch with Christians at the grass roots.

All of this may have little to do with the problem of leftism in the TSM, but it is relevant for Christians who have been involved in movements for social change elsewhere. If the Chinese experience is relevant at all, then an important lesson is that Christians must discover ways of guarding against the sectarianism of the left in movements for change and renewal. This implies the necessity of maintaining vital links with Christians at the grass roots, and accepting a plurality of beliefs and understandings among those who share common commitments to the church and to the world.[72]

In Chinese Protestantism the principle of mutual respect was designed to create a common ground of commitment around a comprehensive understanding of Christian faith. The problem with Christian leftism was that it had an inadequate understanding of the variety of ways in which Christian faith could be expressed and still remain patriotic and progressive politically. Just as sectarian Protestants excluded from the fellowship those who did not conform to their narrow interpretation of faith and doctrine, so leftism made the reservation of differences in matters of faith increasingly untenable in the years leading up to the Cultural Revolution.

The Cultural Revolution Era, 1966–1976

The challenge posed to the TSM from the left and the right was of an entirely different order from that of the Cultural Revolution. Regardless of whether it is viewed as a power-struggle between different factions of the CPC hierarchy, or as a struggle between two approaches to social and political transformation, or, more commonly in the China of the 1980s, as the eruption of anarchy and "feudalistic totalitarianism," the Cultural Revolution represented a fundamental rejection of a united front approach to religious policy and practice. The framework that to a greater or lesser degree had guided religious policy over the previous seventeen years was in the spring of 1966 abruptly put aside. By that time the UFWD was already under attack, and Li Weihan, its director and a major architect of religious policy, had been removed from all positions of power and influence. By that time also the debate over religious theory and policy had been silenced, and by late August the Protestant, Catholic, Buddhist and Islamic associations had ceased to function. Although as yet there had been no overt attacks against religious believers or places of worship, the Cultural Revolution ushered in a decade during which nearly all visible and institutional expressions of faith were either destroyed or removed from the scene.

The mandate for the subsequent struggle against religion is contained in the famous sixteen-point ''Decision Concerning the Great Proletarian Cultural Revolution'' adopted by the CPC Central Committee on August 8, 1966. Although the main target of this directive was ''those who have wormed their way into the Party and are taking the capitalist road,'' it was also directed against ''bourgeois'' educational and cultural institutions, which would include the Christian churches. Specifically, the first point called for the eradication of ''old ideas, culture, customs and habits'' and the transformation of ''education, literature and art and all other parts of the superstructure that do not correspond to the socialist economic base.''[73] The campaign against the ''Four Olds'' and ''other parts of the superstructure that do not correspond to the socialist economic base'' had, within a matter of days, spilled over into the religious realm, as Red Guards began to break into churches and temples to seize images, scriptures and religious symbols, carrying away and destroying only those things which they could not burn on the spot.

The poster which was reportedly pasted on the former YMCA building in Beijing was typical of the way in which the struggle against religion was now cast:

> There is no God; there is no Spirit; there is no Jesus; there is no Mary; there is no Joseph. How can adults believe in these things? . . . Priests live in luxury and suck the blood of the workers. . . . Like Islam and Catholicism, Protestantism is a reactionary feudal ideology, the opium of the people, with foreign origins and contacts. . . . We are atheists; we believe only in Mao Zedong. We call on all people to burn bibles, destroy images and disperse religious associations.[74]

Over the next three years the persecution of religious believers was severe. In some cities, Protestant clergy were physically abused and paraded through the streets by various groups of marauding Red Guards. Old missionary connections or ''foreign contacts'' were dug up to establish grounds for criticism and attack. Most church buildings were taken over and used as factories, residences or Red Guard command posts. Some ministers were sent to the countryside for reform through labor or locked up in the ad hoc prisons known as ''cowsheds'' and forced to confess their ''crimes.'' Many more were either removed from their homes or were required to share their residences with other families. Christians working in factories and schools were harassed, interrogated, beaten and tortured. A musician in Beijing has described how he was asked to renounce his faith. ''Up until that time,'' he relates, ''I didn't really consider myself to be a Christian. But when they asked me to renounce my faith, then and there I proclaimed Jesus Christ as my Lord.'' It was at this point that his interrogators drove a nail through his upper lip and into his gums.

For many the strain was too great. Some individuals were literally persecuted to death, and others were driven to suicide or even murdered during the Cultural Revolution era. Among the distinguished Christian intellectuals who committed suicide during this period were Fu Lei, the translator of French literature, and his wife. They hanged themselves.[75] Lao She, the celebrated novelist, either took his own life or was murdered in 1966. He was one of the most prominent victims of the Cultural Revolution. What is not so well-known is that Lao She, a patriotic Chinese who returned to China at Zhou Enlai's request in 1949, had been a Christian since 1922. In the 1950s and 1960s, while he continued to participate in Chinese literary circles, Lao She was active in Beijing's Gang Wa Church, where he taught Sunday school for a time.[76]

Most religious institutions were shut down at the very beginning of the Cultural Revolution. Nanjing Theological Seminary closed its doors in June 1966. A few months later Protestant leaders were criticized in "big character posters" as representatives of the bourgeoisie and exploiting classes. In one poster the Three-Self Movement was described as a "conspiracy between Liu Shaoqi and Y. T. Wu" that was designed to portray a sympathetic picture of Christianity. Red Guards later came to the seminary, where they proceeded to ransack the library and to destroy all articles of a religious nature. When they were told that there were also books on Marxism in the library, and that some of the older theological volumes were perhaps the only ones in China, the seminary faculty was given twenty-four hours to select those it wanted to keep and to store them away. Faculty members were then separated into two groups. Half of them went to work in an agricultural commune outside Nanjing, while the other half stayed in Nanjing to tend the seminary buildings and grounds. At the same time, the seminary was taken over as the headquarters of a major Red Guard contingent in the city. The situation became less chaotic in the 1970s, and members of the seminary faculty could begin to undertake more constructive tasks, including the preparation of a Chinese-English dictionary and the translation of U.N. documents into Chinese.[77]

During the years between 1966 and 1969 the Protestants who were the most vulnerable to attack from the outside were the prominent and widely known leaders of the Three-Self Movement. Not only were they in positions of power and influence, useful for the spreading of "bourgeois ideas," but they were also the ones who had promoted a united front between Christians and the CPC. Since this policy was no longer operative, leaders of the TSM found themselves in the most exposed positions in facing the onslaught of the Red Guards. Many of these leaders did what they could to protect the Christian community. Stories are now told about how they helped to hide Bibles, minimize the damage which was done to the churches and care for other members of their community. In some cases Christian leaders volunteered to be criticized, humiliated or imprisoned so as to save others from further abuse.

There were other pastors and Three-Self leaders whose example was not so inspiring. Some denied their faith during the most difficult times of the Cultural Revolution. Others joined in the attack against friends and fellow Christians. The decision to leave the church represented a final break with Christian faith for some of these. But for others the denial of faith was an expression of human weakness that has been part of the Christian experience since the time of the apostle Peter. Intense pressures must have been exerted on the men and women who chose to make such a decision, and Christians who have not been through a similar experience are in no position to question their motives. Chinese Christians now speak of the difference between Peter's denial and Judas' betrayal in such cases. Peter could accept Christ's mercy and the forgiveness of the church, but Judas, convinced as he was of his own guilt, could not. Today in China, all those who have repented and have reaffirmed their faith are welcomed back to the Christian community with expressions of joy and forgiveness.[78]

Chinese Christians endured a great deal of pain and suffering during the Cultural Revolution era, as did tens of thousands of other men and women who had no connection with religious institutions. Stories are told all around China about artists whose hands were broken by the Red Guards; language teachers who lost their hearing during repeated interrogations; and students who were driven mad by the chaos of the times. One of the most diabolical episodes concerns the young man who was taken from his mother's house and shot. A few days later, Red Guards returned to the grief stricken mother and demanded that she pay for the bullet which killed her son, because he was not even worth 10 *fen* of their expense. Countless similar tales of exile and imprisonment, torture and abuse, murder and mayhem have been recounted about the ways in which people from all walks of life were affected by the Cultural Revolution.

Especially severe treatment was reserved for high-ranking party members who opposed the ultra-leftist line. Liu Shaoqi, He Long and Chen Yi died during the struggles of this period. Deng Xiaoping and Chen Yun, Lu Dingyi and Peng Zhen, Hu Yaobang and Zhao Ziyang, and many other top leaders were either exiled or in disgrace during the Cultural Revolution era. Leading cadres of the UFWD and the RAB who had worked most closely with Chinese religious leaders were singled out for their advocacy of a "revisionist" or "capitulationist" approach to the religious question. Supporters, friends and family members were guilty by association. These included Deng Pufang—the son of Deng Xiaoping—who was permanently crippled after he was thrown out of a third story window during an interrogation session. A full list of prominent individuals, government leaders and party cadres who were attacked during the Cultural Revolution would fill many volumes.

Throughout this period there were party and government leaders who tried to resist the ultra-leftists. When Liu Shaoqi's own children began participating in house searches to weed out the "four olds," he stopped them.

Taking out a copy of the constitution of the People's Republic of China, he had said, 'If you want to destroy the four olds, I don't oppose you.

But you can't go to search people's houses and beat people. I am the head of state. I am responsible for implementation of the constitution. Many democrats cooperated with our party for dozens of years, and that is the important fruit of our work with the United Front. It was not easily won, and we can't let it be destroyed in one day. . . . I am responsible for your actions.''[79]

The leader who did more than anyone else to protect religious, cultural and intellectual life was Zhou Enlai. In travels around China in the early 1980s, I was repeatedly told how Zhou had "personally" sent off a telegram ordering the protection of this temple or of that individual. He must have played an important role in the minimizing of potential damage caused by rampaging Red Guards, especially when they threatened to encroach upon institutions that contained valuable and often irreplaceable cultural artifacts. Zhou may also have been responsible for the reemergence of some prominent non-party intellectuals, including "religious personages," after the death of Lin Piao in 1971.[80]

Although in some places an effort was made to eradicate all signs of religion—officials in Wenzhou at one point wanted to declare their city a "non-religion district"—there is little evidence for a systematic Cultural Revolution policy against religion as such. The treatment of religion varied a great deal from place to place over the ten-year period. Stories were circulated in the early 1980s about Buddhist monks from remote areas who had never heard of the Cultural Revolution. In some parts of the countryside, and even in many towns, Christians continued to meet for worship in their homes, and they were not bothered by local officials. While such cases are the exception rather than the rule, they indicate how difficult it is to develop an accurate picture of the treatment of religion during the Cultural Revolution for the country as a whole.

What can be asserted is that the Cultural Revolution was not in and of itself an anti-religious movement. Much broader social issues hung in the balance, issues involving China's economic development, organizational structure and political orientation. The ideological struggles during the Cultural Revolution era were over these issues as they were reflected in the leadership and guiding principles of the CPC. Religion was a casualty of these broader struggles, and it was rejected in the same way that cultural and intellectual life were also suppressed.

Any understanding of the experience of Chinese Christians during this time must take this broader picture into account. Unfortunately, the popular view of the Cultural Revolution among Christians *outside* of China centers on the suffering of the devout in a godless society.[81] This raises the question of suffering in a way that is foreign to the Chinese Christians who actually lived through those times. Their suffering was very real, and indeed, as Zhao Fusan has said, represented a "trial by fire" in which all external things were taken away.[82]

Precisely because it was such an extreme situation, the experiences of Chinese Christians during the Cultural Revolution will continue to shape their perspective on the church and the world. Further reflection on this period is required in order to develop a better understanding of its meaning for the Chinese church.

A number of autobiographical accounts have been published in China and overseas in recent years, offering glimpses of how life was experienced during the Cultural Revolution era. One of these, Nien Cheng's *Life and Death in Shanghai*, has become a bestseller in the United States.[83] Cheng, who formerly served as an adviser to Shell Oil's Shanghai office, was arrested in 1966 under a vague set of charges. The story of her experiences over the next ten years reveals a woman of remarkable character and resilience. One cannot but admire an individual who, from the early days of her arrest through her darkest times of solitary confinement, insisted on telling the truth and standing up for her principles. Her struggle continued even after her release from prison, as she unsuccessfully attempted to bring the murderers of her only daughter to justice. Throughout her long ordeal Cheng's personal sense of integrity was buttressed by her prayers, her faith and her sense of Christian integrity.

In the end Nien Cheng left China and settled in the United States, a perfectly natural conclusion to her story, at least in one sense. Yet it is precisely for this reason that hers is not a story with which most Chinese Christians can identify. At times her account suggests that she was the only righteous one in China; thus her experiences during the Cultural Revolution required no change in her old way of life. In the absence of a perspective on the social context of Christian faith, her character finds as much expression in her disdain for the Shanghai masses as in her personal sense of pride and integrity. We must respect Nien Cheng for maintaining her human dignity, but we must also recognize that her story is not one that can inspire renewal and reconciliation in the Chinese church.

Most Chinese intellectuals, Christian as well as non-Christian, who endured the difficult times of the Cultural Revolution have remained in China to work for change. In this respect the story of a dedicated Communist like Yue Dai-yun, a woman who has been through an ordeal just as difficult as Nien Cheng's, is at once more human and more inspiring. Having had all of her ideals challenged, she is still able to say at the end of her story,

> But even as I recalled the disappointments of my own life and the tragic loss of my friends, I realized that some flame still burned in my heart. It had flickered at times but had never been finally extinguished. Surely the hardships, the losses suffered together, would not be redeemed unless we strove to keep that flame alive. I would join in the efforts to rebuild the Party, convinced that whatever its past mistakes, it alone could lead China forward. I was far less confident of its success than in 1949 and far less certain that I could contribute, but I knew that I had to try.[84]

It is for such individuals, and for all who experienced a similar sense of loss but continue to live in China, that one must look for the meaning of reconciliation. It is for them that the suffering and persecution of religious believers needs to be placed in a more inclusive context. There are those who now argue that suffering has become part of what it means to be Chinese. "To be Chinese is to have suffered in China."[85] Although this is not the whole story, it helps to explain why Chinese Christians have not emphasized their own special suffering. To do so would be self-indulgent, and would undermine the solidarity they have now gained with the rest of the Chinese people.

During the Cultural Revolution Christians suffered *with* the Chinese people, not *for* them. In the words of one Protestant leader, "It was a time of testing, and we were called as a Church to enter into the lives of the people. Our experience was similar to that of Paul who (had to depend on others when he) was blinded and confused after his conversion."[86] If Chinese Christians were now to isolate their suffering from the more general human suffering of the times, or if the Cultural Revolution experience were interpreted as primarily a time of *religious* persecution, then the church would have very little to say to those outside.

Even in their suffering, Chinese Christians were able to find a common ground with the rest of the people. What the church can now offer is the understanding that emancipation from suffering must be accompanied by *redemption* from the guilt and fear which hang over from the past and *reconciliation* between God and humanity.[87] In solidarity with the Chinese people, Christians should be able to point a way to a future in which the suffering of the Cultural Revolution, while not forgotten, need no longer be binding.

The Renewal of Three-Self

The termination of nearly all visible and institutional expressions of religious life during the Cultural Revolution era did not mean that Christian faith had ceased to exist. In fact, as has become increasingly clear over the last ten years, the situation was, to almost everyone's surprise, quite the reverse. Whether judged in terms of individual devotion or numbers of adherents, Christian faith deepened after 1966 and broadened to include a significant number of women and men who worshipped and prayed together in their homes. As Chinese Protestant leaders affirmed in 1980, "God's rod and staff were never very far from us as we moved through the valley of the shadow of death. His promise' to Joshua, 'I will always be with you; I will never abandon you (Jos. 1:5),' has been actualized in our midst these years."[88]

The major vehicle for the fulfillment of this promise was the growth of home worship gatherings in cities, towns and rural areas. As has already been indicated, this was the most important ecclesiastical development in Chinese Christianity in the years after 1957. The emergence and growth of new home worship gatherings during the Cultural Revolution era was a spontaneous response to what Chinese Protestants believed to be God's call to the Christian community. The church was quite literally driven underground in many areas, as Christians gathered informally for worship in apartments, courtyards and houses all over China. Most of these were isolated from one another, but a few saw themselves as part of a much wider fellowship and established regular patterns of sharing and communication. Many of the home worship gatherings met irregularly, but the important thing is that they continued to meet, in some cases even during the most difficult years.

Although there were home worship gatherings which were led by ordained clergy or individuals who had been church leaders in the past, many more were organized and carried forward on the initiative of laymen and laywomen. With characteristic modesty, Peter Tsai (Cai Wenhao) has observed,

> I saw during (the Cultural Revolution) that my own faith was weaker than that of many lay Christians. It is they who have now become the motive force of our Church. We would not have survived without the laity during the Cultural Revolution. We were weak, but they continued to do evangelistic work. We were pushed forward by our congregations.[89]

The perseverance of the laity thus became one of the major sources for Christian renewal and evangelical witness during the years between 1966 and 1976.

The full story of China's home worship gatherings will probably never be known. The secrecy of home meetings in the 1950s, 1960s and 1970s; the difficulty in obtaining reliable information about Christian communities at the grass roots; and the absence of written historical resources about Christians in the Chinese countryside all cloud our understanding of this important phenomena.

After 1972 it became possible for Christians to meet more openly in rural areas due to the relative political relaxation following the halcyon days of the early Cultural Revolution period. The greatest numbers of Chinese Protestants are today found in the provinces of Henan and Zhejiang, and we may conclude that here, and in other east coast provinces, the strength of the home worship gatherings has been greatest. Generalizations such as these, however, are of limited usefulness. It is more meaningful to rely on the individual stories which can be told and retold in the oral tradition which has served the Christian church so well.[90]

In Nanjing there were as many as twenty-five home worship gatherings in the late 1970s. Some of these were deliberately small and informal, but the largest had an average attendance of more than 150 people and met in the courtyard of an active layman. One of the most moving stories to come out of the Christian experience in Nanjing concerns one home worship gathering which was led by a woman evangelist. She was so convinced that the church on Mo Chou Lu would someday reopen that she preserved in her own small home the large communion table, which had stood in front of the sanctuary. More than thirty members of the community that she led began to tithe in the late 1960s in the hope that the money they saved could eventually be used for Christian work in China. Sometime before the Mo Chou Lu Church reopened for its first Christmas Eve service in 1979, the men and women who had tithed for so long returned the communion table and presented the money they had saved, which by then amounted to almost 20,000 *yuan*, as their offering for the repairs and restoration necessary. Many stories from other places could be told about the ways in which the home worship gatherings kept Christianity alive during the Cultural Revolution era, and how they began to resurface after 1979.

Taken as a whole, the emergence of home worship gatherings is difficult to analyze and interpret. We are not only hampered by a lack of reliable information, but by the great diversity which is revealed in what information is available. Raymond Fung's observations on the basis of a study of forty-two communities in eleven provinces in the early 1980s are, in this respect, balanced and informative. His conclusions are threefold. First, the local Christian communities are Chinese and are very much a part of their society. Second, they are Christian with many of the same strengths and weaknesses of Christian communities elsewhere. This is important to remember in order to guard against romanticizing the home worship gatherings and thereby turn their testimonies into "success stories" of Christian witness. Finally, Fung concludes that, although there are tensions between different traditions in Chinese Christian communities, "nowhere have we discovered the kinds of division that lend support to the theory that there are two Protestant churches in China, the 'Three-Self church' and the 'house churches.' "[91]

This last point bears repeating, because as we saw earlier, there are still those who promote the view that there is a "house church movement" which stands over against Three-Self. There is certainly a range of perspectives in Chinese Christianity regarding the TSM, from the active supporters to the stubborn resisters. There are Protestants who have real greivances against local Three-Self organizations, just as there are those who try to sow seeds of opposition against the Christian leadership. However, Chinese Christians cannot be systematically grouped according to the place where they meet for worship. The same tensions which exist within local Christian communities, in China or anywhere else, are reflected in the church as a whole. Published reports from Chinese and foreign visitors all across China over the past ten years testify to the fact that the church situation continues to improve. The vast majority of Chinese Christians are thankful that they can again worship openly, whether in homes or restored churches, at designated meeting points or in the new churches they have built with their own hands.

The home worship gatherings began to grow during a time of increasing political and social pressure against religious belief. Christians were for the most part in situations of extreme isolation. As we shall see in the next chapter, this contributed to the spread of superstitious practices and heretical teachings in many rural areas. The very same things which help churches survive in difficult times—a reliance on "miracles," a tightly knit small community and authoritarian individual leaders—also prove to be limiting and divisive in the long run. In China, when it became possible for Christian communities to resume a more normal existence after 1979, they revealed their vitality and power for renewal. But they were also subject to the same jealousies, divisions and mistakes which have been with the church since New Testament times. An understanding of this negative side of China's home worship gatherings is needed for historical perspective, as well as theological understanding.

Efforts to restore the institutional life of the church followed from the experience of the home worship gatherings. The only Protestant church which was reopened during the Cultural Revolution era was that on Rice Market Street in Beijing. Weekly worship services resumed on Easter 1972, but they were mainly for foreigners in the diplomatic community.[92] The first church to reopen after the fall of the "Gang of Four" was the *Bainian Tang* in Ningbo.[93] It began to hold worship services for overflow crowds in April 1979, only four months after the close of the Third Plenum. At about the same time the national offices of the RAB and the UFWD were reestablished under a reconstituted united front oriented religious policy. In August four Protestants were members of the first religious delegation to travel to North America. Then, almost simultaneously, churches began to reopen in Shanghai, Tianjin, Beijing, Guangzhou, Nanjing and other major cities. Visitors reported that church services were jammed to capacity, while Chinese church leaders confirmed the reimplementation of the policy of religious freedom. All of this was important for the Christian response to the restoration of social and cultural life in China following the close of the Third Plenum of the CPC in December 1978.[94]

An enlarged standing committee of the TSM met in February 1980, for the first time in almost fifteen years. It reaffirmed the principle "Love-Country–Love-Church," but laid special emphasis on the pastoral needs of the church. These were to include the printing of the Bible; the development of new Christian publications; the training of new leaders; and the more effective implementation of religious policy. In order to undertake these responsibilities, the standing committee called for the formation of a new national organization which would be particularly concerned with ecclesiastical matters alongside the TSM, which would continue to function as a patriotic mass organization of Chinese Christians. The role of the new organization was introduced in the pastoral letter sent to Christians all over China on March 1.

> We greatly need to strengthen the pastoral work of our Christian communities. This is an urgent task which calls for our deep commitment and leads us in a most concerted way to see the necessity of the formation of a Christian national structure. After earnest prayer and long deliberation we have decided to proceed with the preparatory work for this organization. This organization aims at giving the necessary pastoral help to Christians and Christian communities across China. It is above all a serving agency. In any question that has to do with our faith our principle is to practice mutual respect and not to interfere with or make uniform our beliefs.[95]

This new organization was set up at the Third National Christian Conference, which met in Nanjing October 6–13, 1980. One hundred and seventy-six delegates gathered from all over China, mostly older Christian leaders who had been involved with Three-Self since the 1950s. It was an emotional reunion of men and women, many of whom had not met together or seen one another for twenty years. They had all suffered during the Cultural Revolution, but now they were intent on preparing a way for the church in the future. The conference was symbolic of the renewal and reconciliation which was already taking place in Chinese Christianity. Both Xiao Xianfa, then director of the RAB, and Zhang Zhiyi, deputy director of the UFWD at that time, spoke before the gathering on the reassertion of religious policy based on the united front. The delegates also heard reports on the growth of Christianity in China and on the pressing needs of churches and Christian organizations. The conference reaffirmed the Three-Self road and the policy of mutual respect; adopted a new Constitution for the TSM; and elected a new standing committee.[96] But its most important decision was the creation of the China Christian Council (CCC).

The China Christian Council was envisioned as an organization to serve the pastoral and ecclesiastical needs of Chinese worshipping communities. According to Article 2 of its Constitution, the objective of the CCC is,

> To unite all (Protestant) Christians who believe in one Heavenly Father and confess Jesus Christ as Lord, and who, under the guidance of the Holy Spirit and abiding by the common Bible, with one mind and in cooperative efforts, seek to further the cause of a self-governing, self-supporting and self-propagating Church in our country.[97]

The China Christian Council is both a reaffirmation of Three-Self and an institutional expression of the TSM on a different level. Neither a national church nor a superstructure imposed on local churches, it is intended to be a servant organization for the promotion of church-building according to the Three-Self principle.[98] Like the TSM, the CCC is a voluntary organization of Chinese Christians. It assumes a comprehensive understanding of faith according to the principle of mutual respect in matters of belief, and has functioned as an agency of reconciliation for the ecclesiastical renewal of Chinese Protestantism.

The relationship between the Council and the Three-Self Movement has been described as that between "two hands of one body."[99] Their respective constitutions emphasize the cooperation and division of labor between the two organizations. Although the current standing committees of the two organizations are, with the exception of Bishop K. H. Ting, completely different, leadership at the provincial and local levels tends to overlap, and local councils and TSM committees will often work together on common concerns. In negotiating for the return of a church building, access to printing facilities or the organization of lay training classes, for example, both organizations would naturally be involved. This is an expression of their essential unity. The difference is that the patriotic and ecclesiastical emphases in Chinese Protestantism are now represented by two separate organizations. With the establishment of the China Christian Council, Chinese Protestants have acted upon their "long-cherished hope," nourished since the mid-1950s.[100] They now have an organization specifically designed to meet the ecclesiastical needs of the churches, needs that were first articulated at the Second Plenum of the TSM standing committee in 1956.

The pastoral needs of the churches were more fully addressed at the Fourth

National Christian Conference in 1986. Two hundred sixty-six men and women gathered in Beijing from August 16–23 representing Protestants from every province, municipality and autonomous region of China except Taiwan and Tibet. The major theme of the conference was the need to deepen the principles of self-government, self-support and self-propagation (the three "selfs") by emphasizing good-government, good-support and good-propagation (the three "goods"). This is a reconciling theme, for the emphasis is on building up the Body of Christ in love (Eph. 4, 15, 16). At the closing worship service, Bishop Ting said,

> Three-self needs upholding, but it also needs implementing. We want to implement three-self by building up the body of Christ. The correctness and necessity of three-self is proven by the fact of improvements in the life and witness of our church. Today there are places where some Christians harbor certain misgivings towards Three-Self, not so much because they are opposed to the three-self principle as because they somehow feel that certain things done in the name of Three-Self seem not to be building up the church but rather harming it. As Three-Self considers the building up of the church as its task, Christians will support it wholeheartedly and the justness of the cause of Three-Self will be taken for granted.[101]

As we shall see in the next chapter, the movement from "three-self" to "three-goods" continues to shape the pattern of renewal for the pastoral life of Chinese churches, as well as theological and publication work.

At the Fourth National Christian Conference Bishop Ting was reconfirmed as president of the CCC and chairperson of the TSM committee. Mr. Shen Derong is Secretary General of the TSM with Rev. Shen Cheng'en, editor of *Tian Feng*, as his deputy. Although Bishop Zheng Jianye continues to serve as CCC General Secretary, his declining health has meant that day-to-day responsibilities are in the hands of Associate General Secretary Ms. Cao Shengjie. The CCC also has two executive vice-presidents. Rev. Shen Yifan, pastor of Shanghai Community Church, has major responsibilities for domestic affairs, and Mr. Han Wenzao, General Secretary of the Amity Foundation, is concerned with international ecumenical work.[102]

If the emergence of the home worship gatherings is the main source for the renewal of Three-Self *from below*, then the reorganization of the Three-Self Movement and the China Christian Council over the past decade must be regarded as the primary expressions of the renewal of Three-Self *from above*. Reform and renewal at both levels are needed. The spontaneity and lay participation of the home worship gatherings (from the masses) requires the organization and theological leadership which only Three-Self can provide (to the masses). If there had been no home worship gatherings, Christian community life would have been snuffed out during the Cultural Revolution era. But without the restoration of the TSM, there would have been little possibility for individual congregations to establish a more normal institutional life or meet their larger needs by relying on their own resources. Because of the CCC it is again possible to speak of a Chinese Christianity which is both rooted in its own soil and ecumenically related. But, as Peter Tsai and so many others have testified, the leadership of the Chinese church is sustained and pushed forward by the faith of its lay members.

What that leadership has been able to accomplish during this time has been nothing less than miraculous. A few hundred men and women, most of whom are in their 60s and 70s have helped to reestablish an ecclesiastical and organizational structure for Chinese Christianity. This is clearly evident from the statistical report issued by the CCC and TSM in August 1987. (See Table 2.)

Table 2
The Protestant Church in China, 1980–1987[103]

Churches (reopened)	2,977
Churches (newly built)	1,067
Family meeting points	16,868
Christians	3,386,611
Baptisms in 1986	151,062
Professional church workers	4,575
New church workers in 1986:	
Ministers ordained	69
Elders ordained	172
Evangelists appointed	376
Lay church workers	26,336
Theological students	594
Lay Training programs in 1986	401
Participants in these programs	14,891
Christians known	
to have been awarded	
in their work units in 1986	7,713

This table reveals both the vitality of Chinese churches and the importance of lay leadership for their pastoral work. Most of the more than sixteen thousand family meeting points, which are regularized home worship gatherings, are led by lay church workers. Training programs have been organized for lay leaders since 1980, and specialized publications offer instruction in theological and pastoral matters. The awards given to Christians from their work units are for excellence in service or job performance. As we shall see in the following chapter, they represent an important form of witness in China today.

Lay leadership and the home worship gatherings depend upon the work of the TSM and CCC at various levels. The lay training programs are important, but the churches also need an ordained clergy. Almost six-hundred students are now under training at China's eleven seminaries and theological training centers. Bibles, New Testaments, hymnals and theological literature are also needed, and the TSM and CCC have carried out an ambitious publication program since 1980. By the end of 1987 Chinese Protestants had printed and distributed more than 2.9 million Bibles and New Testaments with Psalms.[104]

Chinese Protestants have been saying over the last several years that they are more united now than they have ever been before. This testifies to the reconciliation and renewal which has come from the home worship gatherings and the organizational structures of the Chinese Christian community. But Chinese Protestants are not only more united than ever before; they are also more numerous. (See Table 3.)

Table 3
The Protestant Population of China, 1949–1987[105]

	Total Population	Protestants	Percentage
1949–50	483,870,000	936,000	0.19
1986–87	1,000,175,288	3,386,611	0.34

"Document 19" claims that although the absolute number of *all* religious believers has increased since 1949, there has been a decline in growth as a percentage of the total population.[106] However, this has not been the case with Chinese Protestants (see Table 3). Their numbers have significantly increased as a percentage of the population since the departure of all Western missionaries. Chinese Christians, still only a tiny fraction of the entire population, have shown a remarkable resilience in the course of four decades as the gospel has become incarnate in the Chinese context.

In this light, the debate among Christians overseas over the number of Protestant Christians in China has very little meaning.[107] It is fraught with theological and political overtones and assumptions about the relationship between the two kinds of renewal that we have been discussing. Chinese Protestants themselves do not dwell on the question of church growth. Without entering into the wider debate, let it be said that the figures represented here, although conservative, do indicate an order of magnitude. They are based on the best calculations which are currently available from China. However, Christian faith does not rise or fall on the numbers of Chinese who profess to believe in Jesus Christ. The important thing is that Christianity is growing, and this is evidence of the renewal and reconciliation which is taking place in Chinese Protestantism.

Conclusion

The restoration of institutional Christianity and the Three-Self Movement since 1979 is in part a result of the reaffirmation of China's united front policy, which had been dormant since the 1960s. A similar pattern of restoration has also been underway among Buddhists, Catholics and Muslims. The democratic parties, the national capitalists, ethnic minorities and returned overseas Chinese have also regained their place under the auspices of a reinvigorated patriotic united front. In chapter 3 we traced the organization and development of the united front over the past thirty-five years. In chapter 4 we showed how the united front has been applied to religion and religious policy. In chapter 5 the TSM was treated as a mass organization of Chinese Protestants within the united front that helped to establish a working relationship between Christians and Communists in the 1950s according to the principle of "seeking the common ground while reserving differences." The discussion of the rejection and renewal of Three-Self in the present chapter now leads us to some concluding observations on the development of Three-Self as a *Chinese* movement over the last three decades. Specifically, how are we to understand the TSM of the 1950s in comparison with Three-Self in the 1980s?

The first thing which must be emphasized is the *continuity* between the 1950s and the period since the Third Plenum of the CPC. The similarity between the policies of pre-1957 and post-1978 China has been emphasized in all areas of Chinese society and the TSM is no exception. Since 1979 it has reaffirmed "Love-Country–Love-Church," the Three-Self road and mutual respect, all of which were principles first articulated in the early 1950s. The understanding of Three-Self as a patriotic movement of Chinese Christians has in this sense been reappropriated, finding its fullest articulation in K. H. Ting's "Fourteen Points" (1980). This statement was intended to clarify the stance of the TSM for Christians overseas who entertained the prospects of a new missionary endeavor in China. As many Chinese Protestant leaders have observed since then, their desire is to return to the guiding principles of the 1950s, not of the 1940s.

The major accomplishment of Three-Self in the 1950s was the identification of Christianity with the goals and aspirations of the broader society. Through the severing of relationships with the foreign mission boards, the launching of the "Christian Manifesto," and the denunciation and study movements, Protestants were able to organize themselves into a patriotic mass movement. At the Third National Christian Conference in 1980 K. H. Ting declared that the TSM had succeeded in doing three things over the past decades: it had made Chinese Christians into patriotic Chinese citizens; it had made Christianity into a Chinese religion; and it had "helped persons in various circles of society to change their impressions of Chinese Christians and of Christianity."[108] These are significant achievements, and they provide a basis for the creation of a truly indigenized Chinese Christianity. Unlike the 1950s, Christianity is today accepted as a Chinese religion and the churches are regarded as legitimate expressions of Chinese social life.

The theological implications of the sinicization of Christianity will be explored more fully in the next two chapters, but here it must be recognized that this process has been accomplished on an institutional level through the efforts of the TSM. Without the foundation laid by the first generation of Three-Self leaders in the 1950s, it is unlikely that Three-Self could have emerged out of the Cultural Revolution era with the strength and vigor it has shown over the last few years. If further evidence is needed, then one need only turn to the very different situation of Chinese Catholics. They did not have a very strong mass organization in the 1950s and are only now dealing with many of the problems that Chinese Protestants faced thirty years ago.

The TSM of the 1950s was not without its shortcomings. The excesses and abuses of the TSM during the national campaigns were a result of the impatience, inexperience and lack of discernment among some sections of the leadership in the movement's formative years. These same leaders were also handicapped by persistent difficulties with the penetration of the TSM into the grass roots, and with problems over the formation of local organizations in the countryside. We have seen that Three-Self was subject to the ever-present danger of leftist sectarianism from the beginning. Leftist sectarianism has by no means been eradicated in the 1980s, for there continue to be reports about abuses by Three-Self leaders at the local level. However, greater awareness and better safeguards have limited their impact on the Chinese Christian community.

It will be a future generation of Chinese Christians who will finally write the book on the achievements and shortcomings of Three-Self in the 1950s. They will acknowledge how much they owe to the first generation of leaders, but when they think of the weaknesses of the movement in its first decade, they would do well to bear in mind the words of the poem which Bertolt Brecht wrote "To Posterity."

> You, who shall emerge from the flood
> In which we were sinking,
> Think—
> When you speak of our weaknesses,
> Also of the dark times
> That brought them forth.
> For we went changing our country more often
>   than our shoes.
> In the class war, despairing
> When there was only injustice and no resistance.
> For we knew only too well;
> Even the hatred of squalor
> Makes the brow grow stern.
> Even anger against injustice
> Makes the voice grow harsh.
> Alas, we
> Who wished to lay the foundations of kindness,
> Could not ourselves be kind.
> But you, when at last it comes to pass,
> That man can help his fellow man
> Do not judge us
> Too harshly.[109]

There is continuity between the TSM of the 1950s and of the 1980s, but there are also significant differences. As Wang Zhen said in 1983, Three-Self has been changing. The leadership is older and more experienced now, and it is aware of the problems and shortcomings which have been noted above. Because of this, the reemergence of Three-Self in 1979 was not simply a picking up from where the organization had left off twenty years before. A great deal had happened in between, and this has shaped the pattern of the restoration of the TSM.

The Cultural Revolution era, the proliferation of home worship gatherings, the growth of Protestant Christianity, and the new international situation all meant that the TSM was responding to a very different reality in 1979 than that it faced in the 1950s. There has been a renewed appreciation of home worship gatherings as authentic expressions of an indigenous Chinese Christianity. Their claims have been defended on the floor of the CPPCC and in other forums by the Protestant leadership.[110] There is also an increased awareness of the dangers of ultra-leftism. The efforts of K. H. Ting, Zhao Puchu and other religious leaders on behalf of the new constitutional article on religious freedom is perhaps the clearest example of this, but there are other examples as well, including the ongoing criticism of ultra-leftist views of religion in the Chinese press and continuing efforts for the improved implementation of religious policy. As a result of these efforts, the TSM is better able to function as a mass organization of Protestant Christians in China.

Even more significant, however, are the new initiatives that have been taken in pastoral renewal, symbolized by the creation of the China Christian Council. All along the TSM has been something more than a Chinese mass organization. It has never claimed to be a church, but it has promoted and responded to the development of Christian faith in China. The patriotic and ecclesiastical emphases have interacted in the TSM in such a way that Chinese Christians have identified with their people as they have witnessed to Jesus Christ in their midst. The subject of this witness and the source of its power are derived from Christian faith. Thus the growth of Christianity in China does not imply the burgeoning of a mass organization, but rather the church in the power of the Spirit. Any treatment of the TSM limited to a consideration of Three-Self as a patriotic movement is, therefore, inadequate.

The reawakening of interest in Christianity in China over the past several years has raised questions in many people's minds about the understanding of the church in a socialist society. We have tried to indicate the framework and social context of a Chinese Christianity which is "seeking the common ground." As we now turn to consider Three-Self as a *Christian* movement, it becomes necessary to take up the "reserved differences" of Christians within the united front by engaging in a dialogue between the 1950s and the 1980s. In what sense has there been continuity and change in the understanding of "Love-Church" in Chinese Christianity? How are unity and selfhood being interpreted by Chinese Christians? What new theological initiatives have come out of the Chinese Christian experience? The answers to these questions can only be discovered by retracing our steps to a consideration of the efforts for church renewal in the 1950s.

PART FOUR

THREE-SELF AS
A CHRISTIAN MOVEMENT

7

Faith and Works

I do not aim to imply that the Christian Movement in China will be sinified in any complete sense of that term. It will, however, cease to be alien propaganda, and will be merged into China's religious experience. This merging will necessitate mutual modification of both China's historical experience and Christianity. This mutual modification cannot be foretold in detail. For Christianity in China, however, it will certainly involve the following factors. (1) Chinese experience of God will be direct and not mediated in any sense by Western Christians. (2) The expression of that experience will become Chinese in intellectual and literary terms and forms of worship. (3) The initiative and dynamic of Christian effort in China will be China-centric.[1]

—Frank Rawlinson, 1927

In order to spread the gospel in China, we should proceed apace with the reform of our churches' internal life so that they may be appropriate for the context of New China. Just think how many of our fellow Chinese have today doubted, cast aside or refused Christian faith because of the darker side of the churches and the poor ethical behavior of Christians. True, it is by faith that we are justified and all of our good works cannot save us. But our unethical behavior can certainly do harm to others. It can obstruct them from believing so that they cannot be justified by faith! There is a close connection between the ethical nature of our actions and whether others will be led to Christ and justified by faith. Just think how many more Chinese Christians there would be if our preachers were able to act in greater purity and justice, clearly distinguishing between right and wrong. So let our actions become those of new men and women in this beautiful age. Let the people see our good works illumined by the light of the Church, to the glory of our Father in heaven.[2]

—K. H. Ting, 1954

Axiologically speaking, it is the Christian purpose of the TSM which must be regarded as the primary one. Patriotism, support for the leadership of the CPC and a sense of identification with the Chinese people have been very precious for Chinese Christians as the *context* for their unity within the common ground. Patriotism mediated a new understanding of the Christian purpose, just as it provided new opportunities for Christian witness. Although patriotism in the Chinese context became the necessary condition for the development of the Three-Self Movement, it did not and could not supersede the ultimate purpose for which Chinese Protestants wanted to become self-governing, self-supporting and self-propagating in the first place. That purpose has defined Three-Self as a Christian movement, which has promoted the selfhood, unity and witness of the Chinese church.

The Chinese word for witness is composed of two characters meaning "to see with one's own eyes" and "to provide proof or give testimony." Chinese Christians have taken this kind of Christian witness very seriously. Cao Shengjie says of her own experience:

> Previously I worked as a pastoral worker in the church. My only contact with those outside the church was as objects of evangelization. It seemed I always assumed a higher status. With the Cultural Revolution, I worked in a factory for eight years. This was a completely new life for me. It took more than ten of us cooperating in the workshop to complete the day's duties. I was just an ordinary worker in the collective. We worked together. We exercised, rested, studied and laughed together, and became true friends. . . . At the factory, I never kept my faith a secret. I feel that factory life helped me grasp more deeply why, at Jesus' birth, the angels first announced the good news to shepherds tending their flock. Jesus' exhortation to "preach the gospel to the poor" has a deep significance for us. At the same time, I discovered that the workers understood me and because of this began to come into contact with the reality of Christian faith. When the churches were reopened, some people said to me, "Is it all right if we go to church with you?" Of course they were welcomed.[3]

This simple testimony sums up so much of what Chinese Protestants have been saying about their faith over the last four decades—the importance of the change in evangelical orientation, of immersion into the Chinese socialist context, of seeing with one's own eyes and giving testimony on the basis of what the Bible teaches. For Chinese Christians the gospel message has been a great deal more than simply a reserved difference within the united front. Cao Shengjie speaks of it as the power of God for salvation (Rom. 1:6).[4] Belief in this message and a commitment to bear witness (Lk. 24:48) has characterized the Christian purpose of the Three-Self Movement all along.

The most ambitious attempt to articulate this purpose programmatically was

Y. T. Wu's call for the "Three Witnesses and the Ten Tasks" at the Second Plenum of the TSM Committee in 1956.

> As Christians, our basic mission is to bear witness to the saving gospel of Jesus Christ. At the same time, we, God's children who have received His grace, must witness to God's works and will for the age in which we live. Today, God has done wonderful things in China and in the Chinese Church, and we who have seen this cannot but bear witness to that which we have seen.[5]

The "Three Witnesses and the Ten Tasks" called upon Christians to witness *in* and *through*: (1) the realization of selfhood for the church; (2) participation in socialist reconstruction; and (3) the safeguarding of world peace. Y. T. Wu observed that the struggle for Three-Self created new opportunities for Chinese Christians to "unearth the hidden treasures of the gospel." Christian participation in socialist reconstruction was thus both an affirmation of the struggle for liberation and the context for evangelization and witness-bearing. Similarly, commitment to peace was a basic Christian principle as well as an expression of a more universal understanding which united Christians with those outside the church. These "Three Witnesses" were spelled out more concretely in the "Ten Tasks" which outlined a program for reform and renewal in the mid-1950s and were picked up again in the 1980s when the challenge had become even more urgent.

The Three-Self Movement has affirmed the positive social changes which have come with the Chinese revolution. In urging Christians to witness in and through the Chinese socialist experiment, the TSM has been saying that God's grace is active outside the church as well as within it. This understanding provided "new light" in interpreting the biblical conviction that all good things come from God (Jas. 1:17). It meant that Christian witness did not always require a sense of over-againstness to the secular world. Christians should therefore be committed to the success of the Chinese revolution because of the contribution it could make to humanization and social change. In the 1950s an increasing number of Chinese Protestants came to realize that the message of humanization expressed in their witness through the revolution did not mean the abandonment of the message of salvation, which still had to be proclaimed in that historical context.

This understanding of the relationship between humanization and salvation does not require a radical reinterpretation of the Christian message. In some respects it is similar to Karl Rahner's perspective on the unity between the love of neighbor and the love of God. His interpretation of the continuity that exists between these two forms of love, especially as the former relates to the "anonymous Christianity" implicit in the creative moral activity of non-Christians, can help to explain the relationship that Chinese Christians were striving for. According to Rahner, "wherever there is an absolutely moral commitment of a positive kind in the world and within the present economy of salvation, there takes place also a saving event, faith, hope and charity, an act of divinising grace.'' This is so even when the explicit motive and act do not spring from the positive revelation of God's Word.[6] Those who perform such acts in accordance with conscience are what Rahner terms ''anonymous Christians,'' and their ethical activity is a message of humanization. Christians who find themselves in a minority situation may find comfort in the objectivity which an understanding of anonymous Christianity carries. It does not obviate the need for Christian witness, but it allows the task of proclamation to be viewed in a new light.[7]

Chinese Protestants have not spoken of an anonymous Christianity implicit in the Chinese revolution, but they have affirmed the positive moral value of its efforts for humanization. The Chinese Christian commitment to witness through the revolution has meant neither the baptism of the entire Communist program nor the replacement of Christian faith with a revolutionary soteriology. There were admittedly tendencies in this direction among the Chinese Protestants who affirmed a form of Christian leftism in the 1950s. But the more-reasoned judgment of the Christian leadership was to view the revolution as a movement of humanization and to interpret Christianity in terms of the fulfillment and deepening of revolutionary understanding.

Several years ago, K. H. Ting told an audience at Uppsala University in Sweden,

> There are situations in which the Church has to tell the inquirer: ''Go and sin no more.'' But quite often the Church's message is to encourage the people to carry on their valuable work and to relate it to the loving purpose of God in all his work of creation, redemption and sanctification, and thus to gain a new and fuller sense of its value. Then, the undertakings acquire a deeper grounding and are in tune with the love which is the reality at its deepest level, and thereby giving the Christian a peace, a confidence, a calm, a faith, a lack of fear that is the result of his or her consciousness of being at one with the ultimate. We think this is the kind of transcendence or spirituality which endorses involvements in history and does not discount but enhances the quality of good earthly undertakings. In this way, Christ again comes to fulfill and not to destroy.[8]

For Christian witness to be credible on these terms, a great deal depends on the ones who are bearing witness. This is especially the case in China, and for at least two reasons. Given the extremely small number of Christians in society as a whole, people's impression of Christianity might very well be based on an encounter with one or two Christians. As Cao Shengjie noted in the essay cited above, this put a tremendous responsibility on Chinese Christians to witness through their actions. ''Model'' ethical activity would provide Christians with the opportunity to explain their faith to those who became interested. In contrast, unethical behavior would alienate non-Christians and lead them away from what might have been their only chance to hear the gospel interpreted.

This is related to a second factor which is derived from Chinese culture. An ethical understanding of Christianity makes faith more accessible to men and women from a society in which the moral and relational dimension has played such a prominent role in philosophy and social thought. If Chinese thinking, Confucian as well as Marxist, is more practical and this-worldly than mystical and other-worldly in its basic orientation, then we should expect that Chinese Christianity might be best expressed in a similar practical and this-worldly way. In this sense Frank Rawlinson's prediction that Chinese Christians would eventually "interpret religion in terms of ethical relationships between men and men, and between men and God, and consider the aim of religion to develop, in cooperation with God, the full possibilities of human personalities"[9] has been borne out in the experience and theology of Chinese Christians.

Throughout the 1950s the Three-Self Movement called upon Chinese Protestants to reexamine their works, not for the purpose of bestowing praise and blame, but in order to discover the form of Christian witness that would be appropriate for the new society.[10] As a result, Protestants became more self-critical, more humble, and more willing to learn from the example of non-Christians. This resulted in a renewed commitment to Christian witness and ecclesiastical reform, as is evidenced by the call for the "Three Witnesses and the Ten Tasks" in 1956. In this chapter and the next we will consider different themes and emphases that have received attention in the Three-Self Movement since the 1950s. As we take up the questions of selfhood, unity and theology in Chinese Christianity, it will be important to bear in mind the tension between faith and works in the development of Three-Self as a Christian movement.

Christian Selfhood

Selfhood can never be the most basic theological category for the existence of the church. It may even suggest the wrong orientation if independence and autonomy are meant to imply the priority of human initiative over divine grace in the Christian life (1 Cor. 3:6-8). The church has no other foundation than that which was laid by Jesus Christ (1 Cor. 3:11). It is therefore in Christ that the church must discover its true selfhood (Matt. 16:24ff, *NEB*), and this is always understood as both a gift and a task. It is a gift, for the existence of the church is assured by grace and founded upon the message of Jesus Christ. But it is also a task insofar as the church is continually called to communicate that message and participate in its own renewal.

Anything that detracts from its true selfhood or inhibits the communication of the gospel presents an obstacle to the witness of the church. It has been argued that there is already an intrinsic foreignness of the gospel that convicts human beings of sin and makes its acceptance hard for women and men. The church, therefore, should not make its acceptance even harder by embracing that which detracts from its witness. In this light the removal of obstacles to the witness of the church is a movement toward the recovery of the church's true selfhood for the sake of the communication of the gospel message. Whether interpreted as a movement for indigenization, contextualization or three-self, such a movement contributes to the original purpose of the church, and its "builders" may be regarded as fellow workers with God.

When Chinese Protestants began to organize the Three-Self Movement, they saw that if the church were to continue to bear witness, it would have to initiate a cooperative process of reform and renewal among the various denominations. This was necessary because of the predicament in which Chinese Christians now found themselves. As Zhao Fusan argued in 1951,

> How many churches have there been over the past 20 or 30 years which relied on American money and influential officials rather than on the movement of the Spirit in calling all people to Jesus Christ and the church, thereby turning the pursuit of the Kingdom of God and His justice into mere words? This is what millions of believers and good pastors who sincerely love the Lord and follow Him in all things find profoundly distressing. But still there are some laypeople and clergy who have fallen so deeply into bad habits that they think this is as it should be. They think that it is affecting a high moral tone to speak of the independence and self-support of the church. They may also promote independence and self-support, but draft plans saying it will take 10 to 15 years. To this we can but say with distress that a church's ability to rely on the Spirit and unify fellow Christians is in inverse proportion to their dependence on American funding. Our faith in God, our faith in working together with God, has been paralyzed by American funds, and this is a sin![11]

Zhao goes on to say that Three-Self was expressing both the judgment and the grace of God by calling the churches to repentance and renewal. It was indicating a return to the true foundation of the church, rejecting the foundation which had been built with power and money. The TSM was testing what sort of work each person had done (1 Cor. 3:11–13). Now was the time for Chinese Protestants to wake up those who had been asleep to the church's problems, acknowledge their own sinfulness and give themselves up to the cause of the church's true selfhood.

One image of the church that is popular among Chinese Christians is that of the seven golden lampstands mentioned in the Book of Revelation (1:12–20). A lampstand is not a decorative item or something added on; it is that which gives light and is the bearer of light. Similarly, the church's function in society is to bear witness to the light which is Jesus Christ. Writing in 1953 Shen Yuehan argued that the church had lost its true function due to its association with imperialism. It was therefore unable to bear witness to the light, and the lampstands had been taken away. In order to recover the church's original purpose, the TSM would have to break the relationship between Christianity and imperialism so that the true light of Christian faith could once again shine forth (Matt. 5:14–16).[12] This was another way of saying that the Chinese church needed to recover its selfhood.

Chinese Protestants have not spelled out the full meaning of selfhood in any systematic way, nor have they developed a "theology of selfhood." What they have tried to do is promote the realization of selfhood through their faith and through their works. The TSM has taken practical steps toward the recovery of the selfhood of the Chinese church which have far-reaching significance for Christians all over the world. Often responding out of necessity, Chinese Protestants have accomplished many things which have been little more than subjects of ecumenical discussion in other countries, especially in the area of self-support.

A self-supporting church whose goal is self-propagation would naturally be self-governing as well. In the early 1950s this meant the establishment of institutions and church structures that would be appropriate for Christianity in the new situation.[13] It was related to other questions, including church unity, voluntary church work and lay participation. Insofar as these questions are dealt with elsewhere in this book, our discussion of the selfhood of the Chinese Protestant church will be limited to a treatment of self-support and self-propagation.

Self-Support

Self-support was one of the most urgent questions facing Chinese Protestants in the late 1940s. It was related to the more general problems of widespread poverty and unequal development in the nation as a whole, but it also had a character of its own. Many churches and Christian institutions did what they could to respond to human need through educational, medical and social-service programs, but the systemic nature of the problem meant that these efforts had little effect on the overall situation. It is true that the NCC and some Protestant leaders spoke out against government corruption and social injustice,[14] but their statements seem in retrospect to have said too little too late. Part of the problem was that the churches, especially congregations in the countryside, had their own financial difficulties. Some of them had been devastated by the war, and many others had never been able to support themselves or their pastors.

Churches and denominations that were related to the foreign mission boards had access to funding which was unavailable to the population as a whole. Foreign funds enabled Christians to run schools and hospitals, but they also helped to shore up the mainline churches and guarantee their institutional identities. This set the churches and Christian institutions apart from the rest of society and was in large measure responsible for their image as foreign organizations. Even some of the indigenous churches profited financially from their relationships to churches overseas. The "Little Flock," for example, received financial support from England in the 1940s, in the form of direct contributions and proceeds from the sale of Watchman Nee's books.[15] Moreover, Chinese Christians enjoyed the prospects of scholarships, overseas travel and jobs which were not easily secured by those who lacked a church connection. It was this use and availability of foreign financial assistance against the background of poverty and social injustice that brought the question of the churches' self-support to a critical juncture in the years leading up to 1949.

Chinese Protestants soon realized that until the question of the churches' self-support was resolved, they would be unable to deal with many other related issues. So much was involved in this very basic question. There was the problem of rice Christians who "ate the foreign religion" for nothing more than satisfying their material interests. Moreover, as long as the churches were dependent on financial assistance from abroad, they would have difficulty responding to the criticism that Christianity was a semi-foreign reflection of "compradore" culture and imperialist interests. A third problem was that of denominationalism. It had been introduced from the West and was perpetuated by funding and support from a large number of competing foreign mission boards. Finally, there was the question of the relationship between voluntary and professional church workers in the future of the Chinese church. An editorial which appeared in *Tian Feng* in 1950 argued that there would be no possible way of resolving any of these difficulties until the question of self-support had been dealt with. It put the question even more sharply by relating self-support to the basic character of the Christian church.

There are those who attribute the problems (associated with self-support) to a lack of love, faith or unity within the Chinese church. Of course they are correct, but we must ask why is the Chinese Church lacking in these things? Moreover, what shall we do to correct the situation? Is it enough just to "give everyone a little encouragement"? It has not been enough in the past. Was that because no one wrote an essay or a speech encouraging everyone? This sort of viewpoint clearly confuses cause and effect. It does not begin from practice and it is not scientific. In looking at the "question of self-support," some people, especially those who want to use the above methods in dealing with their own concerns, may see it as just a "practical question" and therefore as just a "secondary question." However, precisely because it is a "practical question" it is therefore a "question of primary importance." Although looking down on practical questions and speaking emptily of ideology may appear to be attractive on the surface, it is no way of solving any problem in actuality. Just take theology as an example. We all know that the Chinese Church has fallen behind in this area. There is no one who is concerned about a Chinese theology because everything depends upon foreigners. If China has not even a church of her own, how can she then produce a Chinese theology?[16]

Less than a year after these questions were raised, all foreign funding had been cut off from the Chinese churches, and the question of whether or not to be self-supporting had been answered. What Protestants had originally envisioned as a gradual process unfolding over a period of years now came upon them all at once. With the outbreak of the Korean War and the entry of Chinese troops into the conflict, relationships between Christian institutions and the foreign mission boards were abruptly severed. There was no longer the possibility of Chinese Protestants running schools and hospitals; they were without funds to support such organizations. All hospitals, orphanages, social service institutions and schools were turned over to the government.[17] We have seen that government regulations which mandated self-support also included provision for continuing financial support through the remission of taxes and rental on church buildings no longer in use. Although this income provided the churches with some measure of financial independence, it did not make them self-supporting from the Christian point of view. For that to happen, it was necessary for Chinese Christians themselves to take the initiative in providing for their support and development.

In the early 1950s Chinese Protestants were responding to a radically new situation, and there was a good deal of confusion and misunderstanding as the efforts for consolidation and cutting back proceeded. There is little information about the progress of self-support in the pages of *Tian Feng* or *Xie Jin* after 1951. The subject was discussed at the national meetings of the Preparatory Committee and the TSM, but most reports offer little insight into how self-support was being structured. However, several interpretations of self-support from a Christian point of view were published. One of these, written by Xie Yongqin in 1951, offers insight into a conservative churchman's view of the subject. As the leader of the Chinese Jesus Independent Church, which had been self-supporting since 1904, Xie came to play an important role in the Three-Self Movement, and his thoughts on the subject deserve our careful attention.

He begins with the observation that the building up of the church is more dependent on the nurture of "spiritual workers" than it is on money or material resources. Self-support therefore should be of secondary consideration in any independent church. The China Jesus Independent Church was based upon three principles. First, the initiative of Christians in the local area to gather together for worship took precedence over their understanding of ecclesiology, ritual and forms of organization. Christian communities arose when three or four people gathered to pray, and it did not matter whether they met in "grass huts or tiled houses." Xie maintained that "most of our churches began as home worship gatherings, which little by little constructed a church building and finally established a formal church." Second, the church depended on the efforts of an active laity. "We promote voluntary church work. We do not worry about forms, but we do concentrate on faith, which church workers should have in abundance." For the individual congregation, voluntary work also meant shared responsibility and a common concern for financial support. Xie's third and final point was that the expenses of the local church should correspond to its income. The congregation should neither borrow money nor seek outside sources of support, but should rely solely on the contributions of church members.[18]

These three principles describe what appears to be a congregational understanding of church order. They were never adopted by the TSM, but the growth and development of many home worship gatherings after 1958 embodied a similar understanding of self-support. The emphasis throughout was on local initiative, an active laity and a community oriented self-reliance.

However, Xie Yongqin did not take into account the disparity which existed between churches in different parts of China. This was especially a concern of the larger denominations. In urban areas and in some parts of the countryside, the economic conditions were such that individual congregations would be able to achieve complete self-support with little difficulty after 1949. But in other areas this was not yet possible. What could be done to assist churches in the poorer parts of the Chinese countryside?

The standing committee of the TSM addressed this question in a 1956 resolution calling for concrete steps to help churches and pastors in situations of financial difficulty.

> According to our economic understanding, we believe that the basic resolution of problems with self-support depends upon the enthusiastic giving of Christians from each church. But at the same time, this meeting proposes that we consider how to mobilize Christians around the country on a voluntary basis to develop the spirit of mutual aid and assistance in order to solicit contributions to help some churches become self-supporting. This would be similar to those churches in the apostolic age which helped the church in Jerusalem, expressing their love as parts of one body, and thus excelling "in this gracious work (of giving) also" (2 Cor. 8:7).[19]

The principle being expounded was still one of self-support for all congregations, but this was combined with the responsibility of Christians in the cities to support churches which were experiencing financial difficulties. The following year a stronger program was implemented for churches which still faced financial difficulties. It established a special supplementary assistance fund to which churches around the country could apply for economic assistance. The money for this fund was to be raised by national and provincial offices of the TSM.[20] Despite the variety of ecclesiologies and denominational structures, *all* Protestant congregations were seen to have a Christian and moral duty to support one another.

There were other obstacles to the full implementation of self-support in the churches. In the most detailed report on the subject to appear on the pages of *Tian Feng*, H. H. Tsui described four such difficulties.

1. *Difficulties brought upon the Chinese church by the mission board system.* The denominations had given insufficient attention to the actual conditions of China, and in many places they had built more churches than were really necessary. As a result, some churches now faced serious problems because they were without outside means of support. This was compounded by the fact that some Christians had little feeling of responsibility for the support of their own churches, or they lacked experience in dealing with financial matters.

2. *Difficulties brought about by natural disasters in the countryside.* Prob-

lems such as flooding and drought not only took their toll on church buildings, but also affected agriculture and made it difficult for peasants to support their churches because of their own financial problems.

3. *Difficulties in fully realizing the potential for self-support among churches themselves.* According to Tsui's statistics, congregational giving averaged only 2 RMB per person in 1956–1957, but it could conceivably be increased to 6 RMB, extending from a high of 11 RMB to a low of 0.2 RMB per year, depending on the area of the country. Rental income could also be increased by attending to needed building improvements and then charging higher monthly rentals.

4. *Miscellaneous difficulties*, including the lack of effective church leadership; waste; the inadequate understanding of religious policy and the prejudices of local officials.[21]

Most Chinese Christians had not had to worry about the self-support of their own congregations before 1949, because they could "shake the money tree" which had been planted overseas. In urging Christians to take greater responsibility for self-support, Tsui reminded them of its basis in New Testament teaching (1 Cor. 9:14; Gal. 6:6; Rom. 15:27; Heb. 13:16). Tsui also reasoned that if the church were better able to minister to Christians' spiritual needs, then congregations would regard the church as their spiritual home and they would take up the responsibility for its support. He was saying, in effect, that if Christians discovered the gift of God's grace in the life of their church, then they would take upon themselves responsibility for its support and renewal. A self-supporting church would in this way become a self-propagating one. While it is impossible to determine how far this understanding was accepted by local congregations, it was very much a part of the TSM's view of the subject in 1957.

Protestant thinking on self-support was also being shaped by their participation in socialist society. In the report just cited, H. H. Tsui urged pastors to take part in productive labor, not only to meet their own financial needs, but also so that they would better understand the changes which were taking place in China under socialism. It would help them to identify with the masses and contribute to the material well-being of the whole country. A few months later there was a lively debate on the question of the pastor's participation in productive labor in *Tian Feng*, with the consensus being that it would be good for the individual, the church and the nation.[22] In the years after 1958 Christians from all walks of life were assigned to work in factories and communes alongside everyone else, an experience that provided them with greater understanding of what would be entailed in the creating of self-supporting Christian communities in a self-reliant China.

Support for socialism meant that Chinese Protestants were developing a new outlook on *all* economic questions, and not only on those which directly affected the church. From 1949 Christian thinking on economics would naturally and unashamedly be cast in a socialist mold. For some, this meant that the link between Christianity and Marxism would have to be made more explicit. All

Christians learned that self-supporting churches would share fully in the economic life of the nation as a whole, for seeking the common ground meant the identification of Christian material interests with the general economic interests of the Chinese people. By not seeking to differentiate themselves from the rest of the people on the basis of economic well-being, Chinese Protestants would continue to bear witness in self-supporting communities and *through* their participation in socialist society.

Self-Propagation

If self-support was the most pressing institutional question facing Chinese Protestants in the first few years after 1949, self-propagation was by far the most important theological concern for the future of the Chinese church. Whether understood in terms of mission, evangelism, preaching or theological reorientation, it pertained to the very nature and purpose of Christian witness. For Chinese Protestants, self-propagation became a question not so much of Who? or of Why? but of How? and To what end? How was the Christian message to be understood, interpreted and communicated in the new situation? To what end should the gospel be preached? K. H. Ting said that the basic question Chinese Christians should be asking themselves is, Does the purpose of our speaking serve to build up or to obstruct faith?[23] Such questioning led to a reexamination of all aspects of life in the church, and to a rethinking of what Christian existence would mean in the new situation. As we shall see in the next chapter, self-propagation was also related to the theological fermentation which was beginning at the grass roots. Articulated in a variety of ways in the 1950s, self-propagation has been of crucial importance for the Three-Self Movement ever since.

The point of departure was the decision to seek the common ground as the context for Christian witness in and *through* the Chinese revolutionary movement. This came to be interpreted by Chinese Protestants in different ways. Borrowing from the language of liberation theology, Chen Zemin declared in 1981 that Christians in China had chosen to ''opt for the people,'' for the welfare of their country and for a better social system than China had ever before experienced. This option opened up ''an extensive vista to our theological thinking,'' and enabled Christians to develop new insights about their faith in a radically new situation.[24]

In contrast, Jiang Peifen understood patriotism, support for the leadership of the CPC and identification with the Chinese people as the context for a new understanding of evangelism. In her own words, she gained ''new light'' through her reading of the Bible in the early 1950s, especially in her understanding of Jesus' words in the good shepherd passage of the Gospel of John, ''I have other sheep, that are not of this fold; I must bring them also, and they will heed my voice'' (Jn. 10:16).[25] For Sister Jiang seeking the common ground meant a movement beyond the narrow religious context in which she had been living, enabling new forms of encounter with those who were not of the Christian fold. Beyond what this meant for her own learning and sense of identification with the common people, it also provided her with the opportunity to introduce non-Christians to the gospel message.

Seeking the common ground pushed Protestant churches into a different understanding of their future. In a sermon entitled "The Call Forward," Wang Shenyin interpreted the situation of the Chinese church in light of Moses' call to lead his people through the wilderness (Ex. 14:15). Moses was an Israelite, but he had been raised in the Pharaoh's household and was taught everything he knew by the Egyptians. As he came of age, Moses had to decide whose side he was on. Did he support the Pharaoh in his oppression of the Israelites? Or did he support his own people? When he killed the Egyptian who was beating one of the Israelite slaves (Ex. 2:11-12), Moses answered that "he refused to be called the son of Pharaoh's daughter" (Heb. 11:24). For the rest of his life he was continually called to go forward and lead his people. Moses endured forty difficult years in the wilderness, but despite all of his setbacks and disappointments, his faith kept him with the Israelites. Wang's conclusion is that Chinese Christians should be like Moses. They cannot long for the missionary past and the fleshpots of Egypt, but must go forward with their own people.[26]

After 1949 the propagation of the Christian message could not go on as it had before. It was not that Chinese Protestants had found the gospel wanting, but that they saw it was being interpreted and expressed in ways that separated them from their own people. Literally dozens of essays were published in *Tian Feng* during this time criticizing both the form and content of pre-Liberation evangelism.[27] The central point was that Chinese Christianity had been shaped by biblical, theological and political interpretations that served foreign interests rather than the Chinese people. Because of this, preaching and evangelism from the missionary era communicated a message that was neither by nor for Chinese Christians. The question was not who was doing the preaching, but whose interests the preaching was serving. Faith and piety had been interpreted in ways that may have been appropriate for Western countries, but they were decidedly inappropriate for a people struggling to free themselves from a "semi-feudal and semi-colonial" past. The Protestant message had been too individualistic, too idealistic, too other-worldly and defeatist, and Christian faith had become divorced from the struggles which ordinary people were facing in their day-to-day lives. It was no wonder that many people had grown suspicious of Christian piety and felt alienated from the church. This was the argument that Three-Self put before the Chinese churches in the early 1950s, an argument that challenged past assumptions and called the Protestants to look at the difficulties which were before them.

What was being rejected was the political and social understanding of Protestantism that had been brought to China by the foreign missionaries. Both the "reformism" of the progressives and the "transpolitical" understanding of the evangelicals detracted from what the gospel had to offer in the new situation.[28]

Reformism perpetuated the semi-colonial system and made fundamental change impossible. Lacking a deep sense of religious conviction, it was, moreover, unable to meet the atheist challenge to Christian faith.

The transpolitical interpretation of the evangelicals, in contrast, *did* have a strong religious message, but it represented a response to the political situation that was even more inadequate than that of the progressives. By separating both individuals and the church from the struggles of society, by giving inadequate attention to the social-justice orientation of prophetic Christianity, and, in the case of the large number of pre-millenarians, by suggesting that there was no hope for ever changing the world, evangelical Protestants were distorting the gospel and preaching a message which was irrelevant for a society in the midst of revolution. It was this latter, transpolitical view of Christian faith that came under greater scrutiny and criticism on the pages of *Tian Feng* in the early 1950s, probably because it was more influential for Chinese Protestants at the grass roots.[29]

The this-worldly turn in self-propagation provided a needed corrective for evangelism in the early 1950s. Unfortunately the critique also resulted in a tendency to blend preaching too much with current political themes, especially for the "Christian leftists." Writing in 1953 one author criticized those who viewed the Bible as a political text.

> They do not begin from the spirit of the Biblical text in elucidating the truth, so that believers in search of spiritual life find (their sermons) dry, insipid and stereotypical. . . . For example, some are empty of spiritual content, only copying off mechanically phrases which are popular in the church. Some speak only of the historical Jesus, but they deliberately avoid speaking of the Jesus of faith, the Son of God. Some not only lower Jesus to the position of an historical personage, but they even force the society of Jesus' time to fit the mold of our 20th century knowledge. . . . They simply make Jesus into a socialist revolutionary strategist. Some take a verse or passage of the Bible as their topic, but rather than develop its meaning, they merely shout about some political slogans of the times.

The writer also criticized those who wrote on spiritual nurture in an attempt to transcend political questions:

> Some writers seem to have no feeling for our social environment since liberation. Intrinsic changes have taken place, but they still use phrases like "the darkness of the world," "the evil in men's hearts," "the church has been tempered," "humanity is without hope," etc., as subjects of their essays. They act as if there had been no change at all.[30]

Self-propagation meant a new understanding of evangelism, one which embraced neither the reformism nor transpolitical interpretations of the missionary era, and one which also avoided the temptation of politicization. It would allow Christians to witness in the Chinese socialist experiment in such a way that the gospel would not become irrelevant, and through the revolutionary movement without it becoming a syncretistic blend of Marxism and Christianity. Self-propagation meant that Christian faith could neither be unrelated to politics nor taken over by a purely political message. In the 1950s the concern for a truly self-propagating Chinese Protestant movement was expressed over and over again by the Three-Self leadership, but by 1957 progress toward this goal had been at best fragmentary.

This was the conclusion of Bishop Z. T. Kaung who reported his views on the subject in a speech before the standing committee of the TSM in 1957.[31] He began with the observation that there were three points concerning self-propagation which were commonly recognized. First, the "purification of Christian faith" had necessitated the criticism of imperialism and the eradication of its influence on biblical interpretation. Second, the Bible was the unchanging and eternal word of God, whose truth is revealed anew in every age. The truth of the Bible does not change, but people's understanding of it does. This suggests that Christian faith may be expressed differently in different times, as the Christian message develops according to new insights which emerge in the course of history. Third, mutual respect in matters of faith was acknowledged by Kaung to be a basic principle of the Three-Self Movement.

On the basis of these three points Kaung described the contemporary situation as one in which the deep spiritual needs of Chinese Christians posed new questions for self-propagation. Was belief still necessary? Is Christianity idealistic? Is it opposed to science? Should time be taken off from labor for attending worship services? Pastors in the local church were doing what they could to address such questions, but there were problems in how they were responding. Some pastors seemed unable to reinterpret the meaning of Christianity for the present situation. Others had become too political. Still others were neglecting various aspects of pastoral work, including Sunday schools, visitations and women's organizations. Given this situation, Kaung suggested several possibilities for future work, including greater attention to the theological questions which Christians had been raising at the grass roots and the creation of an organization for the promotion of self-propagation. His suggestions must have been discussed by the Three-Self standing committee, but the onset of the Anti-Rightist movement and subsequent events made further progress impossible.

It appears, then, that by 1957 little had been achieved in terms of self-propagation. The critique had been made of the missionary era, and there was a new understanding of the nature of self-propagation, but the question as to how the propagation of the gospel would actually proceed had been articulated only in a vague and general way. This, however, was only part of the story. On a very different level self-propagation was already being practiced and lived out in the lives of ordinary Christians. In a practical and this-worldly fashion, one that allowed Christians to make their faith manifest in works, Protestants from all walks of life were discovering that they could participate in socialist reconstruction and bear witness to Jesus Christ at the same time. Evidence for this assertion comes chiefly from the stories and reports of Christians who were selected as models in their working units.[32]

With the support and encouragement of the TSM, Christians who became "Model Teachers" or "Advanced Workers" or "Outstanding Students" were contributing to a new understanding of self-propagation in the Chinese church. In 1956 Shanghai Three-Self leaders spoke of the significance of the large number of Christian model workers.

> At the Second Representative Assembly of the Shanghai Christian Three-Self Patriotic Movement in May of this year, many Christians spoke in the plenary session about their own work at their posts. There were workers, teachers, health workers, government employees, store clerks, industrialists, businessmen, literary workers and neighborhood committee workers among them. All have been commended by their leaders, and some have been named model workers or advanced workers. These workers, who love country and church, said that the reason they were able to work like this was, on the one hand, the leadership of the CPC in our motherland, striving for the well-being of the people. The rapid progress of the motherland in the last six years has enabled each person to realize our nation's brilliant future. On the other hand, the Bible has taught them that a Christian should love God and humanity, and so must take an active part in socialist reconstruction. In this way, they can give glory to Jesus Christ and be good Christians. They all felt deeply that due to the fact that they enjoy the freedom of belief, they have a deeper love for their motherland.[33]

Models have been of fundamental importance for the process of transformation in Chinese society. The belief that people are socialized and educated primarily through the imitation of models may owe as much to Confucian moralism as it does to Communist ethics; it has important implications for the structure of social life in the PRC nonetheless.[34] Through the designation of political, educational and ethical models, particular individuals are held up as positive examples whose behavior others should try to emulate. This practice was adopted by the CPC in Yanan, and although its function may no longer be as emphatic as it once was, models such as Lei Feng and Zhang Haidi continue to receive prominent attention in the media and in the educational system. At the local level, models from schools and factories are regarded as potential leaders, and they tend to exert a greater influence on fellow students and colleagues than do those who have not been so designated.

In the 1950s Christians who became model workers helped to change the image of Christianity in the eyes of the Chinese people. They also created an interest in their faith among those around them. For a Christian to be a model worker meant that he or she could not be a "running dog" of American imperialism, for his or her efforts represented a contribution to socialist construction. This could not but lead others to question their understanding of, or, as the case may be, misunderstanding of Christianity. If a Christian could be a model worker, then it meant that there must be some value in Christian faith. This was both an affirmation of and a challenge to socialism. It suggested that men and women who held a worldview other than Marxism-Leninism could be motivated for the good of the people and of the nation to make a social contribution. Christians themselves pointed to the models of the Old Testament prophets and of Jesus and his disciples to indicate their own understanding of faith.[35] By so doing, they stressed the continuing relevance of Christianity to their own individual and corporate lives in a way that did not lead to a false syncretism between religion and politics.

There is no way of measuring the impact that Christian models have had upon self-propagation. Stories are now told and retold about the exemplary behavior of some committed Christians during the Cultural Revolution era, and of how their personal witness led others to Christian faith. But there are other cases in which Christians' behavior was not so exemplary, not to mention the countless examples of Communists and others who had no connection with the church whose spirit of serving the people testified to a different source of faith. For the Christian, faith cannot be reduced to morals or ethics, nor can the lives of individual Protestants imply the superiority of the Christian persuasion. But the faith and works of Christian model workers can suggest an appropriate form of witness-bearing in the Chinese context. Their witness is one that allows others to see with their own eyes the proof of the model worker's faith. In this way the Christian as ''model'' constitutes a lasting contribution to self-propagation in the Chinese church.

Christian Unity

It is generally acknowledged that the Protestant missionary movement of the nineteenth century paved the way for the ecumenical movement which came to fruition in the twentieth. The disunity of Protestant missionary efforts in Asia, Africa and Latin America not only caused confusion among the people whom the missionaries went to serve; it also weakened the common witness of the new churches in what then were called mission fields. It was therefore the missionaries and Christians from the Third World who first began to stress the need for interdenominational cooperation and church unity. Their theological point of departure was Jesus' words to his disciples in the high priestly prayer of the Gospel of John.

> I do not pray for these only, but also for those who believe in me through their word, that they may all be one; even, as thou, Father, art in me, and I in thee, that they may also be in us, so that the world may believe that thou hast sent me (Jn. 17:20-21).

This text has shaped ecumenical thinking for much of the present century. It brought the concerns for mission and unity together, as the meaning of the word ecumenical came to be understood in both its worldly and its churchly sense.[36]

The passage from John's Gospel was very much on the minds of the delegates who gathered in Edinburgh in 1910 to attend the First World Missionary Conference. Edinburgh was significant for interpreting Christian mission and unity as these terms came to be understood in China. The official report of the conference questioned the proliferation of separate Christian communities, which detracted from the mission of the church and undermined visible Christian unity in non-Christian countries. More than joint action and coordinated efforts among mission societies was needed. The aim of missionary work should be "to plant in each non-Christian nation one undivided Church of Christ."[37]

The report goes on to speak of a "notable expression" of this idea in the declaration on church unity from the Centenary Conference held in Shanghai three years earlier. The desire for unity was taking shape not only among foreign missionaries, but "under the influence of the growing national consciousness" of Christians in some countries, an influence which was felt most strongly, the report noted, among the Christians of China. This observation is substantiated by the testimonies of a number of China missionaries, including Bishop Logan Roots, who linked the question of Christian missions to that of patriotism.

> The leading Christians of China undoubtedly believe that one reason why they should be Christians and propagate Christianity in China is that they will therefore render the greatest service to their country; and therefore Christian zeal has become to many a matter of patriotic obligation.

Roots maintained that Christian unity was essential in order to strengthen the church in the service of the Chinese nation and to more effectively propagate the Christian gospel.[38]

Similarly, Cheng Chingyi (Cheng Jingyi), who was already one of the outstanding ecumenical leaders of his generation, addressed himself to the question of unity at the Edinburgh Conference. In his now famous seven minute speech, Cheng spoke from the floor about the importance of the Christian federation movement, which had already begun in some parts of China.

> Since the Chinese Christians have enjoyed the sweetness of such a unity, they long for more, and look forward for yet greater things. They are watching with keen eyes, and listening with attentive ears for what this conference will show to them concerning this all important question. I am sure they will not be disappointed. Speaking plainly, we hope to see, in the near future, a united Christian Church without any denominational distinctions. This may seem somewhat peculiar to some of you, but, friends, do not forget to view us from *our* standpoint, and if you fail to do that, the Chinese will remain always as a mysterious people to you!

Such unity was essential for three reasons. (1) It would help to promote the self-government and self-support of the Chinese church; (2) denominationalism was of little interest to the Chinese; and (3) unity would help to build up the defenses of the Chinese church against "the powerful force of heathenism from without, and the feebleness of the Church from within."[39]

Both Roots and Cheng recognized that Christian unity was important in China for practical as well as theological reasons, but not unity on Western terms. Neither the Western powers nor the denominational structures could determine the pattern of national or Christian unity in China, as developments over the next forty years would indicate so clearly. The increasing ecumenical activity during those decades did bear fruit—the formation of the Holy Catholic Church of China (Anglican), the National Christian Council and the Church of Christ in China were significant in this regard—but these efforts had little connection with what was taking place in the rest of society. Because the ecumenical movement did not deal with the emerging Chinese national consciousness, it lacked Chinese roots. Latourette was correct when he observed, "Chinese Protestantism was being integrated in the Ecumenical Movement and so was not being absorbed by Chinese nationalism."[40] But this was precisely the reason why ecumenical Protestantism could not be the source for initiatives in Christian unity after 1949.

In the early 1950s ecumenical unity was never articulated as the goal of the Three-Self Movement, and to the extent that it was achieved, it was largely a function of other factors. No meetings were held to discuss doctrinal differences or to promote organic union, but there was a great deal of practical cooperation among Christians working together. An editorial in *Tian Feng* asserted that there was but one body of Christ, and that Christians should therefore be unified. But of more immediate importance was the movement for practical cooperation arising from the concrete needs of the situation: "The most important thing at present is not 'unity' but 'whole-hearted cooperation' and 'close relations plus mutual love.' Everyone must first put aside their prejudices so that we may have something of 'mutual tolerance.' . . ."[41] The assumption was that Protestants could not come together all at once, but they could at least practice tolerance, forgiveness and mutual respect in relating to one another.

Some form of cooperation was absolutely necessary in the early 1950s because the disunity of the churches posed serious practical problems for the Protestant churches.[42] Competing denominations had spawned institutions and social programs which Chinese Christians, left to rely on their own resources, were no longer able to support. Such divisions weakened the Christian community in the eyes of those outside and made it difficult for the government to relate to Chinese Protestants as a group that shared common concerns. This was reinforced by the foreign identity of Chinese churches whose divisions seemed to suggest the competition of the various powers in "semi-colonial" China. There was also reason to believe that such divisions could be exploited by the GMD in the service of its own political interests.

Chinese Protestants criticized their own disunity theologically, arguing that an unwillingness to practice tolerance and forgiveness was an expression of narrow self-centeredness and arrogant individualism. One author warned Christians not to close themselves off like Elijah (1 Kings 19) and believe that they were the only faithful ones left in Israel.[43] Chinese Christians have tended to believe that an understanding of the church as the Body of Christ should promote a cooperative, not an individual, journey of faith. The point was made over and over again that disunity implied arrogance and selfishness; a perspective that put one's own interests and concerns above those of the community; an expression of self-interest that elevated itself over the interests of the group; and thus an understanding of faith that neglected the teachings of God and the Bible.

The unity that the TSM was most interested in promoting in the early 1950s was the political unity of a mass organization. But for this to be effective, some interdenominational coordination and interconfessional acceptance was absolutely necessary. On one level, unity was interpreted in terms of "Love-Country–Love-Church" and voluntary efforts for cooperation, renewal and political participation. In this sense unity within the TSM could be understood as an expression of national unity, a rejection of which for whatever reason would *ipso facto* have direct political implications.[44] On a very different level there were the practical concerns facing the institutional churches and the long-standing desire for a united Protestantism. Taken together, one is left with the impression that Chinese Protestants became increasingly unified in the 1950s, as much by the exigencies of the situation as by any conscious desire for ecumenical cooperation. Although separate denominational structures would be maintained at least through 1958, the necessity of Christian cooperation made them increasingly insignificant in the life of the Protestant community. Their vastly reduced profiles, combined with the creation of new union seminaries and the prominence of the Three-Self Movement as a mass organization for all Protestants, further diminished the structural importance of the denomination.

Given the lack of a viable social base for separate Protestant structures, as well as what many church leaders had observed to be a general disinterestedness in denominationalism even before 1949, the surprising thing is that the denominations lasted as long as they did. They were foreign imports and in no way intrinsic to Christian witness. Northern Chinese became Southern Baptists, Protestants in Sichuan identified themselves as Swedish Lutherans, Christians all over China were compelled to choose from among the various expressions of Protestantism which had come into existence over political and religious controversies in Europe and America since the sixteenth century. If Chinese Protestants were in some ways forced by their situation to come together after 1949, then they had also been forced into separate Protestant divisions since the nineteenth century. The scandal of this situation had been apparent for some time, but whatever had been accomplished by the various unions and associations had still left the Chinese churches largely separated from one another and divided among themselves. Chinese Protestant leaders had been saying for years that there was no justification for denominationalism in China. When the end finally came it should therefore have surprised no one.

The Unification of Worship

Relatively little can be said about the unification of worship services which came about in 1958.[45] Attendance at worship services had been on the decline for the past several years, hastened by the energies which were directed toward the Great Leap Forward and the criticism of all activity that was felt to be "unproductive." Pastors were increasingly involved in labor and other secular activities, and churches in many cities stood empty. Combined with the prevalent anti-religious propaganda, all of this put pressure on the Protestant churches to consolidate their activities. Beginning in August, independent reports on the unification of worship services were received from many cities. In Beijing sixty-five places of worship were reduced to four, one in each quarter of the city. The rest of the buildings were turned over to the government. Cheng Guanyi, Cheng Chingyi's younger sister, reported on the meetings that had decided on the unification of worship, commenting that such action was both an expression of Chinese Christians' long cherished hope for unity and a contribution to the nation as represented by the more economical use of resources.[46] It was also a practical necessity.

There were similar reports from other cities. In Shanghai, where there had previously been more than two hundred Protestant churches, unified services began on September 7 in twenty-three places of worship.[47] In Nanjing and Guangzhou four churches continued to hold services of worship, while in middle-sized cities such as Nanchang, Shenyang and Yangzhou, ten or more churches were reduced in number to one or two.[48] Although the unification process varied from place to place, the regulations which were passed in Taiyuan may have been typical of those from other cities. They were published in *Tian Feng* and are translated here in full:

On the Plans for Unification

Worship in the city of Taiyuan shall be unified with a ministerial staff of three to four. Except for the ministerial staff and fellow workers in the Three-Self office, all other church workers shall throw themselves into the socialist construction of the motherland. The physically weak and the elderly may retire. All real and movable church property and church funds shall be turned over to the Three-Self committee to be administered in common.

On the Reform of Church Organization

1. Church organization: All former church committees, governing committees and boards and all administrative organs shall cease operations. The administration of the churches shall be unified under the Three-Self Patriotic Movement committee.

2. Ritual, regulations and church order:
  a. Worship shall be unified. No church shall stress its own religious ritual.
  b. Hymns used in worship shall be unified and a hymnal committee established to undertake reform of hymn content.
  c. Examination and criticism of all books and publications used by churches in interpreting the Bible shall be undertaken. Those containing poisonous material shall be rejected without exception. Teachings which promote cooperation and which accord with socialism should be encouraged. At the same time, a critical approach shall be taken towards all material received from abroad.
  d. Negative and pessimistic doctrines such as the Last Days and the vanity of this world should no longer be stressed. Efforts should be made to bring into play the principle of the unity of faith and practice and to inspire in believers a consciousness which upholds the dignity of labor, the control of nature, a recognition of the division between ourselves and our enemies and of the distinction between right and wrong.
  e. Belief and unbelief shall not be an issue in marriage.
3. Reform in individual churches:
  a. The Little Flock shall abolish its women's meetings, its weekly breaking of the bread and its outdated rule against women preaching. Members shall no longer be required to submit to an interview before the breaking of the bread.
  b. The Salvation Army should no longer stress its military regulations.
  c. The Seventh Day Adventists shall abolish their daily morning prayers. Beneficial good works and economic production may be done on the Sabbath. The clergy shall not be supported by the tithe system in Shanxi. The unification of accounts shall be abolished and local churches shall manage themselves.
  d. YMCA secretaries shall temper themselves by taking part in productive labor or change jobs so as to effectively enter into socialist construction. The closing of the Taiyuan YMCA as a separate organization is presently under consideration.
  —The Taiyuan Christian Three-Self Patriotic Movement Committee.[49]

If these regulations are in fact typical, then it appears that the unification of worship proceeded in a heavy handed way, more by the administrative order of the local Three-Self Committee than through a process of democratic consultation characteristic of the united front. The Taiyuan plan confuses religious and political categories, and brushes aside many of the distinctive features of individual denominations that should have been safeguarded through the policy of mutual respect. The influence of leftism in the practice of the TSM is clear in these regulations, and indeed it is prominent in the whole unification process. A brief report from Wenzhou published in the same issue of *Tian Feng* put the unity question in terms of the "awakened political consciousness" of Christians who "recognize the necessity of their participation in labor." The transition to a post-denominational Christianity was, to say the least, quite abrupt. The whole unification process should have been more thoughtful and gradual, although in view of the times in which it took shape, this was hardly possible.

The political climate shaped the efforts for the unification of worship services, even though party and government officials may not have been directly involved in its implementation. In Cheng Guanyi's report from Beijing, the RAB director is specifically said to have made no recommendation about the question.[50] Likewise, when Zhao Fusan was asked whether there was government pressure on the churches for unification, he replied: "Not at all. To my knowledge no one has ever suggested that the government interferes in any way in matters of church order. There has been some movement towards unity from the top, as it were. But the main impetus has come from the congregations themselves, all over China."[51] The movement from the top refers to the efforts of the TSM. The national committee and local organizations must have been in close touch with one another, for it would be difficult to explain why the unification process took place almost simultaneously in separate cities if they were not. It is also likely that the national committee and local organizations consulted with the RAB and government officials about the process. As a mass organization the TSM would have a responsibility to do so. It would also be involved in promoting common efforts among the denominations, especially in so significant an event as the unification of worship services. The relationship between the movement from the top and the impetus from the congregations themselves probably varied from place to place, but most evidence suggests that the former took precedence.

The unification of worship may not have meant the complete elimination of denominational differences, but it did indicate the end of separate denominational structures. Visitors from the Australian Free Churches were told in 1959 that unification was a process of "dissolving denominational division without the loss of distinctive emphasis."[52] Exactly what this implied is not clear, although it seems to suggest a reaffirmation of mutual respect within the context of overall Protestant unity. Structurally speaking, the dissolution of denominational differences meant that various levels of the TSM were replacing separate denominations in matters of church order. Buildings and church properties were turned over to the local Three-Self committees to administer, and these same committees have been involved with church administration ever since. In retrospect, the radical reorganization of church life which was effected with the unification of worship was perfectly consistent with other aspects of social and political life in the late 1950s. However much it may have reflected the real needs and aspirations of Chinese Protestants, the abrupt termination of denominationalism went beyond the platform of the Three-Self Movement as it was originally conceived.

Be that as it may, the unification of worship meant that the Chinese church entered a post-denominational era in the late 1950s. Protestants joined together for worship, in churches and in their homes, and they have stayed together, through the difficult times of the Cultural Revolution era and in the restoration and renewal of Christianity since 1979. The China Christian Council is, according to its constitution, an organization designed to promote Christian unity and Three-Self. It is neither an ecclesiastical structure nor an expression of church unity so conceived. To speak of the Chinese church, therefore, is to speak of the community of Christian congregations in China, whose unity, holiness, catholicity and apostolicity are derived from the authority of the Bible, the proper preaching of the Word and the right administration of the sacraments. The unity of the Three-Self Movement does not insure the theological unity of Chinese Christians, but the ecumenical cooperation it has sought to promote must certainly be understood as a step in the right direction.

Mutual Respect

In the 1950s mutual respect became the principle for the interpretation and mediation of differences among men and women from a variety of denominational and theological backgrounds within the Three-Self Movement. It was concerned with the relationship between unity and diversity in matters of faith among Protestants who were increasingly unified as a mass organization, but for whom organic union was not yet a possibility. The principle of mutual respect was inserted into the 1954 Constitution of the TSM in order to reassure theological conservatives, but it was subsequently endorsed and promoted by the entire membership. Although apparently turned aside during the period in which worship services were unified, mutual respect remained a basic theological consideration for Chinese Protestants through most of the 1950s, and it has been strongly reaffirmed in the 1980s.

H. H. Tsui highlighted the importance of this principle in an authoritative statement made in 1955:

> The most distinctive feature of our unity is that it is based on the principle of mutual respect in matters of faith. We are all aware that although there are many different schools of theology within Christianity, our faith is yet fundamentally the same. The reason we must have mutual respect, therefore, is that among Christians, the knowledge, understanding and experience of this similarity in matters of faith varies in intensity, in depth and in emphasis. Put in another way, this means that the faith of each denomination or group preserves "small differences" within a "great unity." It is inevitable that there be differences within unity, but small differences present no obstacle to unity. The situation is similar to that of brothers and sisters (within the same family); they are fundamentally the same, but there are individual differences in ears, eyes, mouth, nose, complexion and height. These differences do not stand in the way of their relationships. Suppose everyone were completely uniform in faith from fundamentals to particulars. What need would there then be to speak of mutual respect?[53]

Tsui maintained that mutual respect did not mean the "mutual blending" or "mutual exchange" of faith and belief. Chinese theologies did not have to become unified or syncretistic. On the contrary, one of the most precious things about Christianity is the diversity of life in which "a hundred flowers bloom." Christian unity could accordingly be conceived as a symphony in which each plays his or her own part, and this symphony would suffer or become monotonous if all played in the same way.[54] Using the same analogy, a symphony had to be harmonious, for each musician could not go off to play his or her own tune. Mutual respect was designed to create the conditions for harmony within the overall unity of the Three-Self Movement.

As might be expected, there was a strong ethical component implicit in the principle of mutual respect. At the first National Christian Conference, and again in response to Wang Mingdao, K. H. Ting argued that mutual respect was primarily a question of the Christian's love and regard for others whose understanding of faith differed from his or her own.[55] He quoted Paul's words from the second chapter of the Philippians, a passage which has served as an important text for Chinese Protestants: "Do nothing from selfishness or conceit, but in humility count others better than yourselves. Let each of you look not only to his own interests, but also to the interests of others." Mutual respect is thus related to the example of Christ, whose self-giving action and unselfish servanthood should guide the faith and practice of brothers and sisters within the Christian community. As a working principle, this bears a strong similarity to T. T. Lew's well-known motto, first articulated at the 1922 meeting of the Church of Christ in China, "We should resolve to differ and agree to love."[56] The ethical emphasis is the same in both cases.

If mutual respect was an important principle for individuals within the Christian community, then it was even more important for shaping the character of a community like Nanjing Union Theological Seminary, where students and faculty from eleven independent seminaries came together to create one union seminary in September 1952.[57] Located on the campus of the old Presbyterian Girls' Bible School, the seminary opened with an enrollment of 103 students and 59 faculty members from the former institutions. The seminaries were all in East China and ranged from conservative-fundamentalist to mainline-ecumenical in theological orientation. The general principles for union were five in number:

1. Nanjing Union Theological Seminary takes the Bible, both Old and New Testaments, as the basis of faith.
2. The Common Program of the Chinese People's Political Consultative Conference is the basis of the facilities, pedagogy and life of the school.
3. Nanjing Union Theological Seminary accepts the leadership of the Preparatory Committee of the Chinese Christian Resist-America–Aid-Korea Three-Self Patriotic Reform Movement Committee.
4. Nanjing Union Theological Seminary adopts the principles of toler-

ance, mutual respect and mutual study towards different theological points of view.

5. Nanjing Union Theological Seminary believes that the special characteristics and traditions of each denomination in the church are gifts of grace given to believers by the Holy Spirit in different historical periods. Thus, there should be mutual respect for and mutual study of each church's tradition, order, organization, and ritual.[58]

The principles of the new union seminary were a clear expression of the general outlook on unity in the Three-Self Movement. It was committed to educating a new generation of leaders who would support the patriotic stance of Chinese Christians. But this did not mean the encouragement of a uniform theological viewpoint, and there was no theology of unity in the Chinese Protestantism of the 1950s. It is therefore important to note the emphasis given to mutual respect (Point 4) and respect for different theological and denominational traditions (Point 5) in the above guidelines. As a training center for future leaders of the church, the seminary became a laboratory for experimentation on unity in diversity in Chinese Christianity.

The seminary curriculum was designed to safeguard different expressions of Christian faith. There were two different tracks in bible and theology courses, one for conservatives and one for progressives, each taught by faculty members who maintained contrasting points of view. Likewise, there were different courses of instruction for the policy of the various churches and denominations, and each denomination looked after its own teachers and students at the seminary. K. H. Ting, who has been the principal of the seminary since its founding, noted in 1953 that the purpose of all this was to foster mutual respect. Evangelicals would become better evangelicals, progressives would become better progressives, and both would be enriched in the process of being with one another and participating in school life.[59] To encourage this, daily worship services were not divided, although there was ample opportunity for students to meet for worship and prayers on their own if they so desired. Moreover, decisions were made in common so that the entire faculty and student body would feel that they were part of the community and understand that the TSM was not directing everything.[60] The principle of mutual respect served as a stabilizing influence in this situation. It allowed individuals to work together on matters of common concern, but it did not infringe upon different expressions of faith.

For a new and experimental approach to diversity in unity in theological education, such a stabilizing influence was very much needed. There were many problems and misunderstandings among students and faculty in the early years of the new seminary, but this was to be expected. Never before had people from such radically different traditions come together to form a theological community in China. In the past fundamentalists and liberals would not even speak with one another, let alone worship together, sit in the same classroom or live with one another. Compelled to make decisions about the future of theological education by the exigencies of the situation, the formation of a new union seminary was a practical necessity that afforded new opportunities for understanding the nature of Christian unity.

For some churchmen it also meant a renewed emphasis on the biblical approach to unity. On the first anniversary of the founding of the seminary in 1953, Bishop T. K. Shen (Shen Zigao), one-time secretary of the Anglican House of Bishops, preached on the nature of the seminary's union from the first and third chapters of 1 Corinthians. The Corinthians of Paul's time, like the different schools that came together to form Nanjing Seminary, were divided into different parties. Bishop Shen noted three things that stood out in Paul's advice to the Corinthian church: For the sake of unity, all parties should humbly seek to learn from one another. They should also develop a perspective on the gospel in all of its variety. And they should cooperate with one another by virtue of their common faith in Jesus Christ. A diversity of perspectives has been characteristic of the history of the Christian church, and this diversity should be accepted in Chinese Protestantism. Yet amid the diversity, there is a oneness of faith, which is even more important. In order to more fully realize this oneness, Bishop Shen urges Chinese Protestants to work together toward a common witness.[61]

The principle of mutual respect did not break any new theological ground or establish a framework for church union. It was, however, founded upon recognized biblical and theological teaching on the importance of unity in diversity. Diversity was just as important as unity for the well-being of Three-Self as a Christian movement in the 1950s. The establishment of a confessional or liturgical formula for a united church would have been unnecessarily divisive, for there was no way that *all* Protestants could agree to enter into a formal ecclesiastical union. Mutual respect was in some sense a second-best option developed in order to insure the continuing relevance of diversity among Christians who joined together in the TSM.

Mutual respect never meant the absolute toleration of any beliefs that claimed to be Christian. There are always limits to what can be accepted theologically, although these were purposely vague in the TSM of the 1950s. The only evidence we have of a creed among Chinese Protestants after 1949 is the simple four-point statement of faith that students entering Nanjing Seminary had to subscribe to. Although not all Christians would agree that this was a *sufficient* expression of Christian faith, very few would doubt that each article was *necessary* for Protestant belief. The statement reads:

1. All scripture is inspired by God. It includes everything necessary for salvation and (is) the basis of the Christian's faith and the standard of conduct.

2. The one God is the creator of all things and the Father of humankind, full of justice and love.

3. Jesus Christ is the Son of God who became flesh and was crucified in order to save humanity, who rose from the dead to become head of the Church and savior of the whole world.

4. The Holy Spirit is the third person of the Trinity, the source of regeneration and sanctification, and in the Church, gives believers every kind of grace.[62]

This simple statement contains the basic elements of historic, trinitarian faith. The creed was only used at the seminary in Nanjing, and its wording allowed wide latitude for diverse interpretations.

For most Christians the question of the acceptable limits of theological diversity did not pose a serious problem to relationships within the Three-Self Movement. However, the central issue for Protestants who rejected the TSM from the right was the validity of diversity in the first place. By stressing the marks of a "true" church and the limits of "correct" doctrine, they were narrowing the possibility of differences in matters of belief. The same was true of the Christian leftists, although their standards were more explicitly political in nature. Sectarian Protestants of the right and the left rejected the principle of mutual respect because they did not believe that theological diversity was important for Chinese Christianity. In so doing they not only undermined the possibility of a common Christian witness in the PRC, but they weakened the prospects for ecumenical unity as well.

Those who reject the principle of mutual respect could argue that there is no *absolute* mandate for this position in the Bible, and they would be correct. On one level mutual respect may be understood as the ecumenical counterpart of "seeking the common ground while reserving differences," with the accent firmly on the differences. Its adoption as a principle of the TSM was as much a function of the movement's practical needs as it was a product of wrestling with the message of the Bible. The question is whether this was very different from the experience of Christians in other times and places. The Three-Self Movement had a different purpose from other movements for union and ecumenism, but does the fact that the principle of mutual respect could never have been derived *sola scriptura* invalidate its significance? Clearly the answer to this question must be no.

In his seminal study of unity and diversity in the New Testament, James Dunn concludes,

> There never was such a unity which could truly claim to be rooted in the New Testament; the unity of the great Church in earlier centuries owed more to sociological factors than to theological insights and could be justified theologically only by ignoring or suppressing alternative but equally valid expressions of Christianity.[63]

The same could be said of the adoption of the principle of mutual respect in the TSM. As a principle it was no more or less valid than contextually conditioned ecumenical formulae from other times and places. The more basic consideration, however, was its power to generate new forms of ecumenical cooperation. For any Christian movement this power depends on an understanding which comes from the mind of Jesus Christ.

Dunn concedes that there is no single normative form of first-century Christianity, but he also speaks of the "integrating center" for diverse expressions of Christianity in "the unity between the historical Jesus and the exalted Christ."[64] It is a continual challenge for any Christian community to express this unity in its faith and work, even though, using this yardstick, all movements seem to fall short. To the extent that mutual respect has been more than a principle, it may serve as one way of moving toward the "integrating center" of Protestant faith in the Chinese experience.

Ecumenical Relations

With the departure of Protestant and Catholic missionaries from China in the early 1950s, all visible expressions of international ecumenical relations with Chinese Christians were effectively brought to a close.[65] The renewal of those relationships has been bracketed by considerations of a political nature which are part of a complex international picture ever since.

The unity of Christian faith and fellowship is a gift of God's grace which extends beyond national boundaries. It does not depend on regularized channels of ecumenical exchange, nor is it limited by human barriers which have been set up between ideologies, nations and churches. However, such barriers do impede the full realization of the unity which we already share, and ecumenical communication is needed for the task of healing the divisions that we have created among ourselves. There is no clearer example of this than that of ecumenical relationships with Chinese Christians during the 1950s.

The renewal of ecumenical relationships with the Chinese Protestants was frustrated by the politics of the Cold War, which created divisions and misunderstandings on all sides. Although some Western Christians, including a few former missionaries, tried to maintain contacts with Chinese Christians through the TSM, the overwhelming majority adopted a skeptical or even anti-Communist view of the Chinese situation. This helped to isolate the Chinese church from the world community. For their part, Chinese Christians responded with repeated charges that American imperialism was exploiting Christianity through the missionary and ecumenical movements.[66] Moreover, in seeking to shed their foreign image and identify themselves with the Chinese revolution, they considered ecumenical ties to be highly problematic, and not at all desirable. For Westerner and Chinese alike, therefore, there were difficulties in confronting the ecumenical situation facing the churches. Some of these were beyond the power of churches to influence, let alone control, but others were of their own making.

As with so many other aspects of their experience in the 1950s, the Korean War was critical for the international relationships of Chinese Christians. It created fears and tensions in all corners of the globe, and in China it shaped the context for the departure of missionaries, the denunciation movement and the rising tide of patriotism. The Korean War was also the occasion for the severing of relationships between Chinese Christians and the World Council of Churches, a division that to this day has not been fully healed.

Delegations from several Chinese denominations were present at the Amsterdam Assembly of the WCC in 1948, where T. C. Chao was elected as one of its first presidents. Chao was widely known and respected in the West as a creative theologian, and his election symbolized what many thought to be an emerging sense of unity and mutuality between the "younger" and "older" churches. His resignation from the World Council three years later was regarded as a tragic loss, because it meant that Chinese Christians would no longer take an active part in ecumenical organizations, and that therefore the unity of the fellowship had been broken.

At the time of Chao's resignation Christians from the West generally assumed that the situation in China had forced the Chinese churches to withdraw from the ecumenical movement.[67] This interpretation is true as far as it goes, but only if it is recognized that the Chinese decision was related to questions posed to the churches in East *and* West by the Cold War and the Korean conflict. Just as Chinese Christians supported their government in the Korean War, so Christians from the United States tended to support theirs. The issue for the World Council was not which government to support, but how to develop a Christian response to the situation as an ecumenical fellowship representing member churches.[68]

Less than a month after the outbreak of the Korean War the Central Committee of the WCC gave its answer in a statement on "The Korean Situation and World Order," which was approved at its regularly scheduled meeting in Toronto. The statement took a strong stand in favor of the United States'–sponsored U.N. "police action" in Korea, urging member nations to support the United Nations "for its prompt decision to meet this aggression and for authorizing a police measure" in response to the North Korean attack. The statement then characterized the world situation in the following way:

> Post-war totalitarianism relies not only on military pressures but also on a policy of exploiting the distress of the poor, the resentments of subject people, discrimination on grounds of race, religion or national origin, the chaos of badly governed nations, and the general disunity between nations. The Korean attack may well be one of a possible series of thrusts at such weak points in world society. Since the world is still filled with these injustices and disorders, a mood of complacency is both wrong and politically dangerous. Overcoming these evils is therefore the most important means for rendering the world morally impregnable to totalitarian infiltration.[69]

If Korea was a testing ground in the ideological conflict between communism and liberal democracy, then the World Council had decided whose side it was on. In terms of both its tone and content, the political posture of this statement put the WCC into the Western camp in the emerging Cold War. The influence if not the hand of John Foster Dulles is clearly visible in the paragraph just cited. The implication is that a worldwide Communist movement would take advantage of situations of social injustice, and that this challenge had to be met with force, presumably under the leadership of the United States and its allies. In a few short sentences the post-war situation in Europe was seemingly linked to the aspirations of peoples in the Third World.

Chinese Christians could not support the statement because it did not reflect their views on the questions of peace and justice involved. T. C. Chao resigned from the presidency of the WCC in April 1951 in response to the action of the Central Committee on the Korean situation. In retrospect, it should not be too difficult to understand why he would conclude "that the World Council of Churches had fallen into being used as a tool of American imperialism."[70]

Although the United States' policy of containment and the rivalry between the United States and the USSR were underlying causes of the Korean War, it is not necessary to accept the Chinese government's contention that the police action was *solely* an instrument of American power politics in the Far East. Nor need we endorse the Chinese charges, supported by Chinese Protestants, that the United States used germ warfare in Korea.[71]

International politics are rarely reducible to clear-cut questions of right and wrong. In light of all the uncertainties and political implications of the Korean conflict, the World Council should not have passed the statement that it did. Josef Hromadka was correct when he said that the Central Committee could have and should have adopted "a stand of critical non-commitment" urging a peaceful resolution of the conflict. As it turned out, the WCC remained an object of deep mistrust on the part of Chinese Christians throughout the 1950s. After visiting with Chinese Christians, Hromadka observed,

> The Chinese brothers are still unable to understand (and I agree with them on this point) how the Central Committee could have arrived at such an unfortunate decision, pulling the World Council of Churches into one of the warring camps. The authority and purity of the church community is passing through a difficult test precisely at these moments of fateful decisions. The World Council of Churches in Toronto, 1950, lost much of its moral prestige, and has put a load upon itself for a long time. All who know the details and documents of the Korean question before June, 1950, and since, are aware of the fact that all reasons of "international morality and justice" used to justify the Korean "police action" were only the facade needed to camouflage the struggle for power in Asia. The Chinese brothers are waiting—although with a certain amount of skepticism—for the Central Committee to revise its resolution.[72]

It should be added that the resolution was never revised, and that this has been a contributing factor in the decision of Chinese Christians to remain aloof from the WCC. Throughout the 1950s Chinese Christians asked whether the W in the WCC stood for "World" or "Western." When it was pointed out that Christians from the Soviet Union and Eastern Europe were playing an active role in the World Council, the Chinese responded that the comparison was unfair because of China's semi-colonial missionary past. Christians from the USSR did not face a possible return of Western missionaries, it was argued, whereas Christians from China did.[73] Today Christians from the Third World have a much stronger voice in the World Council of Churches than they did in the 1950s, and it is doubtful that a resolution similar to the one on Korea could be approved. Yet the WCC faces a continuing dilemma as to how it may be both a world body, representing member churches, and a Christian fellowship committed to making statements on controversial questions facing the world. In this regard the experience with Chinese Christians over the Korean question is still relevant.

After the Korean War ended, it was not until 1956 that Chinese Protestants again began to explore the possibilities of renewing international ecumenical contacts, largely through channels other than the WCC. There had been a few foreign Christian visitors to China before that year—the Endicotts and Hewlett Johnsons had made highly publicized visits in 1952—but it was not until the Second Plenum of the TSM Committee that a broader spectrum of Christian visitors began to be invited to China as official visitors. In 1956 there were visits from J. L. Hromadka and Bishop Janos Peter from Eastern Europe; G. Nystrom, a former Swedish missionary in China; Bishop Rajah Manikam of India, who went to China representing the WCC; Bishop and Mrs. R. O. Hall from Hong Kong; a delegation of Australian Anglicans; as well as return visits from the Endicotts and Johnsons. Besides meeting with Chinese church leaders, the visitors also met with government officials, including Premier Zhou Enlai, and toured the country. Most of them later published reports noting the social and economic progress which China had made in a few short years and sharing their impressions of church life in China.[74]

Also in 1956 the TSM sent several individuals abroad. K. H. Ting and his wife Kuo Siu-may (Guo Xiumei) attended the Lambeth Preparatory Conference, and Ting attended a meeting of the WCC Central Committee prior to a visit to Hungarian churches. Together with Huang Peiyong and Zhao Fusan, Ting and Kuo were also present at a 1956 meeting of the World Student Christian Federation in Tutsing.[75] All four were members of an International Affairs Committee that had been set up by the TSM under the leadership of Tu Yuqing.[76]

The very fact that such a committee had been set up made 1956 an important year for the exploration of renewed ecumenical contacts. The reasons behind this initiative included an improved international situation and the participation of Chinese Protestants in the Eastern Bloc's movement for world peace. At the Second Plenum, where the decision was made to explore the possibility of renewed international contacts, Phoebe Shi (Shi Ruzhang) declared,

Chinese Christians, like Christians in other nations, live in the real world, and changes in the international situation have a close influence on our life and work. The distinguishing feature of the international situation at present is this: the tense situation has eased and the power and influence of peace has spread, but the American military clique has no plans to abandon the Cold War, quite the opposite, preparation and provocation for war continue. Because of this, the peoples of the world must continue to work together for world peace. We feel that Christians of the world must have a clear stand and a positive attitude on the peace issue, because we preach the gospel of redemption which is also the gospel of peace. Jesus Christ is our savior. He is also the Lord of Peace. Through Him, God allows people to abandon their enmity and return to harmony. Thus, Christians must work to safeguard world peace.[77]

This statement indicates that Chinese Protestants had a very different perspective on international relationships from that which prevailed in the ecumenical movement. Because of their emphasis on "Love-Country–Love-Church," Chinese Christians approached international questions both as Chinese who were concerned with their nation's position in world affairs, and as Christians who recognized that they were part of a fellowship that extended beyond national boundaries. World peace was a central concern on both counts, but this is precisely where the problem lay. In Shi's statement world peace meant the pursuit of China's international interests. But the theological understanding of peace can never be defined as an extension of one nation's policy. If the WCC statement on Korea was one example of how the Cold War affected ecumenical relationships, then the peace efforts of Chinese Protestants was another. In other words, the international activities of Chinese Protestants in the 1950s seem to have been more a function of their patriotic stance than of a genuine concern for ecumenical relationships. This may be one aspect of the international character of religion within the united front, but it also hinders international Christian fellowship within the ecumenical community.

Internationally the most important political factor affecting ecumenical relationships with Chinese Protestants in the 1950s and 1960s was the enforced isolation of the People's Republic of China from the family of nations. The extremely limited nature of contacts between almost one-fourth of the world's population and the rest of the world could not but serve to increase misunderstandings and international tensions. This isolation only increased after the Sino-Soviet split and the onset of the Cultural Revolution, despite China's repeated overtures to other nations in the Third World. All during this time a central issue was the place of the PRC in the United Nations. The denial of China's rightful seat in that body was due to the strong position of the United States in favor of the Nationalist government on Taiwan. This position was increasingly challenged in the 1960s, as United States foreign policy was being tested in Vietnam where the role of China was also an issue.

It is unfortunate that the WCC did not address the question of China's place in the United Nations in the 1950s. "Not a word of critcism has been said about the support of Chiang Kai-shek's rule of Taiwan, about the morally and politically absurd support Chiang Kai-shek's regime is receiving in its actions against the Chinese mainland," Hromadka charged in 1956.[78] Some action of the WCC on this issue might have demonstrated to the Chinese that they were included in the prophetic witness of the World Council. However, it was not until 1960 that the WCC even spoke to the question of China's international political situation, and even then, it was initially done in the most equivocal fashion.[79]

In the United States the National Council of Churches was more prompt and forthright in calling for the recognition of the PRC. At the 1958 meeting of the Governing Board, and repeatedly since that time, the NCCUSA called for the seating of China at the United Nations and the recognition of the People's Republic by the United States. The 1958 NCC message to the churches noted:

> The exclusion of the effective government on the mainland of China, currently the People's Republic of China, from the international community is in many ways a disadvantage to (the international) community. It helps to preserve a false image of the United States and of other nations in the minds of the Chinese people. It keeps our people in ignorance of what is taking place in China. It hampers negotiations for disarmament. It limits the functioning of international organizations. We have a strong hope that the resumption of relationships between the peoples of China and of the United States may make possible also a restoration of relationships between their churches and ours.[80]

While this message did not reflect the opinions of all or even most American Christians, Robert Smylie is correct when he suggests that it was perhaps the first statement of a major American social organization to call for a new China policy.[81] It did not result in the immediate recognition of the PRC, but along with subsequent statements of the NCCUSA and member churches, it helped to promote a changed atmosphere.

The restoration of more normal ecumenical relationships with Chinese Christians was also hampered by China's turbulent domestic politics, especially after the beginning of the Anti-Rightist campaign. The flurry of visitations in 1956 was not repeated in subsequent years, and contacts with Chinese Christians became increasingly limited. The one significant exception was the presence of K. H. Ting, Zhao Fusan and Li Shoubao at the First All-Christian Peace Assembly in 1961, where many of the issues dividing the People's Republic of China from the rest of the world were again brought to the surface.[82]

As the 1960s wore on, the influence of ultra-leftism effectively prevented the further development of ecumenical relationships. This influence is evident in a number of essays written by Chinese Christians themselves. Y. T. Wu's "The 'New Strategy' of the American Imperialist 'Missionary Enterprise,' " which appeared in *People's Daily* in 1962, seemed to reject almost any form of international ecumenical cooperation. [83] With the outbreak of the Cultural Revolution the door on international ecumenical relationships was banged shut. It would not be opened again until the domestic and international situation of China had begun to change, so that Chinese Christians could take the initiative in expressing their ecumenical unity with Christians from around the world.

Selfhood and Unity in the 1980s

Chinese Christians emerged from the Cultural Revolution era deeply wounded, but with their selfhood intact. The home worship gatherings, which grew up in China during those difficult years, were all self-governing, self-supporting and self-propagating Christian communities. The restoration of the Three-Self Movement, the reopening of churches in towns and cities and the establishment of the China Christian Council served to reaffirm the Three-Self principle, which Chinese Protestants have upheld since the early 1950s. In public statements and in private conversations, in churches open for public worship and in home worship gatherings, one message has been repeated over and over again: The Chinese church is, by the grace of God, alive and growing. It has moved toward self-government, self-support and self-propagation, so that Protestant Christianity has at last become a Chinese religion.

The selfhood of the Chinese church has been received as both a gift and a task. It is only by the grace of God that Christians were sustained individually and in home worship gatherings during the Cultural Revolution era, and it is by God's grace that the institutional church has undergone a process of restoration since that time. Chinese Christians realize that they cannot take God's grace as their own possession, lest they become a community closed off from the rest of society. Thus the gift of selfhood in the life of the Chinese church means much more than what has happened in the experience of the Chinese Protestant community. It also extends to what God has done through the Chinese revolution in which they too have had a share. According to K. H. Ting, Chinese Christians have discovered,

the immanence of the transcendent God in history, in nature, in the people's movements and in the collectivities in which we find ourselves. After all, the God who is worthy of our worship and praise is not so small as to be concerned only with a few million Chinese who profess to believe in him. God's love and care is for the whole of humanity and the whole of the Chinese people. He does not mind terribly much if many, for good reasons, do not recognize his existence. We know to believe that God is loving and at the same time almighty is difficult anyway, if one is serious about one's belief. But I think liberation in China, with all the material and cultural elevation it has brought to our people, does make it more possible for our people to ponder such a God. We hope we are able to be an instrument for introducing this God to our people. [84]

To serve as such an instrument means that Three-Self must also be regarded as a task. Since 1979 Chinese Christians have been trying to transform self-run churches into well-run churches.[85] The major task of the TSM and the CCC was the work of rebuilding, restoration and reconstruction in the period between the Third National Christian Conference (1980) and the Fourth National Christian Conference (1986). Since that time the emphasis on rebuilding the Christian community has shifted to an emphasis on building-up the Body of Christ.[86] The energy with which Christian leaders and laypeople proceeded with such varied efforts as the reopening of churches, the writing of a new hymnal and theological training in the early 1980s testifies to the seriousness with which they approached the many problems that the church still faces. Now, with the work of rebuilding basically completed, attention has focused on the quality of church support, Christian outreach and church order.

Self-support was the most urgent question facing Chinese Christians in the early 1950s, but it is no longer so today.

> Among the three "wells" it should be noted that "supporting well" is the least difficult, since churches in China operate on small budgets. Also a number of the present clergy live on pensions they are already receiving from previous work units. Their retirement benefits include medical care and other insurance. They serve the Lord with commitment, some entirely on a voluntary basis and some with only minimum stipends. But this situation will change as the number of newer, younger clergy increases in the future. We must realize that Christians in present day China love their church very much. With the national economy improving, people give generously to the church, and this has helped to meet the financial needs of the churches. Of course there are churches in the rural areas that still face some difficulties in self-support. With gradual improvement in the countryside, they too will solve their problems eventually. As long as the church is able to nurture the spiritual life of the congregation and minister to the needs of the people, the church in China will not only be able to support itself, but to do it well.[87]

Most Chinese Christian communities are today basically self-supporting and financially independent. The TSM has no desire to solicit material contributions from abroad, although local churches and the China Christian Council agree to accept "certain contributions from friendly church groups and persons overseas with no strings attached and with due respect for the independent stance of our Church, simply as an expression of the universality of our Christian fellowship."[88] This means that the TSM has not closed the door on *all* contributions from Christians overseas, but that they will basically depend upon their own material resources.

The principle of self-support has been a sound one, and although there were difficulties with its implementation in the 1950s, the Chinese Christian leadership views that experience in a positive light. Today the Chinese Protestant community is one of very few major Christian groups in the Third World whose mission and material well-being does not depend on the beneficence of Christians from Western Europe and North America. This is no small achievement for a small church in a poor country.

The major problem with self-support is not the adequacy of existing resources but their distribution. This problem in turn revolves around the relationship—or contradiction—between the city and the countryside. We have seen that churches in the Chinese countryside have historically had greater financial needs than those in the cities. Today there are still rural Christians who are without churches in which to worship, trained pastors to guide them or an adequate supply of Bibles. Given the current economic program, it is likely that the disparity between the city and the countryside will increase rather than decrease in the years ahead, although there is also likely to be greater prosperity for all sectors of society.

In response to the economic reforms some churches have begun to run their own enterprises and shops. In the report cited above, Sun Xipei includes a word of caution about such enterprises because of their implications for the role of the church in society. The distribution issue itself raises all sorts of similar questions. How should the Three-Self Movement and the China Christian Council respond to the inequities in levels of self-support in churches around China? Should self-support be understood congregationally or on a church-wide basis (2 Cor. 8-9)? Should a supplementary assistance fund be set up similar to the one that was established in 1957? Is the availablity of material contributions from overseas a temptation for Chinese Christians to forsake what they have been struggling for? We may expect that Chinese Christians will seek answers to these questions in ways that will be instructive for the Christian community the world over.

Self-propagation and propagating-well are questions which concern the overall development of Chinese Christianity in the future. Chinese Protestant leaders have said repeatedly over the past several years that the task of self-propagation and evangelism is the responsibility of the Chinese church.[89] This task is being carried out through the printing and distribution of the Bible, publications work, the training of new leadership and the witness of Christian model workers, but a great deal remains to be done, especially for Christians in rural areas.

The rural church was the major subject on the agenda of a joint meeting of the CCC and TSM Committee in August 1987 in Chengdu. At this meeting the delegates passed a resolution on rural church work which identified six particular tasks:

    1. Acceleration of the nurture of rural church workers and volunteers by organizing, in addition to the existing short-term training programs, specialized theological education programs and Bible schools in provinces, cities and autonomous regions which are able to do so;

    2. Publication of reading materials suitable for Christians in rural areas;

3. Continuing assistance to the government in the implementation of religious policy in order to establish churches and meeting points in ways which are beneficial to production and convenient for daily life so that all rural Christians can worship and gather together in an appropriate way;

4. Set up Three-Self and church affairs organizations in county churches where possible, with management committees and leaders responsible for churches and meeting points;

5. Raise the ability of rural Christians to resist heterodox teachings, illegal activities and infiltration from overseas, by strengthening their nurture according to the true teachings of the Bible, and promoting education about three-self patriotism and religious policy;

6. Christian Councils and Three-Self Committees at the provincial, city and autonomous region levels should do their best to organize visits to assist in rural church work in areas which are especially short of pastors.[90]

In China, churches in rural areas have traditionally been the fastest growing but the most understaffed. In the West they have also been the least understood. Scattered reports from observers with inadequate understanding of the Chinese countryside have not enabled us to develop a realistic picture of the life and faith of rural Christians.* The six areas of concern outlined above reveal some of the problems facing churches in rural areas. However, it is difficult to say more about the extent of these problems, or how they are being dealt with.

One problem which continues to pose particular difficulties to Chinese Christians is the efforts of well-financed evangelistic organizations from overseas that have been involved in "bible smuggling" and other clandestine activities. Not only is such activity forbidden by the Chinese constitution, but it goes against everything that the TSM has been struggling to achieve. Any unilateral effort on the part of Christians overseas to organize activities inside China without the cooperation of the Chinese Protestant leadership therefore represents a challenge to a church which has only recently emerged from the shattering experience of the Cultural Revolution. With little understanding of China's social and political context, overseas groups, including those based in Hong Kong, acting on their own initiative can also do great harm to the Chinese Protestant community.[91]

For Christianity to again become identified as a "foreign religion" acting outside the law and dependent on the initiative of Christians overseas would be

---

*In this regard, the reporting of Deng Zhaoming stands out as the exception. His stories and accounts of Christians in rural areas on the pages of *Bridge* magazine have provided a consistent, balanced and generally well-informed source of information on church life in China today. Although there may be disagreements over his interpretation, we are all indebted to him for his labors.

tragic. Protestant leaders have therefore called attention to Paul's words, "My ambition is to preach the gospel not where Christ has already been named, lest I build on another man's foundation" (Rom. 15:20) as an illustration of the apostle's respect for the selfhood of other churches.[92] In an age of mutuality in mission and interdependence, many churches would have little difficulty in accepting such a position. The challenge for those who do not is to do nothing in the absence of the call from Macedonia.

The activities of groups from overseas may also exacerbate the sectarianism of Christians in the countryside. Chinese Christians in rural areas are hampered by isolation, inadequate education and insufficient leadership. For more than a century sectarian religious groups have been emerging in the Chinese countryside. In the eyes of the government this is a problem of "feudal superstition," which carries political implications for the entire community. There are many local officials who still see it as a problem that must be met with coercion. From a Christian viewpoint, sectarian heterodoxy that deviates from normal standards of Christian belief is more of a theological concern. It is one which involves self-propagation and an understanding of the historical tenets of Trinitarian faith.

In recent years there have been a number of widely reported sectarian challenges to the selfhood and unity of the church in China. The most notable of these was the "yeller movement," an apparently unorthodox form of pentecostalism, which has spread in the rural areas of Zhejiang, Fujian and Henan. Inspired by the writings of Witness Li (Li Changshou), a former follower of Watchman Nee, who now resides in California, the yellers are said to believe that a new age of the Spirit is ushered in through shouting the name of the Lord at ecstatic worship gatherings. This releases the Spirit and allows the Christian to do just about anything that will enhance his or her "sense of life." Although very little is known about the yellers beyond the Chinese countryside, the TSM was sufficiently alarmed by this phenomenon to issue a forty-page refutation of their beliefs and practices.[93] Local Christian leaders have also tried to integrate former yellers into the broader Christian community.[94]

There have been other cases of sectarian challenges to Christian unity in China. One group from Western China sought to exclude all parts of the Bible except the four gospels, while another group wished to combine Christian and Daoist teachings. It is not known how many similar groups exist. Sectarianism of this sort will always represent a potential danger to the churches of China, and in all likelihood, it will be around for many years to come.

Although the problems faced by churches in the countryside may be more serious, some of the same problems are also confronting Christians in urban areas. In towns and cities, however, self-propagation has been strengthened through the continuing witness of Christian model workers. Conversations with Christian leaders in China suggest that the number of Chinese Christians who have been selected by their peers as models is out of all proportion to their representation in society as a whole. More than forty model workers were recognized at the Fourth National Christian Conference as outstanding lay leaders, and their individual testimonies make inspiring reading.[95] The witness of such individuals shows that self-propagation is taking place on many different levels.

Propagating-well involves the broader question of the nature and purpose of Christian witness and evangelism. It is a question to which we shall return in the next chapter. Here it should be noted that the experience of the 1950s is relevant both in terms of the witness of Christian model workers and the theological fermentation at the grass roots. To what extent should the experience of the 1950s be reappropriated for the 1980s? How can a local Christian leadership be trained to deal with sectarian challenges patiently and with wisdom? What will be the positive content of self-propagation in the future? Can a minority Christian community challenge and affirm the Chinese socialist experience without becoming either irrelevant or syncretistic? These are some of the important questions which Chinese Christian leaders will have to ponder as they deepen their understanding of selfhood for the church of tomorrow.

Self-government and governing-well, theologically understood, are concerned with questions of church unity and church order. Since 1979 Chinese Protestant leaders have stressed again and again that the Protestant community in China is more united now than it has ever been before. This is a unity which has been achieved without either a clear confessional basis or a strong liturgical center. Unity does not mean uniformity in the practice of Chinese Protestantism, for there are still historical and theological differences that separate Chinese Christian communities from one another. These differences are not as sharp as they once were, nor are they reinforced by separate denominational structures. The Cultural Revolution experience helped to bring Christians together, reinforcing their common faith and strengthening their sense of identification with the rest of the Chinese people at the same time.

The renewal of more institutionalized forms of church life has also meant a renewed interest in denominations among some Christians. Seventh Day Adventists no longer insist on being called Adventists, but they do meet for worship on Saturdays. Former Baptists continue with their practice of baptism by immersion, and indigenous church groups continue to worship in their own way. While such diversity is a good thing, it may also result in the consolidation of differences in particular communities. This may be behind the warning against revived denominationalism in a 1987 resolution on Christian unity.[96]

Unlike efforts toward Christian unity in other parts of the world, Christian unity in China was not achieved through a lengthy process of planning and theological discussion. Beginning in 1951 it took place almost all at once, primarily as a result of the practical and concrete needs of the churches. A theological articulation of Christian unity was not desirable in the beginning, because any theological controversy would have been divisive. But if church history is any guide, then there will come a time when Christian unity in China will have to be interpreted more clearly. The recent publication of a short Christian catechism may indicate that the time has already come.[97] There will be a need to determine what can and cannot be subject to mutual respect and still be called Christian, a need to develop a clearer understanding of the tolerable limits of Christian diversity. The point is not to argue for a rigidly defined confessional orthodoxy—that would seem to go against the grain of the Chinese Christian experience up to this point—but to articulate a theological and ecclesiological center for Christian unity in China.

The parallel between the Chinese Protestant experience and Anglican comprehensiveness has been suggested at several points in this book. Bearing in mind the fundamental differences between the British situation and united front oriented Marxism-Leninism, we have observed that the Anglican practice of church-state relations is also similar to the patriotic emphasis in Chinese Protestantism. In the Three-Self Movement there is an interpenetration between religious and political realms combined with a wide tolerance for diverse expressions of Christian beliefs. The Anglican idea of comprehension seems to suggest a pattern of "unity without uniformity" that would be helpful for Chinese Christians struggling with the question of unity. Such an understanding entails a broadly unifying theological vision "based not on the *compromise* of 'consensus theologies' but on the *comprehensiveness* of a theological thinking in which truth is ever coming to be in a dialectical way."[98] In this light the following definition of comprehensiveness, proposed at Lambeth in 1968, bears repeating:

Comprehensiveness demands agreement on fundamentals, while tolerating disagreement on matters in which Christians may differ without feeling the necessity of breaking communion. In the mind of an Anglican, comprehensiveness is not compromise. Nor is it to bargain one truth for another. It is not a sophisticated word for syncretism. Rather it implies that the apprehension of truth is a growing thing: we only gradually succeed in "knowing the truth." It has been the tradition of Anglicanism to contain within one body both Protestant and Catholic elements. But there is a continuing search for the whole truth in which these elements will find complete reconciliation. Comprehensiveness implies a willingness to allow liberty of interpretation, with a certain slowness in arresting or restraining exploratory thinking. We tend to applaud the wisdom of the rabbi Gamaliel's dictum that if a thing is not of God it will not last very long (Acts 5:38–9). Moreover, we are alarmed by the sad experience of condemnation in the past (as in the case of Galileo). For we believe that in leading us into all the truth the Holy Spirit may have some surprises in store for us in the future as he has had in the past. "The only authority in the Catholic Church which can ultimately preserve the truth is the power of the Holy Ghost to guide theologians in the end to a true understanding of the faith."[99]

In the Anglican tradition comprehensiveness is grounded upon a strong ecclesiology, adherence to the "Thirty-nine Articles," the authority of the bishop and the centrality of the liturgy. A Chinese Protestant ecclesiology would not be Anglican, and so it would not have to contain all of these elements. But it seems that it would have to be grounded upon a strong and theologically well-educated leadership. Initially this might involve the consecration of bishops, who would be the visible expressions of Christian unity. Chinese Protestants are well aware of the problem of future leadership, and they recognize the difficulties of moving from a post-denominational Protestantism to a united church. How will they then proceed?

The CCC and the TSM committee passed a "Resolution on the Promotion of Self-Government Through the Formulation of a System of Church Order" in August 1987.[100] This resolution called upon local and provincial Christian councils and Three-Self committees to formulate guidelines for church order, and it also established a committee headed by Peter Cai and composed of eight men and women representing different ecclesiastical traditions to draft a plan for a united church. A future united church would embrace elements of various Protestant traditions, including the historic episcopacy, although bishops would not be diocesan or administrative.

Although consideration of such a plan had begun as early as 1985, the proposal has met with resistance, according to conversations with Protestant leaders. Some Chinese Christians object to the idea of an ordained clergy, let alone bishops. The ecclesiology of other Protestants would prevent them from entering into any church union. How will such objections be handled in the movement toward a united church? Can the principle of mutual respect become a means for allowing a Chinese "free church" tradition? A comprehensive understanding of a self-governing Christian church of China will require great patience and sensitivity to questions of church order. Chinese Christians will have to learn from the experience of other churches in other times, but they will have to break new ground in discovering the meaning of Christian unity in a Chinese setting.

Developments toward church unity in China will also have significance for Christians in other parts of the world. Over the last nine years there have been more church visits and exchanges with Chinese Protestants than there were in the previous thirty. Relationships have been established between the China Christian Council and church organizations from almost thirty countries. New contacts with Chinese Christians are in part related to changes in the international situation and open policy of the Chinese government. But they are also due to the changing perspectives of Christians in China and from other parts of the world.

In 1981 an international conference with Chinese Christians on "God's Call to a New Beginning" was held as an expression of the changes which had taken place. Sponsored by the Canada China Programme of the Canadian Council of Churches, the conference brought together a delegation of Chinese Protestants and Catholics to meet with Christians from other parts of the world and to discuss matters of common concern in light of the Chinese experience. The major impact of this conference was in developing understanding and goodwill between Christians in China and overseas—a significant achievement in its own right. Since 1981 other meetings have been held with Chinese Christians, including a conference on ecumenical sharing sponsored by the NCCUSA and a separate conference organized by the Baptist World Alliance, both in Nanjing in 1986.[101]

Chinese Protestants have expressed an increasing interest in bilateral relationships with both ecumenical and evangelical Christians from overseas. Their principle in establishing such relationships is one of "differentiation." Groups which are willing to relate to the China Christian Council on the basis of mutual respect, equality and friendship are welcomed, while those which remain hostile are either excluded, or they exclude themselves.[102] In practice this means that a distinction is drawn between Christians from overseas who recognize the authority of the China Christian Council to speak for Chinese Christians and those who do not.

Although they participate in the World Conference on Religion and Peace, Chinese Protestants have not made any effort to join either the Christian Conference of Asia or the World Council of Churches. There are several reasons for this. Although the WCC and Chinese Protestants have come a long way since the 1950s, a structural relationship would be open to criticism in China by those who continue to oppose the WCC on either political or theological grounds. It must also be remembered that Chinese Protestants have a great deal to attend to at home, leaving them little time and few people to participate in international gatherings. For the time being, therefore, it appears unlikely that the China Christian Council will pursue international ecumenical relationships very far.

Since 1985 the Amity Foundation has also promoted ecumenical relationships through a variety of education, health and social projects in China. Amity is an independent people's organization, initiated by Chinese Christians in order to contribute to China's socialist modernization; make Christian involvement in society more widely known to the Chinese people; and serve as a channel for sharing and international people-to-people relationships. Not being a church organization, Amity welcomes the participation of non-Christians in all of its work. The Foundation has invited language teachers to China from overseas church-supported sponsoring agencies; supported the upgrading of facilities at selected medical and welfare institutions; and, in cooperation with the United Bible Societies, established a printing press in Nanjing.[103]

Ecumenical relationships with Chinese Christians have developed rapidly over the last decade, often without sufficient theological reflection as to their significance. We have thus far said little of the Catholic church in China, but it too must be included in future ecumenical contacts. What prospects are there for relationships with Chinese Catholics and a rapprochement with the Vatican? How can Protestants and Catholics learn from the ecumenical experience in other parts of the world? What should be the position of Christians outside China who wish to develop a greater sense of critical solidarity with Chinese Christians? How will "Love-Country–Love-Church" shape the ecumenical stance of Chinese Protestants in the future, and what should be the Christian response from overseas? How should Christians approach opportunities for participation in educational and social service work in China? These are questions which Christians from China and other parts of the world must raise with one another as we look toward the development of deeper and more extensive relationships in the years ahead.

8

Theological Reorientation

Our experience and understanding, although fragmentary and incomplete, are yet neither chaotic nor isolated. We are in a turbulent era, a society brimming with creative power, a period of rapid historical advance, and many things are progressing by leaps and bounds. Due to the sluggishness of our faith and the cloudiness of our vision, however, our understanding frequently lags behind reality. The revelation of God shows itself in earthquake and in fire, but in our weakness, we cover our ears and hide our eyes; we dare not face it. But we can in no way escape the advance of the torrent. Our faith is merely sluggish—it has not died; our eyes are cloudy—but we have not grown blind. In the mighty streams of history we are pushed forward by an irresistible force, and from among the many shattered whirlpools and spray flying in all directions, we can discern the path of the main current. If we examine the crumbs scattered on the floor, we shall see the loving face of the Giver of Life when we have filled 12 baskets with them. Spiritual hunger urges us to grope forward, and the path we follow is but the finger of God leading us.[1]
—Chen Zemin
August 1957

The movement for theological fermentation at the grassroots which took place in Chinese Christianity during the 50s was spontaneous, not organized by anybody. But it had a very strong mass character and was extensive. Having entered the historical stage of New China, thousands upon thousands of grassroots Christians, though aroused by patriotism, did not want to give up their Christian faith lightly. But they were unable to keep intact a lot of the theological viewpoints instilled in them in the past. At a time when they were establishing their new political standpoint, they had to do some hard theological thinking themselves, so that they could not only face up to the political reality but find a viable theological position as well. This was a movement from the bottom up. At first, not too many clergymen were involved. Far more numerous were

those who found themselves on the border between church and society,
those who were drawn into the current of the times, such as Christian
workers, peasants, teachers and other intellectuals, and some of the pas-
tors at the grassroots who were close to these people.[2]

—K. H. Ting
September 1982

There has been very little theological reflection of a systematic nature in China over the last forty years. Caught up in the turbulence of change and revolution, Chinese Christians have had neither the time nor the inclination to reformulate the Christian teaching which they inherited from their Protestant forebearers. The writing of a distinctively Chinese theology still awaits its author.

This is partly due to the particular nature of the Chinese Protestant experience, which has been described in the foregoing chapters. But it is also related to the situation of the church and theology in China before 1949. It was the opinion of foreign missionary and Chinese Christian alike that the country was almost totally lacking Chinese theologians and Christian theological writings. Even T. C. Chao, who by almost everyone's account was the outstanding Christian thinker of his generation, could write in 1948,

Not many intellectual Chinese Christians think much of theology; some have no use for any theology whatever, thinking that such a thing has long been defunct. This constitutes a great weakness of the Body of Christ in China, which has thus far not produced a real theologian.[3]

This judgment notwithstanding, there had been a movement toward the development of an indigenous Chinese theology at least since the early 1920s. Beginning in response to the changes that were taking place in culture and society following the May 4th Movement, Chinese Protestant thinking became increasingly concerned with the two related issues of indigenization and national reconstruction. Christian theologians as diverse as Hsu Pao-ch'ien and T. T. Lew, T. C. Chao and Wu Lei-chuen, Y. T. Wu and Hsieh Fu-ya, addressed the question of indigenization in the 1920s in an attempt to show how Christianity could be recast in a Chinese way. Initially the arguments were designed to reformulate the Christian message in terms of China's cultural heritage in order to present intellectuals with the challenge of a Chinese Christ.[4] The problem was that Confucianism and traditional Chinese culture were themselves under attack as obstacles to the creation of a New China. It soon became evident that any theological effort that represented a purely cultural response to the intellectual and social ferment of the times would be a futile attempt to relate the Christian message to a tradition which was no longer vital. Although indigenization and national reconstruction were never completely separate issues, the emphasis had shifted by the mid-1930s as Chinese theologians came to address themselves more directly to questions of a socio-political nature.[5]

They wished to demonstrate the relevance of Christian faith to questions of social change and national reconstruction.[6] Unless Christianity could be shown to offer a social contribution to New China, then it would be regarded as of little use by the population as a whole. The church, therefore, was compelled to take positions on questions of war and aggression, democratic politics and national unity, especially after the full-scale Japanese invasion.

For Protestant theologians the social relevance of Christianity was especially important in the post-war years leading up to 1949. Yet despite the fact that the individuals involved came up with different solutions to the problems China faced, the options they selected tended to be Christianized versions of particular secular philosophies. Whether liberal or Marxist, they revealed the limitations of the various contextual theologies that were being developed in Chinese Protestantism, rather than the contribution which theology and the church could make to social reconstruction. This is the conclusion of Ng Lee-ming, who adds,

In only being able to Christianize a secular social approach, Chinese theologians were in fact admitting that no specific Christian contributions could be made in terms of concrete social action. A Christian could do or should do only what others did. This was, of course, only an admission of the fact that we were not supermen. But in the particular situation of China at that time, it amounted to an admission of failure, the failure to satisfactorily answer the question, "Why should I become a Christian?" against the background it was posed.[7]

This sobering judgment indicates one reason why a fundamental theological reorientation was necessary after 1949. The theological positions that had been taken prior to that time were simply unable to relate themselves in a creative and distinctively Christian way to the new situation. This was not simply a question of deciding upon a particular political option, although a political choice was explicit in the decision to seek the common ground. Equally important was the need to reformulate theological questions in light of a changing situation. This was to involve both a new approach to theological discussions and a different context for theological reflection. It was an approach and context, however, for which most Chinese theologians were unprepared.

There is no better example of the radical discontinuity of theological efforts in China before and after 1949 than the experience of T. C. Chao.[8] At first Chao appeared to welcome the Communists' victory. Along with many other liberal intellectuals, he was critical of the chaos and corruption of the old order, and he realized that the GMD no longer had the sympathy and support of the people. Writing to a friend shortly after the liberation of Peiping (Beijing), Chao expressed the hope that after a period of adjustment the churches would eventually be allowed to continue with their activities. For this to happen, however, Christians had to come to a new sense of awareness.

Groups of poor Christians in China are still unconsciously much too bourgeois in outlook and sentiments. They need to be thoroughly shaken to realize that a new day has dawned and that a change of ways, of life, and communication, is necessary. They need to learn, perhaps less from missionaries than from the present situation, that the task before them is one of practical and concrete demonstration that God in Christ is tremendously real. Reality is never unrelated, and therefore the task is an interpretation of the faith in relation to Marxism and Chinese culture; absorption of science and its limitations; and a theology of creative thinking and living.[9]

Chao went on to describe the challenge to Christians in the new situation. In eight points ranging from the dissociation of the "genuine gospel from historical accretions" to a program of self-support, he was suggesting many of the things which the TSM would be involved in over the next several years. He seemed to be on the right track.

In 1949 and 1950 T. C. Chao was very much involved in promoting the new order. Although he continued to express his reservations about communism, Chao was a Christian representative at the First CPPCC; he was one of the church leaders who met with Zhou Enlai in Beijing; and he was among the initiators of the "Christian Manifesto." Less than two years later, however, he came under severe criticism during the *sanfan* campaign. Students, faculty and staff at the Yenching (Yanjing) School of Religion accused Chao of promoting "cultural aggression" against China and of making a "dishonest" and inadequate confession when so confronted. Although he had resigned his presidency of the World Council of Churches in 1951, Chao was also challenged for his connections with overseas "imperialists." The final blow came with the announcement on March 17, 1952, that Chao's bishop had suspended his clerical privileges and had made a request to the Anglican House of Bishops that his Holy Orders be revoked.[10]

Although the reasons behind all of these actions against Chao remain unclear, it may be assumed that they are related to his hesitancy to fully endorse the Communist program.[11] Similar to many actions of the time, his rejection by the Anglicans and the TSM are unjustifiable from the Christian point of view. Still, Chao continued to be a leader of the Three-Self Movement, and in later writings and conversations, he defended China against charges of religious persecution which were being made by former missionaries.[12] As a leading voice in Chinese theology, however, T. C. Chao's influence was at an end.

Why was it that after initially welcoming the challenge of liberation, T. C. Chao had such difficulties in relating himself theologically to the new order? To interpret Chao's declining influence in terms of the political excesses of the times is at best only a partial explanation. It is more useful, in this regard, to consider his theological approach and the way in which it would be tested in the new situation. Although Chao published practically nothing of a theological nature after 1950, Winfried Gluer has identified two basic problems with Chao's theological perspective, both of which are related to Chao's earlier efforts at contextualization.

Gluer observes that Chao's theological anthropology was determined by a dialectic between Confucian humanism and God's saving act in Christ, a position which he had been developing since the 1920s:

> He maintains a Christian socio-political responsibility matched with the Confucian quest for unity in knowing and acting, and relates it to the demands of the historical moment in the Chinese Revolution.

This is good as far as it goes, for the emphasis on practice has been shown to be a continuing theme in Chinese thinking—Confucian, Christian and Marxist. The problem is that after 1949 Chao was unable to develop his theological position any further with the result that the dialectic of faith and practice was eventually dissolved into practice alone.[13]

Because a theology based upon Christian responsibility and Confucian humanism had no place to go, only Chao's ethics remained. Thus in 1956 he could write, "Our duty to Christ is to love men in a practical way, in practice, and again in practice." Or again, speaking in 1973, "Religion has no name in China today; it is not based on doctrine, dogmas or hypotheses, but practice."[14] Chao was evidently not aware of the home worship gatherings, which were even then emerging all over China. He also seems to have accepted all the limitations imposed by the current situation. Although it is incorrect to assume that he finally gave up his Christian faith, it is clear that Chao gave up his theology.[15] Or perhaps more correctly, he surrendered theology to his context in a way that other Chinese Christians did not.

Gluer also points out the inadequacy of Chao's personalistic concept of ethics. Throughout his writings Chao's emphasis is upon socio-political responsibility as the concern of the individual, not the church or the community. Christianity might have some role to play in the spiritual rejuvenation of society, but its major contribution was the motivation of individuals who would in some way then exert a decisive socio-political influence. As theology was reduced to an ethic of Christian practice, so the church became for Chao primarily a source for individual spiritual cultivation.[16]

Although the social and institutional role of the church has been minimized in China over the last three decades, Christian faith has not been relegated to personalistic ethics and individual spiritual cultivation. We shall see how an important arena of reorientation in the 1950s was relating Christian faith and ethics in a positive way to socialism and the struggles of the Chinese people. As Christians sought to seek the common ground while reserving differences, the church became the context for the new areas of theological inquiry that were emerging at the grass roots. Moreover, the growth and vitality of local Christian communities has meant that the church continues to exercise a powerful *communal* witness to the rest of society. It is for these reasons that Chinese

Christian leaders who have been in closer touch with Christian life at the grass roots could begin to speak of a theological reorientation in the 1950s in a way that T. C. Chao could never understand.

More than anyone else, Y. T. Wu helped to promote this reorientation by virtue of his own theological journey, his leadership of the Three-Self Movement, and his involvement in the Chinese Revolution. The theological perspective that he had begun to develop in the 1930s and 1940s remained intact, but it was broadened to include a whole new theological program. "The one great cause for the difficulties some Christians in China are facing," he wrote in 1952, "is their inability to appreciate the true meaning of God's omnipresence. They are bewildered because they refuse to see God's light which comes through unexpected channels."[17] One such channel was, for Wu, the Chinese Communist Party. This did not mean, as has so often been charged, that he identified the achievements of New China with the advent of the kingdom of God. Rather, he was striving for a fuller understanding of God's work in nature and society, confidence in human achievements as gifts of God's grace, and the realization that all good works come from God (James 1:17). He believed that communism could be the vehicle for human betterment, and that Christians could learn from people, even atheists, who did not confess the name of Jesus Christ. For Wu the important thing was commitment to the struggle for social justice and *doing* the will of God (Matt. 7:21). Christians had to be fully involved in the historical process in order to live out a life of a faith which was justified by grace, but also proven in the "test of works."[18]

Wu went very far in developing a Christian perspective on Marxism, almost to the point of advancing a synthesis between communism and Christianity. But he took the continuity between faith and society beyond the point to which other Christian thinkers were prepared to go. Wu believed that communism and Christianity were like two rooms, separated by a wall. The purpose of theology was to take down the wall so that the essential unity between the two could be discovered. Although such a perspective may pose serious questions about the adequacy of Wu's theological judgment, it does not indicate that he compromised his theological integrity. As Ng Lee Ming has demonstrated so clearly, Wu's position was not hastily arrived at, but rather was the result of an honest and existential wrestling with Christian faith in light of the situation in which he found himself.[19]

Y. T. Wu never lost faith in the basic truth of the Christian message. Writing in 1954 he expressed his view of the future of Christianity in China.

Since liberation, we frequently hear Christians saying, "Has Christianity any future?" That is a strange question to be upon the lips of Christians. What has happened to our Christian faith? Do we believe that the eternal God who made heaven and earth exists today and will not exist tomorrow? Have we forgotten that the Christ whose life was full of mercy and truth is the same yesterday, today and forever? Do we believe that the Holy Spirit who has hitherto enlightened and guided our hearts, will now suddenly stop working? Not so. The eternal Triune God does not change with the times. It is not the faithfulness of God that we need be concerned about, but our own faithfulness. If we have deeds to match our faith, if we make an effective witness for Jesus Christ, then all our anxieties will have been found to have been needless.[20]

Wu never departed from these convictions, and unlike T. C. Chao, he never surrendered theology to his context.[21]

Although Y. T. Wu helped to establish the context for theological reorientation in China, he was neither its source nor its inspiration. Because his writings were so individual and idiosyncratic, going far beyond the accepted beliefs of the average Christian or the more conservative church leaders, his theology did not attract a wide following. To speak of theological reorientation in the China of the 1950s, therefore, does not mean the inauguration of a new theological system or school directed by Y. T. Wu or anyone else. That would have gone against the principle of mutual respect which the TSM had as its basis, and it would imply a greater sense of clarity and direction than was possible for Chinese Protestants at the time. What was important in the 1950s, theologically speaking, was that ordinary Christians at the grass roots began to raise questions about how to reconcile their Christian faith with the new social reality then emerging in the PRC. This was something which took place among pastors and laypeople in churches all around China, and not only in seminaries and universities. Although the theological discussions which will be described in this chapter came to an end in the late 1950s, they are significant insofar as they foreshadow a new way of "doing" theology which continues to be practiced in China and other parts of the Third World.

A great deal has been written about the "living theology" that has emerged out of the Asian context in the last few decades. It has been described as Asian contextual theology, rooted in particular Christian situations and growing out of an encounter between faith and contemporary historical reality.[22] An issue-oriented form of reflection, "living theology" seeks to create a dialectic between the biblical message and Asian culture and society in such a way that the latter is both taken seriously in its own right and called into question by the Christian gospel. This presupposes a sense of involvement in one's historical situation as well as the necessity of critical reflection about one's involvement. The aim of "living theology" is neither the articulation of a final statement of faith nor the writing of a new theological system, but rather the discovery of the meaning of faith in particular situations of suffering and struggle.

Chinese theology has never been cited as a forerunner of this type of reflection, but the theological fermentation that began to take place in the 1950s was also a type of "living theology." At the time it went practically unnoticed among Western theologians.[23] This was in part because of the isolation of Chinese Christians, in part because of the nature of the questions being considered, and in part because it represented a radically different understanding of the theological enterprise. In order to reclaim and understand the importance of the

Chinese "living theology" of the 1950s, it is its context and orientation which must first claim our attention.

The Context and Orientation of Theological Reflection

In order to understand the theological reorientation which began in China after 1949, it is necessary to briefly recall the past 150 years of the history of the Protestant effort in that nation. As has been stressed over and over again in this book, the association between the missionary enterprise and foreign imperialism was responsible for the prevailing view that the church was a foreign or semi-foreign institution. Because Christians had played practically no role in the revolution, and because the interests of the foreign missionaries in China seemed to lie with the perpetuation of the status quo, the extent to which Chinese Christians supported the government and were committed to social change was open to question, especially after the onset of the Korean War. Under these circumstances the TSM became the means by which Chinese Protestants could make a break with their missionary past and seek the common ground with the rest of the Chinese people under the political leadership of the CPC. The starting point for theological reorientation, therefore, was not 1807 and the arrival of Robert Morrison on the South China coast, but 1949 and the determination of Chinese Protestants to witness in and through the Chinese revolution.

In this light we can understand why Chinese Protestants have said that pre-liberation Chinese theology tended to be "a reflection of our alienation from our own people."[24] There could be no genuine *Chinese* theology before 1949 in the sense of a theology created by and for Chinese Christians. Western missionary leadership of the Chinese church had resulted in a distance between Christianity and the Chinese people, isolating Chinese Christians and making their theology an expression of cultural alienation. The efforts toward an indigenous theology that began in the 1920s were not continued in the 1950s because the questions they raised were no longer relevant for the new situation. The theological controversies introduced to China with the missionary movement were even more irrelevant, for they all had their roots in the historical situation of nineteenth- and early twentieth-century Europe and North America. Thus the fundamentalist-modernist controversy, the emergence of crisis theology, the rise of neo-Thomism, and even the theologies which sought to interpret the Christian-Marxist relationship presupposed a historical and cultural background that was foreign to Chinese Christianity.[25] These were not "universal" theological problems, but expressions of particular contextual theologies that were not recognized as such.

In all of this the basic consideration was the way in which Christianity should be expressed in a radically non-Christian context. It was natural that most of the early Protestant missionaries felt alienated by the non-Western societies which they entered in the nineteenth century. Their response was to create a new context which emphasized the fundamental discontinuity between Christian faith and the people whom they came to convert. They built Christian schools, Christian hospitals, Christian social organizations and Christian churches modelled after institutions with which they were very familiar in their home countries. In China the problem was that this created a Christian sub-culture that separated the new believers from their social and cultural environment. At its worst this sub-culture resulted in a "ghetto mentality" among Chinese Christians who set themselves above or apart from the sufferings and struggles of their fellow Chinese. As Francis Price Jones has rightly observed:

It may come as a surprise to some missionaries to find their previous contribution to the Chinese church put in the world denying category, but there is some reason for this classification. Missionaries were inclined to stress the heathen nature of the Chinese social environment, and to demand a greater break with that environment than is demanded of Christian converts in America. Moreover, since the church was such a tiny segment of society, it could not hope to effect the course of events, and so Chinese Christians were not encouraged to take part in civic enterprises. They did in fact hold aloof from political and social questions to such an extent that the attitude of being above "politics" has been one of the accusations now most frequently made against Chinese preachers.[26]

This was the result of a Chinese Christian movement that was not self-governing, self-supporting and self-propagating prior to 1949, and it was this history that Chinese Protestants began to put behind them.

The term "new light" appears repeatedly in the pages of *Tian Feng* in the 1950s as an expression of the new understanding that was being developed from the biblical message. In contemporary terms this would be referred to as a new hermeneutic and interpretive framework. The year 1949 had created a *new* context for theological reflection, in *light* of which the direction of theological inquiry was being reoriented. "New light" did not signify a new source of revelation, but rather the leading of the Holy Spirit toward a more complete understanding of the revealed truth of the Bible. K. H. Ting seemed to associate the term "new light" with the growing realization of truth which is expressed in the Gospel according to John (13:7; 16:12–13).[27] Others spoke of the need for Christians to affirm the goodness and truth that was revealed in nature and history. One preacher compared the confusion of Christians in the new situation to the disciples' failure to recognize Jesus walking with them along the Emmaus road (Lk. 24:13–21). "We have a worried expression when we should be rejoicing; our eyes are blinded when we should see clearly; our minds are troubled when we should be thinking carefully."[28] The point was that the Chinese revolution brought with it a new understanding of Christian faith. It was not that God's eternal truth was somehow changing and developing, but that people's perception of it should grow through the movement of history.

For Chinese Christians involved in the Three-Self Movement, this resulted in an effort to revise and rethink the theological task. Nanjing Theological

Seminary has been the most important center for this endeavor, from the time of its inception in 1952 up until the present. Although the theological fermentation we shall be looking at arose outside of this institution, it was at Nanjing Seminary, the first union theological institution organized by the TSM, that the prospects of such a reorientation began to be discussed, developed and introduced to a new generation of theological students. Both conservative and progressive faculty members came to alter the ways in which they approached theological questions. In the pages which follow, we shall be dealing largely with the work of Nanjing theologians, drawn primarily from the pages of *Tian Feng* and of the *Nanjing Union Seminary Journal*, which they edited between 1953 and 1957. Although there were comparatively few essays of a theological nature published in China in the 1950s, their number is sufficient to indicate the new context and orientation of Chinese theological reflection. Our point of departure will be the two-part essay by Chen Zemin that was cited at the beginning of this chapter.

In this essay Chen Zemin, who is at present the dean of Nanjing Theological Seminary, attempts to identify the central issues for theological reflection in the Chinese church. After considering the problems with Chinese theology before 1949, Chen lists seven particular factors that gave rise to a "theological awakening"—the "new light" in which the Bible could now be understood. Taken together they constitute a summary of the self-understanding of the context of theological reflection in the 1950s.

1. *Independence*. No longer fettered by Western mission boards and foreign missionaries, Chinese Christians could now begin to determine their own agenda for self-propagation and theological construction. This is spoken of as a "spiritual exodus";

2. *A Critical View of the Missionary Enterprise*. The church's newfound independence meant that Chinese Christians could more clearly understand the damage done by the missionary movement and its obstruction of Chinese theological development;

3. *Identification with the Chinese People*. This included Christian participation in socialist construction, and the realization that the social life of the church cannot be separated from its spiritual life;

4. *Unity and Mutual Respect*. Protestants from different theological backgrounds and denominational traditions had begun to find a common basis for their life together. They were also discovering that they were enriched by their diversity, which was guaranteed by the principle of mutual respect;

5. *Materialism and the Christian Faith*. Materialism compelled Christians to come to a better understanding of the theological basis of their belief. Christians could no longer take their faith lightly, but needed to develop a better approach to the task of evangelism;

6. *Affirmation of the Revolution*. Both church and society were caught up in a movement of change and revolution. Christians could accept and affirm the positive changes which were taking place, and find in them new directions for theological understanding;

7. A Refusal to Accept the Limitations of Contemporary Western Theology.
Chinese Protestant theologians now approached their task differently from theologians in the West. They also had different questions. Chen is especially critical of the existential and "irrationalist" strain in Western theology, indicating
that it had no relevance for the Chinese situation. This did not mean that Chinese
Christians meant to discard the Western theological tradition, for Chen Zemin
is quite clear in distinguishing the theological inheritance of Protestantism from
the harmful influence of the missionary movement.[29] Accepted Protestant beliefs on the nature of the Trinity, revelation, sin and redemption have not been
challenged by Chinese Protestants, although there has been some redefinition
of terms.

In these seven points Chen Zemin is describing what was involved in the
creation of the Three-Self Movement. He has summarized the developments
that had taken place over the previous seven or eight years and has indicated
their importance for the theological task. It must be emphasized that in this
understanding Chinese Christians were not adapting their theological program
to reinforce Marxism-Leninism. On the question of materialism, for example,
Chen is not affirming the materialist criticism of Christian faith. Rather, he is
saying that insofar as materialism is the ideology of the social context in which
Christians now found themselves, it must be studied to determine its positive
value, its impact on theology and its inherent limitations. Likewise, in affirming the revolution Chen Zemin is not calling for a theology of revolution, but
for a new understanding of the theological task in light of the acceptance of the
positive changes that were coming to society. In each of the seven points the
principle of seeking the common ground while reserving differences is embodied in approaching the social context of theological reflection.

In the second part of the essay Chen Zemin attempts to discern the parame-
ters of theology by using Melanchthon's idea of mapping the theological locus.
For Chen, theology traces out the figure of an ellipse whose two foci are God
and "man." The shape of the ellipse varies because its form is determined by
the distance between its two foci. The church, as it moves through history, is
sometimes at a point on the ellipse closer to God and at other times closer to
"man," depending on the relative emphasis given to the divine and the human
in the theological task. Between the two foci, however, there must always be
both a relationship and a certain distance.

The ideal would be for the ellipse to be gradually transformed into a circle,
the center of which is Jesus Christ, the God-man, the Word become flesh.
However, the premature or forced identification of the two foci would mean
the complete absorption of God by "man," resulting in a form of absolutism,
the extremes of which are either pantheism, where God is everywhere, or humanism, where God is nowhere. On the other hand, if the distance is increased
to infinity, then there is an absolute gulf which separates man from God, in
which case human beings are either pitted against God or led to deny his existence. Although the distance between them varies, the two foci are not equal,
for God is always the active center and "man" is the acted upon. Chen admits

that the geometrical model is not entirely satisfactory, but he argues that it does help to clarify the relational dimension of the theological task.[30]

The figure of the ellipse can help to explain the theological concerns of Chinese Christians. Here the central question is the relationship between what is termed "continuity" and "discontinuity" in the theological enterprise. Should the direction be toward the identification of the two theological foci or toward their absolute separation? To what extent should continuity and discontinuity be emphasized in relationships between the transcendent and the immanent, revelation and reason, church and society, Christian faith and other religions, eternity and history, the kingdom of God and the present world? In our understanding of God, for example, do we speak of the "wholly other" or of "God with us"? If emphasis is placed on the former, then redemption must be understood as the purpose of creation and essentially discontinuous with the created world. If, on the other hand, we speak of "God with us," then redemption is better understood as the completion of creation. The point is not to opt for one or the other, but to determine in which direction God calls the church to move in a particular situation. After criticizing what he sees as an overemphasis on discontinuity in contemporary Western theologies, especially neo-orthodoxy, Chen concludes that Chinese theology needs to move further in the direction of continuity.[31]

What Chen Zemin seems to be suggesting is the recovery of a this-worldly emphasis without the reduction of theology into an ethic of Christian practice. In each of the relationships mentioned above, the emphasis would be on the human dimension, or the sense of continuity between God and "man." Chinese Christians had to discover what God was doing in the Chinese revolution and to see Christian faith not as the negation of this, but as its fulfillment. Chinese theologians would thereby accept the doctrine associated with St. Thomas that grace represents the perfection and not the abolition of nature. Nevertheless, for Chen Zemin the active focus is still God in Jesus Christ, for without God theology would be reduced to humanism. Learning from the Communists, therefore, could never result in the collapse of faith into ideology.

In this understanding ethics is important as a way of bearing witness and as a means of interpreting Christian faith to people outside the church. Frank Rawlinson's prediction about the future of Chinese theology bears repetition at this point: "When (Chinese) do their own theological thinking, they will interpret religion in terms of ethical relationships between men and men, and men and God, and consider the aim of religion to be to develop, in cooperation with God, the full possibilities of human personalities."[32] This is precisely the point being made by Chen Zemin. It should be added that there has been a similar concern among Chinese religious thinkers, Christian as well as non-Christian, for centuries.

For theological conservatives reorientation meant a broadening of their understanding of God and God's world. This made it possible for Christians to affirm some of the things that were taking place around them. Jiang Peifen has already been cited as one conservative evangelical who came to accept the positive changes that were taking place in China as gifts of God's grace. Another theological conservative is Sun Hanshu, professor of theology at Nanjing Theological Seminary, who strongly affirmed God's calling to Chinese Christians in the new situation.

> The church has been through a long historical journey. We have also come a long way over these past months and years, but we have now finally arrived at this new age. "This is the way, walk in it" (Isa. 30:21). This command, full of grace, now has a new meaning. It calls us to look back on the past and ask ourselves if we were then truly walking on the right road. It also points us in the right direction from this time on, and gives us the strength we need.[33]

Implicit in the theological reorientation of conservative theologians is the understanding that the world in which they were living was not completely fallen. There was not a total disparity between divine grace and the natural world, for then even the incarnation would be impossible. We will return to this subject shortly, but it is mentioned here in order to indicate that a sense of continuity between God and "man" was also being outlined by theological conservatives.

Although staunch conservatives such as Sun Hanshu could never be termed theological liberals, there is a definite similarity between some of the Nanjing theologians and the liberal theology of the nineteenth century. In both cases there is a healthy spirit of open-mindedness, an acceptance of historical progress and a strong emphasis on Christian humanism. Liberal theology also embraced a sense of continuity between the Christian message and the natural or historical world. Despite these similarities, however, there are fundamental differences. Chen Zemin argues that Chinese theology should accept neither liberalism's naive belief in human freedom (a product of the bourgeois age) nor its denigration of biblical revelation. On both counts Chen claims to agree with neo-orthodoxy's critique of liberalism, but he then asserts that he does not follow it to the same conclusions.[34]

It is especially in their understanding of sin and redemption that Chinese theologians would part company with liberalism. Although Christians wished to affirm the social and political programs of the Communist party, they did not equate progress and humanization with Christian salvation. Nor did an emphasis on the continuity between the divine and the human mean that human beings could become gods and angels under a different social system. Socialism does not obviate the need for salvation, which is in Jesus Christ, and it does not eliminate the problem of sin. As K. H. Ting wrote in 1957,

> We should welcome a social system that shows itself able to raise the level of moral life. But the change of a social system can only limit the effectiveness of sin, it cannot solve the problem of sin. Sin can only be

healed by forgiveness, salvation and grace. It is not a matter of social progress.[35]

Likewise, the Marxist understanding of the social sources of sin provided a needed corrective for an overly individualistic emphasis, but it could never resolve the fundamental problem of human estrangement from God.

Chen Zemin is equally explicit:

> On the one hand, we must frankly recognize the problem of sin. We must not approach it circuitously nor stick our heads in the sand like ostriches to deceive ourselves. At the same time, exaggerating and absolutizing the problem so as to prevent us from doing anything about it are of no use. We should clearly recognize that there are undoubtedly social factors in the root of evil, but in spiritual terms, it still represents humanity's incompleteness and pride before the face of God. Therefore, the spiritual problem cannot be resolved by a change in the social system. Evil will never disappear because social morality has been raised. Evil represents a hideous side of humanity and will hasten humanity's eternal search for God and salvation.[36]

Chen also introduces an understanding of redemption which emphasizes the need to begin with the love of God rather than with a sense of hopelessness in the world. This is consistent with the evolving understanding of the relationship between creation and redemption and between nature and grace.

> In our understanding of redemption, we oppose making sin the foundation of the gospel or basing the future of the church on human despair. . . . Rather, we find the source in the just and loving nature of God. The necessity of the gospel and the future of the church are not based on the hopelessness of this world or of humanity, but on the fact that God, in His plan of creation, chose redemption as His method. It was not humanity's utter depravity that caused God to seek us, but that humanity is the crown of creation, created in the image of God to help God oversee this world. It is only because of all this that we are worthy of God's redemption.[37]

The continuity between creation and redemption is most clear in this passage. Chen is saying that if Christian faith were built on a sense of hopelessness, cynicism and despair for the created world, then conversion could mean little more than an escape from historical worries, beyond the social context in which Christians found themselves. Besides representing an individualistic bias, such an understanding of conversion is thoroughly ahistorical and unbiblical. In contrast, Nanjing theologians wanted Christians to move in the direction of involvement as Christians in the struggles of history, with the biblical message always pointing beyond the status quo. Christians could witness *through* the

Chinese revolution—where they could see God at work—but they also had to witness in it, testifying to the incarnation, death and resurrection of Jesus Christ. In this way the concern for humanization and salvation were brought together, but not unified. They could co-exist, but one could not be subsumed under the other.

A sense of continuity between creation and redemption combined with an adherence to basic principles of Protestant belief provided a way in which Chinese theologians could interpret their sense of identification with the Chinese revolution and the Chinese people. We have already alluded to the importance of the understanding that grace represents the fulfillment and not the removal of nature, which has been especially significant in this regard. This is related to the question of how history evolves and the relationship of the church to that history. In China the church has never played much of a role in the evolution of history, and yet things have happened in history and society that Christians can affirm. To interpret this affirmation theologically Chinese Christians have emphasized the continuity between nature and grace. Nature is not just fallen, for it also bears the promise of God's grace. The relationship between faith and society, revelation and reason, Christians and non-believers can all be seen in some way related to the question of nature and grace. Liberation in 1949 may also be interpreted as part of the process of God's involvement in the history of nature. By making grace not so absolute, and by affirming nature as something more than a realm of sin, Chinese Christians were able to relate themselves theologically to a program of social transformation in which Christianity had only a limited significance.

As with all theological positions, there is a danger of one-sidedness in the Chinese approach. This danger was revealed time and again as Chinese Christians too readily identified their Christian faith with current political and social themes. This did not result in a rejection of Christian faith but in the de-emphasis of that which is unique in the Christian message. More specifically the question became one of theological perception and the confusion of religious and political categories. Goodness and truth in nature *may* be interpreted as signs of God's grace, but an overemphasis on these tends to neglect the importance of the cross and the resurrection. Likewise it *was* important for Chinese theologians to emphasize the continuity between reason and revelation, but this could easily lead to the substitution of one for the other. It is just as possible to err on the side of continuity as to overemphasize discontinuity, and this seems to have been a major problem for some Chinese theologians in the 1950s. It explains why Chinese theological writings could so often be misinterpreted as an expression of politicizing the Christian message, and it is of course related to the ongoing problem of ultra-leftism.

But here we are getting beyond ourselves. Awareness of existing problems with a theological position should not lead to a premature rejection of the direction in which that theology was moving. The difficulties with Chinese theology in the 1950s in no way invalidate the very important ways in which Chinese theologians were trying to respond to a creative new context for theological reflection. It was at Nanjing Theological Seminary that many theologians began to reflect on their theological inheritance in light of the changes that were taking place around them. However, to discover the real source of these changes it is necessary to turn to something which was very new for Chinese Protestant theology—the phenomenon of theological fermentation at the grass roots.

Theological Fermentation at the Grass Roots

There are a number of possible approaches to the theological enterprise, different ways of "doing theology," all of which depend upon the context, orientation and understanding of the theological task. Theology is first and foremost a participatory form of reflection in which reason is enlightened by faith, and faith is rooted in the Bible and the experience of the Christian community. A particular theological orientation depends not only on the way in which the truth of the Bible is interpreted, but also on the social, cultural and intellectual factors that give rise to such interpretation. Finally, the context of theological reflection—both the Christian context and the social context—shapes and is shaped by the mind of the theologian. Whether one is a professional or lay theologian, whether one's realm of discourse is the church, the university or the broader society, the theological task is one of critical reflection on Christian faith in light of the relationships in which one stands.

In the China of the 1950s an important area of reorientation was the shift in the creative edge of theological reflection from the university of the professional theologian to the church at the grass roots. This shift has been described as a theological fermentation which emerged from below, one in which laypeople and local pastors raised questions that were rooted in their experience of the encounter between Christian faith and the Chinese revolution. Discussions began to take place in local churches about the meaning of Christian faith in a radically new situation. Similar to the group study that was being introduced at all levels of society, the discussions which emerged in the churches represented a mass phenomenon that depended on local initiative. While it is impossible to estimate the scope and extent of such discussions, they were reflected in thousands of letters and articles that were sent to Christian organizations and publications in the mid-1950s. Many of these were crudely written and in poor Chinese, but that does not alter their significance as an expression of a new type of theological questioning and reflection.[38]

Today Chinese Christian leaders are seeking to reaffirm the importance of this phenomenon. However, very little was written about such grass roots theological reflection as it was actually going on. The process was no doubt related to the various campaigns and political movements of the early and mid-1950s, and yet the theological fermentation also had a character all its own. The best evidence for this is the discussions and theological essays that were carried in *Tian Feng* between 1954 and 1957. Some of these involved the criticism of individuals such as Wang Mingdao and his interpretation of the relationship of Christians and non-believers. Others were the product of Christians wrestling with the meaning of faith in a world in which Christianity had been put on the defensive. The questions raised in all of the discussions must have been very immediate for Chinese Protestants, who were learning what it was to live as Christians in a radically non-Christian context.

To say that the theological fermentation emerged from below does not mean that there was no leadership. On the contrary, theological discussions were guided and encouraged by the Three-Self Movement, whose leaders believed that they promoted local participation and new thinking. The essays and articles that were printed in *Tian Feng* were generally written by local pastors and those seminary professors who were responding to questions raised in the churches. This was in some ways a Christian counterpart to the more general approach of from the masses to the masses. Men and women who were closely in touch with the local situation and themselves involved in the changes taking place were especially important in this regard. They included Huang Peiyong, his brother Huang Peixin, Wang Weifan, Jiang Peifen and many others.[39] To borrow a term from the Italian Marxist Antonio Gramsci, they were ''organic intellectuals'' rather than traditional intellectuals of the old order.[40] This means that they consciously tried to relate themselves to people at the grass roots, and that their work was done in response to the questions that were being raised there.

These questions had to do with the redefinition of what was a generally conservative understanding of Christian faith. K. H. Ting has summarized some of the theological issues that were being raised in the 1950s in terms of the following series of questions.

> Is this world in the hand of the devil? What is the status of the world in the mind of God? How should Christians look at history? Should Christians only be concerned with questions of belief and unbelief and of life after death? Should Christians be concerned with issues of right and wrong? Should they differentiate good from evil? What is meant by being spiritual? Should Christianity negate and deny reason? What is the scope of God's care and love and the work of the Holy Spirit? How does one assess the true, the good, and the beautiful outside the realm of the church? How should Christians think of the nation? Of patriotism? What is the place of the Bible in divine revelation? How should one look at the holiness of the church in the face of the many evil deeds being exposed there? How to recognize anew the holy love of God, His intentions in carrying out the ongoing work of creation, redemption and sanctification? In this providence of God, how to understand the role of Christ as revealed in Colossians and Ephesians?[41]

Many of these issues became the subject of wide-ranging discussions on the pages of *Tian Feng, En yu*, a Christian youth magazine, and elsewhere. One can see from these discussions why Chen Zemin interpreted theological reflection in terms of continuity and discontinuity between Christian faith and the world; all of the questions concerned the Christian's approach to history and society. For the Three-Self leadership such questioning pointed toward greater Christian involvement in this-worldly concerns, and thus in the direction of Christian participation in the new order.

For example, the question was raised as to whether it was appropriate for Christians to differentiate right from wrong in matters of ethics and morality. This may seem to be a question with a very obvious answer, but it had to do with issues of righteousness and unrighteousness, justice and injustice, good and evil *outside* the Christian community. Was "man" born in original grace as well as in original sin? Was righteousness completely lost at the time of the Fall? These were questions that many Protestants were asking themselves. There were apparently some Christians who contended that the only real question was whether or not one had life in Christ, and that all other concerns were besides the point. They maintained that Christians should only "touch life" in Jesus Christ, and need not "touch issues of right and wrong."[42] In this view there was no residue of original righteousness in non-Christians, and the social and political world thereby became irrelevant. Should Christians work to improve the world? Are there standards of truth and righteousness in the natural order? Can Christians learn from non-Christians? None of these questions made any sense unless right and wrong could be differentiated.

In this particular issue one can see the way in which Christian faith was being recast in the language of the broader environment. The Communists were emphasizing the need to distinguish right from wrong in the ideological realm, and this had a bearing upon all mass organizations in China.[43] However, although the language was borrowed from the context, the discussion itself was argued from the Bible.

In a three-part biblical reflection entitled "Distinguishing Between Right and Wrong," Xie Yongqin contends that the crux of the matter is that truth and righteousness are related to the economy of salvation. Anything which embodies truth, justice or righteousness, from whatever source, expresses God's will for humankind and should be welcomed by Christians. The implication is that Christians should relate themselves positively to the efforts going on around them, because they were bringing changes for the better in Chinese society.

> Righteousness and unrighteousness are fundamentally irreconcilable, but due to the influence of the context, it is sometimes difficult to draw a clear line between the two. For example, class oppression and exploitation are inherently unrighteous, but in the context of the old society, we did not feel the injustice. Praise the Lord, He has helped us to distinguish right from wrong. God gave us a standard with which to measure righteousness and unrighteousness, which is written in the three texts just quoted (1 Cor. 13:16; Rom. 1:18; 2 Thess. 2:12). These texts teach us that whatever accords with truth is righteous and whatever obstructs truth is unrighteous. Whoever loves truth will be blessed, whoever loves injustice will be called a sinner.[44]

It may be argued that Xie, who was the leader of the China Jesus Independent Church, does not go very deeply into his subject, and that he is still operating on the basis of a pre-critical hermeneutic. The same criticism could be made of most of the theological essays which were carried in *Tian Feng*, for most of them lacked a penetrating theological analysis of the issues involved. The point, however, is not that the theological fermentation which emerged in the 1950s represented a radical breakthrough in the world of ideas, but that it heralded a new approach to the theological enterprise. It would be inappropriate to term this a "people's theology" if by that is meant a theological version of people's democracy. But it was a theology which developed from the questions that people were raising in local churches, and the discussions were carried on for their benefit. In this sense the theological fermentation was something new for China, similar in some ways to the type of dialogue which Ernesto Cardenal has recorded in *The Gospel in Solentiname*.[45] In both cases the intention was to encourage lay Christians to participate in the task of theological reflection.

In the pages which follow we shall describe two of the discussions that were carried in *Tian Feng* in 1956. The first of these concerns the Christian understanding of the world, and the second deals with the relationship between Christians and non-Christians. Although both concerns were developed in a number of essays and articles written after 1949, the 1956 discussions are especially significant insofar as they present the issues in terms of an organized theological forum.

Christianity and the World

The most fundamental area of theological reorientation in the 1950s was the Christian's view of the world and his or her relationship to it. The question was basic, for it had to do with one's understanding of creation and redemption, as well as one's interpretation of history and society. The Christian's view of the world is behind all of the questions raised by K. H. Ting a few pages back. The Bible could be interpreted to emphasize either involvement in the world (Jn. 17:15) or separation from it (Jn. 2:15), and different preachers were urging their congregations in different directions. How should the Christian situate himself or herself in a world of change and revolution? What guidance could be expected from the Bible?

The question of Christianity and the world was not posed in a general and metaphysical way, but arose out of the particular existential situation in which Chinese Christians now found themselves. They were interpreting the Bible and asking questions about their faith on the basis of their encounter with the Chinese revolution. For the Three-Self Movement the Christian view of the world was central to what it would mean to bear witness in and *through* the Chinese revolution.

As early as 1952 Huang Peiyong was urging greater Christian involvement in the world according to John 17:15 and passages in the Old and New Testaments that emphasized the goodness of creation (Gen. 1:31; Ps. 19:1; 1 Tim.

4:4, etc.). He maintained that Chinese society had been improving since 1949, and that Christians had a responsibility to take part in efforts that led to the bettering of human life. When the Bible refers to the world as sinful and fallen, it is concerned with the sinfulness of the flesh and that which is evil in God's sight (Jas. 4:3–4; 2 Pet. 2:20). The distinction between the goodness of creation (the world which God loves) and the world of sin (the world which is hostile to God) are brought together in passages that urge Christians to reject the evil and strive for the good (Jn. 17:14; 1 Pet. 1:14–15; Is. 1:16–17).[46] Huang Peiyong was reaffirming the world as a realm in which God works. Christians have a duty not only to the church, but to society, and therefore they must take seriously their historical involvements and all efforts aimed at improving the world.

This same understanding is developed more fully in the discussion which was carried in *Tian Feng* in the first part of 1956. More than a dozen essays were published over a three-month period under the general title, "How Should Christians Approach the World?" The editors of *Tian Feng* were urging men and women to reconsider the Bible in light of their new situation. They argued that in old China the world was disparaged as an area of Christian involvement, and Christians were discouraged from playing an active role in the revolutionary movement.[47] In the new situation it would be possible to reclaim and recover the significance and meaning of the "world" in its original biblical understanding.

Several of the essays in the series concentrate on different usages and interpretations of "the world" (*kosmos*) in the Bible. Thus, Xie Shouling, a professor at Yanjing Theological Seminary, distinguishes between the created world in which we live (Gen. 1:26ff), the inhabited world or humanity (Jn. 3:16) and the fallen world of sin. Christians should respond differently to the three different understandings of the world. In the first instance we are asked to manage and order the world, as God's stewards. In the inhabited world Christians should love one another as God loves us. In the fallen world of sin Christians should separate themselves from good and evil.[48] The concern is to differentiate between various usages of the world in the Bible and to take sides in the struggle between good and evil. People's understanding of the world changes with the social and historical situation in which they live. Before 1949 a world of exploitation and oppression resulted in a fundamental discontinuity between Christian faith and the world, but the changes brought by socialism should lead to a reinterpretation of history and creation. Now it should be more possible to speak of a sense of continuity between creation and redemption, and to recognize creation as a realm of God's saving acts.[49]

Because the world was created to be good, Christians should not seek to transcend the world but to improve it: "The Bible teaches that God not only wants human beings to live in the created world, but to live more abundantly; in order to attain this more abundant life, human beings must participate in labor, for we cannot only rely on that which God has arranged for us."[50] Improvement of the world did not mean the removal of sin, but it did underscore the creative functions of labor. The dignity and importance of labor were persistent themes in the China of the 1950s as Chinese Protestants came to regard work as an important principle of human spirituality. Labor or production was considered to be an expression of one's faith in God, a means by which men and women could work *with* God in carrying out the work of creation. The social emphasis on production was thus tied to a Christian belief in the goodness of creation, and participation in the world was important in order to achieve a more abundant life.

A third aspect of the *Tian Feng* discussion on Christianity and the world was the association made between the goodness of creation, the love of God and the love of one's neighbor. If God so loved the world that he sent his only son, then Christians should love their neighbor as an expression of their love of God. This was why Jesus linked the two expressions of love in response to the question on the greatest commandments (Matt. 22:37–40). In the same way, one author argues that if we do not show through our words and our deeds the love of our fellow human beings, then we have no love of God.[51] Similarly Luo Zhenfang contrasts the people who are opposed to Jesus in John's gospel (15:18–19; 16:20; 17:14) with the people whom Jesus loves and who love Jesus (Lk. 22:6; Acts 2: 46–47; 1 Thess. 3:12). His point is that all people are objects of God's love.[52] This is not to deny the reality of sin, but to redefine the Christian's relationship to non-believers. We shall see in the next section how the love of neighbor was broadened to include the whole question of how Christians should function in the world and among a people for whom Christianity did not set the terms.

As Francis Price Jones observed, the theological reorientation of Chinese Protestants was similar to the metamorphosis from world-denial to world-affirmation which characterized the early church after the conversion of Constantine.[53] The circumstances were vastly different, but in both cases there was a movement from non-involvement or hostility to the political realm, toward a sense of identification and active cooperation with the new order. Although Christianity never became the unifying ideology of the Chinese state, Christians in China, as in Rome, wished to demonstrate that they were not subversives, and that they could be constructive participants in the new society. In both cases the dialectical relationship of Christians to the world shifted from a position of basic opposition to one of general affirmation.

This shift implied a change in approach to the question of Christian eschatology. In the People's Republic of China, as in the third-century Roman Empire, world-affirmation resulted in a downplaying of apocalyptic and eschatological themes in Christianity. At the time of liberation in China many Christians spoke of the Chinese revolution as a chiliastic event which signalled the catastrophic destruction of the final days preceding Christ's imminent return. The Communists were attacked in apocalyptic terms, identified with the Gog and Magog of Ezekiel or the Beast of the Book of Revelation. As Christians began to develop a positive appreciation of creation and society, the feeling of impending doom was replaced by a sense of hope for the future. In the words of

Wang Weifan, Christians came to "realize that this world is Christ's very own garden. It is not a world full of thorns, but one in which the hundred flowers proclaim Christ's loving heart."[54]

A sense of continuity between the present and the future was contrasted to the radical discontinuity between the present and the past. This change was reflected in the discussion of Christianity and the world, which has here been under discussion. While there was no explicit TSM policy of prohibiting preaching on eschatological themes, apocalypticism was downplayed because of the practical reorientation of Christians toward the world. As Chen Zemin later added, "Why speculate on last things when history is just beginning?"[55]

Some conservative Protestant theologians also began to experience an inner adjustment in the eschatological perspective. The story is told of Ding Yuzhang (Ting Yu-chang), a staunch conservative and, after 1952, vice-president of Nanjing Theological Seminary, and his conversion from pre- to post-millenialism.

> He began to tell us a story about a carpenter who was an ardent believer in the immediate second coming of Jesus Christ. Somebody asked this carpenter, "How can you reconcile your belief in his imminent coming with the fact that you try to do so well in your carpentry? Since Jesus Christ will be coming tomorrow, why do you still have to make strong and durable desks and chairs?" He answered, "I want to prepare my soul so I could meet Jesus Christ tonight or tomorrow, but I must work with my two hands as a carpenter to produce furniture that would be good for use for a hundred years or even five hundred years." This story represented his attempt to arrive at some sort of reconciliation between his pre-millenarian faith in the imminent return of Jesus Christ and his desire to affirm what human beings in China were doing. Later he took a further step by becoming a post-millenarian and taught that Jesus Christ would return to this earth only *after* one-thousand years of peace and prosperity.[56]

There was also a change in interpreting the Christian response to suffering. The affirmation of Christian involvement in the struggle to improve the world meant that the notion of suffering as a passive acceptance of the will of God had to be challenged. Chinese Christians did not shrink from this task. In 1959 Mrs. Charles E. Cowman's *Streams in the Desert*, a devotional work which enjoyed considerable popularity among Chinese Protestants—and still does— came under attack as a pessimistic rendering of the biblical message which emphasized suffering to the exclusion of human efforts for social change. This work was criticized as being reactionary, for it represented an understanding of Christian faith and suffering that reflected a social background in which people had become passive in the face of injustice.[57] What was at issue was the primitive and other-worldly theological view of suffering as either an instrument of divine retribution or as a means of spiritual discipline. Chinese theologians were saying that insofar as Christians were participants *with* God in the ongoing work of creation, they should not hold a passive attitude toward human needs.[58] World affirmation meant that suffering had to be confronted as a problem rather than accepted as a matter of fate.

Theologically this was based on a fuller understanding of the love of God. As Wang Weifan later wrote,

> Chinese Christians no longer play up and beautify suffering because we know that Christ is the fulfillment of all and not someone who simply fills in the cracks in our spiritual lives. God wishes to remove the sadness, crying and tears from history at the end of time. He does not wish to use suffering as the only means of disciplining his children.[59]

This was not an attempt to deny suffering as part of the human condition and fundamental to the biblical doctrine of salvation. The question was the Christian's *response* to suffering. Chinese Protestants were saying that a pessimistic perspective on history and society, one in which hope is seen as an escape from worldly concerns and suffering is to be met with patience, does not provide a very solid foundation for Christian faith. Rather, it was important to look into the origins of suffering in history and society and to discover the biblical message of liberation and this-worldly hope. In this light the criticism of *Streams in the Desert* was not only well-founded, but also a significant expression of the this-worldly reorientation in Chinese theology.

Theological reorientation toward the world represented a positive turn in the dialectic between biblical faith and Chinese society in the 1950s. It was a turn in the direction of secularization that reflected a sense of continuity between the Chinese revolution and the biblical promise of humanization. The essays that were published in *Tian Feng* express a reclamation of the world as a realm of God's care and concern. Human sinfulness and the world hostile to God were never negated in this discussion, but they were overshadowed by a new emphasis on the affirmation of history and society. The essays in *Tian Feng* showed that a denial of the possibility of human progress, other-worldly apocalypticism and the passive acceptance of human suffering have no place in Christian faith. The New Testament does not teach either the negation of history or contempt for this-worldly social involvements. Its message is faith in Jesus Christ, the Lord of history, who has overcome the world.[60]

It is on this very point, however, that the discussion carried on in *Tian Feng* appears to be lacking. Christians must indeed be reconciled to the world as a proper sphere of their activity and concern. But the New Testament teaches that the world has been reconciled by God in Christ (1 Cor. 5:19), and this understanding sets the terms for Christian worldliness. The tension is not between world-denial and world-affirmation, but between affirmation and transformation. When Paul says that "the form of this world is passing away" (1 Cor. 7:31), his purpose was not to steer Christians away from active involvement, but to give them a new perspective on change and transformation in a world redeemed by Jesus Christ. This same idea is expressed in his admonition, "Do not be conformed to this world, but be transformed by the renewal of your mind, that you may prove what is the will of God, what is good and acceptable and perfect" (Rom. 12:2). In the discussion in *Tian Feng* the writers pick up the theme of world affirmation, but they do not carry it to the point of world transformation. Therefore, in comparison with the Pauline approach, the essays from *Tian Feng* seem to be static and without a cutting edge.

Given all the other changes which were taking place in Chinese Protestantism in the 1950s, it may be unfair to expect a more incisive approach to the transforming dynamic of Christian faith. For one thing, Chinese Protestants were only beginning to understand the revolutionary implications of the socialist program. In a very real sense their this-worldly hopes for the future of society were embodied in the common ground they shared with the rest of the Chinese people. At the same time Chinese Protestants continued to challenge the world by their commitment to bear witness in the revolution and not only *through* it. The very existence of the church held open the possibility of Christian transformation. Still, the absence of a theological perspective able to move from world affirmation to world transformation represents a serious limitation in the theological reorientation of the 1950s. It raises the question of the theological significance of the Protestants' reserved difference within the united front, a question that is intimately related to the other discussion in *Tian Feng* which we must now consider.

Christians and Non-Christians

The relationship between Christians and non-Christians was an urgent and immediate concern for Chinese Protestants in the 1950s. It was one aspect of the question of human relationships in socialist China, a question which was basic to the whole approach of "seeking the common ground while reserving differences." For Christians, it concerned the relationship between a tiny Protestant minority with the people around them. We have seen how Wang Mingdao was criticized in his use of 2 Corinthians 6:14–18 to justify his rejection of relationships with non-Christians, but the question remains as to how Christian faith *should* inform the relationships between Protestants and the rest of the population. Should non-Christians be regarded primarily as objects of evangelism, or were they brothers and sisters in the same sense that fellow Christians were? How should Christians deal with atheists and atheism in their day-to-day lives? What did it mean to bear witness to Jesus Christ in a world in which Christianity was primarily associated with foreign imperialism?

All of these questions were behind a second theological discussion which appeared on the pages of *Tian Feng* in 1956. Almost twenty letters and essays on the subject of "The Relationship Between Christians and the People" were published between July and November of that year.[61] Initiated by the editors of *Tian Feng* in response to the ongoing questioning in the Chinese church, this forum generated a discussion that was livelier and more interesting than the earlier one. There was a greater diversity of opinion and more argument between different points of view. At issue was the way in which Christians should regard their unity with the people—the common ground—despite their reserved difference in matters of belief and worldview.

Although there was considerable diversity of opinion in this discussion, there was also a consensus on certain fundamental points. In a concluding comment the editors of *Tian Feng* expressed the consensus in this way:

> The relationship between Christian faith and the people should be one of friendship. Christians should follow Christ's teachings to love others as oneself. Separating ourselves from others, having no dealings with them even to the point of discriminating against non-Christians—such attitudes should be criticized.[62]

The emphasis on friendly relations between Christians and non-Christians was important, for it implied that evangelization should not create an "us" and "them" mentality around the axis of belief and non-belief. Thus matters of faith and worldview should not become the pretext for separating oneself from society.

However, this skirts the issue of how non-Christians should be viewed theologically, and in this area there was considerable disagreement. On the one side there were those who emphasized what may be termed a universalistic approach, in which relationships were determined solely on the basis of doing justice. Basing his views on Matthew 12:46–48, Xie Yongqin argued that anyone who does the will of God should be regarded as a "brother," the term which had previously been used to refer only to fellow Christians. Christians should strive to live peaceably with all (Rom. 12:17–18). There should be no distinction between Christians and non-Christians, but only between justice and injustice. This represents a strong theological critique of religion and of the cultic aspects of Christian faith, argued by one who was a strong supporter of the ethical claims of Jesus Christ. In his conclusion Xie opens up his theological understanding to include all human relationships based on justice:

> Brother is a common form of address in relationships of affection. It is not limited to a particular meaning inside the church. To express a brotherly relationship, like that between relatives and friends, we can also call all those who respectfully do the Father's will and do good works, Brothers.[63]

The same point is reiterated in a number of other essays. Wan Fulin argues that God is the Father of all people, and since all people are included in his love (Jn. 3:16), Christians should have brotherly relationships with all.[64] Another essay emphasizes the arrogance implicit in the claim that only Christians "see the light." This was said to be an incorrect view, which was no longer appropriate in New China.[65] In each instance the authors are de-emphasizing the distinctively Christian element in human relationships, which they believed to be too narrow and restrictive.

Luo Zhenfang is also opposed to a narrow interpretation of Christian–non-Christian relationships, but his perspective is not quite so universalistic. Basing his argument on the story of the Good Samaritan, Luo maintains that love and justice should transcend all religious barriers and obstructions to mutual cooperation. In the New Testament the Jews regarded the Samaritans as a "party of unbelievers"—an obvious reference to the views of Wang Mingdao—and they refused to have anything to do with them. Jesus' purpose in telling the story of the Good Samaritan is to criticize this narrowness and introduce a more open-minded interpretation of human relationships. On this basis Luo urges Christians to learn greater tolerance from the example of Jesus' own ministry.[66] Similar to his interpretation of loving one's neighbor mentioned earlier, Luo is concerned with a broader understanding of Christian faith. However, unlike Xie Yongqin, the broadening of faith is not expanded to include all who do justice. Luo seems to be more intent on maintaining faith as a "reserved difference."

A more conservative approach is represented by those who wished to draw a clearer distinction between Christians and non-Christians. Matthew Tang, a popular Baptist preacher from Guangdong, argued that Jesus himself drew distinctions between his disciples and the rest of the people, as in his high priestly prayer shortly before his death on the cross (Jn. 17:9, 21, 23). Of course God loves all people, and the distinction between Christians and non-Christians does not have to create a barrier to mutual understanding. God's love is most fully expressed in the reconciling action of Jesus Christ (2 Cor. 5:19), and it is therefore the mission of Christians to promote reconciliation as Jesus' disciples did. But while it is important to regard all people as one's friends, it is also necessary that they come to recognize Jesus as the Christ. This was Paul's view in 1 Corinthians 9:20–22.[67] Tang highlights the evangelical dimension of the Christian relationship with others, while the issue of justice is not really dealt with at all.

Similarly, Huang Xianglin challenges the view that the biblical understanding of universal brotherhood somehow supersedes the relationship Christians can have with one another as brothers and sisters in Christ. Although he agrees that the major criterion for Christian faith is to do God's will, Huang maintains that this means a great deal more than doing justice. Prior to any other consideration must be a willingness to receive God's grace (2 Tim. 1:9). This sets Christians apart as heirs to God's promise (Heb. 6:17), as those who have received new life in Christ (Jas. 1:18) and as men and women who understand the unity of all things in Christ (Eph. 1:9–10). Doing the will of God must be expressed in one's words and actions. But there is also a distinctively Christian understanding of the meaning of faith, and this perspective must be included in any discussion of the will of God. This is not to say that Christians should build walls between themselves and non-Christians, for the Bible teaches that whosoever is not against us is for us (Mk. 9:40).[68] While rejecting the idea that all who do justice should be regarded as "brothers," Huang affirms both the unity of Christians with non-believers and the uniqueness of the Christian message.

Huang Xianglin and Matthew Tang had a very different view of the relationship between Christians and non-Christians than that of Xie Yongqin, Tian Yunzhen and others. Tang and Huang wished to assert a stronger sense of Christian identity in society, but not one as divisive as it had been in the past. Theirs was a conservative Christocentric position, which sought to maintain a definite emphasis on the *religious dimension* of Christian faith. In contrast, the more universalistic approach stressed social justice and tolerance as important to the *ethical dimension* of Christianity. This view tended to be more theocentric, minimizing the contradiction between Christians and non-Christians while highlighting the possibilities of mutual interaction. Whereas the former position appears to be more in the direction of discontinuity on the basis of "reserved differences," the latter viewpoint tends toward a sense of continuity between Christian faith and the "common ground." Both positions were represented in the leadership of the Three-Self Movement, and the differences between them notwithstanding, each had a contribution to make in understanding the relationship between Christian faith and secular society.

The differences in the discussion in *Tian Feng* were not as sharp as the theological controversies that emerged in the West. The theological liberals in China were more ready to acknowledge the acceptability of the conservative position, while conservatives emphasized that differences in matters of belief should not cause divisions within the common ground. The two positions were able to co-exist in the TSM because of the principle of mutual respect. In chapter 1 it was observed that Christians who chose to work deliberately in socialist China pointed more directly to the ultimate in their situation than those who did not. This is precisely the point, and it highlights the basic difference between the theological reorientation in the China of the 1950s and the perspective of those who were putting theological questions to the Chinese church from afar. In the case of Chinese Protestants, liberal and conservative alike, there was a basic affirmation of what was taking place in Chinese society, and this made all the difference in the world.

This has important implications for understanding the relationship between Christianity and Marxism in the Chinese experience. On one level theological reorientation in China was a movement in the direction of continuity, the more liberal and universalistic position that has been under discussion. The approach of seeking the common ground while reserving differences did not emphasize the contradiction or encounter between two rival "faiths," but rather the co-operation possible among people holding different worldviews. However, the fact that Chinese Protestants spoke of nation and church, of continuity *and* discontinuity, of Christians *and* non-Christians, meant that they were also acknowledging the difference between Christianity and Marxism. An explicit Christian-Marxist dialogue was deliberately avoided among Chinese intellectuals, Christians and Marxists alike. But an indirect dialogue was always implicit as Christians came to consider how they should relate themselves to the world, to non-Christians and to the task of socialist construction.

Marxism is not explicitly dealt with in either of the theological discussions that we have considered, and it was not a subject for theological reflection at the grass roots. However, one cannot read the essays we have been looking at without some understanding of the social and political fermentation which lies behind them. For example, Huang Peixin's contribution to the discussion of relationships between Christians and non-Christians takes its point of departure from the story of the Good Samaritan. As with Luo Zhenfang, he affirms that Jesus told this story in order to emphasize the need for openness beyond a narrow religious viewpoint. He adds that the Jews of Jesus' time had a great deal to learn from the despised Samaritans.

> The Bible shows us that the Samaritans were not as the Jews pictured them, hopeless people without a single good point. On the contrary, there were those among them who genuinely thirsted after truth (Jn. 4); there were those who understood gratitude even more than the Jews (Lk. 17:11–19); there were Samaritans blessed by God who were even better than the Jewish priests and Levites (Lk. 10: 25–37). Our Lord Jesus actually wanted the Jewish lawyer to take the Samaritans—despised by the Jews—as models. "Go and do likewise" (Lk. 10:37).[69]

No Chinese Christians reading this account in 1956 could fail to see the implications which this had for their own relationships to members of the Chinese Communist Party.

The same author also wrote one of the very few essays published in the 1950s dealing explicitly with the Christian-Marxist relationship as a theological problem. As we might expect, his argument is that socialism and Christianity are not really talking about the same thing, and that, therefore, a comparison between the two misses the mark.

> Christianity and socialism belong to two entirely different frameworks, and they cannot be compared. Those who say that Christianity is socialism or that Christianity contains socialism are making forced analogies which violate history. Christianity may of course be said to support socialism, but we must assert that Christianity itself has no concrete plan for social transformation, for this is not the problem which faith seeks to resolve.[70]

Huang contends that the question was neither one of developing a Christian form of socialism nor of maintaining that Christianity and socialism stood in absolute opposition. In the latter view Christians were said to have no way of living in a socialist society, and if a Christian lived happily under socialism, then there was either something wrong with his faith or his spiritual life was weak. For Huang Peixin, the question was how a Christian should live in socialist society. The theoretical problem of Christianity and communism is transformed into a practical problem for Chinese living in the PRC.

Huang then makes two observations. First, Christianity is the acceptance of new life in Christ, and it is not necessarily linked with any particular kind of social system. Just because Christianity had been introduced to China before 1949 does not mean that Christians should thereby favor the social system of old China. His second point is that Christians should be able to endorse many of the views which socialism advances. For example, the Bible teaches that all people are equal before God, and Christians should be able to support a social system that seeks to bring an end to class and racial oppression. People are not only equal before God, but they are very precious to God. Jesus was sent to redeem human beings, and his parables of the lost sheep, the prodigal son, and the lost coin are examples of his care and concern for human life. Should not Christians, therefore, be able to support a social system which is more humanizing than any which China had seen before? Should not Christians also be able to support a social system which seeks to bring greater material blessings to all people?[71]

The point is that Christian faith and moral conscience should, at the very least, allow Christians to accept socialism. This is not to say that Christianity should be replaced by socialism, but that it is important that they find some common ground between them. It is not Huang Peixin's intention to baptize a particular social system, but to argue that Christians had every reason for supporting the positive changes that had come with liberation. Although he is more explicit than most in treating the Christian-Marxist relationship as a theological problem, even Huang Peixin avoids the deeper philosophical issues one might expect from such a discussion. He is more interested in demonstrating the *minimum* possibility for Christian-Marxist cooperation than he is in dealing directly with a comparison contrast between two different worldviews.

What then is the theological significance of the Christians' reserved difference within the united front? This was the question raised at the end of our discussion of Christianity and the world, and it is one to which we must now return. Does the stress of the reservation of differences mean that Christians should direct their attention to the so-called religious realm and leave the rest of the world to the Communists? Or is it that Chinese Christians should have the same social involvements as anyone else but interpret their activity in a different light? And if the latter is the case, does it not mean that the only theological significance of the reservation of differences is kept in the heart of the individual Christian, or at best in the worshipping life of the church as a whole?

It is true that Chinese Christians did not advance an independent perspective on social transformation after 1949. This was consistent with Y. T. Wu's rejection of the possibility of an independent social program for the Chinese church on the grounds that it would be limited by the ideological framework of bourgeois Protestantism. It is also a recognition of the essential weakness of Chinese Christianity in the China of the 1950s, when Chinese Protestants and the Three-Self Movement appeared to be on the defensive as far as social questions were concerned. Even though Christians were included within the united front, it always seemed necessary to prove that they belonged there. This did not make for a very creative environment in which to pursue theological inquiry.

Despite such limitations, however, the united front did provide a context for theological reorientation in China, and this proved to be extremely important for the adaptation of Christians to a radically new situation. The overall impact of this reorientation was to move Christians to a greater acceptance of the world as a realm of God's concern, a movement which made possible an appreciation of the changes which were taking place in Chinese society. It is in part for this reason that Chen Zemin and others argued for a greater sense of continuity between God and "man" in the theological enterprise.

The existence of a reserved difference in the form of adherence to basic principles of Protestant belief, however, also meant that there was a fundamental discontinuity between Christianity and Marxism. This accounts for the biblical character of most Protestant theology in the China of the 1950s. Not only theological conservatives but all Protestants rejected the atheism that was explicit in Marxism-Leninism. The point was that the church should retain its basic sense of Christian purpose and that Christians should play an active role in society. Yet the question of the theological significance of the reserved difference still remains. How could church and society be theologically related and still allow for the integrity of Christian witness in China?

In a speech before seminary students in 1957, K. H. Ting gave his answer to this question in the form of an eloquent defense of Christian theism. The speech need not be summarized here, for it is widely known in the West.[72] However, one particular part of this speech has a bearing on our discussion. Ting argues that theists and atheists needed to find a way of getting along with one another in the People's Republic. Christians could hardly expect that all atheists would be converted all at once, even though this remained an ultimate hope and expectation. For the present it was only necessary to discover which social system would be best for the common life of atheists *and* theists.

China, Ting asserts, had found such a system in socialism. Yet socialism does not and cannot obviate the need for the salvation that is in Jesus Christ. Nor can it remove the problem of sin and human estrangement from God. The question of atheism is still problematic, but it must be addressed in a new way.

> Atheism has for a long time existed alongside the church; it is not something which the church has just met within the last few years. We must not be alarmed, we should recognize the right of all shades of atheism and agnosticism to exist, we should become accustomed to living with them, learn how to avoid being seduced by them, while at the same time, profiting by their criticism of religion, and learn how to present the gospel to people who have been influenced by these theories.[73]

Maintaining Christian theism meant that there would always be discontinuity in continuity, reserved differences within the common ground, an *implicit* dialogue and contradiction between Christianity and Marxism in China. The existence and propagation of Christian faith has remained a challenge to individuals and society in China, not only in the 1950s, but during the Cultural Revolution era and right up to the present. There is no question that Christianity within the united front has in some ways been limited by its context, but this has not prevented the continuing relevance of Christianity and the Three-Self Movement to the Chinese revolution. Although it has not yet led to a uniquely Chinese Christian perspective on social transformation, theological reorientation has provided a perspective which was acceptable and workable for a broad community of Chinese Protestants in the 1950s.

All of this was possible in the TSM as long as a united front oriented approach to religious policy remained operative. With the growing influence of leftism leading up to the Cultural Revolution, however, the theological fermentation at the grass roots came to a halt. The *Nanjing Seminary Journal* ceased publication in 1957, after only seven issues had been released, and there were no more theological discussions in *Tian Feng* after 1959. As with so many other aspects of life in the Chinese Protestant community, all theological activity was suspended from the early 1960s until 1979.

Chinese Theology in the 1980s

The Cultural Revolution has not been a subject of theological reflection among Chinese Protestant thinkers. There has been no "theology of the wounded" comparable to the "literature of the wounded," which was developed by Chinese intellectuals after the fall of the "Gang of Four." In novels, short stories, poems and plays written between 1977 and 1981, Chinese writers exposed the wounds of the Cultural Revolution era in order to explore its meaning for history.[74] Although the Cultural Revolution also left scars and wounds on Chinese Christians, there has been no similar movement within the church. Perhaps because the experience is still too close, or because developments since the Third Plenum have presented tasks that are too immediate, or because they have not wished to emphasize their particular hardships as unique, Chinese Protestants have not written about the theological significance of the Cultural Revolution era. However much those of us outside China might hope for a theological perspective on the Cultural Revolution, the fact that Chinese Christians have not developed a "theology of the wounded" makes it impossible for us to explore the implications of such a theology *for* them. No one is entitled to write a theology of someone else's experience.

Yet it is possible to discern the ways in which the Cultural Revolution experience has influenced Chinese Christians' understanding of their faith. Gao Ying, who was in the first class of students in Nanjing Union Seminary after the Cultural Revolution, preached a sermon in which she referred to the testimony of a woman who had suffered throughout the years leading up to the Cultural Revolution.

The husband of a devout Christian woman was wrongly arrested as a counter-revolutionary during the three-anti's and five-anti's campaigns, and died in prison soon after. She was made to return to her home in the countryside with their three young children. They had no means of support and were politically branded as members of a counter-revolutionary's family. Life was extremely difficult for them, but even in the midst of such bitter suffering, she never lost faith in God, for she believed in God's promise for her children: "A bruised reed he will not break, and a dimly burning wick he will not quench." During those days she loved most to recite Psalm 23. Often, she would take her children up to the hillside to gaze at the blue sky and pray through her tears: "O God on your heavenly throne, I raise my eyes to you. How does the servant gaze upon the master's hand or the serving girl upon the hand of her mistress? Even so do we gaze upon Yahweh, our God." Thus did this sister, in faith, raise her eyes to the Lord and wait. Finally God's promise was realized to her. Today, not only has her husband been cleared, but two of her daughters have been called to study theology. When she came to church and recited Psalm 23 for the first time together with the other brothers and sisters there, she could not help weeping. After twenty years and more of waiting and hoping, their faith has finally gained God's promise for them. They are blessed and their hearts are filled with gratitude and praise to God.[75]

This same theme—the abundance of God's grace in Jesus Christ—has been presented in countless other sermons preached in churches and home worship gatherings all over China since 1979. "For if many died through one man's trespass, much more have the grace of God and the free gift of the grace of that one man Jesus Christ abounded for many" (Rom. 5:15). Chinese Christians have paid particular attention to the "much more" in this verse, for it expresses both the experience of grace within the Christian community and the grace which extends to God's work outside the church.[76] It emphasizes the belief that we are born not only in original sin but in original grace as well. There is no better example of this two-pronged interpretation, one which combines the grace of humanization with the grace of salvation, linking the experience of Chinese Protestants in the 1950s with the 1980s, than the story behind a recently published Chinese hymn entitled "Winter Is Past."

The words of the hymn were written by Wang Weifan, an evangelical theologian at Nanjing Theological Seminary. After graduating from Nanjing Seminary in 1955, Wang served in a local church and was involved in the grass roots theological fermentation discussed in the previous section. Sent to the countryside during the Anti-Rightist campaign, Wang Weifan lived and worked there for the better part of the next eighteen years. A patriotic Chinese who was also a committed Christian, his experience during those years was similar to that of many other Chinese intellectuals who came of age in the 1950s. Yet despite all of his hardship and suffering, he never lost hope. In his own words, "One needs to see the suffering in history in the same way that one views the suffering of childbirth. In the end, a child is born." With this understanding, Wang was able to maintain this faith in God and humanity and to deepen his sense of identification with those around him during his eighteen years in the countryside.[77]

In the spring of 1957, before the Anti-Rightist campaign had begun, Wang Weifan wrote three verses of a hymn, which he was not able to complete. It is based on a passage from the Song of Solomon (2:10–14) a book usually regarded as an interpretation of the covenant relationship and love that God has for and with his people. On another level the Song of Solomon has been seen as a celebration of the beauty of creation cast in the language of love between man and woman. Wang Weifan's use of this passage from Old Testament wisdom literature combines both interpretations. The three verses of the hymn represent his implicit affirmation of the changes that were then taking place in China, although there is no specific mention of this context.

> The winter is past, rain is done.
> Flowers fill the earth, birdsong in the air.
> Why do you wait? Why do you hesitate?
> My fair one. Come away with me.

> Let me see your face, hear your voice,
> For your voice is sweet, your face comely,
> O my dove, come away with me.

> My beloved, I'll follow you,
> Away from the rocks and the cliffs,
> In the birdsong, among the flowers,
> I'll follow your steps, I'll go with you.

One can detect a certain elusiveness about these verses, especially when they are sung to the melancholy and lilting melody which accompanies them.[78] The hesitation, the dove out of reach, the unnamed person whom the author seeks to follow—in each verse one is left with the impression that something is missing. Twenty years after these verses were written, after the book had been closed on the Cultural Revolution, Wang Weifan discovered this hymn among his papers at Nanjing Seminary. A great deal had transpired in between, but his experience since 1957 now enabled Wang Weifan to write the chorus and have the whole piece set to music. This is the refrain which he wrote in 1982.

> My Lord Jesus, Source of my Love.
> My body, my soul, forever yours,
> In darkest valleys, I long for you,
> I will go with you, Spring has come again!

The elusive questioning in the first three verses is somehow answered as the chorus connects Old and New Testaments. It brings together the experience of Chinese Protestants in the 1950s with their experience of today. Throughout this hymn the sense of continuity between creation and redemption, salvation and humanization, ultimate and penultimate is expressed, and in the chorus, these find fulfillment in identifying Jesus Christ as the source of faith, hope and love. The hardship and suffering of the Cultural Revolution era are implicit in the words of the third line, and hope for the future is expressed by the words, "Spring has come again!" Without reading too much into the story behind this hymn, it is possible to see it as one expression of the renewal of Christian spirituality in China since 1979.

How the Chinese Christian experience will be developed and put on a firmer intellectual footing remains a fundamental theological challenge for the future. Several years ago Zhao Fusan observed that China needs a "Christian intellectuality" to complement the deep spirituality so evident in churches and home worship all around the nation.[79] As we have seen, a revitalized Christian faith has been accompanied by a tendency toward heterodoxy and superstition, especially in the Chinese countryside. In some areas of northern Jiangsu, for example, Christian faith has been blended with popular folk beliefs, including the incantations of witches and shamans. Such practices make the task of spiritual nurture, pastoral care and biblical theological study extremely urgent.

This is one reason behind the publication of the recently prepared Christian catechism. Chinese Protestant leaders know that they must draw on the strengths of the spirituality that has emerged from below. But they must also provide it with a sounder theological foundation. For this purpose they have been developing programs over the last few years aimed at the education of the laity, the training of a new generation of church leaders, and the encouragement of theological reflection.

The task of training the laity has been taken up with a vigorous program of theological education and Christian publication. Beginning with the republication of "How to Study the Bible" in the first issue of *Tian Feng*, a conscious effort has been made to provide laywomen and laymen with the theological tools they need to lead their communities in the future. *Jiao cai* (Curriculum), a new publication from Nanjing Seminary with a circulation of more than forty thousand, was created with this in mind. It is in effect a biblical and theological correspondence course, although there are neither examinations nor certificates of completion. The publication includes commentaries and introductions to books of the Bible; essays on Christian life and faith; a question and answer section; and articles on various aspects of the church in China today.[80] The overwhelming majority of subscribers are lay leaders of home worship gatherings in towns and the countryside.

There are also short-term training courses for the laity, organized by the Protestant seminaries as well as by local churches and provincial Christian Councils. These courses are designed to meet current leadership needs by deepening the theological foundation of largely uneducated Protestant communities in the countryside.[81] It is too early to predict whether such programs and publications will again result in a theological fermentation at the grass roots, but they do represent a significant attempt to broaden the theological base of church leadership.

A second task is the education and nurture of a professional clergy. There are now eleven seminaries and theological training centers in China. Provincial level training centers have been set up in Guangzhou, Fuzhou, Shenyang, Hangzhou, Hefei and Jinan. Regional theological schools are located in Beijing, Shanghai, Chengdu and Wuhan. Nanjing Union Theological Seminary is regarded as a country-wide institution, under the leadership of the China Christian Council and the Three-Self Movement Committee. In 1984 Nanjing Seminary resumed publication of the *Nanjing Union Seminary Journal*.[82] Two years later a theological publications committee was established under the leadership of Shen Yifan. It will oversee the continuing library and publication needs of the TSM and the CCC, including the importation of books for Chinese seminary libraries. In 1983 Zhang Jinglong became the first theological student sent by the Chinese church to study overseas since 1949. He received his degree from the Toronto School of Theology in 1986 and is now teaching on the staff of Nanjing Seminary. Several other recent graduates have since been sent to study theology abroad.

By the time of the Fourth National Christian Council more than 280 seminary students had been enrolled at Nanjing Seminary alone.[83] The seminary curriculum is similar to that of other theological institutions in Asia, with a strong emphasis on biblical studies. A distinctive feature of the seminary is the incorporation of both liberal and conservative perspectives into the courses that are taught on theology and the Bible. Unlike the 1950s, however, there are no longer separate courses for conservative and progressive students. Rather, two different professors teach the same course so that students can be exposed to different points of view. This is based on the principle of mutual respect, and it affords all students an introduction to different views on many of the controversial questions that are facing the Chinese church. The students come from both Christian and non-Christian homes, and they represent a wide variety of beliefs and experiences.[84] Although their ministry is only beginning, these students will shoulder the main burdens of church leadership within a decade, as they assume their responsibilites from an aging generation of Protestant clergy.

One of their responsibilities will be to give direction to the ongoing task of theological reflection. Chinese theologians and church leaders have been saying for the past several years that they need to give more attention to the development of a distinctively Chinese theology. Numerous essays have been published on the subject since 1979, as Christians in churches all over the world have become familiar with the names of K. H. Ting, Chen Zemin, and Shen Yifan, among others. Chinese theological reflection, however, cannot be limited to the ideas of a few outstanding church leaders. As K. H. Ting told overseas readers in his preface to the first *Chinese Theological Review,*

> With all the importance given these days to contextualization, it may not be in fashion to say that in our view, theology must be in conversation not only with the social and cultural context within which the church finds its being, but also within the minds and hearts of the masses of the Christians within the folds of the church. A "contextualized theology" appreciated only by socially conscientized intellectuals abroad but foreign to its own church constituency right at home is an anomaly. . . . We write first of all for domestic consumption, that is, for Chinese Christians' nourishment and edification. We meet them where they are in ways they can accept. We do not impose on them anything they are not ready for. Theological changes are definitely taking place, but these changes, instead of attuning themselves to elitist tastes elsewhere, must reflect and push forward changes—slow as they may seem—in the spirituality and intellectuality of the masses of Chinese Christians.[85]

Although it is still not possible to discern the shape of this "spirituality and intellectuality," it will surely be built upon the foundation which was laid in the 1950s. Thus in preparation for the Fourth National Christian Conference, a special collection of significant theological writings from the past thirty years was published by *Jiao cai.* Entitled "Rod and Staff," adapted from Psalm 23, the short pamphlet contains essays and articles by many of the theologians whom we have been discussing in this chapter.[86] This collection gives some indication of where the church has come from and where it is going. Theology is still in the process of articulation in the Chinese church, and the earlier efforts of the TSM are only gradually being introduced to a new generation of leaders at Nanjing Seminary. But the legacy of the 1950s, to the extent that it is critically reappropriated for the 1980s, provides a source of continuity between the theological enterprise of yesterday and tomorrow.

One important indication of this continuity was the first theological consultation after the Cultural Revolution, which was held in Shanghai in the summer of 1981. Because it was a theological discussion of an exploratory nature, the papers that were presented by Protestant pastors and theologians at this gathering have not been published. The meeting represented an initial attempt on the part of the TSM-CCC to deal theologically with some of the issues that had emerged in the church over the previous decades.

In a letter written to participants in the theological discussion, K. H. Ting expressed the hope that they would take up questions that would promote a new departure in Chinese theology.[87] In the past there had been resistance to such a theology from the right as well as the left. Those on the right tended to dismiss all who did not believe with them as unbelievers, while many on the left politicized the situation and rejected the possibility of any positive function for Christian theology. As a result, theology in China had suffered from a lack of attention, and Christian thinking had not grown. Ting argues that theology should not be confused with politics, but the two should be seen to complement one another.* Moreover, "following from changes in our knowledge of and feelings toward the motherland, some adjustments in our theological views are natural, inevitable and normal." It is therefore important to deal theologically with the changes which are taking place in society, and to reformulate areas of theological inquiry. While maintaining the principle of mutual respect, theology should not be regarded as a closed system, but should be enhanced by drawing on recent cultural and intellectual developments, as well as biblical knowledge and Christian doctrine. This will help to promote the articulation of a uniquely Chinese theology, one which at the same time takes seriously the theological contributions of other countries.

Following this introduction, Ting lists six important areas that were the subject of open discussion at the 1981 meeting. These are cited here insofar as they appear to represent some major questions Chinese theology will have to address in the years to come.

1. Theological explanations of the major questions currently facing Chinese Christianity. For example, the function and contribution of Christianity in a socialist society; the Three-Self approach to denominationalism; the responsibility and jurisdiction of preaching the gospel in China; the ecumenical nature of the Church and the international relations of the Chinese Church; how Chinese Christianity can make the transition to the united Church of tomorrow.
2. The history of theological thinking in China:
a. Pre-liberation: primarily Chinese theological thinking in retrospect, from the May 4th Movement to 1949;
b. Post-liberation: the course of theological thinking in China over the last 30 years.
3. How are we to regard the nation, patriotism and the social system?
4. How are we to regard the questions of freedom and human rights?
5. How are we to regard atheism?
6. The question of nature and grace.

This list is by no means exhaustive, but it does present a full agenda for the task of theological reflection in the Chinese church. Many of these subjects have been explored by Chinese theologians since that 1981 meeting. Some of

---

*Ting gives his definition of theology in: *How to Study the Bible*, pp. 35–36. "Theology is the summary and systematization of the spiritual insights which successive generations of Christians from many different cultural backgrounds received from God. Its function is to guide us in our spiritual quest. If theology does not arise out of the experience of the church, then it becomes inflexible dogma. But if experience neglects the guidance of theology, then it remains primitive and easily prone to subjectivist abuses. The purpose of theology is to direct our seeking along the right path so that we may not be led astray. It is the responsibility of theology to examine and protect the precious resources accumulated by the whole Church in past generations, and to guide the lives of individual churches and Christians."

these same questions were important for Protestant theologians in the 1950s. A great deal has taken place since then, and the experiences of Chinese Protestants during that time will help to redefine the way in which theologians approach their work. Their efforts will help us to understand what a self-propagating Chinese church has to say about the gospel of Jesus Christ, not only to the Chinese people, but to fellow Christians the world over.

Conclusion

In helping to transform Christianity into a Chinese religion, the Three-Self Movement has made Christian faith more accessible to the average Chinese and the church more acceptable within Chinese society. This stands as the singular achievement of the TSM over the last forty years.

What does it mean to say that Christianity has become a Chinese religion? And how is one particular expression of Christian faith, in this case Chinese, related to what Christians believe to be the universal truth of the gospel message? These questions suggest that the Three-Self Movement has a deeper meaning, one which is related to a more general understanding of Christianity in the modern world. To the extent that any movement has genuine historical and theological significance, its importance lies beyond the conscious religious and political objectives which the movement itself has tried to embody. In venturing to discern its particular significance, one is compelled to probe beneath the surface understanding of ideas and events and reflect upon their meaning in a more universal light.

The Particular in the Universal

The Japanese must absorb Christianity without the support of a Christian tradition or legacy or sensibility. Even this attempt is the occasion of much resistance and anguish and pain. Still, it is impossible to continue by closing one's eyes to the difficulties. No doubt, this is the peculiar cross which God has given the Japanese.[1]

The Catholic novelist Shusaku Endo wrote these words as an expression of the struggle in his own heart to come to terms with the meaning of Christian existence in a radically non-Christian context. He speaks of Christianity as a "ready-made suit," one which he was unable and unwilling to throw off, but one that always made him feel as if he was wearing borrowed clothes. In searching for a better fit, there was always the danger that what Endo terms the "mud swamp" of Japan—the capacity of Japanese culture to suck in and ab-

281

sorb all sorts of religions and ideologies—would transform Christianity into itself and distort it in the process.[2] Still, the challenge was for Christianity to find a new suit of clothes and thereby discover an understanding of faith that was more meaningful for the Japanese. What does it mean for Christian faith to lose its Western identity and enter into a Japanese or a Chinese context? More specifically, what does it mean to say that Christianity has become a Chinese religion?

In chapter 2 of this study Maurice Freedman was quoted as saying that religion in traditional China was a civil religion achieved without a church. Based upon a view of the interpenetration of religion and society, it was assumed that there could be no bifurcation of secular and sacred authority, and so religion in traditional China generally adapted itself to the political order. The People's Republic of China is vastly different from the imperial Chinese state, but with regard to the relationship between religion and society there are also significant parallels. Although it is based upon political rather than cosmological considerations, the united front approach to religion and religious policy also assumes the interpenetration of religion and society. It presupposes that a successful handling of the "religious contradiction" is essential for the unity and stability of the Chinese nation. Similarly, in becoming a Chinese religion Protestant Christianity has assumed a role in the People's Republic of China that is in many ways comparable to that which we have described as the "place" of religion in traditional China.

The Three-Self Movement has sought to develop *a functional working relationship between Marxism and Chinese Christianity*. In the realm of ideas, ethics and social life, there has thus emerged a matrix of mutually supportive and interdependent relationships between Christians and Communists. This has been the purpose of Three-Self as a mass organization within the united front. The possibility of such a relationship is also involved in the theological reorientation which was presented in the last chapter. The desirability of establishing a functional working relationship is implied in the overall commitment of the TSM to seek the common ground and identify with the Chinese people. However, such a relationship does not mean the articulation of a Christian-Marxist synthesis, anymore than there was a Confucian-Buddhist synthesis in traditional China. Nor should it suggest the collapse of faith into ideology. The reservation of differences within the common ground has meant that the theological understanding of Chinese Protestants continues to create space for a distinctively Christian position within socialist China.

Chinese Protestants accept the political leadership of the Chinese Communist Party, and they have learned that it is possible to work together with men and women whose atheistic worldview they categorically deny. This is why the Three-Self Movement can endorse Christian participation in a united front for socialist modernization.

What Jose Maria Gonzalez-Ruiz has said of Roman Catholics in another context also applies to the experience of Protestants in the PRC.

In building the new "secular city" for which we all yearn, people cannot be subject to discrimination because of their belief or disbelief in God. Moreover, believers should have no difficulty in collaborating in social, political and economic movements, even when these originated in a philosophical vision that was atheistic and that they find thoroughly unacceptable. Here we have one of the major intuitions of Pope John XXIII: "It is perfectly legitimate to make clear distinction between the false philosophy of the nature, origin and purpose of men and the world, and economic, social and political undertakings, even when such undertakings draw their origin and inspiration from that philosophy" (*Pacem in Terris*, no. 159). . . . The pope leaves Catholics free to embrace such movements on condition that they do not accept the philosophical doctrines that gave rise to such movements. The only further condition the pope sets down is that such political, economic and cultural movements should not impede or smother the spiritual values that the Church regards as essential for the preservation of Christian beliefs.[3]

Although the possibility of a functional working relationship presents a challenge to Christians and Marxists alike, the burden of responsibility for the development of such a relationship in the future lies with the CPC. For most of the last forty years it has been religious believers, rather than atheists, who have been most subject to legal abuses and discrimination in the PRC. The Cultural Revolution was only the most overt attempt to smother the spiritual values of Chinese Christians, but the danger of an ultra-leftism which rejects the possibility of a common ground between people holding different faiths and worldviews lingers on. The Three-Self Movement has made a significant contribution to socialist China, and it is one that must now be recognized if the relationship between Christians and Communists is to improve in the years ahead.

Chinese religion has traditionally been non-exclusive. This accounted for a pluralistic approach to the co-existence of religious ideas in imperial China, and it inhibited the emergence of well-defined religious dichotomies. Christianity, in contrast, is an exclusive religion based upon the life, death and resurrection of Jesus Christ. Although the China Christian Council upholds the uniqueness of Christian faith, it has also developed *a non-exclusive approach to interconfessional relationships and interreligious tolerance.* The principle of mutual respect in post-denominational Protestantism has created the context for a more inclusive, tolerant and accepting relationship among Christians from different historical and theological backgrounds.

We have seen that mainline and evangelical Protestants are closer to one another in China than they are in most other parts of the world. They have to be, for they share a common future as a minority faith in a secular society. Progressives in China are not as radical in their approach to biblical revelation and traditional Protestant beliefs as their non-Chinese counterparts. Evangelicals in China are more open to other points of view and more willing to learn from non-Christians than they tend to be elsewhere. This is something "ecumenicals" and "evangelicals" from overseas can learn from the experience of Chinese Christians. It is probable that Chinese Protestant theologies will become even closer in the future, as a new generation of leaders is educated together at the Protestant seminaries. If this happens, it will further enhance the ecumenical unity of post-denominational Protestantism and diminish the interconfessional dichotomies that remain.

The Three-Self Movement has also promoted a pluralistic approach to religious toleration, because freedom of religious belief is important for all religious minorities in China. Although there has been relatively little interreligious dialogue in the People's Republic, Christians, Muslims and Buddhists do work together on matters of common concern relating to religious policy and relationships between believers and non-believers.[4] Christians in some Asian countries have drawn a sharp line between themselves and the religions around them, almost as if they were defining themselves primarily on the basis of their differences with non-Christians. In contrast, Chinese Christians have tended to emphasize the common ground they share with other religious believers, although this has not led to any movement toward interreligious syncretism. One does not encounter an "us" and "them" mentality among most Chinese Christians or among the other religious groups in China.[5]

A third similarity between religion in traditional China and contemporary Chinese Protestantism is that *the experience of faith tends to be more diffuse than institutional*. We have referred to the Chinese church as the community of Christian congregations in China. Although the formation of the China Christian Council was an attempt to meet the pastoral and ecclesiastical needs of the churches at a local level, it in no way represents a national church structure. Institutionally the Chinese church is very weak, lacking both a consistent ecclesiology and a rationalized system of church order. Although there may be some advantages in the variety of expressions of Christian existence possible in the absence of a clearly defined institutional center, it also means that individual Protestant communities are only loosely related to one another, primarily through the Three-Self Movement and the China Christian Council. They are likely to remain so, even if the movement toward a united church materializes.

The diffuse nature of Christian existence in the PRC leads us to a fourth and final parallel with the relationship between religion and society in traditional China. Just as folk religion once provided a source of millenarian ideas and alternative structures during times of peasant rebellion, so it is likely that *"folk Protestantism" will continue to pose problems to social order in the Chinese countryside*. Independent churches and sectarian groups created problems for Christian and national unity in the 1950s, largely because of their unwillingness to accept the type of social relationship the TSM was trying to establish. As home worship gatherings proliferated during the Cultural Revolution era, especially in smaller towns and rural areas, there was also a growth in heterodox teachings, superstitious practices and sectarian Protestant communities in the Chinese countryside. The phenomenon of "folk Protestantism" may indicate the influence of traditional folk religion on Chinese Christianity, especially in cases in which there is a syncretistic blending of Christian and non-Christian elements. For the Three-Self Movement and the China Christian Council it underscores the urgent need for theological training and more effective pastoral leadership for the diffuse and widely separated Christian communities in the Chinese countryside.

The problem of "folk Protestantism" illustrates what is perhaps the major division in the Protestant community in China. It is not primarily a theological division, for although tensions between progressives and evangelicals do remain, both perspectives can be accommodated within the framework of Three-Self unity. Nor is it primarily a political division, because almost all Christians have come to recognize and accept the political leadership of the Chinese Communist Party. Rather, it is a sociological division of long standing, one which is also reflected in many other areas of Chinese life. We are referring to the division between Christians in the cities and in the countryside.

The Three-Self Movement began as an urban-based mass organization whose leadership was drawn from the university educated sections of the national capitalists and the petit-bourgeoisie. In 1949 most urban intellectuals knew very little about the concrete conditions in the Chinese countryside, and it is likely that the Protestant leadership was also unfamiliar with the overall situation of rural Christianity. In the 1950s the TSM had a difficult time forming effective local organizations in rural areas, and such difficulties persist. Mao Zedong termed the division between rural and urban China a basic contradiction in Chinese society, and a similar division is apparent in all other areas of the Third World. The way in which this contradiction is resolved will be a continuing concern for the Three-Self Movement and the China Christian Council as they attempt to guide a unified Protestant community into the future.

In helping to transform Christianity into a Chinese religion, the TSM has established a social relationship for which there are historical precedents in Chinese history. As an expression of indigenous Chinese Christianity the experience of the Three-Self Movement is relevant for other efforts at contextualization now going on in different parts of the Third World. However, the point is not that the Three-Self Movement is in any sense a paradigmatic example of Christian existence, which Christians in other cultures and societies should follow. On the contrary, the particularity of the Chinese Protestant experience mitigates against any attempt toward its universalization. The question which must therefore be asked is how this particular expression of contextualized Christianity is to be understood in terms of the universal truth of the gospel message.

The Universal in the Particular

Every correct, regionally or temporally limited historical self-interpretation of man's supernatural relationship to God has therefore an intrinsic dynamism towards universalism, towards the mediation of an ever more adequate religious self-understanding for all men, although it might not be aware of this dynamism.[6]

If the Protestant community in China is both identifiably Christian and distinctively Chinese, does this imply that it is still Christian only in the most formal sense? If Chinese Protestants are no longer wearing borrowed Western clothes, then have they been sucked into the "mud swamp" of Chinese society and culture? Or to put it another way, in becoming a Chinese religion, has the particular—China—swallowed up the universal—Christianity—so that all that remains of the incarnation are the flesh and bones of a body which no longer lives? Not all the grains of wheat that fall into the earth and die bear fruit. Has Chinese Christianity come to enjoy the same patronage and protection of a national-ethnic minority and thereby ceased to be a creative movement? Will Chinese Protestants one day represent a cultural curiosity whose message is tolerated but no longer challenging?

For the believing Christian, faith is a choice of life. More important, it is an expression of God's righteousness and grace for all of humankind (Rom. 1:16–17). Chinese Christianity has discarded the spurious universalism of the ready-made suit it once wore, and it lives on as a particular expression of Christianity in the Chinese context, which points toward a more genuine understanding of the universal. By virtue of its very existence and historical visibility, it states a general proposition about the relevance of Christian faith to the meaning of life. Chinese Protestantism is not a closed community in danger of being sucked into the "mud swamp" of society as a whole. On the contrary, we have tried to demonstrate throughout this book that there has been a continuing sense of faithfulness and vitality in the Protestant community of China. This is why the number of Christians has grown dramatically in the years since 1949. Although it is unlikely that China will ever be "Christianized" in the sense that missionaries of a bygone era once dreamed, the Chinese Christian community will continue to reach out and bear witness to those around them.

The particularity of Christian faith in the Chinese Protestant experience is markedly different from the social expression of Christianity as it has developed in the West. At least since the time of Augustine there has been the belief that the church might eventually become coextensive with society as a whole, that it might absorb, transform and perfect human society.[7] This was a fundamental assumption behind Christendom and the *corpus christianum*. Christianity, extending from the top down and the bottom up, would create a Christian society, a Christian culture, a Christian politics, a Christian world. After the

Protestant Reformation there were different understandings of what this might mean, but the idea of Christendom remained intact. In different ways and in varying degrees, Christian churches in China before 1949 were extensions of this idea of the *corpus christianum*.

The Three-Self Movement turned this idea of Christendom on its head. After 1949 the Chinese churches were absorbed and to a certain extent transformed by society, a process which took place relatively quickly, but one that represented a pattern of adaptation which was not so dissimilar from the sinification of Buddhism. Christianity in China lost its self-centeredness and unburdened itself of a form of Christian existence that could not survive. It is for this reason that the starting point for the Three-Self Movement was for Christianity to become a Chinese religion, based not on compromise or expedience, but on a self-conscious immersion into the historical movement of the Chinese people. Christianity became absorbed and transformed through the Three-Self Movement, so that in time it might work its own process of transformation and perfection from within. It may be said that the Chinese church lost itself in the world in order to save itself for the world.

In this way Three-Self has come to combine apparently contradictory elements—passivity and activism, yielding and firmness, weakness and strength. The Chinese Christian community since 1949 has never been in a very strong position. No longer protected by the missionaries, without financial support from overseas, challenged by the atheism of the CPC, attacked during the Cultural Revolution, hampered by continuing difficulties over the implementation of religious policy, the church has had more than its share of difficulties. To say that Christianity was in some ways transformed and absorbed by society— that it yielded—sounds like a negative and passive response. But this is so only if one sees the movement for humanization represented by the Chinese revolution in a negative way. It was otherwise with Chinese Christians who chose Three-Self. Conscious of all the potential difficulties involved, the yielding of Three-Self to the movement for revolution and reconstruction was also a positive and active response of those who would continue to bear witness in and through the Chinese revolution. It is true of both Christianity and Daoism that in weakness there is strength and a different kind of power. This is the particular significance of Chinese Christianity in the Three-Self Movement.

This sense of particularity expresses the universal in a way that is similar to what some Catholic theologians have begun calling "universalism by induction." Since Vatican II there has been a shift in Catholic thinking from the ecclesiology of the *universal church* to an ecclesiology of a *universal communion* of particular churches. The particular church expresses a universal truth, even though it is not the whole church. Its wholeness depends upon its relationship to the whole church, the church ecumenical.[8] There is thus a tension between particularity and universality in any expression of Christian existence. The truth of this form of universality is not deduced from a generalized understanding of the unity of Christendom, but rather it is expressed in terms of the inductive unity of particular churches which have an intrinsic dynamism toward a more universal communion.

Bishop Anseleme Sanon of Upper Volta has written:

> We are invited to join in a universality lived at the base, in local or individual churches as a way of creating a new experience of universality which transcends all particularity. This places the Mediterranean or Western example in its context, recognizing it as a valuable source of inspiration and in some points normative. Inductive catholicity will give priority to individual churches so that they can preserve their local character and an openness in their mission to the catholic communion.[9]

Although this understanding presupposes a Catholic ecclesiology and the primacy of the Holy See, its perspective on universality in particularity is similar to a Protestant approach to ecumenicity. This in itself is a sign of universalism by induction, that a particular understanding of universality from tradition may have implications for interpreting the experience of Christians from other communions. Although a perspective on universalism by induction may be even more useful for understanding the particularity of Chinese Catholics, who still are without direct ties to Rome, it is also helpful for reflecting on the experience of Chinese Protestants.[10]

To speak of the universal significance of a church in one nation recognizes the concrete historicity of the Christian church, which exists only as a community of believing men and women in a particular time and place. Moreover, it establishes a tension among particular churches and between the particular church and the universal communion. This is the tension between rootedness and relatedness spoken of in chapter 2. Particularity defines in practice the nature of the communion that exists between particular churches. Particularity is necessary to promote this communion, but the communion allows the particular church to recognize its own inadequacies and limitations. Finally, particularity is always the product of inculturation and incarnation. It is this that enables the uniqueness and universality of God's Word in Jesus Christ to enter into a particular culture and society, and thus to renew and revitalize that society and culture.[11] All of this serves to underscore the importance of Christian particularity for the existence of the Three-Self Movement in China.

However, it also establishes a tension with that particularity. Universalism by induction is not a *confirmation* of all that Chinese Protestants have been trying to do as much as it is a *challenge* to embrace a greater sense of openness to the universality of the Christian communion. The universal in the particularity must be understood as both a gift and a task. The very fact that Christian faith in the Chinese experience points toward a genuine understanding of the universal claims of Jesus Christ makes it important for the Chinese context to be understood and interpreted in light of the universal communion. It is not enough that a particular Christian community see itself moving in the direction of the universal. It is also necessary that it see itself from the perspective of the universal Christ and discover what that means for its life and work as the church in the world. The vehicle for gaining such a perspective may be an encounter with other Christians within the universal communion of particular churches.

It was demonstrated in the last chapter that Chinese Protestant thought has never developed a theological understanding that was able to move from world affirmation to world transformation. This stands as one example of a limitation in the Chinese Protestant position, one which becomes apparent when the particular understanding of the Three-Self Movement is viewed from within a more universal perspective on change and transformation. It is related to other questions about the Chinese Protestant experience that have been raised at different points in this study. For example, the Chinese understanding of patriotism, though by no means nationalistic, seems to exaggerate the theological importance of national identity. Given such an understanding, would Chinese Christians ever find it appropriate to say, "We must be Christians first and Chinese second?" Also, the Chinese perspective on prophetic Christianity has barely been touched upon in this study. Yet the question must be asked, How is prophecy to be understood in the context of seeking the common ground? These are some of the questions that can be raised about China, but they can only be raised *with* Chinese Christians and *within* a more universal fellowship and communion.

Lesslie Newbigin has observed that there is a special need for Christians in the contemporary world to see themselves through the eyes of Christians from other cultures and societies.[12] This is needed in order to see ourselves from a more universal Christian perspective, to guard against our own universalistic pretensions and to recognize our own inadequacies and limitations. For if Christianity as a ready-made suit is no longer appropriate for China or Japan, then it has become increasingly apparent that it is no longer adequate for Christians from Europe and North America either. If we discard the suit, we may be in danger of becoming a European folk-religion or a North American cult. But we may also encounter Christ as the stranger walking with us along the road. As we see ourselves through the stranger's eyes, we will gain a clearer vision of what it means to be a particular church within a universal communion.

This is why the perspective of Christians from the People's Republic of China is so important for Christians from the rest of the world. Their experience has for too long been neglected or misinterpreted in ecumenical circles. Chinese Christians have a great deal to say to us about what it means to be a Christian community in the modern world. They can surely raise questions with us about the limitations and inadequacies of European or North American Christianity. But just as they may be more aware of the universalistic pretensions of Western Christianity than we are, so they may also be overlooking some of the possibilities for dialogue and mutual understanding that we see. The question to be asked is this: Can we create the context for a critical encounter between the Chinese church and churches from other nations and traditions, so that we all might be challenged by a more holistic perspective on the universal truth of the gospel message? This is the ecumenical challenge that China forces us to consider.

Such an encounter would go beyond the new beginning that was represented by the Montreal consultation in 1981. It would explore the theological significance of diversity we Christians have within *our* common ground of faith in Jesus Christ. What does it mean to seek the common ground while reserving differences in an ecumenical perspective? How can the creative tension between rootedness and relatedness be maintained within the universal communion of churches? In what ways are we enriched and limited by our own particularities? None of these questions is new for the ecumenical movement, but when they are asked in light of the experience of Chinese Christians, they create new possibilities for dialogue and understanding. The perspective of each and every Christian particularity changes the way in which the universal is understood, and the universal allows a particular church to gain new insight into its existence as a church in the world.

The encounter we envision would be theological rather than political in nature, one which concerns the future of the Christian community in the PRC as well as Christian communities elsewhere. But it would also have an impact on the political situations in which all of us are involved, including that of socialist China. For almost forty years Chinese Protestants have been seeking the common ground while reserving differences, and they have succeeded in establishing Christianity as a Chinese religion. During this time they have made a not insignificant contribution to socialist reconstruction and national unity in China. We can now ask: For the very same reasons that Chinese Christians have been seeking the common ground, might it not someday be necessary to seek differences in order to move the Christian-Marxist encounter in China to a new level?

Seeking differences while reserving the common ground should not threaten the political leadership of the CPC, nor would it upset the fragile unity of the Chinese Protestant community. Rather, it would be a way by which Christians could make their own special contribution to Chinese society. If it is true that Chinese socialism represents an advanced stage of historical development, then the Marxist has nothing to lose by accepting a challenge from Christians whose faith has not yet died a natural death. At the very least Marxists would be able to discover the extent to which Christianity has been transformed under socialism, and Christians would be able to share their vision of a future which belongs to all the Chinese people.

This study has been based on the conviction that what is happening in China and in the Chinese church is important for the world. All Christians need to gain a better understanding of what China has to say to the world, and particular churches need to be able to share their understanding of the gospel message within a more universal communion. China challenges us to take seriously our own particularity, but it also forces us to see ourselves from the perspective of the universal truth of Jesus Christ. We must learn to accept one another as we challenge one another, for it is only together that we can begin to express the universality of Christ's message. This message is represented by the unity of the church, a unity we have received as a gift, so that the world may believe.

Notes

Introduction

1. K. H. Ting, "A Call for Clarity: Fourteen Points from Christians in China to Christians Abroad,"*CF* 24 (March 1981), p. 46.

2. Zheng Jianye, "Repent, for the Kingdom of God is at Hand,"*TF* 204 (March 11, 1950), p. 111.

3. Eugen Rosenstock-Huessy, *Out of Revolution: The Autobiography of Western Man* (Norwich, VT.: Argo Books, 1969), pp. 6–7.

4. The "Resolution on Certain Questions in the History of Our Party Since the Founding of the PRC" terms the 11th Plenum "a crucial turning point of far-reaching significance." *BR,* 27 (July 6, 1981), p. 26.

5. The slogan *qiu tong cun yi* was first articulated by Chinese Premier Zhou Enlai at the Bandung Conference of non-aligned nations in 1955. "The Chinese delegation," Zhou told the delegates, "has come to seek the common ground, not establish differences. Is there a basis among us for seeking the common ground? There is. It is that the majority of nations and peoples of Africa and Asia have in the modern age suffered from and even now are suffering from the bitterness and sufferings brought on by colonialism. From the common ground of eradicating the bitterness and suffering of colonialism, we can come to mutual understanding and respect, mutual sympathy and support, not mutual suspicion and fear or mutual exclusion and opposition." He went on to relate this same principle to the religious question, in part because he was addressing a number of leaders from Muslim countries: "The principle of freedom of religious belief is commonly acknowledged by modern nations. We Communists are atheists, but we respect people of religious belief. We hope that religious believers would also respect those who do not believe. China is a country in which there is freedom of religious belief. We not only have seven million Communist Party of China members, but tens of millions of Muslims and Buddhists, and millions of Protestants and Catholics. This Chinese delegation includes a faithful Muslim Imam. Since this situation does no harm to domestic unity in China, why should not religious believers and non-believers join together in the great family of nations from Africa and Asia? The era of religious disputes should be in the past, because we would not be among those who would benefit from such infighting." See, "Premier Zhou Enlai's Supplementary Remarks," *Xiejin* (May 1955), p. 14.

6. Quoted in John Leith, *An Introduction to the Reformed Tradition* (Atlanta: John Knox Press, 1982), p. 96.

7. Philip Wickeri, "Seeking the Common Ground: Protestant Christianity, the Three-Self Movement and China's United Front." Ph.D. diss., Princeton Theological Seminary, 1985.

8. Parig Digan, *The Christian China Watchers: A Post-Mao Perspective* (Brussels: Pro Mundi Vita, 1978), p. 15.

9. Beginning on January 1, 1956, the journal became a biweekly, although initially each issue was about twice as long as the former weekly edition. *TF* suspended publication for eight months from June 1960 (*TF* 603) until February, 1961 (*TF* 604–05) when it resumed as a monthly. Beginning in 1964, *TF* was issued irregularly until May 1965. According to Shen Derong, who had been editor since 1951, another issue was scheduled for publication, but it was never released due to the Cultural Revolution. After a lapse of more than fifteen years, *TF* resumed publication as a quarterly at the end of 1980 and became a bimonthly with the first issue of 1983.

10. For understanding the TSM and the united front, the most important of these were the *Xin shidai xuexi congshu* (*New age study series*) published by the YMCA Press in 1950 and 1951. Twelve short study manuals were issued, designed to be used in local study groups. Each contained a series of articles and questions for discussion on subjects such as the new democracy, Christianity and patriotism, the denunciation movement and the united front.

11. For some of the more important missionary accounts, see Kenneth S. Latourette, *Christianity in a Revolutionary Age* (New York: Harper and Row, 1962), vol. V, *The Twentieth Century Outside Europe*, pp. 398–99.

12. The most important of these are *Shijie zongjiao yanjiu* (*Research on world religions*) and *Shijie zongjiao ziliao* (*Resources on world religions*), both published by the Institute for the Study of World Religions of the Chinese Academy of Social Science in Beijing. *Zongjiao* (*Religion*), a journal that represents a different perspective, began to be issued by the Institute for Religious Studies of Nanjing University in 1981.

13. Cf. Franz Schurmann, *Ideology and Organization in Communist China* (Berkeley: University of California Press, 1971), pp. 63–68. For a description of the classification of news for public consumption and internal circulation see Fox Butterfield, *China: Alive in the Bitter Sea* (New York: Times Books, 1982), pp. 184–92.

14. *Heliu* and *heyi* are theological terms, the former referring to the joining together of two streams of theological thought, the latter to Christian or organic church unity. However, *heyi* is too strong a term for the unity that has thus far been achieved by Chinese Protestants, for it would suggest union into a single national church. They therefore use the word *tuanjie*, which is less forceful and all-embracing, to refer to practical unity around a concrete project. *Tuanjie* may also be used in a political sense, as in "unity under the leadership of the CPC." *Lianhe* is unity in the sense of federation or alliance, as in "Workers of the world, unite!" Finally, there is *tongyi*, or broad-based political unity, as in *tongyi zhanxian*, the united front. *Tongyi* also refers to the as-yet-to-be-achieved unity with the province of Taiwan.

Chapter 1

1. Dietrich Bonhoeffer, *Ethics*, trans. N. H. Smith (New York: Macmillan, 1979), pp. 124–27.

2. Samuel E. Boyle, *The Church in Red China "Leans to One Side"* (n.p., Hong

Kong, 1950), pp. ii, 27–29, 152; "Is the Chinese Church a 'True' Church?" *CB* 10 (May 23, 1960), pp. 1–2.

3. Leslie Lyall, *Red Sky at Night* (London: Hodder and Stoughton, 1969), pp. 115–16.

4. Carl Lawrence, *The Church in China: How It Survives and Prospers Under Communism* (Minneapolis: Bethany House, 1985), p. 151. Leslie Lyall's reformulated position is contained in *New Spring in China* (Grand Rapids: Zondervan, 1980).

5. Jonathan Chao, "Prospects for Future Mission Work in China," *Evangelical Perspectives on China*, ed. Donald Douglas (Farmington: Evangelical China Committee, 1976), pp. 102, 108–9.

6. Jonathan Chao, "The Witness of a Suffering Church," *China and the Church Today* 5:5 (September–October, 1983), pp. 8, 12.

7. Jonathan Chao, "Flowering from House to House," *Christianity Today* (June 18, 1982), pp. 24–26.

8. Franklin Woo, "A Response to Jonathan Chao," unpublished manuscript, p. 2.

9. Charles West, *Communism and the Theologians: Study of an Encounter* (New York: Macmillan, 1958), pp. 47–50.

10. This is not recognized even by such sensitive observers as David Adeney. See his *China: The Church's Long March* (Robesonia, PA: OMF Books, 1985), pp. 179–85 and passim.

11. Harold Matthews, comp., "Lessons to be Learned from the Experience of Christian Missions in China," NCCUSA: New York, 1951.

12. Donald MacInnis, "The North American Churches and China, 1949–1981," *International Bulletin* 5 (April 1981), p. 50.

13. In Great Britain a similar though less strident position was taken by Victor Hayward, the last foreign head of the NCC in Shanghai and later secretary of the China Study Project of the British Council of Churches, among other ecumenical positions. For a summary of his booklet "Ears to Hear: Lessons from the China Mission" (1955) see Francis Price Jones, *The Church in Communist China: A Protestant Appraisal* (New York: Friendship Press, 1962), pp. 120–24. Also see Hayward, *Christians and China* (Belfast: Christian Journals Ltd., 1974).

14. Wallace Merwin, "Can the Church Survive in China?," *The Christian Century* 70 (November 4, 1953), p. 1257.

15. Wallace Merwin, "What is Happening to the Church in China?" *IRM* 48 (1959), pp. 297–301. The same perspective is reflected in developments after 1949 in the author's otherwise useful account of the Church of Christ in China, *Adventure in Unity* (Grand Rapids: Eerdmans, 1974), pp. 172–94.

16. Frank Price, *Marx Meets Christ* (Philadelphia: Westminster Press, 1957). Also "Christian Presuppositions for the Encounter with Communism," *The Theology of the Christian Mission*, ed. Gerald Anderson (New York: McGraw-Hill, 1961), pp. 158–67.

17. Frank W. Price, *China—Twilight or Dawn?* (New York: Friendship Press, 1948), pp. 102 and 99ff.

18. Ibid. p. 156.

19. Price, *Marx Meets Christ*, p. 75.

20. Price, "Christian Presuppositions for the Encounter with Communism," p. 163.

21. Jones, *The Church in Communist China*, pp. 62 and 97ff.

22. *CB* 9 (April 13, 1959), p. 2.

23. Price, *Marx Meets Christ*, p. 87 and passim.

24. Walter Freytag, "Meeting Christians in China," *IRM*, 46 (1957), p. 416; Jones, *The Church in Communist China*, p. 113.

25. M. Searle Bates, "It's the Long Pull that Counts," *CN* 16 (Spring 1978), p. 24.

26. Leslie Newbigin, "Mission to Six Continents," *The Ecumenical Advance*, ed. Harold Fey (London: S.P.C.K., 1970), p. 173.

27. R. O. Hall, *Missionary Artist Looks at His Job* (New York: International Missionary Council, 1942), p. 18. David Paton is best known for his *Christian Missions and the Judgment of God* (London: SCM Press, 1953). Also see his "The Church in the World: The Uitlander in No Man's Land," *The Missionary Church in East and West*, ed. David Paton and Charles West (London: SCM Press, 1958), pp. 43–57.

See Randolph Sailer, "Co-operative Thinking Between Americans and Chinese," *CN* 17 (Spring 1979), pp. 67–69. Also, "Randolph Clothier Sailer (1898–1981): Memory and Hope," *CN* 19 (Fall 1981), pp. 180–84. A tribute to Sailer has also been published in China, *Dr. Sailer in China* (Beijing: World Knowledge Publications, 1985).

For a discussion of the Canadians' special role in promoting better relationships with the church in China see Katharine Hockin, "Canadian Openness to the Chinese Church," *IRM* 71 (1982), pp. 368–78.

28. Stephen Endicott, *James G. Endicott: Rebel Out of China* (Toronto: University of Toronto Press, 1980), p. x.

29. "Vilified in the 1950s, Endicott receives church's apology," *Toronto Globe and Mail*, 13 August 1982, p. 1.

30. Paton, *Christian Missions and the Judgment of God*, pp. 18–19, 35.

31. Ibid. p. 41.

32. Sydney Ahlstrom, "The Radical Turn in Theology and Ethics: Why It Occurred in the 1960's," *Religion in American History: Interpretive Essays*, ed. John Mulder and John Wilson (Englewood Cliffs: Prentice-Hall, 1978), pp. 445, 449, 452.

33. M. M. Thomas and Paul Abrecht, *Christians in the Technical and Social Revolutions of Our Time* (Geneva: WCC, 1967), p. 49, paragraph 6.

34. Committee of Concerned Asian Scholars, *China! Inside the People's Republic* (New York: Bantam Books, 1973). The theologians were Ray and Rhea Whitehead.

35. See "The Rise of China," *Student World* 60 (1967) and also the WSCF Working Party Reports, unpublished manuscripts, 1967–68.

36. LWF/PMV, *Christianity and the New China* (South Pasadena: Ecclesia Publications, 1966), II, pp. 17–21, I, p. 4.

37. *Christianity and the New China*, I, pp. 123, 130. For a treatment of the same topic from a Roman Catholic point of view, see Richard Madsen, "The New China and the New Self-Understanding of the Church," *Christianity and the New China*, I, pp. 167–86.

38. "Christ, Salvation and Maoism," *China and Christianity*, ed. James Whitehead et al. (Notre Dame, IN: University of Notre Dame Press, 1979), p. 236.

39. "Interview with Dr. and Mrs. K. H. Ting," reported by Eugene Stockwell, Nanking, October 22, 1976 (unpublished manuscript).

40. Paton, "The Church in the World," p. 54.

Chapter 2

1. See Roger Garaudy, *From Anathema to Dialogue: A Marxist Challenge to Christian Churches*, trans. Luke O'Neill (New York: Herder and Herder, 1966). Also Paul Mojzes, *Christian-Marxist Dialogue in Eastern Europe* (Minneapolis: Augsburg Pub-

lishing House, 1981); Ans van der Bent, *Christians and Communists: An Ecumenical Perspective* (Geneva: WCC, 1980).

2. Mojzes, *Christian-Marxist Dialogue in Eastern Europe*, pp. 28–31.

3. It is not as significant as it once was, but the European-centered Christian-Marxist dialogue has continued through a variety of publications, meetings and groups such as the Institute for International Understanding, Christians Associated for Relationship with Eastern Europe (CAREE) and the Christian Peace Conference. See Mojzes, "The Current Status of Christian-Marxist Dialogue," *Varieties of Christian-Marxist Dialogue*, ed. Mojzes (Philadelphia: The Ecumenical Press, 1978), pp. 8ff.

4. Mojzes, *Christian-Marxist Dialogue in Eastern Europe*, pp. 28–31.

5. See Trevor Beeson, *Discretion and Valour* (Philadelphia: Fortress Press, 1982).

6. West, *Communism and the Theologians*, pp. 51ff.

7. See, for example, M. Searle Bates, *Christianity and Communism*, trans. Zhang Shizhang (Shanghai: Association Press, 1939).

8. Philip West, *Yenching University and Sino-Western Relations, 1916–1952* (Cambridge: Harvard University Press, 1976), p. 172.

9. Gustavo Gutiérrez, "Liberation Theology and Christian Faith," *Frontiers of Theology in Latin America*, ed. R. Gibellini, trans. J. Drury (Maryknoll: Orbis Books, 1979), p. 24.

10. The only similar situation in Latin America is that of the Protestant experience in Cuba, although again, the historical contexts are vastly different. Alice Hageman and Paul Deats provide an excellent introduction to the Cuban situation in their unpublished paper, "Marxist-Christian *Encuentro* in Cuba."

11. Jose Míguez Bonino, "Historical Praxis and Christian Identity," *Frontiers of Theology in Latin America*, p. 262. Cf. Chen Zemin, "Reconciliation with the People" in *A New Beginning*, ed. Theresa Chu and Christopher Lind (Toronto: Canada China Programme, 1983), pp. 16ff.

12. Alfredo Fierro, *The Militant Gospel: An Analysis of Contemporary Theologians*, trans. J. Drury (Maryknoll: Orbis Books, 1977), pp. 198, 328, 343–44.

13. K. H. Ting, "The Church in China," a talk given in Uppsala University, November, 1982, unpublished manuscript, p. 2. Also see K. H. Ting, "Inspirations from Liberation Theology, Process Theology and Teilard de Chardin," *The Chinese Theological Review: 1986*, pp. 46–70.

14. Deng Xiaoping, *Socialism with Chinese Characteristics* (Beijing: Foreign Languages Press, 1984).

15. Maurice Meisner, *Li Ta-chao and the Origins of Chinese Marxism* (Cambridge: Harvard University Press, 1967), p. 149 and passim.

16. See Mao Zedong, "Report on an Investigation of the Peasant Movement in Hunan," *SW* 1.

17. Chalmers Johnson, *Peasant Nationalism and Communist Power* (Stanford: Stanford University Press, 1962), p. 11.

18. K. H. Ting, "Fourteen Points from Christians in the PRC to Christians Abroad," *A New Beginning*, ed. T. Chu and C. Lind (Toronto: Canada China Program, 1983), p. 109. Also, by the same author, "Retrospect and Prospect," *IRM* 70 (April 1981), pp. 28–29 and passim.

19. See "Resolution on the History of Our Party," paragraph 35, pp. 36–37.

20. Frederic Wakeman, *History and Will: Philosophical Perspectives on Mao Tse-tung's Thought* (Berkeley: University of California Press, 1977), p. 63.

21. See Raymond L. Whitehead, *Love and Struggle in Mao's Thought* (Maryknoll: Orbis Books, 1977) for a treatment of Mao's ethics. On the religious dimension in Mao Zedong Thought see Chu Mei-fen, "The Religious Dimension in Mao Tse-tung Thought" (Ph.D. diss., University of Chicago, 1977); and C. K. Yang, *Religion in Chinese Society* (Berkeley: University of California Press, 1961), pp. 378–404. Although they approach the subject from entirely different perspectives, Chu and Yang both view Chinese Marxism in religious terms. Part of the problem in both is the vagueness of their understanding of religion as ultimate concern based upon Tillich's definition. Human hope and faith in history may have different sources of motivation, some explicitly historical and others with some reference to a power beyond history. The Marxist believes that his or her hope is historical, while the Christian grounds hope in God and Jesus Christ. For a Christian to speak of the source of Marxist hope as "religious" is to confuse the issue, as any Marxist will tell you. It is also quite dangerous, as the evidence of the Cultural Revolution so clearly shows.

22. See Mao's "Talk at the Enlarged Central Work Conference," *Chairman Mao Talks to the People*, p. 181.

23. Wakeman, *History and Will*, pp. 303–4.

24. "Resolution on the History of Our Party," paragraph 25, p. 26.

25. See "Practice is the Only Criterion of Truth," *Guangming Daily*, November 5, 1978.

26. See Maurice Meisner, "The Chinese Rediscovery of Karl Marx: Some Reflections on Post-Maoist Chinese Marxism," *Bulletin of Concerned Asian Scholars* 17:3 (1985), pp. 2–16. Also Philip L. Wickeri, "Chinese Intellectuals and Humanism," *China and Ourselves* 49 (Spring 1987), pp. 2–7.

27. Cao Yu, "In Memory of Zhao Dan," *Wen hui bao*, October 15, 1980.

28. As quoted in Morton H. Fried, "Review of Marcel Granet, *The Religion of the Chinese People*," *CQ* 69 (March 1977), p. 158.

29. Frederick Mote, "The Cosmological Gulf Between China and the West," *Transition and Permanence*, ed. David Buxbaum and Frederick Mote (Hong Kong: Cathay Press, 1972), pp. 3–21.

30. Chan Wing-tsit, *Religious Trends in Modern China* (New York: Columbia University Press, 1953), p. 144.

31. "Religion," *Cihai* (Taibei: Zhonghua Book Company, 1967), vol. 1, p. 888.

32. Joseph Levenson, *Confucian China and Its Modern Fate* (Berkeley: University of California Press, 1968), vol. 2, p. 98.

33. Marcel Granet, *The Religion of the Chinese People*, trans. and ed. M. Freedman (Oxford: Basil Blackwell, 1975), pp. 148, 153.

34. C. K. Yang, "The Fuctional Relationship Between Confucian Thought and Chinese Religion," *Chinese Thought and Institutions*, ed. John K. Fairbank (Chicago: The University of Chicago Press, 1957), pp. 269ff.

35. Mote, p. 13.

36. James T. C. Liu, "Lecture Notes for East Asian Studies 223," Princeton University, 1975, pp. 48ff.

37. Wing-tsit Chan has suggested several reasons why this has been so. For one thing, all religions were understood to have a positive educational value for society. Religions were therefore treated equally, so that no single one could get the upper hand. Moreover, different ideas were regarded as either complementary (the Daoist concern for individual tranquility is complemented by Buddhist meditation methods) or as identical (Buddhist enlightenment equated with the idea of awakening in Mencius). Finally,

religions were also seen to have both a common source and a common end or purpose in the realization of one's true nature. Chan's reasoning is at this point too simplistic, but he does indicate the *ideal* of harmonizing the three religions of China into one. See his "The Historic Chinese Contribution to Religious Pluralism in World Community," ed. E. J. Jurji, *Religious Pluralism and World Community* (Leiden: Brill, 1969), pp. 121–24.

38. C. K. Yang, *Religion in Chinese Society*, pp. 296–98.

39. Liang Shuming, *The Essence of Chinese Culture* (Hong Kong: Jicheng Book Company, 1963), pp. 8, 49, 53.

40. See Susan Naquin, *Millenarian Rebellion in China: The Eight Trigrams Uprising of 1813* (New Haven: Yale University Press, 1976); Daniel Overmeyer, *Folk Buddhist Religion: Dissenting Sects in Late Traditional China* (Cambridge: Harvard University Press, 1976); and Elizabeth Perry, "Worshippers and Warriors: White Lotus Influence on the Nian Rebellion," *Modern China* 2:1 (1976), pp. 4–22.

41. M. Searle Bates, "The Chinese State and Religion, with Particular Reference to Christianity, 1840–1949," Columbia University Seminar on East Asia (November 29, 1967), pp. 37, 44.

42. Zheng Jianye, "The Han Religious Sense in Light of Comparative Religious Studies," *Xueshu Yuekan* 156 (May 1982), pp. 1–3.

43. Freedman, "On the Sociological Study of Chinese Religion," *Religion and Ritual in Chinese Society*, ed. Arthur Wolf (Stanford: Stanford University Press, 1974), pp. 40–41.

44. A tentative reevaluation of the social contributions of missionaries has begun in the PRC. See Gu Changsheng, *Missionaries and Modern China* (Shanghai: People's Publishing House, 1981), pp. 275–95. Also, Gu Changsheng, "Patriotism, Foreign Religion and the 'Three-Self'—Rethinking Some Viewpoints of Chinese Church History," unpublished manuscript, December 19, 1985; and Song Jianzhi, "Missionaries' Role in China Evaluated," *China Daily*, December 25, 1982.

45. Tang Liang-li, "Missions, the Cultural Arm of Western Imperialism," *Christian Missions in China: Evangelists of What?*, ed. Jessie Lutz (Boston: D.C. Heath, 1965), p. 52.

46. Quoted in West, *Yenching University*, p. 94.

47. Wu Chao-kuang, *The International Aspect of the Missionary Movement in China* (Baltimore: Johns Hopkins University Press, 1930), pp. 239, 244–247. Also, Milton Stauffer, ed., *The Christian Occupation of China: A General Survey of the Numerical Strength and Geographical Distribution of the Christian Forces in China* (Shanghai: The China Continuation Committee, 1922).

48. K. H. Ting, *Christian Witness in China Today* (Kyoto: Doshisha University Press, 1985), p. 6.

49. Paton, "The Church in the World," p. 44.

50. Van den Berg, *Constrained by Jesus' Love* (Kampen: J. H. Kok, 1956), p. 167.

51. Ibid. pp. 190–91.

52. A China Missionary, "First Thoughts on the Debacle of Christian Missions in China," *IRM* 40 (1951), p. 417. That missionary was David M. Paton.

53. Van den Berg, *Constrained by Jesus' Love*, p. 192.

54. Max Warren, ed., *To Apply the Gospel: Selections from the Writings of Henry Venn* (Grand Rapids: Eerdmans, 1971), p. 26.

55. Ibid. pp. 118, 71.

56. Ibid. pp. 28–29.

57. R. Pierce Beaver, ed., *To Advance the Gospel: Selections from the Writings of Rufus Anderson* (Grand Rapids: Eerdmans, 1967), p. 37.

58. J. Verkuyl, *Contemporary Missiology: An Introduction*, trans. and ed. Dale Cooper (Grand Rapids: Eerdmans, 1978), p. 64.

59. Beaver, *To Advance the Gospel*, p. 97.

60. Ibid. p. 15.

61. Peter Beyerhaus and Henry Lefever, *The Responsible Church and the Foreign Mission* (London: World Dominion Press, 1964), p. 56.

62. David Paton, ed., *Reform of the Ministry: A Study in the Work of Roland Allen* (London: Lutterworth Press, 1968), p. 55.

63. Roland Allen, *Missionary Methods: St. Paul's or Ours?* (Chicago: Moody Press, 1959), pp. 184, 192.

64. Roland Allen, *The Spontaneous Expansion of the Church* (Grand Rapids: Eerdmans, 1962), p. 1.

65. Ibid. pp. 32–42.

66. Allen, *Missionary Methods*, pp. 65–81.

67. Quoted in Paton, *Reform of the Ministry*, p. 26.

68. Beyerhaus and Lefever, p. 17.

69. Ibid. p. 133.

70. The verses from Hebrews are cited by a Chinese pastor struggling to understand the need for Chinese Protestants to identify with their people, see Wang Shenyin, "The Call Forward," *TF* 307 (March 29, 1952), p. 179. The verse from Romans was repeated by a young theologian to a missionary co-worker when she left China in 1950.

71. Katherine B. Hockin, "From 'Church to the World' to 'Church for the World,' " *A New Beginning*, p. 121.

72. Merwin, *Adventure in Unity*, p. 203.

73. Quoted in Hans-Ruedi Weber, *Asia and the Ecumenical Movement: 1895–1961* (London: SCM Press, 1966), p. 114.

74. Jones, *The Church in Communist China*, pp. 16–20.

75. Shen Yifan and Cao Shengjie, "The Patriotic Tradition within Chinese Christianity in Light of the Independence Movement in the Chinese Church," a paper presented at the Institute for Religious Studies, Academy of Social Science (Shanghai, 1982), p. 2.

76. Ibid. pp. 2–4. The Chinese Jesus Independent Church continued into the 1950s, when it was led by Xie Yongqin, who became an active, evangelically-oriented leader in the TSM.

77. Ibid. pp. 2, 8–11.

Chapter 3

1. Mao Zedong, "Introducing *The Communist*," *SW* 2, p. 288.

2. Interview with Yan Tingchang, Deputy Director of the Jiangsu UFWD, Nanjing, China, December 8, 1981.

3. In the major work on the subject in English, Lyman van Slyke traces the development of the united front from tactic (1923–1940) to strategy (1940–1949) to ideology (1949–1954) to symbol, concluding that it was no longer anything but a symbol in the abstract sense at the time of his writing. See *Enemies and Friends: The United Front in Chinese Communist History* (Stanford: Stanford University Press, 1967), pp. 255–58 and passim. *Symbol*, as it is being used here, is meant to suggest a function more evocative than abstract.

4. "Resolution on Party History," para. 35.4, p. 37. Also see para. 4.2, p. 12; para. 7.2, p. 13; para. 25.6, p. 28; para. 29.1, p. 30.

5. During the Cultural Revolution era, there was some talk of organizing a revolutionary (as opposed to patriotic) united front. Revolution, in the broadest possible sense, is always the goal of the united front, but a revolutionary united front was conceived as a union of radical elements opposed to "capitalist roaders" (like Liu Shaoqi) and "capitulationists" (like most of the high-ranking officials of the UFWD). This kind of united front is something very different from that analyzed in this chapter.

6. Jorge Larrain, "Ideology," *A Dictionary of Marxist Thought*, ed. Tom Bottomore et al. (Cambridge: Harvard University Press, 1983), p. 220.

7. Kung-chuan Hsiao, *A History of Chinese Political Thought*, trans. F. W. Mote (Princeton: Princeton University Press, 1979), vol. 1, p. 125.

8. Hou Wailu et al., *The Datong Ideal in Chinese History* (Beijing: Science Publishers, 1959), p. 1. Also see *CNA* 1145 (January 5, 1979), pp. 5–8.

9. Robert Tucker, ed., *The Marx-Engels Reader* (New York: W. W. Norton, 1972), p. 362.

10. Georgi Dimitroff, "The Fascist Offensive and the Tasks of the Communist International," *The United Front* (San Francisco: Proletarian Publishers, 1975), p. 31.

11. Monty Johnstone, "The Internationals," *A Dictionary of Marxist Thought*, p. 237.

12. Mao Zedong, "The Great Union of the Popular Masses," trans. Stuart Schram, *CQ* 49 (March 1972), pp. 76–77.

13. Ibid. p. 87.

14. See van Slyke, *Enemies and Friends*, pp. 20–36.

15. Mao Zedong, "Urgent Tasks Following the Establishment of Kuomintang-Communist Co-operation," *SW* 2, p. 41.

16. Mao Zedong, "On Coalition Government," *SW* 3, p. 229.

17. Mao Zedong, "The Chiang Kai-shek Government Is Beseiged by the Whole People," *SW* 4, p. 136.

18. Mao Zedong, "On the People's Democratic Dictatorship," *SW* 4, p. 412.

19. Maurice Meisner, *Mao's China: A History of the People's Republic* (New York: The Free Press, 1977), p. 58.

20. "Who are our enemies? Who are our friends? This is a question of first importance for the revolution. The basic reason why all previous revolutionary struggles in China achieved so little was their failure to unite real friends with real enemies." See "Analysis of Classes in Chinese Society," *SW* 1, p. 13.

21. Mao, "On the People's Democratic Dictatorship," p. 422.

22. For a description of these movements see van Slyke, *Enemies and Friends*, pp. 224–35.

23. The Chinese word for man/woman, *ren*, is not gender specific. In the discussion which follows, "man" will be used as the equivalent of the Chinese *ren*, and it is intended to have an inclusive meaning.

24. Louis Dumont, *Home Heirarchicus: The Caste System and Its Implications*, trans. Mark Sainsbury (Chicago: University of Chicago Press, 1970), pp. 44–45.

25. Donald Munro, *The Concept of Man in Contemporary China* (Ann Arbor: University of Michigan Press, 1977), p. 1.

26. Ibid. pp. 19–21.

27. Ibid. p. 84.

28. Mao Zedong, "Some Questions Concerning Methods of Leadership," *SW* 3, p. 119.

29. Stuart Schram, "Mao Tse-tung," *A Dictionary of Marxist Thought*, p. 300; "Resolution on Party History," para. 30.2, pp. 33–34.

30. Mao Zedong, "On Practice," *SW* 1, p. 300.

31. Mao Zedong, "On Contradiction," *SW* 1, pp. 312–15.

32. Ibid. p. 342.

33. Ibid. p. 321.

34. Mao Zedong, "On the Correct Handling of Contraditions Among the People," *SW* 5, pp. 385, 389.

35. On the Hundred Flowers movement, see Anne Thurston, *Enemies of the People* (New York: Knopf, 1987), pp. 65–72.

36. Mao, "On the Correct Handling of Contradictions Among the People," p. 391.

37. Mao Zedong, "On the Ten Major Relationships," *SW* 5, p. 301.

38. Mao, "Let Us Be United and Clearly Distinguish Between Ourselves and the Enemy," *SW* 5, pp. 80–81. Lu Chih-shen (Lu Zhishen), a character from the popular novel *The Water Margin*, is an ordinary Buddhist monk who later joins an army of peasant rebels.

39. Mao Zedong, "In Refutation of 'Uniformity of Public Opinion,' " *SW* 5, pp. 172–73.

40. Mao Zedong, "On Policy," *SW* 2, p. 442.

41. Mao Zedong, "Current Problems of Tactics in the Anti-Japanese United Front," *SW* 2, p. 424.

42. Zhang Zhiyi, *On the Chinese People's Democratic United Front* (Beijing: People's Publishers, 1958), p. 365.

43. Mao Zedong, "The United Front in Cultural Work," *SW* 3, p. 186.

44. Li Weihan, *The United Front Question and the Nationalities Question* (Beijing: People's Publishers, 1981), pp. 20–21.

45. Ibid. pp. 165–66.

46. Van Slyke, *Enemies and Friends*, p. 113.

47. Zhou Enlai, "On the United Front," *SW* 1, p. 235.

48. Mao Zedong, "On Policy," *SW* 2, p. 444.

49. See Mao Zedong, "On Practice," *SW* 1, p. 307; "The Role of the CPC in the National War," *SW* 2, p. 207; "On the Correct Handling of Contradictions Among the People," *SW* 5, p. 396. Zhou Enlai, "On the United Front," *SW* 1, pp. 231–34. Zhang Zhiyi, *On the Chinese People's Democratic United Front*, pp. 351–56.

50. See Li Weihan, "Preface," *The United Front Question and the Nationalities Question*, pp. 1–2; Yang Jingren, "The United Front in the New Period," *Red Flag* 419 (April 1, 1983), p. 2; and "Resolution on Party History," passim.

51. "Effectively Carry Out the United Front in the New Period," *People's Daily*, March 15, 1982. Li Weihan also cites Zhou's successful implementation of the united front approach, *The United Front Question and the Nationalities Question*, p. 399.

52. Arthur Hummel, "The Art of Social Relations in China," *Philosophy East and West* 10:1–2 (1960), p. 14.

53. Munro, *The Concept of Man in Contemporary China*, pp. 135–37.

54. In the 1950s, and again in the late 1970s, *wu wei* (non-action) was suggested by some people as an effective application of the united front to intellectual and literary questions. The argument ran that it was in the best Maoist tradition to let things take their own course and not to interfere unless it was absolutely necessary. The united

front, which survives on stressing common points and respecting and preserving differences, is a good application of the Daoist *wu wei er zhi* (governance by non-action) spirit as much as the Communist strategy of uniting all so as to isolate the enemy. No less a personage than Chen Yi was said to have urged his cadres to adhere as much as possible to the *wu-wei* principle. Mao's admonition to have faith in the masses was also considered by some to be an expression of the same thing. Intrigued by the whole question, I raised the matter with Huang Zhu (former director of research of the Central UFWD). He replied in no uncertain terms that such an approach was unthinkable for "correct" united front work, implying that it represented a rightist mistake. Nevertheless, the idea is an intriguing one, and Huang Zhu's interpretation is open to question. *Wu-wei* would certainly encourage creativity in all literary and intellectual fields.

55. Mao Zedong, "The Role of the Chinese Communist Party in the National War," *SW* 2, p. 198.

56. Li Weihan, *The United Front Question and the Nationalities Question*, p. 41.

57. Van Slyke, *Enemies and Friends*, p. 223.

58. Interview with Luo Hanxian, Deputy Secretary General of the CPPCC, August 5, 1983.

59. Li Weihan, *The United Front Question and the Nationalities Question*, p. 160.

60. Ibid. p. 190.

61. Ibid. p. 415.

62. Ibid. pp. 20–21.

63. Ibid. p. 411.

64. See Mao Zedong, "Be Concerned with the Well-Being of the Masses, Pay Attention to Methods of Work," *SW* 1; and Zhou Enlai, "Take Better Care of Our Progressive Friends," *SW* 1.

65. Van Slyke, *Enemies and Friends*, p. 114.

66. For a useful overview on Tibet's recent history, see John F. Avedon, *In Exile From the Land of Snows* (New York: Knopf, 1984), pp. 221–359.

67. Li Weihan also speaks of the need to maintain the living standards of religious leaders from the national minorities, see *The United Front Question and the Nationalities Question*, p. 138.

68. Ibid. pp. 433–434.

69. Ibid. Emphasis is added.

70. Talk by K. H. Ting to the Friends of the Federation, Stony Point Center, New York, October 12, 1981.

71. Mark Selden, ed., *The People's Republic of China: A Documentary History of Revolutionary Change* (New York: Monthly Review Press, 1979), p. 187.

72. Gilbert Rozman, ed., *The Modernization of China* (New York: The Free Press, 1981), p. 386.

73. Zhang Zhiyi, *On the Chinese People's Democratic United Front*, pp. 338–40.

74. These groups make up more than half of the 2,036 delegates to the Sixth CPPCC. See *People's Daily*, May 8, 1983.

75. Zhang Zhiyi, *On the Chinese People's Democratic United Front*, pp. 343–344.

76. Interview with Luo Hanxian, for this and the following.

77. Interview with Huang Zhu.

78. Holmes Welch, *Buddhism Under Mao* (Cambridge: Harvard University Press, 1972), p. 11.

79. For information on Li Weihan, see van Slyke, *Enemies and Friends*, pp. 210–11.

80. Luo Zi, "A Critique of Mao Zedong's United Front Strategy," *Ming bao yuekan* 178 (October 1980), p. 28.

81. Li Weihan, *The United Front Question and the Nationalities Question*, p. 15.

82. Van Slyke, *Enemies and Friends*, pp. 216–17.

83. See the important statement by Y. T. Wu that represents an informal presentation of early religious policy in *TF* 176 (August 20, 1949), pp. 43–44, and 177 (August 27, 1949), pp. 55–56. Also see Dong Biwu's speech to YMCA workers as recorded in *TF* 178 (September 3, 1949), p. 67.

84. Welch, *Buddhism Under Mao*, p. 30 and passim.

85. *TF* 249–50 (February 3, 1951), pp. 41–43; *TF* 260 (April 21, 1951), p. 173; *TF* 272 (July 14, 1951), pp. 13–19; *TF* 315 (May 24, 1952), pp. 281–82.

86. *TF*, 438 (November 31, 1954), p. 612.

87. For a short biography of Xiao Xianfa, see *Guangming Daily*, August 29, 1981.

88. Chu and Lind, *A New Beginning*, p. 110.

89. *Fayin*, 1981:2, p. 1.

90. Jean Chesneaux, *China: The People's Republic, 1949–1976*, trans. Paul Auster and Lydia Davis (New York: Pantheon Books, 1979), p. 36.

91. Mao Zedong, "Carry the Revolution Through to the End," *SW* 4, pp. 302–5.

92. Rozman, ed., *The Modernization of China*, p. 306.

93. See K. H. Ting, "Retrospect and Prospect," pp. 26ff. "The Nanchang Uprising," a feature film released in China in 1981, portrays the Protestant pastor of the Anglican Church in Nanchang as a patriot who supported He Long and Zhou Enlai in their efforts. The incident is based on fact (the pastor in real life was Liu Pinggeng), but what is more important is that it emphasizes Chinese Christians as part of the revolutionary effort. Zhou Enlai is even shown lined up next to the pastor in one of the final scenes. This serves to illustrate the way in which the UFWD, which must have been consulted about the production, together with the TSM is attempting to show that Christianity need no longer be viewed as something foreign.

94. Martin King Whyte, *Small Groups and Political Rituals in China* (Berkeley: University of California Press, 1974), pp. 13, 17.

95. Chesneaux, *China*, p. 36.

Chapter 4

1. Li Weihan, *The United Front Question and the Nationalities Question*, p. 184.

2. "The Basic Viewpoint and Policy on the Religious Question During Our Country's Socialist Period," *Selected Important Documents Since the Third Plenum* (Beijing: People's Publishers, 1982), vol. 2, pp. 1228–29. In China it is commonly known as "Document 19."

3. The united front is not even discussed in Francis Price Jones' *The Church in Communist China*, and it is mentioned only in passing in Richard Bush, *Religion in Communist China* (Nashville: Abingdon Press, 1970). Don MacInnis has a short section on patriotism and the united front, but he includes no referencs to the "five characteristics of religion," which are central to united front religious theory, in his otherwise useful documentary history, *Religious Policy and Practice in Communist China* (New York: Macmillan, 1972).

4. *Writings of the Young Marx on Philosophy and Society*, ed. and trans. Lloyd Easton and Kurt Guddat (Garden City: Doubleday, 1967), p. 250.

5. Frederick Engels, "The Peasant War in Germany (Chapter II)," *Marx and Engels on Religion* (New York: Schocken Books, 1967), pp. 97–118.

6. V. I. Lenin, *Religion* (New York: International Publishers, 1933), p. 14.

7. Beeson, *Discretion and Valour*, p. 16.

8. Lenin, *Religion*, p. 10.

9. Ibid. p. 6.

10. Ibid. p. 18.

11. An introduction to the debate and translation of seven major articles are in MacInnis, *Religious Policy and Practice in Communist China*, pp. 35–89. Other interpretations are found in Holmes Welch, *Buddhism under Mao*, pp. 456–458; Winfried Gluer, "Religion in the PRC," *CF* 10 (Autumn 1967), pp. 34–57; and Bush, *Religion in Communist China*, pp. 25–28.

12. MacInnis, *Religious Policy and Practice in Communist China*, p. 38. Also see pp. 43ff.

13. Ibid. pp. 86–87.

14. Ibid. pp. 52, 55, 66, 68.

15. Ibid. p. 70.

16. *Guangming Daily*, September 27, 1977. Written by Ren Jiyu, first director of the Institute for the Study of World Religions, the article is entitled, "Investigate Religion and Criticize Theology." A full translation appears in *CF* 20:3 (1977), pp. 170–76. Ren retired from the ISWR in 1985.

17. *People's Daily*, March 15, 1979. Entitled "Religion and Feudal Superstition," a translation and analysis appear in *CF* 22: 4 (1979), pp. 190–218.

18. Important articles in the first years after the Third Plenum include those in *People's Daily*, October 17, 1979; June 14, 1980; and March 19, 1982; *Guangming Daily*, November 30, 1980 and April 20, 1981; *Red Flag* 5 (March 1, 1981); and 12 (June 16, 1982). Translations and comments on these articles and essays may be found in *Ching Feng* and *Religion in the People's Republic of China: Documentation*.

19. See the translations of essays by Ren Jiyu in *CF* 20:3 (1977), pp. 170–176 and 22:2 (1979), pp. 75–89. For an interview with Ren on religious studies in China, see Chen Weiwei, *People's Daily*, August 10, 1983.

20. The articles by Ya and Sun appear in *Research on World Religions* 1 (August 1979). Material presented here appeared earlier in my review of that volume for *CN* 18:3 (1980), pp. 125–26.

21. See *CN* 3 (April 1965) for a discussion of Yang Zhen, "How Christianity of the West Serves U.S. Imperialism," *Red Flag* (November 21, 1965). Also, Yang Zhen, *An Outline of Christian History* 1 (Beijing and Hong Kong: San Lian Bookstore, 1979), and the extensive review article by Jean Charbonnier in *CF* 24: 1 (1981), pp. 60–68.

22. Hu Yutang, "The Historical Jesus," *Research on World Religions* 1 (1981), pp. 84–100; and Sima Ying, "Jesus and the Origins of Christianity," *Knowledge of Foreign History* 12 (December 14, 1981), pp. 34–36. Hu affirms the existence of the historical Jesus, while Sima denies it.

23. Ren Jiyu, "The Struggle to Develop a Marxist Science of Religion," *CF* 22: 2 (1979), pp. 75ff.

24. Ninian Smart, "Toward a Dialogue at the Level of the Science of Religion: A Reply to Ren Jiyu," *CF* 22: 2 (1979), p. 221.

25. Mao Zedong, "On Practice," *SW* 1, pp. 296–97.

26. Mao Zedong, "Talks at the Yenan Forum on Literature and Art," *SW* 3, p. 74.

27. Ren Jiyu, "Investigate Religion and Criticize Theology," p. 172.

28. Ren Jiyu, "Marxism is the Best Way to Cure Superstition," *China Daily*, July 6, 1982. K. H. Ting's criticism appears in a letter to the editor on July 22, 1983.

29. Ren Jiyu, "Investigate Religion and Criticize Theology," p. 170.

30. Li Weihan, *The United Front Question and the Nationalities Question*, pp. 171–174. The speech was delivered on April 4, 1957.

31. "Document 19" begins with an explication of the protracted character of religion in relationship to the "law of development of religion," pp. 1220–21. Ren Jiyu also speaks of the "law of development of religion" in "The Struggle to Develop a Marxist Science of Religion," pp. 81–83.

32. Mao Zedong, "Report on an Investigation of the Peasants' Movement in Hunan," *SW* 1, p. 47.

33. "Document 19," p. 1220.

34. See Antonio Gramsci, *Selections from the Prison Notebooks*, ed. Q. Hoare and G. Smith (New York: International Publishers, 1971).

35. Wickeri, "The Chinese Delegation at the Third World Conference on Religion and Peace, Princeton, New Jersey, August 28–September 8, 1979."

36. "Document 19," p. 1236. The international character of Catholicism is complicated by the Vatican, which as a political as well as an ecclesiastical entity, continues to maintain diplomatic relations with the Republic of China on Taiwan. For one view of the Vatican's "China problem" see Angelo Lazzarotto, *The Catholic Church in Post-Mao China* (Hong Kong: Holy Spirit Study Centre, 1982), pp. 125ff.

37. See Arthur Wolf, ed., *Religion and Ritual in Chinese Society* for developments in the study of Chinese religion outside the PRC.

38. Zhao Fusan, "Religion, Spiritual Culture and National Unity," *China Study Project: Bulletin* 28 (November 1985), p. 14. Also, "Marxist View of Religion Challenged," *South China Morning Post*, April 10, 1985.

39. Zhao Fusan, "A Reconsideration of Religion," *China Study Project Journal* 2:2 (August 1987), p. 6. A full discussion of Zhao's essay is contained in Robert Whyte, *Unfinished Encounter: China and Christianity* (London: Collins, 1988), Chapter Eight.

40. Ru Wen, "What I Have Gained from Studying Document 19," *Religion* 6 (November 15, 1984), p. 9.

41. Luo Zhufeng, ed., *The Religious Question During China's Socialist Period* (Shanghai: Shanghai Academy of Social Sciences, 1987), pp. 3–4.

42. K. H. Ting, "Religion as Opium?" unpublished paper, October 23, 1981, p. 9.

43. Significantly, this first statement in *People's Daily* (September 23, 1959) carried the "Christian Manifesto," with signatures and editorial comment totaling three full pages. See *TF* 237 (October 28, 1950), pp. 210ff. Also, Welch, *Buddhism Under Mao*, pp. 3–4.

44. *TF* 176 (August 20, 1949), pp. 43–44. The article is summarized in Y. T. Wu, "Religious Liberty and Related Questions in Present Day China," *CB* 1:63 (August 24, 1949).

45. "Document 19," p. 1222.

46. Bush, *Religion in Communist China*, pp. 382ff, and Welch, *Buddhism under Mao*, pp. 42ff.

47. Speech by Lu Dingyi, *TF* 262–63 (May 8, 1951), pp. 202ff., trans. in *Documents*, pp. 29–31. Also K. H. Ting, "Fourteen Points," *A New Beginning*, pp. 108–9.

48. The words in quotation marks are from "Document 19," p. 1222. For an early statement of this position see Chen Qiyuan's remarks in *TF* 249–250 (February 3, 1951), p. 42.

49. "Message from Chinese Christians to Mission Boards Abroad," in *Documents of the Three-Self Movement* (New York: NCCUSA, 1963), p. 15. Several articles on

the question of self-support in light of the CPC victory begin with the one in *TF* 175 (August 13, 1949), pp. 33–34.

50. Philip Wickeri, "Zhou Enlai's Conversations with Chinese Christians: Translation and Introduction," *China Study Project Journal* 2:1 (April 1987), pp. 4–11. The transcript of Zhou Enlai's conversations with Chinese Christians was first published as "Four Conversations on the Question of Christianity," in *Selected Writings of Zhou Enlai on the United Front* (Beijing: People's Publishers, 1984), pp. 180–87.

51. Wickeri, "Zhou Enlai's Conversations with Chinese Christians," p. 11.

52. Mao Zedong, "The Chinese Revolution and the CPC," *SW* 2, p. 312.

53. Xiao's article of January 5 was reprinted in *TF* 201 (February 18, 1950), pp. 71–73. Responses to the article are carried in subsequent issues.

54. Allen Whiting, *China Crosses the Yalu* (Stanford: Stanford University Press, 1960), p. 45; Jean Chesneau, *China: The PRC, 1949–1976*, p. 32.

55. A translation of the regulations appears in *Documents*, pp. 22–24.

56. *TF* 262–63 (May 8, 1951), p. 202.

57. *Documents*, pp. 27–28. "Methods" was formally issued on July 24, 1951.

58. *The Constitution of the PRC* (Beijing: Foreign Languages Press, 1982), p. 32. Also see, "Document 19," p. 1237.

59. *TF* 182 (October 1, 1949), p. 115.

60. Whiting, *China Crosses the Yalu*, pp. 127–30. For a general discussion of this campaign see Theodore Chen, *Thought Reform of the Chinese Intellectuals* (Hong Kong: Oxford University Press, 1960), pp. 24–27.

61. *TF* 260 (April 21, 1951), pp. 173–74. Pu was an Anglican priest before joining the CPC.

62. Numerous examples appear in *TF* between 1951 and 1957.

63. Interview with Wu Gaozi.

64. See, for example, *TF* 477–478 (August 15, 1955), p. 612. Also, Mao Zedong, "Let Us Unite and Clearly Distinguish Between Ourselves and the Enemy," *SW* 5, p. 80.

65. *TF* (NS), 2 (March 20, 1981), p. 19.

66. Bai Hua, "Bitter Love," *Zheng Ming* 44 (June 1981), p. 96.

67. Van Slyke, *Enemies and Friends*, pp. 219–20.

68. See Suzanne Pepper, *Civil War in China: the Political Struggle, 1945–1949* (Berkeley: University of California Press, 1978), p. 217 and passim.

69. Bates, "The Chinese State and Religion," p. 46.

70. Munro, *The Concept of Man in Contemporary China*, p. 163.

71. The articles or clauses on religious freedom are: The Common Program, Article 5, adopted September 30, 1949 (Selden, *The PRC, A Documentary History*, p. 188); The 1954 Constitution, Article 88, adopted September 20, 1954 (*CQ* 62 [June 1975], p. 404); The 1975 Constitution, Article 28, adopted January 17, 1975 (*CQ* 62, pp. 404–5); The 1978 Constitution, Article 46, adopted March 5, 1978 (*Documents of the First Session of the Fifth NPC of the PRC* [Peking: Foreign Languages Press, 1978], p. 167); The 1982 Constitution, Article 36, adopted December 4, 1982 (*The Constitution of the PRC* [Beijing: Foreign Languages Press, 1983], p. 32).

72. Mao Zedong, "On Coalition Government," *SW* 3, p. 263. For the relevant statutes on religious freedom in the Jiangxi soviet see MacInnis, *Religious Policy and Practice in Communist China*, pp. 19–20.

73. Byron Weng, "Some Key Aspects of the 1982 Draft Constitution of the PRC," *CQ* 91 (September 1982), p. 493.

74. Chinese religious leaders spoke with American reporters on their efforts to change

the wording of the 1978 Constitution as early as August 1979. See Wickeri, "The Chinese Delegation at the Third World Conference on Religion and Peace, Princeton, New Jersey, August 28–September 8, 1979," unpublished report.

75. "K. H. Ting Comments on the Constitution," *CN* 20:2–3 (1982), pp. 212–13. Ting adds that there were people who wanted to retain the old wording because they believed that the present wording is too favorable to religion. As the constitution was being discussed by the general public in 1982, it was widely rumored that Ren Jiyu was attempting to put together a coalition in support of the old wording. The RAB and the UFWD, on the other hand, stood on the side of those who favored the newer wording. If this is true, it further confirms the perspective developed in the first part of this chapter.

76. Zhao Puchu in *Fayin* 1 (1982), p. 3; *Fayin* 5 (1983), p. 2.

77. *TF* 421 (July 1, 1954), p. 382.

78. "Report on the Draft Constitution of the PRC," MacInnis, *Religious Policy and Practice in Communist China*, pp. 23–24; and *People's Daily*, April 29, 1982.

79. "Document 19," pp. 1233–34. Li Weihan noted in 1958 that some Hui Party members were theists, some semi-theists and some atheists, with the atheists in an ascending minority, *The United Front Question and the Nationalities Question*, p. 510.

80. "Can Communist Youth League Members Believe in Religion?" *Zhejiang Daily*, May 19, 1980; "Army Onslaught on Christianity," *South China Morning Post*, March 19, 1980; "Religion Not for League Members," *Hong Kong Standard*, December 3, 1980.

81. *The Constitution of the PRC*, p. 31. Other religious policy documents say that what is forbidden is forcing young people into religious belief, for example, "Document 19," p. 1226.

82. The article reads, "A state functionary who unlawfully deprives a citizen of his legitimate freedom of religious belief or violates the customs and folkways of a minority nationality, to a serious degree, shall be sentenced to imprisonment for not more than two years, or to detention," as cited in Lazzarotto, *The Catholic Church in Post-Mao China*, p. 68.

83. Article 35, *People's Daily*, April 28, 1982. Trans. in *China Daily*, April 28, 1982.

84. Zhou Enlai, "Talks at the Forums on Literature and Art and on Film Making," (June 19, 1961), *Wenyi Bao* 2 (1979), p. 2.

85. *People's Daily*, April 29, 1982.

86. "Document 19," p. 1230; Ru Wen, "What I Have Gained from Studying Document 19," p. 14.

87. *TF* 242 (December 22, 1950), p. 273.

88. "Document 19," p. 1230.

89. Welch, *Buddhism Under Mao*, p. 365.

90. Zhang Zhiyi, *On the Chinese People's Democratic United Front*, p. 318.

91. Ibid. p. 318. The essay in which this formulation appears, "Atheists and Theists Can Co-operate Politically and Walk the Road of Socialism," is an excellent example of the united front approach to religious questions as it was understood in the 1950s.

92. Li Weihan, *The United Front Question and the Nationalities Question*, p. 506.

93. Interview with Jiang Wenhan, Vice President of the Standing Committee of the China Christian Council, Shanghai, December 11, 1982.

94. Zhou Enlai, "Several Questions on China's Nationalities Policy," August 4, 1957, *Selected Writings of Zhou Enlai on the United Front*, pp. 383–84.

Chapter 5

1. *TF* 116 (April 10, 1948), p. 4. Translated as "The Present Day Tragedy of Chrisianity," *Documents*, p. 5.

2. *Documents*, p. 16.

3. *TF* 195 (December 31, 1949), pp. 289–91; Zheng Jianye's words are from *TF* 196 (January 14, 1950), pp. 6–8.

4. An early reference to *aiguo-aijiao* is the discussion between Marcus Chen (Chen Chonggu), a staunch conservative-evangelical and formerly president of Chongqing Theological Seminary, and other Protestants and Roman Catholics in Chongqing, *TF* 281 (September 15, 1951), pp. 159–61. In another early reference Liu Liangmo, a progressive YMCA secretary, terms this understanding a prerequisite for the self-propagation of the Chinese church, *TF* 299 (January 12, 1952), pp. 18–19.

5. There is a wealth of material on the theological interpretation of patriotism in the pages of *Tian Feng, The Nanjing Seminary Review, Jiangdao Ji* and elsewhere. It is expressed in essays, sermons and biblical meditations. For a sampling of some of these see Liu Liangmo, "Christianity and Patriotism," *TF* 255 (March 7, 1951), pp. 105–106; Jiang Wenhan, "Church-State Relations," *NSJ* 7 (August 1957), pp. 1–5; Peter Tsai (Cai Wenhao), "The Church in China: Yesterday, Today and Tomorrow," *CCA Consultation with Chinese Church Leaders from China* (Singapore: Christian Conference of Asia, 1981), pp. 13–20; K. H. Ting, "Another Look at Three-Self," *CTR:* 1985, passim; Wang Zhen, "Christian Behavior," *TF* (NS) 16 (July 30, 1983), pp. 1–2.

6. Philip Wickeri, "Sister Jiang: The Story of a Chinese Evangelical," *New World Outlook* (December 1980), p. 30.

7. See J. W. C. Wand, *Anglicanism in History and Today* (London: Weidenfield and Nicolson, 1961), pp. 62–69.

8. William Temple, *Church and Nation* (London: Macmillan, 1915), pp. 56–57. Temple also had this to say about Jesus' weeping for Jerusalem: "No man has ever loved his nation more than the Lord loved Israel, and in the bitterness of disappointment in His lament over Jerusalem we have the measure of His patriotic love for the Holy place of His people" (p. 50).

9. Fierro, *The Militant Gospel*, pp. 71–75.

10. Jiang Wenhan, "Church-State Relations," passim. Also, Jiang's contributions in Chu and Lind, *A New Beginning.*

11. Kenneth Grubb, ed., *World Christian Handbook* (London: World Dominion Press, 1949), pp. 247–49, and 1952 edition, pp. 141–42; Bates, *Gleanings*, p. 101 (Shanghai churches); and Brown, *Christianity in the PRC* (institutions), pp. 78–79. All 1950 statistics are based on *The Directory of Protestant Churches in China* (Shanghai: NCC, December 1950).

12. Kiang Wenhan (Jiang Wenhan), "The SCM in Nanking and Soochow," unpublished paper, pp. 2–3.

13. Frank Price, *The Rural Church in China* (New York: Agricultural Missions, 1948), pp. 1, 221.

14. Ibid. p. 3.

15. Kao Tien-Hsi, "How Shall the Chinese Church Continue Its Work Under the Communist Government?" (Th.M. thesis, Princeton Theological Seminary, 1950), pp. 9ff.

16. Ibid. pp. 80–81. Also, "A Report on Protestant Missions," *Monthly Report* (Shanghai: Millard Publishing Company, December 31, 1949), pp. 9ff.

17. Bates, *Gleanings*, p. 96.

18. "The Experience of the Christian Movement in China with Communism," *CB* 1:77 (January 3, 1950), p. 3.

19. See Ng Lee Ming, "Christianity and Nationalism in China," *East Asia Journal of Theology* 1:1 (1983), pp. 78ff.

20. Quoted in Lynn and Amos Landman, *Profile of Red China* (New York: Simon and Schuster, 1951), pp. 125–26.

21. Mao Zedong, "Friendship or Aggression?" *SW* 4.

22. C. H. Lee, "Why the Goodwill Failed," *CB* 1:67 (September 19, 1949), pp. 1–2.

23. "A Report on Protestant Missions," p. 18.

24. *Documents*, pp. 6–11.

25. Ibid. pp. 1–5.

26. A short biography of Y. T. Wu is contained in Howard Boorman, ed., *Biographical Dictionary of Republican China* (New York: Columbia University Press, 1967), vol. 3, pp. 457–60. For a treatment of Wu's intellectual development prior to his acceptance of communism see Ng, "Christianity and Social Change: The Case of China, 1920–1950," diss. Princeton Theological Seminary, 1970, pp. 175–234. The TSM has published an important collection of essays on Y. T. Wu entitled *In Memory of Mr. Wu Yaozong* (Shanghai, 1982).

27. Ng, "Christianity and Social Change," pp. 179ff.

28. Quoted in Endicott, *James G. Endicott: Rebel Out of China*, pp. 224–25.

29. *TF* 177 (August 27, 1949), p. 56. Wu had expressed the same two years earlier in a talk given to the Chinese SCM: "Since we are Christians and our movement is a Christian movement then we need to have a 'Christian' way of looking at things, and our actions should also be 'Christian' actions. . . . But if we follow this mechanical attitude to its conclusion, what we will have is a 'Christian' formalism. . . . Our goal, at least at the present moment, is no different from that of other people, nor does the method we use in achieving that goal need to be any different." *TF* 98 (1947), p. 7, as cited in Ng, "Christianity and Social Change," p. 238.

30. K. H. Ting, "Forerunner Y. T. Wu," *In Memory of Mr. Wu Yaozong*, p. 90.

31. *TF* 177, p. 55.

32. "The Transformation of Christianity," *TF* 173 (July 30, 1949), p. 9.

33. For the story in his own words see Liu Liangmo, "Shanghai's Anti-Japanese Singing Movement for National Salvation," *Selected Resources on Literature and History* (Shanghai: Shanghai People's Publishers, 1978), First Series, pp. 32–37. Also, Israel Epstein, " 'March of the Volunteers' Echoed Throughout China," *China Daily*, March 11, 1983, p. 5.

34. A short biography of Wu Yifang may be found in Boorman, *Biographical Dictionary*, vol. 3, pp. 460–62. Her obituary appears in *TF* (NS), 38 (February 1, 1986), p. 2.

35. Shen Tilan, who was principal of Medhurst College in Shanghai, is the author of the earliest essay to introduce a perspective similar to the one being developed here to the foreign missionary community. See T. L. Shen, "The People's Movement," *China Christian Yearbook, 1936–1937*, ed. Frank Rawlinson (Shanghai: Christian Literature Society, 1937), pp. 78–82.

36. Kiang Wenhan, *The Chinese Student Movement* (New York: King's Crown Press,

1948), pp. 124–33. For Kiang's views on the Christian-Marxist encounter, see his *Christianity and Marxism-Leninism*, trans. Frank Cooley (New York: Missionary Research Library, 1952).

37. "The SCM in China in the Last Two Years: A View from Peking," *Student World* 44 (1951), pp. 169–74.

38. *TF* 285 (October 13, 1951), p. 206.

39. Paton, "The Church in the World," p. 48.

40. Ibid. p. 49.

41. K. H. Ting, "A Report on the Church Situation in Czechoslovakia and Hungary, with Special Interest in the Light It Throws on China," *CB* 1:69 (October 24, 1949), p. 4.

42. The four official delegates were Y. T. Wu, Cora Deng, T. C. Chao and Zhang Xueyan, editor of the *Christian Forum*. Liu Liangmo had orginally been chosen as a fifth delegate, but he gave up his place and became an alternate so that a Muslim could sit on the religious committee. The three other Protestants were Wu Yifang, Shen Tilan and Chen Sisheng.

43. *TF* 188 (November 12, 1949), p. 200 and *TF* 189 (November 19, 1949), pp. 201–2.

44. Interview with Wu Gaozi.

45. Wu reiterated this position in his report on the visitation teams, see *TF* 204 (March 11, 1950), p. 3.

46. Zhu Chensheng, "Some Impasses Along the Narrow Road," *TF* 214 (May 20, 1950), pp. 221–24.

47. *TF* 233–234 (September 30, 1950), pp. 159–60.

48. Ibid. pp. 155–60.

49. "Comments on the Manifesto," *CB* 1:92 (June 29, 1950), p. 1.

50. *TF* 227 (August 19, 1950), p. 74. The letter and full text of the "Manifesto" appear in *TF* 233–34 (September 30, 1950), pp. 146–47.

51. "Address at a Tea Party Hosted by the Central United Front Work Department," January 20, 1951, *Selected Writings of Zhou Enlai on the United Front*, p. 202. Also see Wickeri, "Zhou Enlai's Conversations with Chinese Christians," p. 11.

52. Translation from *Documents*, p. 19 (slightly revised).

53. *TF* 233–34 (September 30, 1950), pp. 167–80.

54. "The Fourteenth Biennial Meeting of the National Christian Council of China," *The Church* 4:4 (1950), p. 8. Also see Hayward, "Overseas Newsletter VII" (November 1950).

55. The number of signatures on the "Christian Manifesto" increased as follows:

August 1950	1,527	*TF* 233–34 (September 30, 1950), p. 167.
April 1951	180,000	*TF* 262–63 (May 8, 1951), p. 210.
July 1951	250,000	*TF* 274 (July 31, 1951), p. 47.
September 1952	338,552	*TF* 332 (September 10, 1952), p. 539.
September 1953	400,222	*TF* 382–83 (September 24, 1953), p. 543.
September 1954	417,389	*TF* 425–27 (September 3, 1954), p. 431.

56. *Documents*, p. 21.

57. *TF* 233–34 (September 30, 1950), p. 148.

58. One purpose of the editorial which endorsed the "Christian Manifesto" in *People's Daily* was to encourage Chinese Catholics to follow the example of the Protestants. Zhao's remarks are quoted in Welch, *Buddhism Under Mao*, p. 10.

59. Munro, *The Concept of Man in Contemporary China*, p. 54.

60. Lyall, *Come Wind, Come Weather* (Chicago: Moody Press, 1960), pp. 22–26.

61. Charles C. West ("Barnabas"), *Christian Witness in Communist China* (London: SCM Press, 1951), p. 39.

62. This is implied in the concrete methods of the "Manifesto." The Fourteenth Biennial Meeting of the NCC spoke of completing the movement toward Three-Self over a period of five years, and many denominations had a similar timeframe in mind. Also, see *TF* 223 (July 22, 1950), p. 25.

63. On the departure of foreign missionaries from China see Bush, *Religion in Communist China*, pp. 38–68.

64. Because of the Korean War American missionaries were the primary objects of attack in the denunciation movement, although missionaries from other countries were by no means exempt from criticism. For other interpretations of the movement see Jones, *The Church in Communist China*, pp. 63–73; and Bush, *Religion in Communist China*, pp. 187–89.

65. *TF* 262–63 (May 8, 1951) deals almost entirely with the denunciation movement. For the design of the individual denunciation meeting see Liu Liangmo, "How to Hold a Denunciation Meeting within the Church," *TF* 264 (May 19, 1951), p. 233.

66. *TF* 332 (September 20, 1952), p. 541. A three-page listing of major published denunciations through the end of September appears in *Xie Jin* 1:6 (November 1951), pp. 22–24. By September 15, 1953, there had been 227 denunciation meetings in 133 cities, *TF* 382–83 (September 24, 1953), p. 533.

67. April 24, 1951, as reprinted in *TF* 262–63 (May 8, 1951), p. 213. The government also issued several pamphlets on the denunciation movement, such as *Thoroughly Sever the Relationship Between Christianity and American Imperialism* (Beijing: People's Literature Publishing House, 1951).

68. *TF* 262–63 (May 8, 1951), p. 225.

69. See, for example, "Continue to Expand and Deepen the Denunciation Movement," *TF* 276 (August 11, 1951), pp. 73–74; Shen Derong, "Some Ideological Problems of a Minority of Christians Regarding the Present Denunciation Movement," *TF* 277 (August 18, 1951), pp. 93–94 and *TF* 278 (August 25, 1951), pp. 105–6.

70. "Some of My Experiences and Understanding about Denunciation," *TF* 264 (May 19, 1951), p. 232.

71. At the April meeting Price was denounced by Tsui, Luther Shao (Shao Jingsan) and Phoebe Shi (Shi Ruzhang), *TF* 262–63 (May 8, 1951), pp. 214–17. Also, see *TF* 268–269 (June 21, 1951), pp. 300–301 and *TF* 286 (October 20, 1951), pp. 218–19.

72. Frank Price set forth his own position on China in countless articles and books. See especially *China: Twilight or Dawn?*

73. Interview with Zheng Jianye, General Secretary, China Christian Council, Shanghai, April 25, 1982.

74. "Continue to Expand and Deepen the Denunciation Movement," *TF* 276 (August 11, 1951), p. 74. Translation revised from *CB* 1:114 (September 13, 1951), p. 1.

75. Han Wenzao, "The Christian Reform Movement in Nanjing," *TF* 280 (September 8, 1951), pp. 137–41.

76. Zheng Jianye, "How Our Reform Study Class Developed into a Denunciation Meeting," *TF* 299 (January 26, 1951), pp. 52–55.

77. Franz Schurmann, *Ideology and Organization in Communist China* (Berkeley: University of California Press, 1968), 2d ed., p. 317.

78. Interviews with Shen Derong and Zheng Jianye.

79. Interview with Zheng Jianye.

80. Y. T. Wu, "The New Life of Chinese Christianity," *People's Daily*, May 24, 1951, as reprinted in *A Study Manual of the Christian Reform Movement*, ed. Y. T. Wu (Shanghai: YMCA Bookstore, 1952), p. 89.

81. For example, Chen, *Thought Reform of the Chinese Intellectuals*, and Edward Hunter, *Brainwashing in Red China* (New York: Viking Press, 1951). For other views see Robert Lifton, *Thought Reform and the Psychology of Totalism: A Study of "Brainwashing" in Red China* (New York: Norton, 1961); Harriet Mills, "Thought Reform: Ideological Remolding in China," *Atlantic* 204:6 (December 1959), pp. 71–78; and Allyn and Adele Ricketts, *Prisoners of Liberation* (Garden City: Anchor Press, 1963).

82. Ricketts, *Prisoners of Liberation*, p. 265.

83. *TF* 261 (April 28, 1951), pp. 188–89.

84. Interview with Jiang Wenhan, and also Jiang Wenhan, "An Introduction to Land Reform Work in the Shanghai Suburbs," *TF* 293 (December 8, 1951), pp. 324–25. Also see, "Lu Chi-wei on Land Reform," *CB* 1:121 (January 4, 1952), pp. 1–2.

85. Mao Zedong, "Great Victories in Three Mass Movements," SW 5, p. 60.

86. Tu Yuqing, "After Attending the Third Session of the First National Committee of the CPPCC," *TF* 292 (December 1, 1951), p. 311.

87. The first Three-Self leadership training program was held in Shanghai, beginning in early November and lasting until December 21, 1951, *TF* 294–295 (December 22, 1951), p. 338.

88. This is explicitly stated in the record of a discussion among twenty Protestant leaders in December 1951, see "The Question of Ideological Remolding for Christians," *TF* 298 (January 19, 1952), pp. 33–34.

89. Translated in *Documents*, pp. 51–54.

90. Ibid. pp. 55–59.

91. *TF* 288 (November 3, 1951), p. 247.

92. Ibid. p. 248.

93. Robin Chen, "A Summary Report on Shanghai's Three-Self Reform Study Class for Church Workers," *TF* 393 (December 7, 1953), p. 5.

94. Lifton, *Thought Reform*, p. 401.

95. Jones, *The Church in Communist China*, pp. 76–80.

96. Shen Yifan, "What I Have Gained," *TF* 393 (December 7, 1953), p. 698. Another final report from the 1953 Study Class, written from a conservative-evangelical perspective, is also worth reading: see Ke Yuexia, "I Have Received a Precious Key," pp. 699–700.

97. Chu and Lind, eds., *A New Beginning*, p. 41.

98. The proposal for a national conference was first made in *TF* 185 (October 22, 1949), p. 153.

99. *TF* 210 (April 23, 1950), p. 173.

100. For a report on the conference on Christian publications see *TF* 258 (April 7, 1951), p. 145.

101. *TF* 262–63 (May 8, 1951), pp. 226–27.

102. Y. T. Wu, "The New Life of Chinese Christianity," p. 96.

103. Temporary offices for the Preparatory Committee were at 79 Suzhou South Road. In November 1952 the Committee moved to 169 Yuanmingyuan Road, where the NCC was located. This has been the headquarters of the TSM ever since.

104. "Patriotic Shanghai Protestants Mobilize for a Big Meeting," *TF* 245 (December 30, 1950), pp. 320–21; "Learn from the Experience of Guangzhou Christians," *TF* 252 (February 24, 1951), p. 69; "The Third Three-Self Reform Conference in Nan-

jing,'' *TF* 434 (October 25, 1954), pp. 559–60. Nanjing had had two conferences before the First National Christian Conference in Beijing.

105. Y. T. Wu, ''The Second Anniversary of the Chinese Christian Three-Self Reform Movement,'' *TF* 332 (September 20, 1952), p. 541.

106. ''A Working Report on the Preparatory Committee's Visitation Team to Zhejiang and Fujian,'' *TF* 377–78 (August 21, 1953), pp. 461–64.

107. *TF* 425–27 (September 3, 1954), p. 435.

108. Ibid. p. 436.

109. Ibid. pp. 429–30; 473–76.

110. Ibid. p. 436.

111. Ibid. p. 469.

112. Y. T. Wu, ''Report on the Chinese Christian Three-Self Patriotic Movement, July, 1954–March, 1956,'' *TF* 502 (April 16, 1956), pp. 10ff.

113. Y. T. Wu and Cora Deng, ''Observations on the Church Situation in Anhui,'' *TF* 520 (January 14, 1957), p. 12.

114. Marcus Chen, ''Safeguard and Respect Religious Faith,'' *TF* 528 (May 13, 1957), pp. 3–5, 7. Translated in *Documents*, pp. 151–56. The criticism of Chen's statement during the subsequent Anti-Rightist campaign is discussed in the next chapter.

115. Y. T. Wu, ''Some Questions on the Implementation of the Policy of Religious Freedom,'' *TF* 524 (March 18, 1957), p. 305.

Chapter 6

1. Wang Mingdao, ''We, Because of Faith,'' *Documents*, pp. 113–14. The Chinese version of this essay may be found in *Treasuries of Wang Mingdao*, vol. 7, *On Guard*, ed. C. C. Wang (Touliu, Taiwan: Conservative Baptist Press, 1984), pp. 263–333.

2. Wang Zhen, ''My Thoughts Regarding Religious Freedom,'' *TF* (NS) 15 (May 30, 1983), p. 17. Translated in *CF* 26 (August 1983), p. 151.

3. On the characterization of religious sects see Ernst Troeltsch, *The Social Teachings of the Christian Churches*, trans. Olive Wyon (Chicago: University of Chicago Press, 1981), vol. 1, pp. 331ff; H. R. Niebuhr, *The Social Sources of Denominationalism* (Hamden, CT: Shoestring Press, 1959), pp. 17ff; and Bryan Wilson, ''An Analysis of Sect Development,'' *Patterns of Sectarianism*, ed. Bryan Wilson (London: Heineman, 1967), pp. 22–45.

4. J. J. M. De Groot, *Sectarianism and Religious Persecution in China* (Amsterdam: Johannes Muller, 1903), vol. 1, p. 3.

5. See Roger O'Toole, '' 'Underground' Traditions in the Study of Sectarianism: Non-Religious Uses of the Concept 'Sect,' '' *Journal for the Scientific Study of Religion* 15:2 (1976), pp. 146–48.

6. V. I. Lenin, *Selected Works* (London: Lawrence and Wishart, 1947), vol. 2, p. 634.

7. Daniel H. Bays, ''Christianity and Chinese Sects: Religious Tracts in the Late Nineteenth Century,'' *Christianity in China: Early Protestant Missionary Writings*, ed. Suzanne W. Barnett and John K. Fairbank (Cambridge: Harvard University Press, 1985), p.134.

8. Jones, *The Church in Communist China*, p. 16.

9. C. Stanley Smith, ''Modern Religious Movements in Christianity,'' *China Christian Yearbook, 1934–1935*, ed. Frank Rawlinson (Shanghai: Christian Literature Society, 1935), pp. 97, 110.

10. For example, Wang Mingdao, ''We, Because of Faith,'' p. 104.

11. Allen J. Swanson, *Taiwan: Mainline versus Independent Church Growth* (South Pasadena: William Carey Library, 1970), pp. 35–53.

12. Bryan Wilson, *Religious Sects: A Sociological Study* (New York: McGraw-Hill, 1970), pp. 229–33.

13. Paul Abbott, "Revival Movements," *China Christian Yearbook 1932–33*, ed. Frank Rawlinson (Shanghai: CLS, 1934), p. 180.

14. Smith, "Modern Religious Movements in Christianity," p. 99.

15. Abbott, "Revival Movements," pp. 187, 186.

16. The estimate is from Jones, *The Church in Communist China*, p. 19.

17. *TF* 302 (February 23, 1952), pp. 100–103. Translated in *Documents*, pp. 60–65. Local congregations of the True Jesus Church continued to meet in many places through 1958, and they continue to be active in many parts of China today.

18. Francis James, "China: Religion's Carefully Charted Path," *Reports on the Deputation of Australian Churchmen to Mainland China*, ed. Francis James (Sydney: Anglican News Service, 1956), p. 11.

19. See Roderick MacFarquhar, ed., *The Hundred Flowers* (Middlesex: Stevens and Sons, 1960), especially pp. 248–53 and 261–91. Also, Mu Fu-sheng, *The Wilting of the Hundred Flowers* (London: Heineman, 1962), passim.

20. An editorial in *Tian Feng* emphasizes the difference between the case of Gu Renen, who was charged with spying for the American government in 1951, and that of Long Xiangwen, a woman who had been criticized in an earlier issue for her "reactionary thinking." Gu, the editorial claimed, was arrested not for his views, but because of his actions on behalf of the Americans. See *TF* 256 (March 24, 1951), pp. 118–19, and follow-up reports, including a confession, in subsequent issues.

21. D. Vaughan Rees, *The Jesus Family in Communist China* (Exeter: Pater Noster Press, 1959), p. 46. For another portrait of the Jesus Family, emphasizing its "workable Christian Communism," see Wang Shi Peng and H. W. Spillett, "A Christian Communist Settlement in China," *IRM* 40 (1951), pp. 168–78.

22. Y. T. Wu, "The Second Anniversary of the Christian Three-Self Reform Movement," p. 541.

23. Jing Zhendong, "The Words and Actions of Jing Tianying," *TF* 353–354 (February 28, 1953), pp. 102–8.

24. Leslie Lyall, *Three of China's Mighty Men* (London: OMF Books, 1974), p. 79.

25. For the history of the "Little Flock" see Angus Kinnear, *Against the Tide: Watchman Nee* (Eastbourne: Victory Press, 1973); Lyall, *Three of China's Mighty Men*, pp. 45–93; and Swanson, pp. 57–62.

26. A report on Nee's obstruction of Land Reform is carried in *TF* 298 (January 1, 1952), pp. 40–42. In an interview with Tang Shoulin, one of Nee's former associates in Shanghai, an interesting sidelight of this incident was revealed. "Watchman Nee had a great deal of property in Fujian. At the beginning of the Land Reform Movement, he collected 30,000 signatures from 'Little Flock' members on a petition to oppose the confiscation of these lands. They were, the petition claimed, used for church purposes. In fact, the people signed their names twice on two different petitions which were to oppose Land Reform. When one petition was rejected by the government, Nee asked me to turn the other signatures over to Y. T. Wu, saying that they were in support of the 'Christian Manifesto' and that they could be published in *Tian Feng*. Y. T. Wu was both pleased and surprised. However, it later turned out that these names were not in support of the 'Manifesto' at all. Nee had merely used the opportunity to build good relations with the TSM, when he in fact opposed them." Interview with Tang Shoulin,

Vice-Chairperson, Standing Committee of the Chinese Christian Three-Self Patriotic Movement, Shanghai, April 26, 1982.

27. *TF* 498 (February 6, 1956), pp. 9–10.

28. Ibid. p. 11. The next three issues of *Tian Feng* are dominated by reporting on Watchman Nee.

29. Interview with Tang Shoulin.

30. *TF* 498 (February 6, 1956), p. 13; *TF* 503 (April 30, 1956), p. 22.

31. Interview with Tang Shoulin.

32. Jones, *The Church in Communist China*, p. 103. The best source of biographical information on Wang Mingdao is Ng Lee Ming, "Christianity and Social Change," pp. 56–95. Also see the autobiography of Wang Mingdao, *These Fifty Years* (Hong Kong: Bellman House, 1967). A short sketch of Wang Mingdao's life is found in Lyall, *Three of China's Mighty Men*, pp. 97–142.

33. Ng, "Christianity and Social Change," pp. 83–85.

34. *CB* 4:12 (June 7, 1954), p. 3.

35. Interview with Shen Derong. The five older ministers were Robin Chen, Marcus Chen, Xie Yongqin, Zhu Guishen and Z. T. Kaung.

36. The major outside source for Wang Mingdao's arrest and imprisonment is *CB*. Events are summarized in Jones, *The Church in Communist China*, pp. 103–5.

37. The charges are never specified in *TF*. For a general account see *TF* 482–483 (September 19, 1955), p. 682.

38. *TF* 490–491 (November 14, 1955), p. 831.

39. It is Leslie Lyall who calls Wang a "man of iron" in *Three of China's Mighty Men*, pp. 97ff.

40. For this and what follows I am indebted to the discussion in Ng, "Christianity and Social Change," pp. 88–95.

41. Quotation and comment from ibid. pp. 77, 80.

42. Wang Mingdao, "We, Because of Faith," p. 104.

43. Qin Mu, "The True Meaning and Distorted Interpretation of 'Be ye not unequally yoked with unbelievers,' " *TF* 453 (February 28, 1955), pp. 134–138. Qin Mu was a pseudonym used by Huang Peiyong according to *TF* 629–630 (March 31, 1963), p. 23.

44. Qin Mu, "Opposed to 'Modernism' or Opposed to the TSM?" *TF* 473–474 (July 21, 1955), pp. 524–28.

45. This same point is reiterated in Xu Rulei, "Whom Has the *Spiritual Food Quarterly* Been Serving These Past 29 Years?" *NSJ* 4 (November 1955), pp. 20–28.

46. K. H. Ting, "A Stern Warning to Wang Mingdao," *TF* 477–478 (August 15, 1955), p. 608.

47. Ng, "Christianity and Social Change," p. 94.

48. Jones, *The Church in Communist China*, p. 111.

49. Geoffrey Nuttall and Owen Chadwick, *From Uniformity to Unity, 1662–1962* (London: S.P.C.K., 1962), p. 9.

50. *TF* 337 (November 1, 1952), pp. 627–29.

51. "*Gong Bao's* Self-Criticism," *TF* 381 (September 16, 1953), p. 520.

52. See *TF* 469–70 (June 24, 1955).

53. *TF* 529 (May 27, 1957), p. 3.

54. For a general discussion see MacFarquhar, *The Hundred Flowers* and Merle Goldman, *Literary Dissent in Communist China* (New York: Atheneum, 1971), pp. 158–202.

55. As cited in Jones, *The Church in Communist China*, pp. 137, 145.

56. Goldman, *Literary Dissent in Communist China*, p. 204.

57. Shen Derong, "My Understanding of 'Blooming' and 'Contending,' " *TF* 531 (June 24, 1957), pp. 6–7. Shen's essay is based on the talk given by Cheng Zhiming to Shanghai Christian leaders on June 11.

58. *TF* 533 (July 29, 1957), p. 4.

59. "Resolution on Party History," para. 17, p. 19.

60. Most of the reports and criticism from this meeting were not published in *TF*. The source I am using is *Special Edition on the Tenth (Enlarged) Plenum of the Standing Committee of the Chinese Christian Three-Self Patriotic Movement* (Shanghai: TSM Committee, 1957).

61. Ibid. pp. 39–42. The major criticism of Chen, entitled "Unmask Chen Chonggui, Who Says He Supports the Leadership of the Party, but in Fact Opposes It," is signed by twenty-two individuals. One possible explanation for the pettiness of some of the specific charges against Chen is that those involved felt they had to say something, but did not want to say anything too serious against him.

Chen remained a leader of the TSM until his death at the age of 81 in 1963. At that time Y. T. Wu led the funeral committee, which indicates that he must have been regarded as a member of the TSM committee in good standing, see *TF* 629–30 (March 31, 1963), p. 18.

62. Jiang Wenhan's speech at the Tenth Plenum, "On the Manipulation of Christianity by Imperialism," indicates the renewed emphasis on missionaries and imperialism, see *TF* 546 (February 10, 1958), pp. 3–8. There are a number of small pamphlets and mimeographed material from this period contained in the library of Nanjing Theological Seminary.

63. *TF* 604–605 (February 27, 1951), p. 10.

64. Ibid. p. 10. In the "Resolution" and other conference documents, Chinese Christians refer to themselves as a "circle" (*jie*), which is a departure from earlier usage. The employment of this term would tend to de-emphasize the institutional character of Christianity, thus suggesting a diminishing importance of church work in the TSM.

65. See Roderick MacFarquhar, *The Origins of the Cultural Revolution*, vol. 2, *The Great Leap Forward* (New York: Columbia University Press, 1983); William A. Joseph, *The Critique of Ultra-Leftism in China* (Stanford: Stanford University Press, 1984), especially pp. 82–119.

66. Joseph, *The Critique of Ultra-Leftism in China*, p. 231.

67. *TF* 606–7 (April 18, 1961), p. 6.

68. Interview with K. H. Ting (Ding Guangxun), Chairperson, Standing Committee of the Chinese Christian Three-Self Patriotic Movement, and President, China Christian Council, Nanjing, June 29, 1982.

69. NCCUSA, *China Consultation: 1960* (New York: Far Eastern Office of the Division of Foreign Missions, 1960), p. 8.

70. As cited in A Correspondent, "On Understanding the Position of the Church in China," *The East and West Review* 26 (January 1960), p. 21. The correspondent was David Paton.

71. Hu Hua and Lin Daizhao, "The Eradication of 'Leftist' Influences Requires a Thoroughgoing Reform," *The Ideological and Theoretical Contributions of Zhou Enlai*, ed. Hu Hua et al. (Guangzhou: Guangdong People's Publishers, 1982), pp. 159ff.

72. Cf. K. H. Ting, "Preface," *The Chinese Theological Review: 1985*, ed. Janice Wickeri, pp. vi–vii.

73. "Decision of the Central Committee of the Chinese Communist Party Concerning the Great Proletarian Cultural Revolution," *Peking Review* 33 (August 12, 1966), p. 6.

74. As cited in Bush, *Religion in Communist China*, p. 257. Accounts of the experience of Chinese Christians during the Cultural Revolution may be found in *China Notes*, from 1966 on; and Britt E. Towery, *The Churches of China: Taking Root Downward, Bearing Fruit Upward* 2d ed. (Hong Kong: Long Dragon Books, 1987), pp. 17–33.

75. Ye Yonglie, "The Death of Fu Lei," *Here History Ponders: A True Record of 1966–1976*, ed. Zhou Ming (Beijing: Hua Xia Publishers, 1986), vol. 3, p. 179.

76. On Lao She's death see Anne E. Thurston, *Enemies of the People* (New York: Alfred A. Knopf, 1987), p. 137; on his religious beliefs see Shu Bo, "Lao She and Christianity," *NSJ* (NS) 6–7 (September 1987), pp. 130–31.

77. This paragraph is a composite picture based upon informal conversations in Nanjing between 1981 and 1983.

78. "Answers to Thirteen Questions from Evangelical Christians by the Chinese Christian Delegation," (London: October 1982, mimeographed), p. 2.

79. Thurston, *Enemies of the People*, p. 107.

80. For a discussion of Zhou's political role during the early years of the Cultural Revolution see Thomas Robinson, "Chou En-lai and the Cultural Revolution in China," *The Cultural Revolution in China*, ed. Thomas Robinson (Berkeley: University of California Press, 1971), pp. 165–312, especially pp. 169–70 and 279–89.

81. For example, Jonathan Chao. "The Witness of a Suffering Church," pp. 8–12; and Sharon Mumper, "The Church the Gang of Four Built," *Christianity Today*, May 15, 1987, pp. 17–21.

82. Zhao Fusan, *Christianity in China: Three Lectures* (Manila: De La Salle University Press, 1986), p. 29.

83. Nien Cheng, *Life and Death in Shanghai* (London: Grafton Books, 1986).

84. Yue Daiyun and Carolyn Wakeman, *To the Storm: The Odyssey of a Revolutionary Chinese Woman* (Berkeley: University of California Press, 1985), p. 387.

85. Thurston, *Enemies of the People*, p. 300.

86. Interview with Wang Weifan, Instructor, Nanjing Theological Seminary, Nanjing, April 13, 1983.

87. Johann Baptist Metz, *Faith in History and Society*, trans. David Smith (New York: Crossroad, 1980), pp. 126–27.

88. "Open Letter to Brothers and Sisters in Christ Throughout China from the Standing Committee of the Chinese Christian Three-Self Patriotic Movement," *TF* (NS) 1 (October 20, 1980), p. 2. Translated in *CTR: 1985*, p. 49.

89. Interview with Peter Tsai, Vice-President, China Christian Council, Hong Kong, April 7, 1981.

90. The single best collection of stories on the home worship gatherings is Raymond Fung, *Households of God on China's Soil* (Geneva: World Council of Churches, 1982). Also see Whyte, *Unfinished Encounter: China and Christianity* (London: Collins, 1988), Chapter 8; *Bridge: Church Life in China Today*, and *China and the Church Today*.

91. Fung, *Households of God on China's Soil*, pp. vii–ix.

92. Don MacInnis, "Religion and Values in China Today," *CN* 12:4 (Fall 1974), p. 38.

93. Interview with Peter Tsai and other Protestant leaders from Zhejiang, Hangzhou, January 16, 1983.

94. On the restoration of social and cultural activities in China after the fall of the "Gang of Four," see Roger Garside, *Coming Alive: China after Mao* (New York: New American Library, 1981).

95. "Open Letter to Brothers and Sisters in Christ Throughout China," *CTR: 1985*, p. 51.

96. Major speeches and documents from this conference are contained in *TF* (NS) 2 (March 20, 1981), pp. 1–63. Some of these are translated in *CTR: 1985*.

97. *TF* (NS) 2 (March 20, 1981), p. 15. Translation from *CF* 22: 3 & 4 (1980), p. 172.

98. Zheng Jianye, "On the Question of a Church Affairs Organization," *TF* (NS) 2 (March 20, 1981), p. 31. Translation from *CTR: 1985*, p. 47.

99. K. H. Ting, "Retrospect and Prospect," p. 37.

100. Zheng Jianye, "On the Question of a Church Affairs Organization," *CTR: 1985*, p. 42.

101. Translation from K. H. Ting, "Building Up the Body in Love," *CTR: 1986*, p. 104.

102. A full report on the conference has been published as *Collected Documents from the Fourth National Christian Conference* (Shanghai: China Christian Council and Chinese Christian Three-Self Movement Committee, 1986). Also see *TF* (NS) 47 (November 1, 1986), pp. 2–39; and in English, "Love-Country–Love-Church," *China Talk*, 11:5–6 (November 1986).

103. Shen Derong, "A Summary Report on the Activities of the China Christian Council and the Chinese Christian Three-Self Patriotic Movement Committee, August 1986 to August 1987," *TF* (NS) 59 (November 1, 1987), p. 5.

104. K. H. Ting, "Opening Speech at the Dedication of the Amity Printing Press," December 5, 1987.

105. 1950 figures are from Bingle and Grubb, *World Christian Handbook: 1952 Edition*, pp. 141–42. The 1982 population figure is from the recent census, a discussion of which may be found in John Aird, "The Preliminary Results of China's 1982 Census," *CQ* 96 (December 1983), pp. 613–40. The figure for Chinese Protestants is from the report cited for Table 2.

106. "Document 19," p. 1222.

107. For contrasting interpretations of the number of Christians in China see G. Thompson Brown, "How Many Christians Are There in China?" *China News Update* (June 1987), pp. 1, 6; Mumper, "The Church the Gang of Four Built," pp. 17ff.; Howard Snyder and Daniel Runyon, "Ten Major Trends Facing the Church," *International Bulletin of Missionary Research*, 11:2 (April 1987), p. 68; and "How Many Protestant Christians Are There in China?" *Bridge* 25 (September–October 1987), p. 16. A Chinese Marxist theoretician has warned that the hasty use of formulations about religious growth "can easily foster 'leftist' tendencies in our practical work." (Xiao Zhitian, "Some Opinions on the Present Religious Phenomena," *Collected Essays on Religious Research* [Shanghai: Shanghai Religious Studies Association, 1982], p. 122). A similar warning should be in order for those who would draw hasty conclusions about church growth from a Christian point of view.

108. Ting, "Retrospect and Prospect," pp. 28–31.

109. Bertolt Brecht, *Selected Poems*, trans. H. R. Hays (New York: Reynal and

Hitchcock, 1947), p. 177. This poem is also cited in Ting, "Reconciliation," *NSJ* (NS) 5 (December 1986), p. 6.

110. K. H. Ting, "On the Question of Implementation of Religious Policy," *People's Daily*, September 9, 1980.

Chapter 7

1. Frank Rawlinson, *Naturalization of Christianity in China* (Shanghai: Presbyterian Mission Press, 1927), p. 167.

2. K. H. Ting, "Why Should We Be Preachers Today?" *NSJ* 2 (April 1954), pp. 8–9.

3. Cao Shengjie, "Christian Witness in New China," *CCA Consultation with Church Leaders from China*, p. 35.

4. Ibid. p. 29.

5. Wu, "Report on the Christian Three-Self Patriotic Movement, July 1954–March 1956," p. 10. Translation revised from *Documents*, p. 126.

6. Karl Rahner, *Theological Investigations*, trans. Karl and Boniface Kruger (New York: Crossroad, 1982), vol. 6, p. 239.

7. Ibid. p. 396.

8. Ting, "The Church in China," pp. 4–5.

9. Rawlinson, *Naturalization of Christianity in China*, p. 180.

10. In a sermon entitled "Burning and Shining Forth," Shen Yifan develops the importance of the relationship between faith and works by comparing Paul's view of works (Rom. 2:27–28; Eph. 2:8–9; Gal. 5:6) with James' view of faith (Jas. 1:2–4; 6; 5:15). His point is that faith must become active in works, but that works without faith are empty and without grace. See *TF* 455 (March 14, 1955), pp. 176–77.

11. Zhao, "The Three-Self Movement Is a Movement for the Reinvigoration of the Church," *TF* 260 (April 21, 1951), pp. 175, 176.

12. Shen, "My Recognition of the Church," *TF* 269 (June 8, 1953), pp. 334–35.

13. Y. T. Wu, "A New State in the Christian Reform Movement," *TF* 246 (January 13, 1951), p. 2.

14. M. Searle Bates, "The Protestant Experience in China, 1937–1949," *Frontiers of the Christian World Mission Since 1938*, ed. Wilbur Harr (New York: Harper, 1962), pp. 5–6; 15–19.

15. Interviews with Tang Shoulin and Ren Zhongxiang.

16. "The Church's Self-Support," *TF* 212 (May 4, 1950), p. 197.

17. See Bush, *Religion in Communist China*, pp. 69–98.

18. Xie Yongqin, "Our Church's Experience of Independence and Self-Support," *TF* 254 (March 10, 1951), pp. 96–97.

19. "On the Question of Existing Difficulties with Self-Support in Some Churches," *TF* 506 (June 11, 1956), p. 3.

20. "Program of the Chinese Christian Three-Self Patriotic Movement to Assist Churches in Resolving Difficulties in Self-Support in 1957," *TF* 531 (June 24, 1957), p. 8.

21. H. H. Tsui, "Speech on the Situation of Self-Support in the Churches," *TF* 530 (June 10, 1957), pp. 7–10.

22. *TF* 533 (July 29, 1957), pp. 20–22 and *TF* 535 (August 26, 1957), pp. 19–21. Forty-five letters were received on the subject; all but four agreed that pastors should be involved in productive labor. The editor cites the example of Paul's tentmaking ministry, the deepening of one's spiritual experience through manual work and the contribu-

tions that would be made to China's socialist reconstruction as the base of their views. This discussion should not be confused with the 1958 debate over the class background of Protestant ministers, which revolved around the question of whether or not preachers should be regarded as members of the "exploiter class." See *TF* 559 (August 25, 1958), pp. 27–30.

23. K. H. Ting, *How to Study the Bible*, p. 32. This pamphlet was originally published by the Christian Literature Society in 1955.

24. Chen Zemin, "Reconciliation with the People," *A New Beginning*, p. 16.

25. Interview with Jiang Peifen.

26. Wang Shenyin, "The Call Forward," p. 179.

27. Some of the more incisive essays and reports on this subject are Chen Zemin, "The Evangelical Task of Christianity in Light of the Challenge of the New Age," *TF* 204 (March 11, 1958), pp. 102–3; Ding Xiancheng, "An Informal Talk on Evangelism in the New Age," *TF* 226 (August 12, 1950), pp. 62–64; Heng Gang, "Preachers Should Undergo a Self-Criticism," *TF* 258 (April 7, 1951), pp. 146–48; Wang Weifan, "Our Life During Winter Vacation (I)," *TF* 303 (March 1, 1952), pp. 118–19; Chen Chonggui, "What is a Qualified Preacher?" *TF* 405 (March 15, 1954), pp. 138–40 and *TF* 406 (March 22, 1954), pp. 154–56.

28. Zheng Dengguang, "I Accuse American Imperialism of Poisoning My Church," *TF* 275 (August 4, 1951), pp. 68–69.

29. H. H. Tsui, "A Talk on the Question of 'Self-Propagation,' " *TF* 343 (December 13, 1952), p. 719.

30. Shen Yuehan, "A Self-Propagation Miscellany," *TF* 358 (March 30, 1953), p. 177. For other essays criticizing the leftist trend in biblical interpretation see Huang Peixin, "Don't Use the Bible Mechanically in Speaking About Politics," *TF* 293 (December 8, 1951), p. 334; and Si Bo, "My Understanding of Self-Propagation," *TF* 370 (June 15, 1953), p. 354.

31. Kaung, "My Opinions on the Task of Self-Propagation," *TF* 530 (June 10, 1957), pp. 5–7.

32. Testimonies and reports about model workers appear in *Tian Feng* from 1953 on. For a sampling of these, see the three separate reports by a teacher, a peasant and a worker in *TF* 510 (August 6, 1956), pp. 24–26.

33. Z. T. Kaung, et al., "Christians Should Exert Their Utmost in National Construction," *TF* 511 (August 20, 1956), p. 13. Note that the final sentence reaffirms the importance of the policy of religious freedom by linking it to the contributions of Christian model workers.

34. Munro, *The Concept of Man in Contemporary China*, p. 154.

35. Wang Shenyin, "Learn from the Apostle Paul," *TF* 353–54 (February 28, 1953), pp. 100–101; Luo Zhenfang, "The Prophetic Model," *TF* 492–93 (November 28, 1955), pp. 889–90; Lin Guanrong, "Come With Me," *NSJ* 4 (November 1955), pp. 6–9.

36. Barry Till, *The Churches Search for Unity* (Middlesex: Penguin Books, 1971), p. 17.

37. World Missionary Conference (1910), *Co-operation and the Promotion of Unity* (Edinburgh: Oliphant, Anderson and Ferrier, 1910), vol. 8, p. 83.

38. Ibid. p. 85.

39. Ibid. p. 196. Cheng Chingyi (1881–1939) was later to assume positions of leadership in both the National Christian Council and the Church of Christ in China. For a short biographical sketch see *The Chinese Recorder* 70:12 (December 1939), pp. 691–95.

40. Kenneth S. Latourette, *A History of the Expansion of Christianity*, vol. 7 (Grand Rapids: Zondervan, 1971), p. 353.

41. "On the Unity of the Church," *TF* 218 (June 17, 1950), p. 271.

42. Shi Chenghui, "An Obstacle to Church Unity," *TF* 218 (June 17, 1950), pp. 274–75.

43. Tian Yunzhen, "Some Thoughts on the Unity of the Churches," *TF* 441 (December 6, 1954), p. 665.

44. See Marcus Chen's speech before the CPPCC on Christian unity and national unity, reprinted in *TF* 446–47 (January 11, 1955), pp. 18–19.

45. Little can be said because of the paucity of documentary evidence on the unification process. Reports begin with *TF* 559 (August 25, 1958) and continue for the next four or five issues. The subject also comes up in later visits between Chinese Protestants and foreign guests, but these accounts are more interpretive than descriptive.

46. Cheng Guanyi, "Feelings and Hopes on the New Face of the Church in Beijing," *TF* 559 (August 25, 1958), p. 21.

47. Dun Yan, "Thoroughly Change the Semi-Colonial Face of Christianity in Shanghai," *TF* 561 (September 22, 1958), pp. 18–19.

48. "Thoroughly Smash the Imperialist Plot to 'Divide and Rule,' " *TF* 560 (September 8, 1958), pp. 12–13; and M. S. Bates, "China," *The Prospects of Christianity Throughout the World*, ed. M. S. Bates and Wilhelm Pauck (New York: Scribner's, 1964), p. 221.

49. *TF* 561 (September 22, 1958), p. 20.

50. Cheng Guanyi, "Feelings and Hope," p. 21.

51. "Interview with Chao Fusan," *CB* 10–2 (January 18, 1960), p. 1.

52. A Correspondent (David Paton), "On Understanding the Position of the Church in China," p. 26.

53. H. H. Tsui, "We Must Consolidate and Expand Our Unity," *TF* 464 (May 16, 1955), p. 346. For an evangelical perspective on the same subject see Wang Weifan. "Although We are Many, We are Still One Body," *TF* 465 (May 23, 1955), pp. 369, 373.

54. Tsui, "We Must Consolidate and Expand Our Unity," p. 346.

55. K. H. Ting, "Rev. K. H. Ting's Speech (Selections)," *TF* 425–427 (September 3, 1954), p. 453.

56. Frank Price, "Lew, Timothy Ting-fang," *Concise Dictionary of the Christian World Mission*, ed. Stephen Neill et al. (Nashville and New York: Abingdon, 1971), p. 345.

57. The seminaries were Trinity Theological Seminary (Ningbo); Central Theological Seminary (Shanghai); China Theological Seminary (Hangzhou); China Baptist Theological Seminary (Shanghai); Jiangsu Baptist Bible School (Zhenjiang); Ming Dao Bible Seminary (Jinan); Nanjing Theological Seminary; North China Theological Seminary (Wuxi); Minan Theological Seminary (Changzhou); Fujian Union Seminary (Fuzhou); and Cheeloo Theological Seminary (Jinan). Nanjing Union Theological Seminary is not to be confused with the former Nanjing Theological Seminary, an ecumenical theological school and one of the eleven institutions to come together. See *TF* 338–339 (November 15, 1952), pp. 641–49, on the opening of the seminary; and *NSJ* 1 (September 1953), pp. 29–34 and passim, on curriculum, faculty and course of study in the first year.

58. *TF* 330 (September 6, 1952), p. 507.

59. K. H. Ting, "Nanjing Theological Seminary After Six Months," *TF* 358 (March 30, 1953), pp. 174–75.

60. Interview with K. H. Ting.

61. Shen Zigao, "The First Anniversary of Nanjing Union Seminary," *NSJ* 2 (April 1954), pp. 1–3.

62. *NSJ* 1 (September 1953) p. 30. Translation adapted from *CB* 5:1 (January 10, 1955), p. 1. Note the different Chinese terms for God used in this statement, reflecting respect for different traditions within Chinese Protestantism.

63. Dunn, *Unity and Diversity in the New Testament* (Philadelphia: Westminster Press, 1977), p. 377.

64. Ibid. pp. 373, 369.

65. There were a small number of former missionaries who stayed on in China, although none of them was directly involved in church work. Best known among these is Talitha Gerlach. She had come to China as a YMCA worker in the 1920s, but later left the Y to work more directly in progressive social causes. As of this writing she still resides in Shanghai. The last of the more traditional missionaries is thought to have been Ellen Nielson of the Danish Missionary Society. She became a Chinese citizen, and until her death in 1960 at the age of 89, she lived and worked in the countryside around Dagushan, Manchuria. For other accounts of missionaries who remained in China see Bush, *Religion in Communist China*, p. 47.

66. Don MacInnis, "Christian Missions and Imperialism: Views from the Chinese Press," *Occasional Bulletin of the Missionary Research Library* 21:7 (July 1970), p. 5 and passim.

67. This view is represented by "T. T.," "The Situation of the Christian Church in China: An Attempt at Understanding," *IRM* 4:1 (1951), pp. 47–58. "T. T." is described as a missionary who had recently returned from China.

68. For Visser 't Hooft's understanding of the broader issues involved, see "The World Council of Churches and the Struggle Between East and West," *C & C* 9:13 (July 25, 1949), pp. 98–103.

69. "Statement of the Central Committee on the Korean Situation and World Order, Toronto, Canada, July 1950," *The First Six Years, 1948–1954* (Geneva: WCC, 1954), pp. 119–20.

70. "T. C. Chao Resigns from World Council Presidency," *The Christian Century* (August 1, 1951), p. 885. Chao's letter of resignation was originally carried in *Guangming Daily*, July 11, 1951. It was reprinted in *TF* 273 (July 21, 1951), p. 33.

71. In 1952 Hewlett Johnson was presented with four appeals from Chinese Christians condemning the use of germ warfare by United States forces in Korea. The texts are contained in *China's New Creative Age*, pp. 189–194. Johnson supported the germ warfare charges (ibid. pp. 115–123), while most Western observers denied them. A presentation of the issue that accepts the latter point of view is contained in David Rees, *Korea: The Limited War* (London: Macmillan, 1964), pp. 347–63.

72. J. L. Hromadka, *The Church and Theology in Today's Troubled Times* (Prague: Ecumenical Council of Churches, 1956), pp. 64, 65.

73. "Meeting of Bishop R. B. Manikam with Chinese Church Leaders at Peking on Invitations from the I.M.C. and the W.C.C.," March 17, 1956, unpublished manuscript, p. 2.

74. All of these visits were reported in *Tian Feng* and some in the secular press as well. In addition to those cited here, other visitors included a delegation of British

Quakers in 1955; the visit of Walter Freytag in 1957; delegations of Hungarian Christians in 1957 and 1959; a delegation from Australian Free Churches in 1959; and a third visit by the Johnsons in the same year. Brief reports on all of these visits may be found in *Tian Feng* and *The China Bulletin*.

75. *TF* 512 (September 3, 1956), p. 7.

76. *TF* 506 (June 11, 1956), p. 4.

77. Ibid. p. 7.

78. Hromadka, *The Church and Theology in Today's Troubled Times*, p. 66.

79. *Evanston to New Delhi* (Geneva: WCC, 1961), p. 143. Commenting on a report prepared by the Commission of the Churches on International Affairs in August 1960, the Central Committee requested the commission to continue to study the role of China in the international situation and "to help in the creation of conditions which will permit the 650 million people of China to share in the benefits and accept the responsibilities common to all members of the international community."

80. Robert Smylie, "The China Issue: A Review of the Position of the National Council of Churches," *CC* (October 10, 1973), p. 1004.

81. Ibid.

82. See . . . *and on Earth Peace: Documents of the First All-Christian Peace Assembly* (Prague, 1961), pp. 33, 100–109 and passim.

83. Translated in *Documents*, pp. 201–9.

84. K. H. Ting, "Religious Policy and Theological Reorientation in China," unpublished manuscript, from a talk delivered at the University of Toronto, 1979, p. 5.

85. K. H. Ting, "Retrospect and Prospect," pp. 34ff.

86. Xing Wen, "Three-Self Is to Construct the Church Well," *TF* (NS) 52 (April 1, 1987), p. 12.

87. Sun Xipei, "From 'Three-Self' to 'Three-Well,' " *TF* (NS) 54 (June 1, 1987), p. 6. Translation appears in *CTR:1987*.

88. K. H. Ting, "Fourteen Points," p. 116.

89. Han Wenzao, "On the International Relations of the Chinese Church," *A New Beginning*, p. 107; and Han Wenzao, "Friends All Over the World, While Anti-China Forces Plot," *TF* (NS) 59 (November 1, 1987), pp. 15–18. Translated as "A Report on the International Relations of the CCC and the TSM Committee," in *China Talk* 13:1 (January 1988), pp. 2–8.

90. "Resolution on Strengthening Rural Church Work," *TF* (NS) 59 (November 1, 1987), p. 6.

91. An example is Open Doors' "Project Pearl," which sought to smuggle one million bibles off the coast of Swatow. Organized as a para-military operation and led by an American ex-Marine, the bibles were discovered by a Chinese military patrol shortly after arriving at their destination. (See "Risky Rendezvous at Swatow," *Time*, October 19, 1981, p. 81.) Although estimates vary as to the number of bibles actually distributed to Chinese Christians, I have been told that Christians in the Swatow area were put under a great deal of pressure after the incident. Local authorities, who are used to dealing with the smuggling of contraband goods, may very well put the bibles in the same category.

92. Ting, "Retrospect and Prospect," p. 39.

93. Tang Shoulin and Ren Zhongxiang, *Firmly Resist the Heretical Beliefs of Li Changshou*, *Jiaocai* (Special Issue), April 1983.

94. For example, Shen Xilin, "Seeking the Common Ground and Unity," *NSJ* (NS) 6–7 (September 1987), p. 22. Translation appears in *CTR:1987*.

95. See *Collected Documents from the Fourth National Christian Conference*, pp. 124ff. In English translation, Wang Zhu, "To Be a Person With a Beautiful Spirit," *CTR:1987*.

96. "Resolution on Consolidating and Strengthening Unity," *TF* (NS) 59 (November 1, 1987), p. 7.

97. China Christian Council, ed., *A Christian Catechism* (Nanjing: Nanjing Office of the China Christian Council, 1983). This is a short pamphlet of fifty pages divided into separate sections on the Bible, God, Jesus Christ, the Holy Spirit, Salvation, the church and discipleship, arranged in a question-and-answer format. Appended to the text are the Lord's Prayer; the Ten Commandments; Matthew's summary of the law; the Apostle's Creed and the Nicene Creed.

98. MacQuarrie, *Christian Unity and Christian Diversity* (Philadelphia: Westminster Press, 1975), p. 36.

99. *The Lambeth Conference 1968: Resolution and Reports* (New York: Seabury, 1968), pp. 140–41.

100. "Resolution on the Promotion of Self-Government Through the Formulation of a System of Church Order," *TF* (NS) 59 (November 1, 1987), p. 6.

101. See Chu and Lind, *A New Beginning*; Cynthia McLean et al., *Nanjing '86: Ecumenical Sharing, A New Agenda*; and Denton Lotz, ed., *Spring Has Returned . . . Listening to the Church in China* (McLean, Virginia: Baptist World Alliance, 1986).

102. Han Wenzao, "Friends All Over the World, While Anti-China Forces Plot," *TF* (NS) 59 (November 1, 1957), p. 15.

103. For a description of the projects and perspective of the Amity Foundation see *The Amity Newsletter*, 1985–.

Chapter 8

1. Chen Zemin, "The Task of Theological Construction in the Chinese Church (II)," *NSJ* 7 (August 1957), p. 6.

2. K. H. Ting, "Another Look at Three-Self," pp. 29–30.

3. T. C. Chao, "Christian Faith in China's Struggle," *Christian Voices in China*, ed. Chester S. Miao (New York: Friendship Press, 1948), p. 28.

4. The most thorough study of efforts toward theological indigenization in the 1920s is Wing-hung Lam, *Chinese Theology of Construction* (Pasadena: William Carey Library, 1983), especially pp. 27–83.

5. Ng Lee-ming, "The Promise and Limitations of Chinese Protestant Theologians, 1920–1950," *CF* 21:4–22:1 (1978–1979), p. 178.

6. See, for example, Y. T. Wu, ed., *Christianity and New China* (Shanghai: Association Press, 1948), 2d ed. Originally published in 1940, the book contains twenty-seven essays by Hsieh Fu-ya, Hsu Pao-ch'ien, Wu Lei-chuen, T. C. Chao, Jiang Wen-han and others.

7. Ng, "The Promise and Limitations of Chinese Protestant Theologians," p. 181.

8. A short biography of Chao is contained in Howard Boorman, ed. *Biographical Dictionary of Republican China*, vol. 1, pp. 147–48. For a treatment of Chao's theological development see Ng, "Christianity and Social Change," pp. 96–173.

9. T. C. Chao, "Days of Rejoicing in China," *CC* 66:1 (March 2, 1949), p. 226. Two other essays from this period also carry a similar message, see T. C. Chao, "Christian Churches in Communist China," *C & C* 9:11 (June 27, 1949), pp. 83–85 and Chao, "Red Peiping after Six Months," *CC* 66:2 (September 14, 1949), pp. 1066–68.

10. A report of these actions is contained in *Xie jin* 6 (1952), p. 42, translated in *Documents*, pp. 70–71.

11. This is the conclusion of Ng, "Christianity and Social Change," p. 170, and Bush, *Religion in Communist China*, p. 196.

12. "Speech by T. C. Chao," *TF* 502 (April 16, 1956), pp. 21–22, trans. *Documents*, pp. 138–139. This is also confirmed in a letter from R. B. Manikam to Wallace Merwin, in which Chao says he is still in the ministry and "enjoying more freedom, academic and religious, than ever before." The letter is dated May 15, 1956.

13. Winfried Gluer, "T. C. Chao and the Quest for Life and Meaning," *CN* 18:4 (Fall 1980), p. 132. Also see Gluer, "The Legacy of T. C. Chao," *International Bulletin of Missionary Research* 6:4 (October 1982), pp. 165–69; and his more extensive study upon which this latter article is based, *Christliche Theologie in China, T. C. Chao, 1918–1956* (Gutersloh: G. Mohn, 1979).

14. See *Documents*, p. 139; and Franklin Woo, "Another China Visit," *CF* 16:3–4 (1973), p. 157.

15. See Gluer, "T. C. Chao and the Quest for Life and Meaning," p. 132. Also, Luo Zhenfang, "Dr. T. C. Chao's Last Letter to Me," *CTR:1986*, pp. 75–78. This last essay is something of an apologetic attempt to save the legacy of T. C. Chao for the Chinese church. Luo Zhenfang is a professor of New Testament at Nanjing Theological Seminary.

16. Gluer, "T. C. Chao and the Quest for Life and Meaning," p. 132.

17. Y. T. Wu, "Some Thoughts about a New Orientation in Christian Theology," cited in Endicott, *Rebel Out of China*, p. 321.

18. Y. T. Wu, "Freedom Through Truth," *TF* 396–397 (January 11, 1954), pp. 4–5. A partial translation appears in *Documents*, pp. 73–84.

19. Ng, "Christianity and Social Change," p. 243.

20. Wu, "Freedom Through Truth," *Documents*, p. 78.

21. K. H. Ting has written, "I do not know where to find another Christian in China who not only kept his own religious faith steadily but also carried on so persistently and carefully conversations with atheist revolutionary comrades on the truth embodied in Christ," *In Memory of Mr. Wu Yaozong*, p. 100. Also see Y. T. Wu, "My Recognition of the Chinese Communist Party," *TF* 555 (June 30, 1958), p. 12, trans. *Documents*, p. 191.

22. John England, *Living Theology in Asia* (Maryknoll: Orbis, 1982), p. ix.

23. The only essay I have seen that even touches on the emergence of a new Chinese Theology in the 1950s is Francis Price Jones, "Theological Thinking in the Chinese Protestant Church Under Communism," *Religion in Life* 32:4 (Autumn 1963), pp. 534–36.

24. Ting, "Religious Policy and Theological Reorientation in China," p. 7.

25. Chen Zemin, "The Task of Theological Construction in the Chinese Church (I)," *NSJ* 6 (February 1957), p. 25.

26. Jones, "Theological Thinking in the Chinese Protestant Church Under Communism," p. 539.

27. Ting, *How to Study the Bible*, pp. 36–37.

28. Chen Shouzhong, "The Christ Overlooked," *TF* 416 (May 31, 1954), p. 305.

29. Chen, "Theological Construction (I)," pp. 24–27.

30. Chen, "Theological Construction (II)," pp. 6–8.

31. Ibid. pp. 8–10.

32. Rawlinson, *Naturalization of Christianity in China*, p. 180.

33. Sun Hanshu, "This Is the Way, Walk in It," *NSJ* 2 (April 1954), p. 28.

34. Chen, "Theological Construction (II)," p. 11.

35. K. H. Ting, "Christian Theism," *NJS* 7 (August 1957), p. 19, trans. from *Documents*, p. 164.

36. Chen, "Theological Construction (II)," p. 12.

37. Ibid.

38. K. H. Ting, "Another Look at Three-Self," p. 8; interview with K. H. Ting. Also see K. H. Ting, "Theological Mass Movement in China," *Christian Witness in China Today* (Kyoto: Doshisha University Press, 1985), pp. 19–36.

39. All four were frequent contributors to *Tian Feng*. Wang Weifan and Jiang Peifen are now on the faculty of Nanjing Theological Seminary.

40. See Gramsci, *Prison Notebooks: Selections*.

41. Ting, "Another Look at Three-Self," p. 30.

42. Chen Zhong, "Should We Not Touch Right and Wrong?" *TF* 500 (February 29, 1956), p. 21. Chen is directing his comments against the views of Watchman Nee.

43. Mao Zedong, "Let Us Unite and Clearly Distinguish Between Ourselves and the Enemy," *SW* 5, p. 80.

44. *TF* 419 (June 14, 1954), p. 342. The essay begins in *TF* 417–18 (June 9, 1954), pp. 322–23 and concludes in *TF* 421 (July 1, 1954), pp. 383–84.

45. See Ernesto Cardenal, *The Gospel in Solentiname,* vol. 4, trans. Donald Walsh (Maryknoll: Orbis, 1982), p. vii–x.

46. Huang Peiyong, "Lord, Do Not Take Us from the World, but Keep Us from the Evil One," *TF* 333 (September 27, 1952), p. 564.

47. "How Should Christians Approach the World?" *TF* 500 (February 29, 1956), p. 22.

48. Xie Shouling, "Christians and the World," *TF* 500 (February 29, 1956), pp. 23–24. In the same issue see Cheng Zhiyi, "Loving the World and Loving God," pp. 22–23. Also see Yang Jingqiu, "How Should We Approach the World and Things of the World?" *TF* 501 (March 8, 1956), pp. 13–15; and, in the same issue, Huang Peixin, "What Does Not Loving 'the world' Really Mean?" pp. 15–17.

49. Cheng Zhiyi, "Loving the World and Loving God," p. 23.

50. Sun Pengxi, "Christians Should Distinguish Between Love and Hate in Their Approach to the World," *TF* 503 (April 30, 1956), p. 24.

51. Yang Jingqiu, "How Should We Approach the World and Things of the World?" p. 14.

52. Luo Zhenfang, "Christians and the Common People," *TF* 505 (May 28, 1956), p. 17.

53. Jones, "Theological Thinking in the Protestant Church Under Communism," p. 539.

54. Wang Weifan, "Changes in Theological Thinking in the Church in China," *CTR: 1986*, p. 33. Originally published in *NSJ* (NS) 2 (June 1985), pp. 7–10.

55. Chen, "Reconciliation with the People," p. 19.

56. K. H. Ting, "Religious Policy and Theological Reorientation in China," p. 5.

57. The first essay on the subject is Ren Zhongxiang, "My Opinion on *Streams in the Desert*," *TF* 577 (May 25, 1959), pp. 15–16.

58. Ting, *How to Study the Bible*, p. 3.

59. Wang Weifan, "Changes in Theological Thinking in the Church in China," p. 34.

60. Hermann Sasse, *"Kosmos," Theological Dictionary of the New Testament*, ed. C. Kittel, trans. G.W. Bromiley, vol. iii (Grand Rapids: Eerdmans, 1965), p. 895.

61. The Chinese word for *people* used here is a biblical term which may also be

rendered "the common people." The term is somewhat confusing, as it is sometimes equivalent to the Greek *kosmos* (Jn. 3:16), but is also used more specifically to refer to the human world. It is not equivalent to the political term for "the people" in the Marxist sense.

62. "The Relationship Between Christians and the People," *TF* 516 (November 5, 1956), p. 17.

63. Xie Yongqin, "Who Is My Brother?," *TF* 509 (July 23, 1956), pp. 6–7.

64. Wan Fulin, "Christians and the People," *TF* 519 (October 1, 1956), pp. 24–25.

65. Tian Yunzhen, "Should We Be In Conflict With the People Because of That Revealed by Our New Lives?," *TF* 511 (August 20, 1956), p. 19.

66. Luo Zhenfang, "Human Relationships—Brotherly Relationships," *TF* 512 (September 3, 1956), pp. 15–17.

67. Tang Matai, "Believers and People," *TF* 509 (July 23, 1956), p. 708.

68. Huang Xianglin, "The Relationship Between Christians and the People," *TF* 512 (September 3, 1956), pp. 14–17.

69. Huang Peixin, "On Jews and Samaritans," *TF* 515 (October 17, 1956), p. 14.

70. Huang Peixin, "Socialism in Light of Christianity," *NSJ* 5 (July 1957), p. 7.

71. Ibid. pp. 8–10.

72. A translation of Ting's "Christian Theism" is contained in *Documents*, pp. 156–67.

73. Ibid. p. 166.

74. See Lee Yee, ed., *The New Realism: Writings from China After the Cultural Revolution* (New York: Hippocrene Books, 1983), p. 6.

75. Gao Ying, "God's Promise and Human Faith," *CTR:1985*, pp. 145–46. Originally published in *NSJ* (NS) 1 (September 1984), pp. 91–92.

76. Ting, "Religious Policy and Theological Reorientation in China," p. 6.

77. Interview with Wang Weifan.

78. The original words and melody were published in *TF* (NS) 10 (July 30, 1982), p. 28. The Foreign Mission Board of the Southern Baptist Convention released a film on the Protestant Church in China in 1986, taking its title from the hymn, "Winter Is Past."

79. Quoted in Hans-Reudi Weber, "China: Training Leaders Is a Priority for Growing Churches," *One World* 95 (May 1984), p. 4.

80. *Jiao cai* commenced publication in 1981. An incomplete set of the journal is contained in the library of the Christian Study Centre on Chinese Religion and Culture, Kowloon, Hong Kong.

81. See "Resolution on Strengthening Rural Church Work," *TF* (NS) 59 (November 1, 1987), p. 6.

82. The *Nanjing Union Seminary Journal: New Series* commenced publication in September 1984. It was renamed the *Nanjing Theological Review* in June 1986.

83. Chen Zemin, "On Nanjing Union Seminary," *Collected Documents from the Fourth National Christian Conference*, p. 101. Translation in *CTR:1987*.

84. Weber, "China: Training Leaders Is a Priority for Growing Churches," pp. 3–4. Also see K. H. Ting, "Theological Education in China Today," *CCA Consultation with Church Leaders from China*, pp. 47–56.

85. K. H. Ting, "Preface," *CTR:1985*, pp. vi–vii.

86. "Rod and Staff," *Jiao cai* (Special Edition), July 1986.

87. "Letter to Co-workers," mimeo (June 29, 1981).

Conclusion

1. Shusaku Endo, *Silence*, trans. William Johnston (New York: Taplinger, 1980), p. xx.

2. Ibid. p. xix.

3. Gonzalez-Ruiz, *The New Creation: Marxist and Christian*, trans. Matthew O'Connell (Maryknoll: Orbis, 1976), pp. 7–8.

4. See Han Wenzao, "Inter-religious Relations in China Today," *CF* 24:4 (1980).

5. The exception would be the Islamic communities in areas of China where the majority of the population is Muslim. In many cases they still exhibit a strong sense of intolerance toward non-Muslims.

6. Karl Rahner, *Foundations of Christian Faith*, trans. William Dych (New York: Seabury, 1978), p. 251.

7. Peter Brown, *Augustine of Hippo* (Berkeley: University of California Press, 1969), p. 224.

8. John Linnan, "Towards a Theology of a Local Church," unpublished paper, December 3, 1983, pp. 1, 4.

9. Sanon, "The Universal Christian Message in Cultural Plurality," *True and False Universality in Christianity*, ed. Claude Geffre and Jean-Pierre Jossua (New York: Seabury, 1980), p. 89.

10. See Goretti Lau, "A Reflection on 'Particular Churches' Based Upon the Experience of the Chinese Church," unpublished paper, December 3, 1983, 7 pp.

11. These four points are from Linnan, pp. 5–6.

12. See Lesslie Newbigin, *Foolishness to the Greeks: The Gospel and Western Culture* (Grand Rapids: Eerdmans, 1986), Chapter 6 and passim.

Bibliography

Interviews with Author

Cao Shengjie. Associate General Secretary, China Christian Council, Shanghai, PRC. 28 April 1982.

Chen Zemin. Dean, Nanjing Theological Seminary, Nanjing, PRC. 29 November 1982.

Han Wenzao. Associate Secretary General, Chinese Christian Three-Self Patriotic Movement and Associate General Secretary, China Christian Council, Nanjing, PRC. 7 June 1982.

Huang Jianru. General Secretary, Nanjing Christian Three-Self Patriotic Movement Committee, Nanjing, PRC. 20 July 1983.

Huang Zhu. Director of Research, Central United Front Work Department, Beijing, PRC. 4 August 1983.

Jiang Peifen. President, Jiangsu Provincial Christian Council, Nanjing, PRC. 8 May 1980.

Jiang Wenhan (Kiang Wen-han). Vice-President, China Christian Council, Shanghai, PRC. 11 December 1982.

Luo Guanzong. Vice-Chairperson, Standing Committee of the Chinese Christian Three-Self Patriotic Movement, Shanghai, PRC. 24 April 1982.

Luo Hanxian. Deputy Secretary General, Chinese People's Political Consultative Conference, Beijing, PRC. 5 August 1983.

Ren Zhongxiang. Member, Shanghai Christian Three-Self Patriotic Movement Committee, Shanghai, PRC. 26 April 1982.

Shen Derong. Secretary General, Chinese Christian Three-Self Patriotic Movement, Shanghai, PRC. 24 April 1984.

Shen Yifan. Pastor, *Guoji libaitang* (Community Church), Shanghai, PRC. 24 April 1982.

Tang Shoulin. Vice-Chairperson, Standing Committee of the Chinese Christian Three-Self Patriotic Movement, Shanghai, PRC. 26 April 1982.

Ting, K. H. (Ding Guangxun). Chairperson, Standing Committee of the Chinese Christian Three-Self Patriotic Movement and President, China Christian Council, Nanjing, PRC. 20 June 1982.

Tsai, Peter (Cai Wenhao). Vice-President, China Christian Council, Hong Kong. 7 April 1981.

Wang Weifan. Instructor, Nanjing Theological Seminary, Nanjing, PRC. 13 April 1981.

Wu Gaozi (George Wu). Vice-President, China Christian Council, Shanghai, PRC. 11 December 1982.
Xu Rulei. Instructor, Nanjing Theological Seminary, Nanjing, PRC. 13 June 1983.
Yan Tingchang. Deputy Director, Jiangsu United Front Work Department, Nanjing, PRC. 8 December 1981.
Zhang Lingzhu. Staff, Central Religious Affairs Bureau, Beijing, PRC. August 1982.
Zhao Zhi'en. Instructor, Nanjing Theological Seminary, Nanjing, PRC. 12 July 1983.
Zheng Jianye. General Secretary, China Christian Council, Shanghai, PRC. 25 April 1982.

Journals

Bridge, 1983—.
China and Ourselves, 1979—.
China and the Church Today, 1977–1986.
China Bulletin, 1947–1962.
China Bulletin (U.K.), 1979—.
China Notes, 1963—.
China Study Project Journal, 1986—.
Chinese Theological Review, 1985—.
Ching Feng, 1957—.
Jinling xiehe shenxue zhi (Nanjing Union Seminary Journal), 1953–1957.
Jinling xiehe shenxue zhi (New Series), 1984—.
Religion in the PRC: Documentation, 1979–1985.
Shijie zongjiao yanjiu (Research on World Religions), 1979—.
Tian Feng, 1948–1964.
Tian Feng (New Series), 1980—.
Tripod, 1980—.
Xie Jin (New Series), 1951–1954.

Books and Articles

Chinese

Beijing shi jidujiao sanzi aiguo yundong xuexi weiyuanhui, ed. *Jiekai Wang Mingdao de zongjiao waiyi* (Uncover Wang Mingdao's religious cloak). Published October 20, 1955.
Chao, Jonathan, ed. *Zhonggong dui jidujiao de zhengce* (Chinese Communist policy toward Christianity). Hong Kong: Chinese Church Research Center, 1983.
Chao, T. C. "Yanjing daxue de zongjiao xueyuan" (The Yenching school of religion). *Wenshi ziliao xuanji*, ed. National Committee for Research on Literary and Historical Resources of the CPPCC. Beijing: Zhongguo shuju 43 (1981): 106–128.
Chedi geduan jidujiao yu meiguo diguozhuyi de lianxi (Thoroughly sever the relationship between Christianity and American imperialism). Beijing: Renmin wenxue chubanshe, 1951.
Chen Chonggui. *Budao liu zhang* (Six chapters on evangelism). Shanghai: CLC, 1954.
Fung, Raymond and Philip Lam. *Zhu ai women daodi* (God loves us to the very end). Hong Kong: Hong Kong Christian Council, 1981.
Gu Changsheng. *Chuanjiaoshi yu xiandai zhongguo* (Missionaries and modern China). Shanghai: Renmin chubanshe, 1981.
Guan Jiewen. " 'Suixiang' suo yinqi de suixiang—yu Wang Ding tongzhi shangque"

(Random thoughts on "random thoughts"—A response to comrade Wang Ding). Mimeo.

Hou Wailu. *Zhongguo lidai datong lixiang* (The Datong ideal in Chinese history). Beijing: Kexue chubanshe, 1959.

Hu Fuming. "Guanyu woguo shehuizhuyi fazhan de tedian" (Special characteristics in the development of Chinese Socialism). *Shehui Kexue* 2 (1980): 39–55, and 3 (1981): 72–79.

Hu Hua and Lin Daizhao. "Suqing 'zuo' de yingxiang yao zhengben qingyuan" (The eradication of 'leftist' influences requires a thoroughgoing reform). In *Zhou Enlai de sixiang ji lilun gongxian*, edited by Hu Hua et al. Guangzhou 159–171. Guangdong Renmin chubanshe, 1982.

Jian Xue. "Diguozhuyi liyong jidujiao qinlue woguo shihua" (Historical talks on imperialism's use of Christianity to carry out aggression against China). 2d draft. July 1964. Mimeo.

Jiang Wenhan. "Guangxuehui shi zeyang yige jigou?" (What kind of organization was the Christian Literature Society?) *Wenshi ziliao xuanji*, ed. National Committee for Research on Literary and Historical Resources of the CPPCC. Beijing: Zhongguo shuju 43 (1981): 1–42.

———. "Jidujiao qingnianhui zai zhongguo" (The Y.M.C.A. in China). *Wenshi ziliao xuanji*, ed. National Committee for Research on Literary and Historical Resources of the CPPCC. Beijing: Zhongguo shuju 19 (1981): 1–27.

———. *Zhongguo gudai jidujiao ji kaifeng youtai ren* (Christianity in early China and the Jews of Kaifeng). Shanghai: Zhishi chubanshe, 1982.

Kohtoku, Syusui. *Jidu hexu ren ye: jidu moshalun* (What kind of man was Christ: A refutation of Christianity), trans. Ma Cai. Beijing: The Commercial Press, 1982.

Li Weihan. "Mao Zedong sixiang lingdao xia de zhongguo tongyi zhanxian" (China's united front under the leadership of Mao Zedong Thought). *Hongqi* 24 (1983), 14–23.

———. *Tongyi zhanxian wenti yu minzu wenti* (The united front question and nationalities question). Beijing: Renmin chubanshe, 1981.

Liang Shuming. *Zhongguo wenhua yaoyi* (The essence of Chinese culture). Hong Kong: Jicheng Book Company, 1963.

Liu Liangmo, ed. *Jidujiao yu aiguozhuyi* (Christianity and patriotism). Shanghai: Y.M.C.A. Bookstore, 1953.

———. "Shanghai kangri jiuwang de geyong yundong" (Shanghai's anti-Japanese singing movement for national salvation), ed. Shanghai Working Committee on Literary and Historical Resources of the CPPCC 32–37. Shanghai: Shanghai renmin chubanshe 1 (1978).

———. ed. *Shenme shi tongyi zhanxian* (What is the united front?). Shanghai: Y.M.C.A. Bookstore, 1950.

Liu Qingfen. "Huigu guoqu, jianding xinxin, zhanwang weilai, tuanjie qianjin—Tianjin shi jidujiao sanzi aiguo yundong weiyuanhui diwu ji weiyuanhui gongzuo baogao." (Review the past, strengthen confidence, look toward the future, go forward in unity—fifth report on work of the Tianjin Three-Self Committee). *Daibiao huiyi wenjian* (November 1981): 8–24.

Lu Shiqiang. *Zhongguo guanshen fanjiao de yuanyin, 1860–1874* (Reasons behind anti-Christian attitudes of the Chinese gentry, 1860–1874). Taibei: Taiwan Commercial Press, 1966.

Luo Qi. "Ping Mao Zedong de tongyi zhanxian" (An assessment of Mao Zedong's united front tactics). *Mingbao yuekan* 178 (October 1980): 25–28.

Luo Zhufeng, ed. *Zhongguo shehuizhuyi shiqi de zongjiao wenti* (The religious question during China's socialist period). Shanghai: Shanghai shehui kexueyuan chubanshe, 1987.

Shen Yifan and Cao Shengjie. "Cong zhongguo jidujiao zili yundong kan aiguozhuyi chuantong zai zhongguo jidujiao nei de fanying" ("The patriotic tradition within Chinese Christianity in light of the independence movement of the Chinese church). Paper presented at the Institute for Religious Studies, Academy of Social Sciences. Shanghai, 1982.

Sima Ying. "Jidujiao de qiyuan he Yesu" (The origin of Christianity and Jesus). *Waiguoshi zhishi* 12 (12 December 1981): 34–36.

Tang Shoulin and Ren Zhongxiang. *Jianjue dizhi Li Changshou de yiduan xieshuo* (Firmly resist the heretical beliefs of Li Changshou). Nanjing: Nanjing Union Seminary, 1983.

Ting, K. H. et al. *Jiangzhang xinji* (New sermons), 2. Shanghai: Christian Literature Society, 1955.

Wang Chih-hsin. *Zhongguo jidujiao shigang* (Outline history of Chinese Christianity). Hong Kong, 1959.

Wang Ding. "Du 'Shengjing' suixiang" (Random thoughts on the Bible). *Shulin* 2 (1983), 12–13.

Wang Mingdao. *Wang Mingdao wenku: weidao* (Treasures of Wang Mingdao: On Guard). Touliu: Conservative Baptist Press, 1984.

———. *Wushi nian lai* (These Fifty Years). Hong Kong: Bellman House, 1967.

Wu Jing, ed. *Pochu fengjian mi xin wenda* (Eradicating feudalism and superstition). Jiangsu: Renmin chubanshe, 1982.

Wu, Y. T. "Bianzhe de yijian" (The editor's opinion). *Jidujiao yu xin zhongguo* (Christianity and New China). 2d ed., Shanghai: Association Press, 1948, 263–282.

———, ed. *Jidujiao gexin yundong xuexi shouce* (A study manual of the Christian reform movement). Shanghai: Y.M.C.A. Bookstore, 1952.

———. *Meiyou ren kanjianguo shangdi* (No one has ever seen God). Shanghai: Y.M.C.A. Bookstore, 1946.

———. "Xiaguan shijian riji yiye" (A page from the diary on the Xiaguan incident). *Wenshi ziliao xuanji*. Ed. Shanghai Working Committee on Literary and Historical Resources of the CPPCC. Shanghai: Shanghai renmin chubanshe 3 (1979): 77–78.

Xiao Zhitan. "Dui dangqian zongjiao xianxiang de jidian kanfa." (A few opinions on the present religious phenomena). *Zongjiao yanjiu wenli*. Shanghai: Shanghai zonjiao xuehui, 1982, 117–124.

Xin jiaoyu she, ed. *Suqing diguozhuyi de wenhua qinlue shili* (Eliminate the influence of imperialism's cultural aggression). 2d ed. Shanghai: Renmin jiaoyu chubanshe, 1951.

Yang Jingren. "Xin shiqi de tongyi zhanxian" (The united front in the new period). *Hongqi* 419 (1 April 1983).

Ying Yuandao. *Jidujiao de kongsu yundong* (The Christian denunciation movement). Shanghai: Y.M.C.A. Press, 1953.

Zhang Zhiyi. *Shilun zhongguo renmin minzhu tongyi zhanxian* (On the Chinese people's democratic united front). Beijing: Renmin chubanshe, 1958.

Zhang gan ji (Rod and Staff). Special edition of *Jiao cai*. Nanjing, 1986.

Zhao Puchu. "Zhongguo Fojiao xiehui disijie quanguo daibiao huiyi; 'kaimuci' " (Opening speech at the Fourth National Conference of the Chinese Buddhist Association). *Fayin* 1 (1983): 3–4.

Zheng Jianye. "Cong bijiao zongjiaoxue kan hanzu yu zongjiao" (A look at the Chinese people and religion from the standpoint of the comparative study of religion). *Xueshu Yuekan* 156 (May 1982): 1–13.

Zhonggong Zhongyang tongyi zhanxian gongzuobu yanjiushi, ed. *Tongyi zhanxian jiben zhishi* (The united front). Beijing: Minzu chubanshe, 1981.

Zhongguo gongchan dang zhongyang weiyuanhui, ed. "Guanyu woguo shehuizhuyi shiqi zongjiao wenti de jiben guandian he jiben zhengce" (The basic viewpoint and policy on the religious question during our country's socialist period). *Sanzhong quanhui yilai zhongyao wenxian xuanbian.* Beijing: Renmin chubanshe, 1982, 1228–1240.

Zhongguo jidujiao disijie quanguo huiyi zhuanji (Documents from the Fourth National Christian Conference). Shanghai: CCC/TSM, 1986.

Zhongguo jidujiao sanzi aiguo yundong weiyuanhui changwu weiyuanhui de shici (kuoda) huiyi zhuanji (Special edition on the Tenth (enlarged) Plenum of the Standing Committee of the Chinese Christian Three-Self Patriotic Movement). Shanghai: TSM Committee, 1957.

Zhongguo jidujiao sanzi aiguo yundong weiyuanhui, ed. *Huiyi Wu Yaozong xiansheng* (In memory of Mr. Y. T. Wu). Shanghai, 1982.

Zhongguo jidujiao xiehui, ed. *Jidujiao yaodao wenda* (A Christian Catechism). Nanjing: Nanjing Office of the China Christian Council, 1983.

Zhou Enlai. "Guanyu woguo minzu zhengce de ji ge wenti" (On China's nationalities policy). Delivered 4 August 1967. Reprinted *Renmin ribao* 31 (December 1979): 1–4.

———. "Zai wenyi gongzuo he gushipianchuangzuo shang de jianghua" (Talks at the Forums on Literature and Art and Film Making). *Wenyi bao* 2 (1979): 2–7.

———. *Zhou Enlai tongyi zhanxian wenxian* (Selected writings of Zhou Enlai on the united front). Beijing: Renmin chubanshe, 1984.

English

A China Missionary. "First Thoughts on the Debacle of Christian Missions in China." *IRM* 40 (1951): 411–420.

A Correspondent. "On Understanding the Position of the Church in China." *The East and West Review* 26 (January 1960): 20–27.

A Former Missionary. "The Voice of the Chinese Church." *The East and West Review* 17:4 (October 1951): 100–104.

"A Message from the General Assembly of the Church of Christ in China to the Missionary Societies Associated with the Church of Christ in China." 29 November 1950. Mimeo.

"A Report on Protestant Missions." *Monthly Report*, 7:6 (31 December 1949): 1–23.

Adeney, David. *China: The Church's Long March.* Robesonia: OMF Books, 1985.

———. "Division Time in China: To Join the TSPM or Not." *Evangelical Missions Quarterly* 19:3 (July 1983): 201–204; 229.

Ahlstrom, Sydney. "The Radical Turn in Theology and Ethics: Why It Occurred in the 1960s." In *Religion in American History: Interpretive Essays,* edited by John M. Mulder and John F. Wilson, 445–456. Englewood Cliffs: Prentice-Hall, 1978.

Aird, John. "The Preliminary Results of China's 1982 Census." *CQ* 96 (December 1983): 613–640.

Allen, Roland. *Missionary Methods: St. Paul's or Ours?* Chicago: Moody Press, 1959.

———. *The Spontaneous Expansion of the Church.* Grand Rapids: Eerdmans, 1962.

. . . *And on Earth Peace: Documents of the First All-Christian Peace Assembly.* Prague, 1961.

"Answers to Thirteen Questions from Evangelical Christians by the Chinese Delegation." London, October 1982. Mimeo.

Ballou, Earle H., ed. *China Consultation 1960.* New York: National Council of the Churches of Christ in the U.S.A., Division of Foreign Missions China Committee, 1960.

Barnett, Suzanne Wilson and John King Fairbank, eds. *Christianity in China: Early Protestant Missionary Writings.* Cambridge: Harvard University Press, 1985.

Barth, Karl and Johannes Hamel. *How to Serve God in a Marxist Land.* New York: Association Press, 1959.

Bates, M. Searle. "China." In *The Prospects of Christianity Throughout the World,* edited by M. Searle Bates and Wilhelm Pauck, 211–227. New York: Charles Scribner's Sons, 1964.

———. "It's the Long Pull that Counts." *CN,* 16:2 (Spring 1978): 24–25.

———. *Religious Liberty: An Inquiry.* New York: International Missionary Council, 1945.

———. "Religious Liberty in China." *IRM* (1946): 165–173.

———. "The Chinese State and Religion, with Particular Reference to Christianity, 1880–1949." Columbia University Seminar on East Asia, 29 November 1967.

———. "The Outlook for Christianity in China." *C&C* 9:8 (16 May 1949): 59– 61.

———. "The Protestant Enterprise in China, 1937–1949." *Frontiers of the Christian World Mission Since 1938,* edited by Wilbur Harr, 1–22. New York: Harper, 1962.

Beaver, R. Pierce, ed. *To Advance the Gospel: Selections from the Writings of Rufus Anderson.* Grand Rapids: Eerdmans, 1967.

Beeson, Trevor. *Discretion and Valour.* Rev. ed. Philadelphia: Fortress Press, 1982.

Berg, Johannes, van den. *Constrained by Jesus' Love: An Inquiry into the Motives of the Missionary Awakening in Great Britain in the Period Between 1698 and 1815.* Kampen: J. H. Kok, 1956.

Beyerhaus, Peter and Henry Lefever. *The Responsible Church and the Foreign Mission.* London: World Dominion Press, 1964.

Bonhoeffer, Dietrich. *Ethics.* 14th printing. Edited by E. Bethge and translated by N. H. Smith. New York: Macmillan, 1979.

Boorman, Howard, ed. *Biographical Dictionary of Republican China.* New York: Columbia University Press, 1967.

Bottomore, Tom, et al. *A Dictionary of Marxist Thought.* Cambridge: Harvard University Press, 1983.

Boyle, Samuel E. *The Church in Red China Leans to One Side.* Hong Kong, 1950.

Brown, G. Thompson. *Christianity in the People's Republic of China.* Rev. ed. Atlanta: John Knox Press, 1986.

Brown, Homer G. and Muriel J. Brown. *New China as We Saw It.* 1956.

Buege, Gerda. "Are We Trying to Understand the Christians in China?" *Ecumenical Review* 17 (January 1965): 54–61.

Bush, Richard. *Religion in Communist China.* Nashville and New York: Abingdon Press, 1970.

Butterfield, Fox. *China: Alive in the Bitter Sea.* New York: Times Books, 1982.

CCA Consultation with Church Leaders from China. Singapore: Christian Conference of Asia, 1981.

Chan, Wingtsit. *Religious Trends in Modern China.* New York: Columbia University Press, 1953.

———. "The Historic Chinese Contribution to Religious Pluralism in World Community." In *Religious Pluralism and Community*, edited by E. J. Jurji, 113–130. Leiden, 1969.

Chang, Parris H. "Chinese Politics: Deng's Turbulent Quest." *Problems of Communism* (January–February 1981): 1–21.

Chao, Jonathan. "Prospects for Future Mission Work in China." In *Evangelical Perspectives on China*, edited by Donald Douglas, 65–110. Farmington: Evangelical China Committee, 1976.

———. "The Witness of a Suffering Church." *China and the Church Today* 5:5 (September–October 1983): 8–12.

Chao, T. C. "Christian Churches in Communist China." *C&C* 9:11 (27 June 1949): 83–85.

———. "Christian Faith in China's Struggle." In *Christian Voices in China.* Edited by Chester S. Miao. New York: Friendship Press, 1948.

———. "Days of Rejoicing in China." *C&C* 66:1 (2 March 1949): 265–267.

———. "Red Peiping After Six Months." *C&C* 66:2 (14 September 1949): 1066–1068.

Chen, Fu Tien. *The Current Religious Policy of People's Republic of China (January 1, 1976–March 15, 1979): Part I: An Inquiry.* Norwalk, CT, 1983.

Chen, Kenneth K.S. *The Chinese Transformation of Buddhism.* Princeton: Princeton University Press, 1973.

Chen, Theodore. *Thought Reform of the Chinese Intellectuals.* Hong Kong: Hong Kong University Press, 1973.

Chen, W. Y. "The State of the Church in China." *IRM* 36 (1947): 141–152.

Cheng, Nien. *Life and Death in Shanghai.* London: Grafton Books, 1986.

Chesneaux, Jean. *China: The People's Republic, 1949–1976.* Translated by Paul Auster and Lydia Davis. New York: Pantheon Books, 1979.

China Today: Report of a CCA-URM/WCC-URM Visit to the Church and the People. Hong Kong: CCA/URM, 1986.

Chu Mei-fen. "The Religious Dimension in Mao Tsetung Thought." Diss., University of Chicago, 1977.

Chu, Theresa and Christopher Lind. *A New Beginning.* Toronto: Canada China Programme, 1983.

Church Life in China Today. Church Assembly: Overseas Council Research Department, Occasional Bulletin 1 (1960).

Clark, William H. *The Church in China: Its Vitality; Its Future.* New York: Council Press, 1970.

Cohen, Paul. *China and Christianity: The Missionary Movement and the Growth of Chinese Anti-Foreignism, 1860–1870.* Cambridge, 1963.

Committee of Concerned Asian Scholars. *China! Inside the People's Republic.* New York: Bantam Books, 1973.

Conway, Martin. "China: A Moment of Hope and Opportunity." Unpub. paper, September 1986.

Coulson, Gail. "Love Country, Love Church: The Protestant Church in China." *China Talk*, 11:5,6 (November 1986): 1–16.

Covell, Ralph. *Confucius, the Buddha and Christ: A History of the Gospel in Chinese*. Maryknoll: Orbis Books, 1986.

Cowman, Mrs. Charles E. *Streams in the Desert*. 2 vols. Grand Rapids: Zondervan, 1965.

"Decision of the Central Committee of the Chinese Communist Party Concerning the Great Proletarian Cultural Revolution." *Beijing Review* 33 (12 August 1966): 6–11.

Deng Xiaoping. *Fundamental Issues in Present-Day China*. Beijing: Foreign Languages Press, 1987.

Digan, Parig. *The Christian China Watchers: A Post-Mao Perspective*. Brussels: Pro Mundi Vita, 1978.

Dimitroff, Georgi. *The United Front*. San Francisco: Proletarian Publishers, 1975.

Documents of the First Session of the Fifth National People's Congress of the PRC. Peking: Foreign Language Press, 1978.

Documents of the Three-Self Movement. New York: NCCUSA, 1963.

Dunn, James D.G. *Unity and Diversity in the New Testament*. Philadelphia: Westminster Press, 1977.

"EATWOT Visits China, May 2–13, 1986." Ecumenical Association of Third World Theologians, 1986.

Eberhard, Wolfram. *Guilt and Sin in Traditional China*. Los Angeles: University of California Press, 1967.

Elsbree, O. W. *The Rise of the Missionary Spirit in America, 1790–1815*. Williamsport: Williamport Printing Co., 1928.

Endicott, Stephen. *James G. Endicott: Rebel Out of China*. Toronto, Buffalo and London: University of Toronto Press, 1980.

England, John. *Living Theology in Asia*. Maryknoll: Orbis Books, 1982.

———. "Recent Theological Reflection in the Churches of China, 1975–1982: An Annotated Listing of Materials Available in English." *East Asia Journal of Theology* 1:1 (1983): 105–113.

Esmein, Jean. *The Chinese Cultural Revolution*. Translated by W.J.F. Jenner. New York: Anchor Books, 1973.

Evanston to New Delhi. Geneva: WCC, 1961.

Fairbank, John K. *The Missionary Enterprise in China and America*. Cambridge, 1974.

Fenn, William A. *Christian Higher Education in China, 1880–1950*. Grand Rapids: Eerdmans, 1976.

Ferris, Helen. "The Christian Church in Communist China to 1952." Lackland Air Force Base: Air Force Personnel and Training Research Center, Air Research Development Command, January 1956.

Fey, Harold, ed. *The Ecumenical Advance*. London: S.P.C.K., 1970.

Fierro, Alfredo. *The Militant Gospel: An Analysis of Contemporary Political Theologies*. Translated by John Drury. Maryknoll: Orbis Books, 1977.

Fitzgerald, C. P. *The Birth of Communist China*. New York: Penguin Books, 1977.

Fletcher, William C. *Religion and Soviet Foreign Policy, 1945–1970*. London: Oxford University Press, 1973.

Freedman, Maurice. "On the Sociological Study of Chinese Religion." In *Religion and Ritual in Chinese Society*, edited by Arthur Wolf, 19–41. Stanford: Stanford University Press, 1974.

"Freedom of (From?) Religion." *China News Analysis* 1222 (18 December 1981): 1–8.

Freytag, Walter. "Meeting Christians in China." *IRM* 46 (1957): 410–416.

Fung, Raymond. *Households of God on China's Soil.* Geneva: World Council of Churches, 1982.

Garaudy, Roger. *From Anathema to Dialogue: A Marxist Challenge to the Christian Churches.* Translated by Luke O'Neill. New York: Herder and Herder, 1966.

Garside, Roger. *Coming Alive: China After Mao.* New York: New American Library, 1981.

Gernet, Jaques. *China and the Christian Impact.* Translated by Janet Lloyd. Cambridge: Cambridge University Press, 1985.

Gibellini, Rosino, ed. *Frontiers of Theology in Latin America.* Translated by John Drury. Maryknoll: Orbis Books, 1979.

Glasser, Arthur F. "China Today—An Evangelical Perspective." *Missiology* 9:3 (July 1981): 260–276.

Goldman, Merle. *Literary Dissent in Communist China.* New York: Atheneum, 1971.

Gonzalez-Ruiz, Jose Maria. *The New Creation: Marxist and Christian.* Translated by Matthew J. O'Connell. Maryknoll: Orbis Books, 1976.

Graham, Gwen. "The Policy of the Chinese Government Towards the Protestant Churches of China, 1949–1957." Diss., University of Western Australia, 1977.

Gramsci, Antonio. *Selections from the Prison Notebooks.* Edited by Q. Hoare and G. Smith. New York: International Publishers, 1971.

Granet, Marcel. *The Religion of the Chinese People.* Translated and edited by M. Freedman. Oxford: Basil Blackwell, 1975.

Green, H. Gordon. "A Canadian Look at the Church in China." *CC* (24 August 1966): 1038–1040.

Groot, J.J.M., de. *Sectarianism and Religious Persecution in China.* 2 vols. Amsterdam: Johannes Muller, 1903.

Grubb, Kenneth, ed. *World Christian Handbook, 1949 and 1952 eds.* London: World Dominion Press.

Grubb, Violet M. *The Chinese Indigenous Church Movement.* London and New York: World Dominion Press.

Hageman, Alice and Paul Deats. "Marxist-Christian *Encuentro* in Cuba." Unpub. ms.

Hall, R. O. *A Missionary Artist Looks at His Job.* New York: International Missionary Council, l942.

Hansen, Eric. *Catholic Politics in China and Korea.* Maryknoll: Orbis Books, 1980.

Hayward, Victor. *Christians and China.* Belfast: Christian Journals Ltd., 1974.

———. "Overseas Newsletter IV." January 1950. Mimeo.

———. "Overseas Newsletter VII." November 1950. Mimeo.

Hebblethwaite, Peter. *The Christian-Marxist Dialogue.* New York: Paulist Press, 1977.

Hockin, Katharine B. "Canadian Openness to the Chinese Church." *IRM* 70:283 (July 1982): 368–378.

———. "Memories and Impressions of a Revolutionary Period. Mainland China: 1949–1951." Unpub. paper. May 1966.

———. *Servants of God in People's China.* New York: Friendship Press, 1962.

Hromadka, J. L. *The Church and Theology in Today's Troubled Times.* Prague: Ecumenical Council of Churches, 1956.

———. "The Crisis in the Ecumenical Fellowship." *Communion Viatorum* 1 (1958): 18–26.

Hsiao, Kung-chuan. *A History of Chinese Political Thought.* Vol. 1. Translated by F. W. Mote. Princeton: Princeton University Press, 1979.

Hsu, Immanuel C.Y. *China Without Mao: The Search for a New Order*. New York: Oxford University Press, 1983.

Hummel, Arthur W. "The Art of Social Relations in China." *Philosophy East and West* 10:1–2 (April–July 1960): 13–22.

Hunter, Edward. *Brainwashing in Red China*. New York: Viking Press, 1951.

———. *The Story of Mary Liu*. London: Hodder and Stoughton, 1956.

Hunter, Neale. *Shanghai Journal*. New York: Praeger, 1969.

Jack, Homer A. "Some Notes on the Re-emergence of the Religions of China." 30 September 1980. Mimeo.

James, Francis, ed. *Reports on the Deputation of Australian Churchmen to Mainland China*. Sydney: Anglican News Service, 1956.

Jen Yu-wen. *The Taiping Revolutionary Movement*. New Haven, 1973.

Jiang Wenhan. *The Chinese Student Movement*. New York: Kings Crown Press, 1948.

———. "The SCM in Nanking and Soochow." Unpub. paper.

Johnson, Chalmers. *Peasant Nationalism and Communist Power*. Stanford: Stanford University Press, 1962.

Johnson, Hewlett. *China's New Creative Age*. London: Lawrence and Wishart Ltd., 1953.

———. *Christians and Communism*. London: Putnam, 1956.

Jones, Francis Price. *The Church in Communist China: A Protestant Appraisal*. New York: Friendship Press, 1962.

———. "Theological Thinking in the Chinese Protestant Church Under Communism." *Religion in Life* 32:4 (Autumn 1963): 534–540.

Jonson, Jonas. *Lutheran Missions in a Time of Revolution: The China Experience, 1944–1951*. Uppsala: Tvavega forlags, 1972.

Joseph, William A. *The Critique of Ultra-Leftism in China, 1958–1981*. Stanford: Stanford University Press, 1984.

Kao, Tien-hsi. "How Shall the Chinese Church Continue its Work Under the Communist Government?" Th.M. thesis, Princeton Theological Seminary, 1950.

Kinnear, Angus I. *Against the Tide: Watchmen Nee*. Eastbourne: Victory Press, 1973.

Lacy, Creighton. *Coming Home—to China*. Philadelphia: The Westminster Press, 1978.

———. "Protestant Missions in Communist China." Diss., Yale University, 1953.

Lam, Willy Wo-Lap. *Towards a Chinese-Style Socialism: An Assessment of Deng Xiaoping's Reforms*. Hong Kong: Oceanic Cultural Service, 1987.

Lam, Wing-hung. *Chinese Theology in Construction*. Pasadena: William Carey Library, 1983.

Lapwood, R. and W. Lapwood. *Through the Chinese Revolution*. London: Spalding and Levy, 1955.

Latourette, Kenneth Scott. *A History of Christian Missions in China*. New York: Macmillan, 1929.

———. *A History of the Expansion of Christianity*. Vol. 7. Grand Rapids: Zondervan, 1971.

Lawrence, Carl. *The Church in China: How It Survives and Prospers Under Communism*. Minneapolis: Bethany House, 1985.

Lazzarotto, Angelo S. *The Catholic Church in Post-Mao China*. Hong Kong: Holy Spirit Study Center, 1982.

———. "The Chinese Communist Party and Religion." *Missiology* 11:3 (1983): 267–290.

Lee, Renesalaer. "Chinese Communist Religious Policy." *CQ* 19 (1964): 161–173.

Lee, Yee, ed. *The New Realism: Writings from China After the Cultural Revolution.* New York: Hippocrene Books, 1983.

Leeuwen, Arend Th, van. *Christianity in World History: The Meeting of the Faith of East and West.* Translated by H. H. Hoskins. New York, 1964.

Lenin, V. I. *Religion.* New York: International Publishers, 1933.

———. *Selected Works.* London: Lawrence and Wishart, 1947.

Levenson, Joseph. *Confucian China and its Modern Fate: A Trilogy.* Vol. 2. Berkeley: University of California Press, 1968.

———. "The Communist Attitude Toward Religion." *The Chinese Model: A Political, Economic and Social Survey,* edited by Werner Klatt. Hong Kong: University of Hong Kong, 1965.

Lifton, Robert. *Thought Reform and the Psychology of Totalism.* New York: Norton, 1961.

Liu, Kwang-ching. *Americans and Chinese: A Historical Essay and a Bibliography.* Cambridge: Harvard University Press, 1963.

Lotz, Denton, ed. *Spring Has Returned . . . Listening to the Church in China.* McLean, Virginia: Baptist World Alliance, 1986.

Lutheran World Federation/Pro Mundi Vita. *Christianity and the New China.* 2 vols. South Pasadena: Ecclesia Publications, 1976.

Lutz, Jessie. *China and the Christian Colleges, 1850–1950.* Ithaca: Cornell University Press, 1971.

———. *Christian Missions in China: Evangelists of What?* Boston: D. C. Heath, 1965.

Lyall, Leslie. *Come Wind, Come Weather.* London: Hodder and Stoughton, 1961.

———. *New Spring in China.* Grand Rapids: Zondervan, 1980.

———. *Red Sky at Night.* London: Hodder and Stoughton, 1969.

———. *Three of China's Mighty Men.* London: OMF Books, 1973.

MacFarquhar, Roderick. *The Origins of the Cultural Revolution.* Vol. 2, *The Great Leap Forward.* New York: Columbia University Press, 1983.

———. *The Hundred Flowers.* London: Stevens & Sons, 1960.

MacInnis, Donald E. "Christian Missions and Imperialism—Views from the Chinese Press, 1951–62." *Occasional Bulletin from the Missionary Research Library* 20 (July 1970): 1–22.

———. *Religious Policy and Practice in Communist China.* New York: Macmillan, 1972.

———. "The North American Churches and China, 1949–1981." *IBMR* 5:2 (April 1981): 50–54.

MacQuarrie, John. *Christian Unity and Christian Diversity.* Philadelphia: Westminster Press, 1975.

Mao Zedong. *Selected Works.* 4 vols. Beijing: Foreign Languages Press, 1967– 1977.

———. "The Great Union of the Popular Masses." Translated by Stuart Schram. *CQ* 49 (March 1972): 76–87.

Marshall, Richard H., ed. *Aspects of Religion in the Soviet Union, 1917– 1967.* Chicago: University of Chicago Press, 1971.

Martin, Helmut. *Cult and Canon: The Origins and Development of State Maoism.* Armonk: M. E. Sharpe, 1982.

Marx, K. and F. Engels. *On Religion.* New York: Shocken Books, 1957.

———. *The Marx-Engels Reader.* Edited by Robert Tucker. New York: W. W. Norton & Co., 1972.

Marx, Karl. *Writings of the Young Marx on Philosophy and Society*. Edited and translated by Lloyd Easton and Kurt Guddat. Garden City: Doubleday, 1967.

Matthews, Harold, comp. "Lessons to be Learned from the Experience of Christian Missions in China." New York: NCCUSA, 1951.

Mazuri, Ali A. "The Moving Cultural Frontier of World Order: From Monotheism to North-South Relations." *Alternatives* 7 (1981): 1–20.

Mead, Sydney. *The Nation with the Soul of a Church*. New York: Harper and Row, 1975.

"Meeting of Bishop R. B. Manikam with Chinese Church Leaders at Peking on invitations from the I.M.C. and the W.C.C." Unpub. ms. 17 March 1956.

"Meeting of H. E. Chou En-lai, Prime Minister of China, with Bishop Manikam." Unpub. ms. 27 March 1956.

Meisner, Maurice. "The Chinese Rediscovery of Karl Marx: Some Reflections on Post-Maoist Chinese Marxism." *Bulletin of Concerned Asian Scholars* 17:3 (1985): 2–16.

———. *Li Ta-chao and the Origins of Chinese Marxism*. Cambridge: Harvard University Press, 1967.

———. *Mao's China: A History of the People's Republic*. New York: The Free Press, 1977.

Merwin, Wallace. *Adventure in Unity: The Church of Christ in China*. Grand Rapids: Eerdmans, 1974.

———. "Can the Church Survive in China?" *CC* 70:44 (4 November 1953): 1257–1259.

———. "What's Happening to the Church in China?" *IRM* 48 (1959): 297–301.

Metz, Johann Baptist. *Faith in History and Society*. Translated by David Smith. New York: Crossroad, 1980.

Metzger, Thomas A. *Escape from Predicament: Neo-Confucianism and China's Evolving Political Culture*. New York: Columbia University Press, 1977.

Miao, Chester, ed. *Christian Voices in China*. New York: Friendship Press, 1948.

Mills, Harriet. "Thought Reform: Ideological Remoulding in China." *Atlantic* 204:6 (December 1959): 71–78.

Milton, David and Nancy. *The Wind Will Not Subside*. New York: Pantheon, 1976.

Mojzes, Paul. *Christian-Marxist Dialogue in Eastern Europe*. Minneapolis: Augsburg Publishing House, 1981.

———, ed. *Varieties of Christian-Marxist Dialogue*. Philadelphia: The Ecumenical Press, 1978.

Mote, Frederick. "The Cosmological Gulf Between China and the West." In *Transition and Permanence*, edited by David Buxbaum and Frederick Mote, 3–21. Hong Kong: Cathay Press, 1972.

Mu Fu-sheng. *The Wilting of the Hundred Flowers: Free Thought in China Today*. London: Heinemann, 1962.

Munro, Donald J. *The Concept of Man in Contemporary China*. Ann Arbor: The University of Michigan Press, 1977.

Nanjing '86: Ecumenical Sharing, A New Agenda. 1986.

NCCUSA. *China Consultation: 1960*. New York: Far Eastern Office of the Division of Foreign Missions, 1960.

National Christian Council of China. "To the Christians of China." *CC* 67:15 (April 1950): 458–459.

Neill, Stephen. *Colonialism and Christian Missions*. New York: McGraw-Hill, 1966.

Newbigin, Lesslie. *Foolishness to the Greeks: The Gospel and Western Culture.* Grand Rapids: Eerdmans, 1986.

Ng Lee Ming. "Christianity and Nationalism in China." *East Asia Journal of Theology* 2:1 (1983): 71–88.

———. "Christianity and Social Change: The Case of China 1920–1950." Diss., Princeton Theological Seminary, 1970.

Nuttall, Geoffrey F. and Owen Chadwick. *From Uniformity to Unity, 1662–1962.* London: S.P.C.K., 1962.

Orr, Robert C. *Religion in China.* New York: Friendship Press, 1980.

Osmer, Harold H. *U.S. Religious Journalism and the Korean War.* Washington: University Press of America, Inc., 1980.

O'Toole, Roger. " 'Underground' Traditions in the Study of Sectarianism: Non-Religious Uses of the Concept 'Sect.' " *Journal for the Scientific Study of Religion* 15:2 (1976): 146–148.

Outerbridge, Leonard M. *The Lost Churches of China.* Philadelphia, 1952.

Overmeyer, Daniel L. *Folk Buddhist Religion: Dissenting Sects in Late Traditional China.* Cambridge: Harvard University Press, 1976.

———. *Religions of China.* San Francisco: Harper and Row, 1986.

Parker, T. M. *Christianity and the State in the Light of History.* London: Adam and Charles Black, 1955.

Paton, David M. *Christian Missions and the Judgment of God.* London: SCM Press, 1953.

———, ed. *Reform of the Ministry: A Study in the Work of Roland Allen.* London: Lutterworth Press, 1968.

———. "The Church in the World: The Uitlander in No Man's Land." In *The Missionary Church in East and West*, edited by Charles West and David Paton, 43– 57. London: SCM Press, 1959.

Patterson, George. *Christianity in Communist China.* Waco, Texas, and London: Word Books, 1969.

Pepper, Suzanne. *Civil War in China: The Political Struggle, 1945–1949.* Berkeley: University of California Press, 1978.

"Popular Beliefs." *CNA* 439 (28 September 1962): 1–7.

Price, Frank W. *China—Twilight or Dawn?* New York: Friendship Press, 1948.

———. "Christian Presuppositions for the Encounter with Communism." In *The Theology of the Christian Mission*, edited by Gerald Anderson, 158–167. New York: McGraw-Hill, 1961.

———. "History of Nanking Theological Seminary, 1911 to 1961: A Tentative Draft." New York: Board of the Founders of Nanking Theological Seminary. 1961. Mimeo.

———. "Lew, Timothy Ting-fang." In *Concise Dictionary of the Christian World Mission*, edited by Stephen Neill et al., 345. Nashville and New York: Abingdon, 1971.

———. *Marx Meets Christ.* Philadelphia: Westminster Press, 1957.

———. *The Rural Church in China.* New York: Agricultural Missions, 1948.

"Quakers Visit China." *CC* (30 November 1955): 1393–1395.

Rabe, Valentin. *The Home Base of American China Missions, 1880–1920.* Harvard EAS Monograph #75. Cambridge: Harvard University Press, 1978.

Rahner, Karl. *Theological Investigations.* Vol. 6. Translated by Karl H. Kruger and Boniface Kruger. London: Darton, Longman and Todd, 1974.

————. *Theological Investigations*. Vol. 9. Translated by G. Harrison. London: Darton, Longman and Todd, 1972.

Rawlinson, Frank, ed. *China Christian Yearbook, 1932–33 and 1934–35*. Shanghai: Christian Literature Society.

————. *Naturalization of Christianity in China*. Shanghai: Presbyterian Mission Press, 1927.

Rees, D. Vaughn. *Korea: The Limited War*. London: Macmillan, 1964.

Rees, David. *The Jesus Family in Communist China*. London: Paternoster Press, 1959.

"Religion." *CNA* 593 (17 December 1965): 1–7.

Religion in the People's Republic of China: Documentation. 1981—.

"Religious Policy and Popular Religious Practices." *CNA* 221 (21 March 1958): 1–7.

"Resolution on Certain Questions in the History of Our Party Since the Founding of the People's Republic of China." *Beijing Review* 27 (6 July 1981): 10–39.

Rickett, Allyn and Adele. *Prisoners of Liberation*. Garden City: Anchor Press, 1973.

Robinson, Thomas. "Chou En-lai and the Cultural Revolution in China." In *The Cultural Revolution in China*, edited by Thomas Robinson, 165–312. Berkeley: University of California Press, 1971.

Romig, Theodore F. "A Reappraisal of the Missionary Vocation." *Theology Today* 19:1 (April 1952): 55–66.

Rosenstock-Huessy, Eugen. *Out of Revolution: The Autobiography of Western Man*. Norwich, VT: Argo Books, 1969.

Rozman, Gilbert, ed. *The Modernization of China*. New York: The Free Press, 1981.

Sailer, Randolph C. and Robert Brank Fulton. *Suggestions for Working to Understand China and America Better*. September 1977.

Schram, Stuart, ed. *Chairman Mao Talks to the People: Talks and Letters, 1956–1971*. New York: Pantheon, 1974.

————. "From the 'Great Union of the Popular Masses' to the 'Great Alliance.' " *CQ* 49 (March 1972): 88–105.

Schurman, Franz. *Ideology and Organization in Communist China*. 2d ed. Berkeley: University of California Press, 1968.

"Seeking a Broader Dialogue with the Church in China." *One World* 92 (January–February 1984): 16–18.

Selden, Mark, ed. *The People's Republic of China: A Documentary History of Revolutionary Change*. New York: Monthly Review Press, 1979.

Sewell, William. "Religion in China Today." In *China and the West: Mankind Evolving*, edited by Robert Jung et al., 48–64. New York: Humanities Press, 1970.

Shen, T. L. "The People's Movement." In *China Christian Yearbook, 1936–1937*, edited by Frank Rawlinson, 78–82. Shanghai: Christian Literature Society, 1937.

Smith, Huston. "Transcendence in Traditional China." In *Traditional China*, edited by James Liu and Wei-ming Tu, 109–122. Englewood Cliffs: Prentice Hall, 1970.

Smylie, Robert. "The China Issue: A Review of the Position of the National Council of Churches." *CC* 90:2 (10 October 1973): 1003–1007.

Song, C. S. "From Israel to Asia: A Theological Leap." *The Ecumenical Review* 28:3 (July 1976): 252–65.

"Statement of the Central Committee on the Korean Situation and World Order, Toronto, Canada, July 1959." In *The First Six Years, 1948–1954*. Geneva: WCC, 1954, 119–120.

Stauffer, Milton T., ed. *The Christian Occupation of China: A General Survey of the*

Numerical Strength and Geographical Distribution of the Christian Forces in China. Shanghai, 1922.

Stockwell, Eugene. "Interview with Dr. and Mrs. K. H. Ting." Nanjing, 22 October 1976. Mimeo.

Stuart, John Leighton. *Fifty Years in China: The Memoirs of John Leighton Stuart, Missionary and Ambassador.* New York: Random House, 1954.

Swanson, Allen J. *Taiwan: Mainline Versus Independent Church Growth.* South Pasadena: William Carey Library, 1970.

"T. C. Chao Resigns from World Council Presidency." *CC* 68:2 (1 August 1951): 885.

T. T. "The Church in China." *British Weekly.* July 1952. Mimeo.

———. "The Situation of the Christian Church in China: An Attempt at Understanding." *IRM* 4:1 (1951): 47–58.

Temple, William. *Church and Nation.* London: Macmillan, 1915.

Terrill, Ross. *800,000,000: The Real China.* Boston: Little, Brown and Co., 1972.

———. "Conversations in Peking." *CC* 15 (January 1965): 47–50.

The Constitution of the People's Republic of China. Beijing: Foreign Languages Press, 1982.

"The Fourteenth Biennial Meeting of the National Christian Council of China." *The Church* 4:4 (1950): 7–10.

The Lambeth Conference 1968: Resolutions and Reports. New York: Seabury, 1968.

"The Question of Religion and Popular Religious Practices." *CNA* 308 (15 January 1960): 1–7.

"The Rise of China." Special Issue of *Student World* 60:1 (1967).

"The SCM in China in the Last Two Years: A View from Peking." *Student World* 44 (1951): 169–174.

Thomas, M. M. "An Asian Team Visits China: Report and Personal Impressions." Unpub. ms. July 1983.

Thomas, M. M. and Paul Abrecht. *Christians in the Technical and Social Revolutions of Our Time* (Official Report of the World Conference on Church and Society, Geneva, July 12–26, 1966). Geneva: World Council of Churches, 1967.

Thompson, James C. *While China Faced West: American Reformers in Nationalist China, 1928–1937.* Cambridge: Harvard University Press, 1969.

Thurston, Anne F. *Enemies of the People.* New York: Knopf, 1987.

Till, Barry. *The Churches Search for Unity.* Middlesex: Penguin Books, 1972.

Ting, K. H. "A Chinese Traveller in Eastern Europe." *Student World* 42 (1949): 363–369.

———. *Christian Witness in China Today.* Kyoto: Doshisha University Press, 1985.

———. "A Creative Experience for Chinese Students." *Student World* 42 (1949): 22–32.

———. "A Latin American Travel Diary." *Student World* 42 (1950): 258–265.

———. "Behold the Man." *Student World* 44 (1951): 148–155.

———. "Does God Call Us? A Chinese Answers the Question." *Student World* 41 (1949): 318–325.

———. "Facing the Future or Restoring the Past?" Talk given in Toronto, Canada. November 1979.

———. " 'Give Ye Them to Eat' Luke 9:12–17." Sermon delivered at Timothy Eaton Memorial Church, Toronto, Canada. 4 November 1979.

———. *How to Study the Bible.* Hong Kong: Tao Fong Shan Ecumenical Centre, 1981.

———. "Power and its Denial on the Cross." *Student World* 41 (1948): 210–215.

———. "Religion as Opium?" Unpub. paper. 23 October 1981.

———. "Religious Policy and Theological Reorientation in China." Talk given at the University of Toronto. 1979. Mimeo.

———. "Retrospect and Prospect." *IRM* 70 (April 1981): 26–39.

———. "Science, Religion and Democracy in China." Talk given at McGill University, Montreal, Canada. October 1979.

———. "Talk to Friends of the Federation." Stony Point Center, New York, 12 October 1981.

———. "The Church in China." Talk given at Uppsala University. November 1982.

———. "The Task of the Church in Asia." *Student World* 42 (1949): 235–248.

———. "Victims and Sinners." Sermon given at Riverside Church, New York City. 9 September 1979.

Tomkinson, Leonard. *Synopsis of "Reconstruction of the Christian Church in China."* No. 10 in Religion and Life Series. Associated Press of China. April 1950.

Towery, Britt. *The Churches of China: Taking Root Downward, Bearing Fruit Upward.* Rev. ed. Hong Kong: Long Dragon Books, 1987.

Treadgold, Donald W. *The West in Russia and China.* Vol. 2 of *China, 1582–1949.* London: Cambridge University Press, 1973.

Troeltsch, Ernst. *The Social Teachings of the Christian Churches.* 2 vols. Translated by Olive Wyon. Chicago: University of Chicago Press, 1981.

Tsu, Andrew Yu-yue. "Christianity in its Political Setting." *Religion in Life* 24:1 (Winter 1954–1955): 30–43.

U.S. Congress. House Committee on Un-American Activities. *Communist Persecution of Churches in Red China and North Korea.* Washington: U.S. Government Printing Office, 1959.

"Utopia in Chinese History." *CNA* 1145 (January 1979): 5–8.

van der Bent, Ans J. *Christians and Communists: An Ecumenical Perspective.* Geneva: WCC, 1980.

van Slyke, Lyman P. *Enemies and Friends: The United Front in Chinese Communist History.* Stanford: Stanford University Press, 1967.

Varg, Paul A. *Missionaries, Chinese and Diplomats: The American Protestant Missionary Movement in China, 1890–1952.* Princeton, 1958.

Verkuyl, J. *Contemporary Missiology: An Introduction.* Translated and edited by Dale Cooper. Grand Rapids: Eerdmans, 1978.

"Vilified in 1950s, Endicott Receives Church's Apology." *Toronto Globe and Mail* (13 August 1982): 1.

Visser 't Hooft, W. A. "The World Council of Churches and the Struggle Between East and West." *C & C* 9:13 (25 July 1949): 98–103.

Vogel, Ezra. "From Friendship to Comradeship: The Change in Personal Relations in Communist China." *CQ* 21 (January–March 1965): 46–60.

———. "Voluntarism and Social Control." In *Soviet and Chinese Communism: Similarities and Differences,* edited by Donald W. Treadgold, 168–84. Seattle and London: University of Washington Press, 1967.

Waardenburg, J. G. "A Report on Contacts with Protestant Christians in China (Mainland), in November, 1958." 24 April 1959. Mimeo.

Wakeman, Frederic. *History and Will: Philosophical Perspectives on Mao Tse-tung's Thought.* Berkeley: University of California Press, 1972.

Wand, J.W.C. *Anglicanism in History and Today.* London: Wakefield and Nicholson, 1961.

Wang, Mary. *The Chinese Church That Will Not Die*. London: Hodder and Stoughton, 1971.

Wang Shih Peng and H. W. Spillett. "A Christian-Communist Settlement in China." *IRM* 40 (1951): 168–178.

Warren, M.A.C. *Caesar, The Beloved Enemy*. London: SCM Press, 1955.

———. *The Missionary Movement from Britain in Modern History*. London: SCM Press, 1965.

———. *To Apply the Gospel: Selections from the Writings of Henry Venn*. Grand Rapids: Eerdmans, 1971.

Weber, Hans-Ruedi. *Asia and the Ecumenical Movement: 1895–1961*. London: SCM Press, 1966.

Welch, Holmes. *Buddhism Under Mao*. Cambridge: Harvard University Press, 1972.

Weng, Byron. "Some Aspects of the 1982 Draft Constitution of the People's Republic of China." *CQ* 91 (September 1982): pp. 492–506.

West, Charles C. ("Barnabas"). *Christian Witness in Communist China*. London: SCM Press Ltd., 1951.

———. *Communism and the Theologians: Study of an Encounter*. New York: The Macmillan Co., 1958.

———. "The Church Behind the 'Bamboo Curtain.' " *Motive* (November 1954): 32–36.

West, Philip. *Yenching University and Sino-Western Relations, 1916–1952*. Cambridge: Harvard University Press, 1976.

Whitehead, Raymond. "Christ, Salvation and Maoism." In *China and Christianity*, edited by James Whitehead et al. South Bend: University of Notre Dame Press, 1979.

———. *Love and Struggle in Mao's Thought*. Maryknoll: Orbis Books, 1977.

Whiting, Allen. *China Crosses the Yalu*. Stanford: Stanford University Press, 1960.

Whyte, Martin King. *Small Groups and Political Rituals in China*. Berkeley: University of California Press, 1974.

Whyte, Robert. *China and Christianity: Unfinished Encounter*. London: Collins, 1988.

Wickeri, Philip. "Sister Jiang: The Story of a Chinese Evangelical." *New World Outlook* (December 1980): 508–510.

———. "The Chinese Delegation at the Third World Conference on Religion and Peace, Princeton, New Jersey, August 28–September 8, 1979." Unpub. report.

———. "Seeking the Common Ground: Protestant Christianity, the Three-Self Movement and China's United Front." Diss., Princeton Theological Seminary, 1985.

Williamson, H. R. *British Baptists in China, 1845–1952*. London: Carey Kingsgate Press, 1957.

Willis, Helen. *Through Encouragement of the Scriptures: Ten Years in Communist Shanghai*. Hong Kong: Christian Bookroom, 1961.

Wilson, Bryan. *Religious Sects: A Sociological Study*. New York: McGraw-Hill, 1970.

World Council of Churches, Commission on World Mission and Evangelism. *Common Witness*. Geneva: WCC, 1982.

World Council of Churches. *The First Six Years, 1948–1954*. Geneva: WCC, 1954.

World Missionary Conference (1910). *Co-operation and the Promotion of Unity*. Vol. 8. Edinburgh: Oliphant, Anderson and Ferrier, 1910.

"World Student Christian Federation Working Party Reports." Unpub. mss. 1967–1968.

Wu Chao-kuang. *The International Aspect of the Missionary Movement in China*. Baltimore: Johns Hopkins University Press, 1930.

Yang, C. K. *Religion in Chinese Society*. Berkeley, 1961.

———. "The Functional Relationship Between Confucian Thought and Chinese Religion." In *Chinese Thought and Institutions*, edited by John King Fairbank, 269–290. Chicago: University of Chicago Press, 1957.

Yip, Ka-che. "The Anti-Christian Movement in China, 1922–1927, with special reference to the experience of Protestant Missions." Diss., Columbia University, 1970.

Yue Daiyun and Carolyn Wakeman. *To the Storm: The Odyssey of a Revolutionary Chinese Woman*. Berkeley: University of California Press, 1985.

Zhao Fusan. *Christianity in China*. Edited by Theresa Carino. Manila: De La Salle University Press, 1986.

———. "The Penitance and Renewal of the Church in China." In *Essays in Anglican Self-Criticism*, edited by David Paton, 86–98. London: SCM Press, 1958.

Zhou Enlai. *Selected Works*. Vol. 1. Beijing: Foreign Languages Press, 1980.

Index

Adapters to new ideological remolding, 144-145
Ai, N. S., 95
Allen, Roland, 13, 38-39
American Board of Commissioners for Foreign Missions (ABCFM), 37
Amity Foundation, 190; ecumenical relations and, 241
Anderson, Rufus, 37
Anti-Rightest movement, 160
Apocalypticism in China, 264
Atheism: in China, 30; rejection of, 272

Bai Hua, 100
Bastad consultation, 14
Bates, M. Searle, 10, 31, 119
Beyerhaus, Peter, 39-40
Bi Yongqin, 165
Bible smuggling, 236
Boer, Harry, 39
Bonhoeffer, Dietrich, 3, 13
Boyle, Samuel, 4, 9
Brecht, Bertolt, 194
Brunner, Emil, 19

Canada China Programme, 12; of Canadian Council of Churches, 240
Canadian Far Eastern Newsletter, 12
Cao Shengjie, 41, 190, 200, 202
Cao Yu, 27
Cardenal, Ernesto, 261
Chadwick, Owen, 169-170
Chang, Bishop (Wuhan), 174
Chang, Stephen (Zhang Haisong), 172
Chao, Jonathan, 5
Chao, T. C. xxv, 95, 120, 228-229, 244, 245, 246, 247-248, 249; and theology, 246-247

Chen, Marcus (Chen Chonggui), 122, 143, 148, 150, 166, 172-174
Chen, Robin (Chen Jianzhen), 122, 131, 144, 145, 148, 150
Chen Mengnan, 41
Chen Qiyuan, 70
Chen Sisheng, 93, 95
Chen Yi, 46, 182
Chen Yun, 182
Chen Zemin, 210, 243, 252-256, 259, 264, 272, 277
Cheng Chingyi (Chen Jingyi), 216-217
Cheng Guanyi, 219, 221
Cheng Zhiming, 172-173
Chesneaux, Jean, 72
Chiang Kai-shek, 8, 49-50, 121, 136
Chiang Kai-shek regime, 50, 232
Chien Boda, 46
China Bulletin, The (CB), xxv, 9
China Christian Council (CCC), 189
China Inland Mission, 4
China Jesus Independent Church, 207
China's isolation ended, 14
Chinese "Christian problem," 94
Chinese Christianity: incipient nationalism in, 157; and separation from Chinese people, 211
Chinese Christians: ghetto mentality of, 251; organized into mass groups, 98
Chinese Church Research Center, 5
Chinese Communist Party (CPC), xx. See also CPC
Chinese ecumenism and Three-Self, 40
Chinese Jesus Independent Church, 41, 159
Chinese national consciousness: ecumenical movement and, 217

Chinese People's Political Consultative Conference (CPPCC), xxiv

Chinese Protestant community: independence of, 235

Chinese Theological Review, The (CTR), xxv

Ching Tien-ying (Jing Tianying), 160, 164

Christian catechism, 276

Christian churches: and foreign aggression, 95; foreign funding of prohibited, 96-97; and foreign influences after 1949, 20; prohibition of foreigners holding administrative positions in, 97

Christian faith: deepening of, after 1966, 185

Christian "intellectuality": need for, 276

Christian involvement in society: CPC and, 100

Christian Manifesto, 127-133, 129-133, 246

Christian Missions and the Judgment of God (Paton), 12

Christian Reform Movement, 137

Christian selfhood, 203-215

Christian unity, 215-233

Christian witness, 202-203

Christianity: and Chinese context, 27-42; and Marxism, 17-27, 269; and social systems, 271; and the world, 261-266

Christianity and traditional religion, 283-285

Christianity within united front: limits on, 273

Christians: as model workers, 214

Christians and non-Christians: relationship between, 266-273

Church buildings: use of, 99

Church of Christ in China, 4, 40

Church in Communist China, The (Jones), 9

Church difficulties in 1949, 128-129

Church leaders confer with Zhou Enlai, 129

Church Mission Society (CMS), 37

Church-state relations: comparison with Anglican practice, 239

Civil religion in China, 32

Common Program: Protestant study of, 142

Communist Manifesto, The: and united front, 47

Comprehensiveness, 239

Concern for people's well being: and united front, 63-65

Confucianism, 28-29

Contradictions, theory of: and united front, 54-56

Corpus christianum, 35-36, 286-287

Cowman, Mrs. Charles E., 264

CPC: attitudes toward rural church, 119; impossibility of dissent, 101. *See also* Chinese Communist Party

Creation and redemption: continuity between, 256-257

Creator God: absence of concept of, 28

Cultural Revolution era (1966–1976), xxi, xxvi, 179-185; and anti-religious activities, 183; and Christian values, 283; and ecumenical relations, 233; in period of turbulent 1960s in U.S.A., 13; as power struggle, 26; as rejection of united front approach to religious policy, 179; as struggle against religion, 180

Czechoslovakia, occupation of (1968): and Christian-Marxist dialogue, 18

Daniel Group, 165

Den, Kimber, 160

Deng, Cora, 93, 95, 125, 148, 153

Deng Pufang, 182

Deng Xiaoping, 46, 182

Denominationalism, 206, 218

Denominations: renewed interest in, 238

Denunciation movement, 133; Christians' reaction to, 135; CPC understanding of goals of, 135; evaluation of, 138-139; theological interpretation of, 139-140

Denunciation of YM/YWCA, NCC, and CLS, 134

De-Stalinization campaign of 20th Party Congress: and Christian-Marxist dialogue, 18

Deviations in united front work, 59

Digan, Parig, xxiii

Dimitroff, Georgi, 48

Ding Yuzhang (Ting Yu-chang), 264

"Document 19," 88, 106

Dong Biwu, 70

Dong Hongwen, 174

Double standard: moral and religious, 30

Dulles, John Foster, 229

Dumont, Louis, 51

Dunn, James, 226-227

Ecumenical relations, 227-233; development of, with China, 241
Endicott, James G., 12, 230
Endo, Shusnko, 281
Enemies and friends: and united front, 56-58
Engels, Frederick, 47, 76
Eschatology in China, 263
Etiemble, Rene, 28

Fang Aishi, 172, 174
Financial difficulties of church in 1940s, 205
Folk Protestantism, 284-285
Folk religious and peasant rebellions, 31
Foreign mission boards: severing of links with, 147
Four Modernizations, period of (1976–present), xxi
Freedman, Maurice, 32, 282
Freytag, Walter, 10
Fu Lei, 181
Fung, Raymond, 187

Gang of Four, 26
Gao Ying, 273
Garaudy, Roger, 18
Gluer, Winfried, 247
Gonzalez-Ruiz, Jose Maria, 282
Goodness of creation, love of God and love of neighbor: association between, 263
Goodness of creation and world of sin: distinction between, 262
Government corruption in 1940s: church witness against, 205
Grace: as fulfillment of nature, 257
Gramsci, Antonio, 87, 259
Granet, Marcel, 29
Grass roots theology, 258-273
Great Leap Forward: and Chinese Christian church, 175
Guidelines for Christian order, 240
Guo Moro, 96
Gutiérrez, Gustavo, 21

Hall, R. O., 11, 230
Han Wenzao, 125, 137, 190
He Chengxiang, 70
He Long, 182
Hegel, G. W. F., 76
Home worship, 106, 185-187; significance of, 176-177
Hong Xiuquan, 47

Hromadka, J. L., 19, 229-230, 232
Hsieh Fu-ya, 244
Hsu Pao-ch'ien, 244
Hu Yaobang, 182
Huang Peixin, 270-271, 359
Huang Peiyong, 114, 167, 230, 259, 261-262
Huang Xianglin, 268-269
Human and divine in China, 30
Humanization: moral value to Christians, 202

Ideological remolding, 140-146
Ideological struggle of 1950s, 143
Ideological and Theoretical Contributions of Zhou Enlai, The, 178
Ideology: reserved differences possible, 107
Independent Board for Presbyterian China Missions, 4
Indigenization, 40
Indigenous Chinese Christianity: reasons for rapid growth of, 157-158
Institute for Religious Studies, Nanjing University, 89
Institute for Religious Studies, Shanghai Academy of Social Sciences, 89
Institute for Study of World Religions (ISWR), 80
Institutional Christianity and Three-Self: restoration of, since 1979, 192-195
Institutional life of church: attempts to restore, 188

Jesus Family, 40, 157, 160-162
Jia Yuming, 137, 166, 174
Jiang Peifen, 116, 210, 254, 259
Jiang Qing, 46
Jiang Wenhan, xxv, 107, 117
Jinling xiehe shenxue zhi (Nanjing Seminary Journal), xxiv
John XXIII, Pope, 283
Johnson, Edward, 11
Johnson, Hewlett, 12, 230
Jones, Francis Price, 7, 9, 145, 169, 251, 263
Judd, Walter, 4, 121

Kang Sheng, 46
Kang Yuwei, 47
Kiang, Z. T. (Jiang Changchuan), 95, 122, 137, 150, 213
Kiang Wenhan, 125

Korean War: and Chinese Christian international relationships, 227-228; Chinese patriotism and, 24; underlying causes of, 229
Kuo Siu-may (Guo Xiumei), 230

Labor: dignity and importance of, 263
Laity: training of, 276
Land Reform Movement: and Protestants, 142
Lao She, 181
Latourette, Kenneth, 217
Lawrence, Carl, 5
Leadership training classes, 142
Learning from Others: and united front, 60-61
Lee, C. H., 121
Lefever, Henry, 39-40
Left and Right Deviations: and united front, 58-59
Leftism: and reservation of differences in faith, 179
Lei Feng, 214
Lenin, V. I., 76-77
"Letter to Christians Throughout China," 151
Lew, T. T., 223, 244
Li Changshou (Witness Li), 163, 237
Li Chuwen, 170
Li Dazhao, 24
Li Shoubao, 125, 232
Li Weihan, xxv, 58, 61, 62, 65, 68, 69-70, 75, 83-84, 86, 179
Li Xiannian, 128
Liang Hao, 79
Liang Shuming, 31
Liberal perspective: and bias against communism and TSM, 9; and Chinese patriotism, 10
Liberation theology in Latin America, 20-23
Life and Death in Shanghai (Nien Cheng), 184
Lifton, Robert, 144-145
Lin Piao, 46, 182
Ling Eng-hui, 158
Little Flock, 40, 157, 162-164
Liu, James T. C., 30
Liu Junwang, 79
Liu Liangmo, xxv, 93, 95, 124, 125, 148
Liu Lingjiu, 172, 174
Liu Shaoqi, 46, 65, 103, 182
Lo, K. Z. (Guanzong), 125
Louvain consultation, 14

"Love-Country—Love-Church," 114-116
Lu Chih-shen, 56
Lu Dingyi, 97, 182
Luo Hanxian, 62
Luo Zhenfang, 263, 270
Luo Zhufeng, 91
Lutheran World Federation (LWF), 14
Lyall, Leslie, 5, 10, 161

MacInnis, Don, 7
Manikam, Rajah, 230
Mao Zedong, xxv, 14, 45, 46, 48, 54-56, 60, 87, 285; on connection between imperialism and missionary work, 96; on religious freedom, 101
Mao Zedong Thought, 23, 52
Marx, Karl, 47, 52, 76
Marxism: in Chinese experience, 23-28; and Chinese religion, relationship, 30
Marxism-Leninism Mao Zedong Thought, 23-25, 46
Mass Line: and united front, 52-54
Mass organizations, 72-74, 178
May Fourth Movement (1919): and Protestant opposition to unequal treaties, 41; Protestants caught up in nationalism of, 120
Merwin, Wallace, 7, 8
Missionaries: and cultural imperialism, 35; and gunboat diplomacy, 34; and social change in China, 33
Missionary movement and imperialism, 32-36
Missionary Research Library, 7
Modernization, 25
Mojzes, Paul, 18
Monotheism in China, 29
Mote, Frederick, 28
Munro, Donald, 51-52
Mutual respect, 222-227

Nanjing Union Theological Seminary: principles for union, 223-224
National Christian Conference: First, (1954), 117, 147, 150, 151-152; Second, 175; Third, 188
National Christian Council (NCC), xxiv
National Council of Churches in U.S.A. (NCCUSA), 4; call for recognition of PRC, 232
Nationalism in religion, 116
Nee, Watchman, 162-163
New Light, 251-253
Newbigin, Lesslie, 11, 289

Ng Lee-ming, 166, 245, 248
Niebuhr, Reinhold, 19
Nien Cheng, 184
Northern China United Christian Promotion Association, 164
Nystrom, G., 230

One Hundred Flowers campaign: criticism of religious policy during, 153

Paton, David, 11, 12-13, 16, 126
Patriotism, 94, 289
Peng Zhen, 103, 105, 182
Pentecostalism, extreme, 158
People's Political Consultative Conference (CPPCC): functions of, 67-68
Peter, Janos, 230
Politics and the church, 42
Post-denominational Christianity: transition to, 221
Preparatory Committee of Chinese Christian Resist-America—Aid-Korea Three-Self Movement: 148
Price, Frank, 7-10, 136-137
Pro Mundi Vita (PMV), 14
Protestant Church in China: conservative perspective, 4-7; emerging perspectives (1949–1979), 11-16; liberal perspective, 7-11; post-denominational era, xix
Protestant Church in China, 1980–1987: statistics, 191
Protestant institutions in China, 118; decline of, 147
Protestant missionary movement: and ecumenical movement of 20th century, 215
Protestant population of China, 1949–1987, 192
Protestantism: sociological division of, 285
Protestants and Chinese revolution, 117-133
Pu Huaren, 70, 98

Qiao Liansheng, 70

Rahner, Karl, 201-202
Rawlinson, Frank, 199, 203, 254
Reeducation, 140-146
Rees, Vaughan, 161
Rejection of united front: by the Cultural Revolution, 179-185; from the left, 170-179; from the right, 157-170

Religion: definition of, 28; and elimination of social classes, 91; ethnic character of, in China, 87; as a nonantagonistic contradiction, 86; as opium of people, 90; and patriotism, 94-101; and spiritual culture of the nation, 89
Religion and religious policy, 75-109; atheism, religion, and superstition, 78-83; "five characteristics of religion," 83-89; new departure for Chinese religious studies, 89-92; unity of theory and practice, 80
Religion in traditional Chinese society, 28-32
Religious Affairs Bureau (RAB), 70-71
Religious freedom, 93, 101-106
Religious persecution during Cultural Revolution, 180-181
Religious policy: and interpretation of Marxism-Leninism Mao Zedong Thought, 108; rural, 153
Religious Question During China's Socialist Period, The, 91
Religious tolerance, 30
Ren Jiyu, 82
Ren Wuzhi, 70
Reorientation: meaning of, for theological conservatives, 254
Research on World Religions, 81
Resist-America—Aid-Korea campaigns, 98; Protestant participation in, 147
Roots, Logan, 216-217
Rosenstock-Huessy, Eugen, xx

Sailer, Randolph, 11
Sanon, Anseleme, 288
Schurmann, Franz, 138
Sectarian leaders: irreconcilability of, 155
Seeking the common ground, xxi, 210, 253
Self-propagation, 210-215
Self-support, 205-210; major problem with, 235; obstacles to, 208-209
Seminary students, 277
Separation of church and state in China, 31
Separatist religious sects: CPC suspicion of, 155
Shanghai Federation of Philosophy and Social Sciences, 91
Shao Shiping, 128
Sheep stealing, 158
Shen, T. K. (Shen Zigao), 145, 225
Shen Derong, 125, 190

Shen Tilan, 93, 95, 125
Shen Yifan, 41, 145-146, 190, 277
Shen Yuehan, 204
Shi, Phoebe (Shi Ruzhang), 125, 230
Shirob Jaltso, 71
Sin: absence of concept of, 28
Sittler, Joseph, xxii
Smart, Ninian, 82
Smylie, Robert, 232
Snow, Edgar, 14
Social change in 1960s; effect on attitudes toward China, 13
Social injustice: church witness against, 205
Socialism and salvation, 272
Socialist reconstruction, period of (1949–1956), xxi
Song, C. S., 14, 15
Speer, Robert, 37
Spiritual Food Quarterly, The, 164
Statement of faith, 225-226
Struggle between two lines and emerging ultra-leftism (1957–1966), xxi
Stuart, Leighton, 34
Suffering: Christian response to, 265
Sun Hanshu, 255
Sun Pengxi, 174
Sun Ruogong, 81
Sun Yat-sen, 50
Sung, John, 157
Surveillance: by United Front Work Department, 69
Synchronization: of religion and socialist society, 92

Tang, Matthew, 268-269
Tang Liangli, 33
Tang Shoulin, 164
Tenth Plenum of Three-Self: promotion of struggle and division, 174
Terrill, Ross, 14
Theological controversies: introduced into China, 250
Theological disunity, 217-218
Theological diversity: acceptable limits of, 226
Theological reorientation, 243-280
Theology: Asian contextual, 249; Chinese in 1980s, 273-280; continuity of, 278; development of indigenous Chinese, 244; living, 249; open-mindedness in, 255; people's, 261; preliberation, 250; as reason enlightened by faith, 258

Third World Conference on Religion and Peace, xxii, 88
Three Witnesses and Ten Tasks, 152, 201
Three-Self: and accessibility of faith, 281; accomplishments of, 193; affirmation of social changes, 201; as bridge to CPC, 152; as bridge between Protestants and CPC, 117; and China Christian Council, 189; Christian purpose of, 200; comprehensiveness rejected on left, 156; constituted by First National Christian Conference, 117; continuity of pre-1957 and post-1978 periods, 193; contribution of, to socialism, 283; criticised during Cultural Revolution, 181; criticised during Hundred Flowers campaign, 172; from above, 190; from below, 190; and interdenominational tolerance, 218; need for break with imperialism, 204; need for reform and renewal, 204; participation rejected by Wang Mingdao, 164-165; as a patriotic movement, 146-153; Preparatory Committee, xxiv, 137; and pluralistic religious toleration, 284; reaffirmation of, 233; Reform Assembly, 137; renewal of, 185-192; Tenth Plenum marked shift to left and to sectarianism, 173; as united front movement, 154; and unity, 233-242
Three-self idea, 36-42
Three-Self Movement: initiation of, 98
Tian Feng, xxiv, 177
Tian Yunzhen, 269
Ting, K. H., xxvi, 12, 15, 22, 34, 65, 102, 124, 125, 127, 166, 168-169, 176, 189-190, 193, 195, 199, 202, 210, 223, 224, 230, 232, 233, 243-244, 251, 255, 259, 261, 272, 277-279
Ting Yuzhang, 150
True Jesus Church, 40, 157
Tsai, Peter (Cai Wenhao), 186, 191
TSM. *See* Chinese Christian Three-Self Movement
Tsu, Y. Y. (Zhu Youyu), 137
Tsui, H. H., 95, 122, 136, 149, 150, 166, 208-209, 222-223
Tu, Y. C., 95, 125, 142, 148
Two whatevers, 26

United Bible Societies, 241
United Church of Canada: and James Endicott, 12
United front, xxi; Catholic Patriotic Association (CPA), 66; Chinese Buddhist Association (CBA), 66; Christians within, 122-127; during Cultural Revolution era, 64; dynamics of unity, 52-59; early identification with, 126; First (1923–1927), and White Terror of 1927, 49; first attempts to bring Protestants into, 128; in five major campaigns, 51 and KMT (Guomindang) during War of Resistance, 46; historical background, 46-51; ideology and organization, 45-74; Mao Zedong and, 48; mass organizations, 72-74; and national unity, 45; new era after Third Plenum of CPC (1978), 51; organizational framework, 65-68; People's Political Consultative Conference, 66-68; positions of Chinese Protestants outside, 121; rejection of, during Cultural Revolution, 26; and Religious Affairs Bureau, 66, 70-72; and religious policy, 46, 92-94; Second (1937–1945) and War of Resistance, 49; stated as goal of CPC, 51; theory and ideology, 51-52; and Three-Self Movement, 66; United Front Work Department (UFWD), 66; Work Department, 68-70; working style, 60-65; in Mao Zedong's theory, 49-50
United front strategy: adopted by Third Communist International, 48
Unity: without confessional or liturgical basis, 238
Universalism by induction, 287-288

van den Berg, Johannes, 35-36
van Slyke, Lyman, 63, 100
Venn, Henry, 37

Wan Fulin, 267
Wang, Leland, 157
Wang Mingdao, 150, 154, 157, 164-169, 223, 268; arrested as counter-revolutionary, 165; theological critique of, 167-168
Wang Shenyin, 211
Wang Weifan, 166, 259, 264-265, 274-275

Wang Zhen, 154, 166, 194
Wang Zizhong, 131-132
Warren, M.A.C., 37
WCC. *See* World Council of Churches
Wei, Isaac, 159
Welch, Holmes, 68, 106
Wenshi ziliao (Resources on Literature and History), xxiv
Whitby Assembly of International Missionary Council (1947), 36
Whitehead, Ray, 15
Whyte, Martin, 73
"Winter is past," 275
Woo, Franklin, 6
World: Christian view of, 261
World Conference on Church and Society (1966), 13
World Council of Churches (WCC), 4; Chinese Christians and, 228
World Missionary Conference, First, 216
World Student Christian Federation study of China, 14
Worship, unification of, 219-222
Wu, George, 128
Wu, Y. T., xxiv-xxv, xxvi, 9, 93, 95, 113, 122, 124, 128, 129, 139, 142, 148-150, 151-153, 161, 166, 169, 170-172, 173, 175, 201, 244, 248, 249, 271
Wu Lei-chuen, 244
Wu Yifang, 95, 124, 150
Wu Zipu, 128

Xi'an Incident (1936), 49
Xiao Qian, 96
Xiao Xianfa, 70-71, 189
Xie Shouling, 262
Xie Yongqin, 122, 149, 159, 207-208, 260-261, 267-269

Ya Hanzhang, 78, 80-81, 83
Yan Mingfu, 69
Yang Zhen, 79, 81
Yeller movement, 237
YM/YMCAs: criticism of, 125
Yu Guozhen, 41
Yu Xiang, 79
Yue Daiyun, 184

Zhang Haidi, 214
Zhang Jinglong, 277
Zhang Xueyan, 95

Zhang Zhiyi, xxv, 67, 70, 99, 189
Zhao Fusan, 89-90, 125, 204, 221, 230, 232, 276
Zhao Puchu, 102-103, 132, 195
Zhao Ziyang, 182
Zheng Jianye, xx, 32, 114, 125, 190
Zhou Enlai, xxv, 46, 58, 60, 65, 70, 95-
96, 100, 105, 129, 130, 183, 193, 230, 246
Zhou Fuqing, 174
Zhou Qingze, 174
Zhu Chensheng, 129
Zhu Guishen, 122
Zhu Guisheng, 137